THE USMCA AND FREE TRADE AGREEMENTS

Third Edition

Ralph H. Folsom
Professor of Law
University of San Diego
A.B. Princeton University, J.D. Yale Law School
LLM London School of Economics

CONCISE HORNBOOK SERIES™

WEST ACADEMIC

860 Blue Gentian Road, Suite 350
Eagan, MN 55121
1-877-888-1330

Published in the United States of America

ISBN: 979-8-89209-905-9

Preface

Veteran users of my international trade books will note the world-wide coverage of free trade agreements in this Concise Hornbook focused on the North American USMCA agreement. The reason for this global coverage is relatively simple. Despite a geo-political decline commenced by President Trump and continued under President Biden, *free trade agreements (FTAs) of many varieties continue to operate and dominate regional trade.* More than half of all international trade takes place under FTAs. Every country on Earth has at least one FTA, many have dozens.

International rules regarding free trade agreements (FTAs) and customs unions (CUs) are found in Article 24 of the GATT 1947 and GATT 1994 agreements. Article 24 permits, but attempts to regulate their creation, an effort that met failure early on in connection with the European Economic Community Treaty of 1957 (EEC) and various developing world agreements. A sleeping giant for decades, the significance of FTAs was re-awakened by the path-breaking Canada-U.S. FTA of 1989. In 1994, NAFTA triggered an onslaught of FTAs around the world, diminishing the impact of the establishment of the World Trade Organization in 1995.

The hostility of President Trump to free trade agreements like the Trans-Pacific Partnership (TPP-12), the EU and NAFTA caused other countries to negotiate FTAs around the globe. America's traditional trade partners, notably in Asia and Europe, secured free trade deals not involving the USA. Here are examples: TPP-11 (2018, minus the U.S.), the EU-Canada FTA (CETA, 2017), the Japan-EU FTA (2019), the expanded Mexico-EU FTA (2020), the EU-MERCOSUR accord (2020), the China-led Regional Cooperative Economic Partnership with 15 Asian nations (RCEP 2021), the African Continental Free Trade Area (ACFTA 2021), and a host of UK FTAs post-BREXIT (2021 onward).

Meanwhile, despite being characterized by President Trump as "the worst trade deal ever", the United States, Canada and Mexico completed re-negotiation of NAFTA under the U.S.-Mexico-Canada Agreement (USMCA 2020). All this, and more, is covered in this book.

It has been a genuine pleasure to prepare *The USMCA* and *Free Trade Agreement 3d.* I hope that students, academics, lawyers, government officials and people in business will find it a useful and insightful presentation on a timely topic. In preparing this book, I have attempted to address the interests not only of Americans, but also persons located outside North America who are concerned about the law and economics of free trade agreements. Of course, no FTA is totally "free", a theme that repeats throughout this book.

Active links for the e-book and downloadable versions of this Concise Hornbook have been provided throughout.

This Concise Hornbook can be used as a **free** course book under West Academic Study Aids Program.

Your comments and suggestions are most welcome.

Ralph H. Folsom
rfolsom@sandiego.edu

September, 2024

Acknowledgments

I wish to thank my brother, W. Davis Folsom, Distinguished Emeritus Professor of Business Studies at University of South Carolina (Beaufort). Brother Davis extensively tutored me about the economics of free trade agreements and opened many doors to understanding. We initially collaborated with pleasure on *Understanding NAFTA and Its International Business Implications* (1996), an interdisciplinary publication written just after NAFTA 1994 came online, followed by a professional treatise titled *NAFTA Law and Business*.

Our latest joint effort is *The USMCA and Its Business Impacts* in a Nutshell.

I also wish to thank the numerous professors around the world who have supported my international business law writings for many years. For this volume, I am especially indebted to Professors David Gantz, Michael Gordon, and Matthew Schaefer.

Lastly, I very much appreciate the support of West Academic Publishing. They authorized an allotment of pages that permitted reproduction of critical documents.

Acknowledgments

Linked Web Resources

USMCA and U.S. Free Trade Agreements:

- www.ustr.gov/trade-agreements/free-trade-agreements

Free Trade Agreements in the Americas:

- sice.oas.org/agreements_e.asp

Asia Pacific Trade and Investment Agreements:

- www.unescap.org/content/aptiad
- https://aric.adb.org/fta-country

Global Coverage of Free Trade Agreements:

- www.bilaterals.org
- www.wto.org/english/tratop_e/region_e/rta_participation_map_e.htm
- https://en.wikipedia.org/wiki/List_of_free-trade_agreements

About the Author

Ralph H. Folsom has been a Professor at the University of San Diego School of Law since 1975. A graduate of Princeton University, Yale Law School, and the London School of Economics (LLM), Professor Folsom teaches, writes, and consults extensively in the field of international business law.

Folsom has been a Senior Fulbright resident scholar in Singapore and a Visiting Professor at the University of Hong Kong, University of Aix-Marseille, University of Brest, University of Montpellier, University of Paris (Pantheon-Sorbonne), University of Toulouse, University of Puerto Rico, Monash University in Australia, and Tecnológico de Monterrey in México.

Professor Folsom has authored a range of books with West Academic Publishing. These include a popular problem-oriented course book, now in its 14th edition, on *International Business Transactions* (co-author). He has also written Concise Hornbooks on:

International Litigation and Arbitration,

International Trade Law,

Foreign Investment Law and Disputes,

International Business Transactions (co-author), and

The European Union Beyond BREXIT.

About the Author

Summary of Contents

Table of Contents

THE USMCA AND FREE TRADE AGREEMENTS

Third Edition

Chapter 1

THE ESSENTIALS OF INTERNATIONAL TRADE AND TRADE LAW

Table of Sections

NOTE: For much more extensive international trade law and WTO coverage, see my Concise Hornbook on *International Trade Law*. Selected provisions of the GATT 1947 and 1994, various WTO agreements, and the WTO Dispute Settlement Understanding (DSU) are appended in that Concise Hornbook.

INTRODUCTION

§ 1.1 Trade Deficits, Patterns, Treaties and Remedies

The United States is one of a few central players in the world of international trade. It has engaged in foreign trade from the moment of its independence over two centuries ago. Indeed, one of the reasons freedoms were sought was England's imposition of severe restrictions on trade between the colonies and foreign nations, intended to preserve the benefits of international trade for England.

Less than two centuries from achieving independence, the United States became a leading trade power in the world. For over a decade after World War II, the United States was in the envious and economically advantageous position of being the major center of production of finished goods for export. But with extraordinary economic growth in Japan and Europe, by the 1980s the United States no longer dominated world trade. It had to compete for sales abroad, and in the domestic market within the United States. Traditional surpluses in the balance of trade with most nations in some cases began to be reversed. The United States has had to deal with increasingly large trade deficits with Japan, and more recently, the most challenging trade partner—China.

Trade Deficits

The trade surplus of earlier decades has become a trade deficit of disturbing proportions. The deficit status of U.S. international trade in the 1990s and into the new millennium caused trade to be a topic of common conversation. The U.S. trade deficit is often perceived as threatening jobs for American workers and the consequent diminishment of quality of life of the American people. This has generated annual Congressional proposals of an increasingly restrictive nature. U.S. exports have continued to grow, especially in the service and technology areas, but imports of goods have grown more rapidly. Even the periodic fall of the dollar, making U.S. exports cheaper, has not reversed the trade deficit, which escalated under Presidents Trump and Biden.

The importance of trade and its underlying economic relations should be apparent. But the huge capacity of the United States to consume foreign products is out of balance with its ability to find reciprocal consumption for its exports. That is due to many reasons, including problems of quality, real and perceived, problems of barriers to trade imposed by every nation, and problems of government leadership. Those who view the United States from abroad continually point to excessive consumption and inadequate savings, and to the budget deficit, as the principal reasons for the deteriorating U.S. trade position. Congress and the administration hear the complaints but make few corrections. It is easier to blame other nations, a trait President Trump exemplified. After all, the United States still generates a formidable share of world trade and will continue to do so for some time.

Even individual U.S. states have remarkable trade statistics. California alone generates billions of dollars of world trade, making its "gross state product" greater than the gross national products of all but a few nations of the world. In the last few years, however, the per capita standard of living of several other nations has reached and exceeded that in the United States.

Some developed nations are unusually dependent on international trade in goods and services. The Netherlands, for example, depends on exports for over 75% of their Gross Domestic Product (GDP). Roughly 50% of the GDPs of Sweden, Germany and Switzerland derive from exports. Canada, New Zealand, France, and Britain come in at about 25%, China at 19%, with the United States at approximately 12%.

International trade law has a long and controversial history. Many nations, especially in their early stages of development, are fearful of trade across borders. International trade is a competitive force, one that typically shakes up domestic economic interests and results in trade specialization. It is a powerful engine of change, creating winners and losers in its comparative advantage path. It is now certain, for example, that China's admission to the WTO in 2001 contributed to a significant negative impact on U.S. manufacturing jobs and wages in the Midwest, but also shipment to China of 60% of U.S. exports of soybeans. Simultaneously, WTO membership helped lift hundreds of millions of Chinese out of poverty.

Trade is a powerful competitive force increasing the selection of goods and services available in national economies and enhancing domestic market price competition. Wal-Mart's heavy importation of inexpensive Chinese goods, for example, notably reduced U.S. consumer costs, particularly for lower income and displaced Americans. That said, President Trump's America First election revealed deep resentment of the consequences of trade, especially the resulting massive U.S. trade deficit with China, and sizeable trade deficits with Japan, Mexico, and Germany. The Trump and Biden administrations assert that China's trade surplus is the product of unfair trade practices and production subsidies. Forgotten in the political dialogue are modest U.S. trade surpluses with the United Kingdom, Canada, Brazil, Saudi Arabia, and Singapore.

There is a need to "unpack" trade deficit data. For example, roughly 65% of the value of iPhones shipped from China originates in the U.S., yet their full value appears in U.S.-China trade data. Roughly 40% of the value all Mexican goods crossing into the United States is American in origin. Furthermore, U.S. trade deficit numbers tend to be portrayed in goods only (especially by the Trump Administration), omitting trade surpluses in services, and not considering foreign investment capital flows.

Many economists maintain that high overall trade deficit countries like the United States reflect substantial consumer and government spending along with low rates of savings. Low overall trade deficit or surplus countries like Germany and China reflect high savings rates and restrained spending patterns. In short, trade deficits and surpluses do not reflect a win/lose zero sum game. They are instead a reflection of internal, notably fiscal, strengths and weaknesses of various countries. Despite U.S.-initiated tariff wars, U.S. trade deficits rose to record levels in the years of the Trump presidency and in the Biden era. That outcome was clearly not what President Trump had in mind for one of his favorite measurements of international trade success.

World Trade Patterns

Trade traditionally has been measured by the exchange of tangible goods, both raw materials and finished products. This is sometimes referred to as "merchandise trade." The prominence of oil as a trading commodity, and the economic power exerted in the 1970s by the Organization of Petroleum Exporting Countries (OPEC), resulted in a considerable shift of wealth caused by remarkable changes in the price of a single commodity. The power of OPEC diminished in the 1980s and 1990s due to an oversupply of oil and conflict both within the oil industry and within OPEC. Since the millennium, OPEC power and oil prices first rose and then collapsed with the advent of "fracking" and horizontal drilling techniques that generated substantial amounts of U.S. oil and gas production. OPEC+ (Russia plus OPEC) in turn emerged as a more effective cartel, at least prior to Russia's invasion of Ukraine in 2022.

Energy remains the ultimately important global commodity. It played a critical role in the decision of the United States to commence the Gulf and Iraq Wars, and to become engaged in the war against ISIS in the Middle East. Extractable raw materials remain the principal source of wealth for many nations. Nations which produce many natural and agricultural resources, from tin to bananas, have attempted to create cartels resembling OPEC which will give them control of their economic destiny.

Services Trade

In recent years, attention on items of trade and therefore value has shifted from an exclusive focus on tangibles and technology, to an area of trade and economic relations far more difficult to define. That area is trade in services such as advertising, banking, insurance, accounting, consulting, entertainment, construction, tourism, education, and the vast area of computer services. For the most part, trade in services is not subject to tariffs. Nontariff barriers (NTBs), often in the form of licenses or permits, predominate. Cross-border trade in legal services provides an example, particularly by large multinational U.S. and UK law firms. U.S. trade in these "invisibles" is measured in billions annually. Trade in tangibles is marred by an increasing deficit, but U.S. trade in services is marked by an increasing surplus.

Many other nations are eager to develop their own services, and to protect them from encroachment by the developed nations. The negotiations in the Uruguay Round that created the WTO on trade in services were an especially difficult part of the overall trade talks. The industrialized nations, led by the United States, for the most part successfully negotiated lowering trade barriers to services, over the objections of important developing nations such as India and Brazil. These nations fear dominance in ownership of services by the industrialized nations.

The final WTO agreement, the General Agreement on Trade in Services (GATS), reflected many restrictions and reservations by developing nations determined to establish and maintain their own service sectors. The ability of the WTO to govern trade in services is critical to keeping service-oriented nations like the United States a supporter of this important multilateral trade regulating organization.

The Rise of Asia

Viewing the constantly changing world trade patterns as they have developed to this moment, the dominance of the United States which was prevalent decades ago has diminished substantially and is unlikely to reoccur. This trend is attributable to the prominence of Japan in manufacturing and designing products which meet current consumer demands, to the entry of China and re-entry of India in the world trade arena, to the cooperation of the European nations within the European Union, and to the movement through successive stages of development of many nations, especially the "Four Dragons" or "Four Tigers" of Asia—Hong Kong, South Korea, Singapore, and Taiwan.

Increased "world market share" is the goal of every nation, and nations joust over international trade issues. Asian nations, like others, closely regulate foreign investment coming into the country, and create trade incentives to stimulate greater exports to other countries.

The spectacular success of Japan and China as exporters combined with a creativity to block imports led to a sequence of protests and trade sanctions by the United States and the European Union, most notably by President Trump. However accurately Japan or China may be accused of being unfair traders and of using a host of regulatory nontariff trade barriers (NTBs) to keep foreign goods and investment out, the United States sometimes fails to consider that trade imbalances may be as much caused by domestic failures as by foreign intransigence.

Nontariff Trade Barriers

Japan and China are not alone in using nontariff regulatory barriers, such as environmental rules and product and health safety laws. NTBs have arisen to protect domestic industry as the earlier protection by high tariffs has diminished via GATT, WTO, and free trade negotiations. Every nation has developed its own methods of keeping imports at bay.

The United States, for example, has employed agricultural quotas and environmental/conservation regulations in this manner. The French provoked a stream of protest by requiring that documentation for imported goods be written in French. France established a "consultative commission for international trade" charged to watch for "abnormal" and excessive imports and unfair export practices of other countries. Meaning, of course, an agency for domestic business to complain to when affected by imports, regardless of their own efficiency in production. In the United States, similar complaints are filed with the Office of the U.S. Trade Representative.

Other nations have responded in various ways to the impact of imports. Restricted by their agreements to specific tariff levels as members of the WTO, they have carried nontariff barriers to a new height of originality. These barriers may assume the form of health or safety standards, packing or labeling requirements, environmental regulations, and many other rules which may in theory seem justified, but in practice are structured or interpreted to eliminate or reduce imports and benefit domestic industries.

Lawyers retained to deal with these nontariff barriers, as well as subsidies, dumping or rules of origin, have become the major beneficiaries of these complex trade laws. They alone know how to work through the maze of details in lengthy definitions included in trade laws, treaties, and multilateral agreements. For example, foreign targets of a U.S. dumping charge must expend enormous resources responding to such charges, thus making these actions themselves another costly form of nontariff barrier.

Not all nations participated in the GATT 1947 or are members of its replacement, the WTO. By the 1970s, nontariff trade barriers (NTBs) began to be addressed by the GATT, including agreements designed to lessen NTBs, including complex customs valuation procedures, import licensing systems, and product health, safety, and environmental standards. But these GATT NTB agreements were optional, and most of the developing world membership opted out. By the 1990s international trade was at a crossroad.

Trade Incentives

Goods which are sold in one nation are not necessarily either goods produced domestically by locally owned manufacturers, or goods produced abroad by foreign owned manufacturers. They may be goods produced *domestically* by *foreign* owned manufacturers. Or they may be goods produced *abroad* by domestic manufacturers.

Investing abroad is an alternative to exporting goods abroad. Foreign investment shares some benefits of trade. The foreign manufacturer receives the profit, but the host nation of the foreign investment obtains jobs and technology. Raw materials or parts may be sent by the foreign manufacturer, to create what is little more than an assembly plant in the host nation, or raw materials and parts may be purchased in the host nation, adding to the benefits of permitting investment owned by foreign entities. See my Concise Hornbook on *Foreign Investment Law and Disputes*.

While trying to hold imports to reasonable levels, every nation wants to be a major exporter. It is, after all, exports that provide the means to pay for imports. The urge to export leads to another scheme of laws. They are usually laws of encouragement in contrast to laws of discouragement which typify the import rules. They may be fashioned in the way of granting tax benefits, offering export financing or insurance, overlooking trade restraint elements of permitted export cartels, or tying permitted imports to the level of exports.

The United States, for example, in enacting the 1982 Export Trading Company Act (ETC), followed the practice of nations such as Japan in assisting exporters. The ETC Act was designed to permit small and medium U.S. firms to gain information about foreign trade opportunities and techniques, and to have easier access to financing for export activity. Strident debate over renewing U.S. Export-Import

(EXIM) Bank funding continues. Many EXIM export financings have benefited U.S. multinationals such as Boeing and GE.

The Legal Framework of Trade

Every nation engaged in international economic relations develops a legal framework defining its role. That framework will consist of domestic trade laws, including its acceptance of international laws regulating cross-border transactions, and participation in international organizations that establish trade rules. The United States has developed by legislative and executive action an extensive set of domestic rules governing international trade, many reflecting WTO rules. It has also been a major creator and participant in many organizations which influence or govern trade.

Until recently the World Trade Organization, successor to GATT 1947, has been a prominent trade organization. Its "package deal" of about 20 agreements are almost entirely mandatory for its 165 or so member countries and customs areas. Members must incorporate WTO rules into their legal system and obey WTO rules at the risk of authorized retaliation if they do not. Roughly 98% of all world trade is covered by the WTO agreements. But and that is a BIG but, the WTO has been declining in operational importance ever since the Trump and Biden administrations blockaded appointments to its dispute settlement Appellate Body. See my *International Trade Law* Concise Hornbook.

The United Nations has played a disappointingly minor role in trade, although UNCITRAL, the United Nations Commission on International Trade Law, has become an important forum for the harmonization of rules affecting trade, such as the Convention on International Sale of Goods (CISG).

Regional economic relations have increased trade among groups of nations, which is particularly important since the decline of the WTO. The European Union and NAFTA/USMCA are the two most important areas which have reduced barriers to internal trade, although sometimes at the expense of increasing barriers to external trade. Free trade and customs union agreements have been proliferating. See Chapter 5. But however important may be participation in bilateral or multilateral trade agreements or organizations, the will of a single participant to abide by freer trade rules will be expressed in its domestic trade laws and policies. It is under such national laws that international business enterprises operate.

International trade law has a long and controversial history. Many nations, especially in their early stages of development, are fearful of trade across borders. International trade is a competitive force, one that typically shakes up domestic economic interests. It is a powerful engine of change, creating winners and losers in its path. The law of international trade, for better or worse, shapes the scope and direction of this force.

The United States in its early years sheltered "infant" agricultural and industrial sectors behind protective tariffs and regulatory restraints. When the Great Depression of the 1930s arrived, the United States enacted highly protective tariffs under the Smoot-Hawley Tariff Act of 1930. These tariffs were intended to wall off the U.S. economy from foreign competition, in theory "saving American jobs for American citizens." Other nations around the world retreated from international trade through similarly protective laws. Fear of foreign trade (and foreigners) reached a zenith that most economists agree deepened and prolonged the Great Depression. World War II rescued the United States from the Depression but did nothing to remove the Smoot-Hawley tariffs and encourage other nations to do likewise.

Here is a provocative excerpt from a 1930 letter signed by over 1000 economists opposing Smoot-Hawley:

> We are convinced that increased protective duties would be a mistake. They would operate, in general, to increase the prices which domestic consumers would have to pay. By raising prices, they would encourage concerns with higher costs to undertake production, thus compelling the consumer to subsidize waste and inefficiency in industry. At the same time, they would force him to pay higher rates of profit to established firms which enjoyed lower production costs. A higher level of protection, such as is contemplated by both the House and Senate bills, would therefore raise the cost of living and injure the great majority of our citizens.
>
> Few people could hope to gain from such a change. Miners, construction, transportation and public utility workers, professional people and those employed in banks, hotels, newspaper offices, in the wholesale and retail trades, and scores of other occupations would clearly lose, since they produce no products which could be protected by tariff barriers.
>
> The vast majority of farmers, also, would lose. Their cotton, corn, lard, and wheat are export crops and are sold in the world market. They have no important competition in the home market. They cannot benefit, therefore, from

> any tariff which is imposed upon the basic commodities which they produce. They would lose through the increased duties on manufactured goods, however, and in a double fashion. First, as consumers they would have to pay still higher prices for the products, made of textiles, chemicals, iron, and steel, which they buy. Second, as producers, their ability to sell their products would be further restricted by the barriers placed in the way of foreigners who wished to sell manufactured goods to us.
>
> Our export trade, in general, would suffer. . . There are already many evidences that such action would inevitably provoke other countries to pay us back in kind by levying retaliatory duties against our goods. There are few more ironical spectacles than that of the American Government as it seeks, on the one hand, to promote exports through the activity of the Bureau of Foreign and Domestic Commerce, while, on the other hand, by increasing tariffs it makes exportation ever more difficult. President Hoover has well said, in his message to Congress on April 16, 1929, "It is obviously unwise protection which sacrifices a greater amount of employment in exports to gain a less amount of employment from imports.

Almost ninety years later, a letter from more than 1,100 economists revived this message in the face of President Trump's protectionist measures.

Despite its economic power and leadership in the development of modern trade law, the United States retains some of its early fear and concerns about international commerce, notably so under the Trump and Biden Administrations. This is particularly apparent when U.S. free trade agreements are debated and undertaken, but also when the U.S. invokes import trade remedies and export controls of goods and technology. Little wonder that developing nations, many not much more than 50 years old and created out of colonial empires, hesitate to embrace the panoply of modern international trade law.

The need to balance the protection of local industries from harm by foreign competitors and the encouragement of trade across national borders is a recurrent theme in the law of international economic relations. Trade problems associated with the movement of goods across national borders still arise because of restrictive trade devices which impede or distort trade. In most countries, "trade adjustment assistance" to adversely damaged workers has proved inadequate.

Common protective devices include tariff barriers (*e.g.*, normal import and export duties, and special antidumping and subsidy countervailing duties), as well as nontariff trade barriers (NTBs) such as quotas, import and export licensing procedures, safety, environmental, health and other regulatory standards, complex customs procedures, and government procurement policies. For example, France once required that all video recorders entering France had to do so through a small customs post at Poitiers and carry documentation written in French. Product distribution practices have been an effective NTB in Japan. The United States has a host of NTB restraints. See again my *International Trade Law* Concise Hornbook.

Commencing in 1932 under President Roosevelt, the United States began to unwind its Smoot-Hawley tariffs, particularly via reciprocal trade agreements, the first of which was with Canada. World War II ultimately rescued the United States from the Depression but did little to significantly remove high tariffs in Europe, Asia, America and elsewhere. International trade law was at a crossroads.

Trade Treaties

Early efforts by countries to limit disruptive trade practices were traditionally found in bilateral treaties of Friendship, Commerce and Navigation (FCN), some of which remain in force, such as that between the United States and Japan. Such treaties opened the territory of each signatory to greater imports, at times controversially under "unequal treaty" terms favoring European nations and the United States in Asia, for example. Bilateral FCN treaty clauses were usually linked to other preferential trade agreements. Such linkage was most often accomplished through a reciprocal "most favored nation" (MFN) clause. The parties agreed that more favorable trade arrangements are immediately *also* available to the other FCN signatory.

FCN treaties also focused on promoting foreign investment across borders, shipping and basic trade and investment principles of "national treatment"; the right to be taxed, regulated, and generally treated in the same legal manner as domestic businesses.

At this point, the United States has moved beyond many of its FCN treaties to bilateral Trade and Investment Framework Agreements (TIFAs, below), Free Trade Agreements (FTAs, Chapters 4, 5 and 6) and Bilateral Investment Treaties (BITs, Chapter 7). All three can be found at www.ustr.gov. FCN trade and investment law principles, notably MFN and national treatment, carry over into these agreements. TIFAs are centered on dialogue about trade and investment issues. They often precede the more advanced legal regimes of FTAs and BITs.

The United States has numerous TIFAs with individual countries and regional economic groups. The U.S. has TIFAs with:

Angola, Ghana, Liberia, Mauritius, Mozambique, Nigeria, Rwanda, South Africa and the Common Market for Eastern and Southern Africa (COMESA), the East African Community, the West African Economic and Monetary Union (WAEMU) and the South African Customs Union (titled as a Trade, Investment and Development Agreement). The U.S. also has TIFAs with Algeria, Bahrain, the Caribbean Common Market (CARICOM), Egypt, the Gulf Cooperation Council, Georgia, Iceland, Iraq, Kuwait, Lebanon, Libya, Oman, Qatar, Saudi Arabia, Switzerland, Tunisia, Turkey, Ukraine, the United Arab Emirates, Uruguay, and Yemen. Additional TIFAs have been concluded with Afghanistan, collectively with five Central Asian nations, the Maldives, Nepal, Pakistan, Sri Lanka, the ASEAN group (Association of Southeast Asian Nations), Brunei, Cambodia, Indonesia, Malaysia, New Zealand, the Philippines, Thailand, and Vietnam.

GATT 1947 and the World Trade Organization (1995) in Crisis

The most dramatic and far-reaching trade agreements in modern times originate from the General Agreement on Tariffs and Trade (GATT 1947) and its successor, the World Trade Organization (WTO). Commencing in 1995, the WTO package of international trade agreements established a legal baseline for some 165 member states. A list of the WTO agreements, including GATT 1994, is reproduced in Section 1.4.

At this writing, the World Trade Organization is in crisis. It has been unable to complete a Negotiating Round since 1994 (see Section 1.2), and its Dispute Settlement Understanding has been at a standstill from 2020 onward as Presidents Trump and Biden have denied appointments to the WTO Appellate Body (see Section 1.17). For much more on this crisis, which has fueled the growth of free trade agreements, see my Concise Hornbook on *International Trade Law*, Chapter 1.

Normal Bound Tariffs, "Free Trade"

The materials that follow move first to a review of the GATT 1947. The GATT was an international forum among Contracting States which regularly held multilateral trade negotiations (MTN) seeking ways of advancing international trade in goods (and only goods), most notably by diminishing Depression-era tariffs. These periodic negotiations cumulatively reduced tariff barriers by an average of up to eighty percent below those existing in the Great Depression. After the most recent multilateral negotiations completed in 1994, average tariff rates of developed countries on dutiable manufactured imports were cut from 6.3 percent to 3.9 percent. These are the tariffs each country is "bound to" after each negotiating round. They are often referred to as "normal" or MFN tariffs, appearing in the U.S. Harmonized Tariff Schedule (HTS) under Column One.

At their core, "free" trade agreements (FTAs) selectively remove the application of Bound Tariffs as between trade partners. This is permissible under conditions detailed in Article 24 of the GATT 1947/GATT 1994 agreements. See Chapter 2. However, most FTAs permit continued application of special GATT-authorized tariffs not Bound under GATT negotiations. So, even if products qualify for duty free treatment under an FTA, they may still be subject to antidumping duties, countervailing subsidy duties, safeguard duties or non-tariff trade restraints, and national security tariffs or trade restraints as outlined immediately below.

In addition, the United States authorizes unilateral tariffs and trade restraints under Section 301 of the Trade Act of 1974 (below). Use of this provision was prominently made by President Trump as part of his tech-driven trade war with China. President Biden has largely continued these WTO-offending unilateral U.S. tariffs against Chinese goods.

Additional AD and CVD Tariffs

The GATT/WTO system allows certain exceptions to normal MFN tariff levels. The two most important are "antidumping duties" (ADs) and "countervailing duties" (CVDs). Such duties are intended to "remedy" what the GATT/WTO has agreed are unfair international trade practices. Think of them as special tariffs which, in authorized circumstances, are *additional to MFN tariffs*.

Antidumping duties are a permissible trade response where an enterprise prices its goods for sale in the country of importation at a level that is less than that charged for comparable sales in the home country (*i.e.*, at "less than fair value" (LTFV)). Hence AD generally counteract private sector discriminatory pricing. Countervailing duties are a permissible response to certain "subsidies" given in another country that favor its exports in the international marketplace. Hence CVD counteract governmental subsidies. AD and CVD cannot simultaneously be applied.

The WTO system recognizes and permits both antidumping duties and countervailing duties, providing of course the respective requirements are satisfied. Each "trade remedy" also is governed by a separate Agreement ("Code") that provides more detail on the circumstances under which member states may impose these exceptional duties. Because the AD and CVD Codes are mandatory in the WTO system, they provide the foundation for a reasonably uniform body of legal rules for trade remedies among WTO members.

Under the WTO Antidumping Agreement (AD Code) and the WTO Subsidies and Countervailing Measures Agreement (CVD Code), a country may impose a special duty on products of another WTO member state only if two requirements are met. First, the country must find sufficient evidence of an unfair trade practice, either dumping (sales at less than fair value) or prohibited or actionable subsidies. Second, the practice must cause a sufficiently significant injury to a domestic industry. In the case of dumping or subsidies, this requires proof that the practice has caused or threatens to cause "material injury" to a domestic industry, or that it has "materially retarded" the establishment of such an industry. The substantive grounds for the determination of the existence of "dumping" and of a "countervailable (actionable) subsidy" are different, but the domestic injury standard is essentially the same.

Neither of these trade remedies in favor of domestic producers is based on any notion of reciprocity. That is, neither arises because another country has restricted the importation of U.S. goods into its markets. Antidumping and countervailing duties instead address unfair selling prices of dutiable imported goods.

The treaties establishing the European Union notably eliminate AD and CVD duties on internal, but not external, EU trade. See my *European Union Beyond Brexit* Concise Hornbook. In contrast, NAFTA and the USMCA do *not* eliminate AD and CVD on internal trade. See Chapter 5. Most FTAs follow the NAFTA/USMCA approach.

Trade Safeguards

Safeguard and market disruption proceedings are anticipated by Article XIX of the General Agreement on Tariffs and Trade (GATT). A WTO "Safeguards Agreement" emerged from the Uruguay Round of negotiations. In contrast to the statutory remedies against dumping and countervailable subsidies, safeguard proceedings are not targeted at unfair international trade practices. Rather, the goods are assumed to be traded fairly, but imports are in such an unexpected volume that protection is appropriate to *temporarily* allow the domestic industry to adjust to the new competitive environment.

In the United States, businesses may seek protection from import competition by initiating what are known as "escape clause" (safeguard) proceedings under the Trade Act of 1974. Escape clause proceedings can involve imports from anywhere in the world, and are authorized by Section 201 of the Trade Act (19 U.S.C. § 2251). Escape clause proceedings are also typically found in the free trade agreements of the United States.

In addition, "market disruption proceedings" can also provide temporary relief from import competition. Market disruption proceedings concern imports from communist nations and are authorized by Section 406 of the 1974 Trade Act (19 U.S.C. § 2436). They are similar but not identical to escape clause proceedings. Either may result in the imposition of U.S. import restraints, or presidential negotiation of export restraints from the source country.

Import injury relief available under the Trade Act of 1974 is basically of two kinds: (1) Presidential relief designed to temporarily protect domestic producers of like or directly competitive products; and (2) governmental assistance to workers and firms economically displaced by import competition. This assistance is intended to enhance job opportunities and competitiveness. Protective relief tends to be awarded when the President believes that U.S. industry needs time to adjust. Governmental assistance is seen seeks to accommodate the injury caused by import competition. In either case, adjustment to import competition is the longer-term goal, hopefully resulting in more competitive U.S. industries and markets.

The GATT allows, temporarily, "safeguard" or "escape clause" trade remedies for up to a maximum of four years. Such remedies may include additional tariffs, as Presidents Trump and Biden elected to impose on imported solar panels and clothes washers. Safeguard tariffs apply to all the world, not just exporting countries. Since safeguards do not target unfair practices, compensation (often reduced tariffs on the entry of goods into the safeguarding country) must be paid to exporting countries hit by safeguard remedies.

The treaties establishing the European Union also notably eliminate safeguard duties or restraints on internal, but not external, EU trade. In contrast, NAFTA and the USMCA do not eliminate safeguards on internal trade. See Chapter 5. Again, most FTAs follow the NAFTA/USMCA approach.

National Security Remedies

Chapter XXI of the GATT preserves the right of states to act in ways each member considers necessary for the protection of its "essential security interests" relating to fissionable materials, traffic in arms, or taken in time of war or an international relations emergency. President Trump in 2018 placed highly controversial "national security" tariffs on U.S. steel and aluminum imports, triggering retaliatory "re-balancing tariffs" around the globe. The Trump administration asserted that these tariffs are not justiciable under Chapter XXI of GATT, treating that provision as an unchallengeable blank check. Most other WTO members disagreed and filed complaints with the WTO seeking review of Trump's national security tariffs.

In April of 2019, a WTO panel ruled that "national security" issues are justiciable, affirming Russia's right to restrict the flow of Ukrainian goods in transit to Kazakhstan after its occupation of Crimea. The panel found there was an emergency in international relations that justified Russia's trade restraints. *See* Traffic in Transit (Russia), WTO/DS512/7 (2019).

Under the Trump administration and more frequently under the Biden administration, U.S. national security tariffs on steel and aluminum have been lifted or replaced with tariff rate quotas (TRQ). See Chapter 5. TRQs typically apply lower tariffs to imported goods until a designated annual quota is reached, at which point the tariff increases for the remainder of that year.

Unilateral U.S. Trade Remedies

The United States has a history of invoking **unilateral** trade remedies. Section 301 of the Trade Act of 1974 was adopted to confront U.S. frustrations with the GATT agreement of 1947 (below). Use of Section 301, particularly in opening foreign markets to U.S. exports, was influential as the U.S. aggressively sought to obtain approval in 1994 of the WTO package of agreements. Section 301 remedies are decidedly not authorized by the WTO.

For President Trump, Section 301 became the engine behind his tech-driven tariff war with China. China challenged this use of Section 301 before a WTO Panel and prevailed. The Panel ruled in 2020 that Trump's Section 301 tariffs against China violated WTO most-favored-trade (MFN, below) and Bound Tariff (above) principles. In addition, the Panel noted a breach of the U.S. commitment to utilize the WTO Dispute Settlement Understanding (DSU) governing disputes covered by the WTO package of trade agreements. *See* United States—Tariff Measures on Certain Goods from China (WTO/DS543). This ruling entered a legal void created by Trump's denial of WTO Appellate Body appointments.

President Biden has not reversed this denial, nor removed Trump's Section 301 tariffs on Chinese exports. At this writing, additional Section 301 tariffs on highly subsidized Chinese goods (notably EV autos) have been adopted by the Biden administration.

For a much more detailed review of WTO and U.S. trade remedies, see my Concise Hornbook on *International Trade Law*, Chapters 4, 5, 6 and 14.

§ 1.2 The General Agreement on Tariffs and Trade (GATT 1947)

Core Principles

United States, British and other participants in the 1994 Bretton Woods, New Hampshire meetings recognized a post-War need to reduce trade obstacles to foster freer trade. They envisioned the creation of an International Trade Organization (ITO) to achieve the desired result. Fifty-three countries met in Havana in 1948 to complete drafting the Charter of an ITO that would be the international organizational umbrella underneath which negotiations could occur periodically to deal with tariff reductions and other trade law matters. A framework for such negotiations had already been staked out in Geneva in 1947, in what was expected to be only a transitional document, the General Agreement on Tariffs and Trade (GATT 1947) in goods.

Twenty-three nations participated in that first GATT session, India, Chile, Cuba, and Brazil representing the developing world. China participated; Japan and West Germany did not. Stringent trading rules for goods (and only goods) were adopted only where there were no special interests of major participants to alter them. The developing nations objected to many of the strict rules, arguing for special treatment justified on development needs, but they achieved few successes in drafting GATT 1947. Some commenters believe GATT 1947 was in essence a deal struck between the United States and Europe, especially Britain.

The ITO Charter was never ratified. The United States Congress in the late 1940s was unwilling to join more new international organizations. Thus U.S. ratification of the ITO Charter could not be secured. Nonetheless, moving by way of the President Truman's power to issue executive orders, the United States did join twenty-one other countries, as Contracting Parties, in signing a Protocol of Provisional Application of the General Agreement on Tariffs and Trade (61 Stat. Pts. 5, 6) (popularly called the "GATT 1947 Agreement").

One notable feature of this protocol was the exemption of existing trade restraints of the Contracting States. Because of the failure to create the ITO, the GATT 1947 Agreement evolved from its "provisional" status into the premier international trade body, GATT the organization based in Geneva. It was through this organization that tariffs were steadily reduced over the decades by means of increased membership and GATT negotiating Rounds. Today, the GATT 1947 Agreement has been replaced by the substantially similar GATT 1994 Agreement, part of the World Trade Organization "package" of trade agreements that took effect in 1995. See Section 1.4. The United States, having denied the creation of the ITO in the late 1940s, had to wait more that forty years for a second bite at the apple. When that opportunity finally came, the U.S. was among the strongest proponents of the WTO.

Trade in Goods: MFN Treatment

One of the central features of GATT 1947 and 1994 is Article I, which makes a general commitment to the long-standing practice of "most favored nation treatment" (MFN) by requiring each Contracting Party to accord unconditional MFN status to goods from all other Contracting Parties. Thus, any privilege or tariff granted by a Contracting Party to products imported from any other country (not necessarily a WTO member) must also be "immediately and unconditionally" granted to any "like product" imported from any Contracting Parties. Article 1 of the GATT (1947) and (1994) spells out the golden rules of MFN trading:

> "With respect to customs duties and charges of any kind imposed on or in connection with importation or exportation or imposed on the international transfer of payments for imports or exports, and with respect to the method of levying such duties and charges, and with respect to all rules and formalities in connection with importation and exportation, and with respect to all matters referred to in paragraphs 2 and 4 of Article III, <u>any advantage, favor, privilege or immunity granted by any contracting party to any product originating in or destined for any other country shall be accorded immediately and unconditionally to the like product originating in or destined for the territories of all other contracting parties</u>." (emphasis added).

MFN principles essentially ban de jure and de facto tariff and trade discrimination. For leading WTO Appellate Body decisions on the application of MFN rules, *see* EC-Bananas, WT/DS27/AB/R (1997), Canada-Autos, WT/DS139/AB/R (2000). That said, the U.S. and other WTO members suspended the application of MFN rules to many Russian goods following the invasion of Ukraine in 2022.

There are two major exceptions to the MFN obligation of GATT Article I:

- Free trade areas and customs unions (see Chapter 2); and

- Differential and more favorable treatment of goods from developing countries (the 1979 Enabling Clause).

General exceptions contained in GATT Articles XX and XXI, including national security, may also apply.

Trade in Goods: National Treatment

GATT Article III incorporates the practice of according "national treatment" to imported goods by providing, with enumerated exceptions, that they shall receive the same tax and regulatory treatment as domestic goods. In this context, national treatment requires that "like products" of the exporting GATT Contracting State be treated no less favorably than domestic products of the importing State under its laws and regulations concerning sale, internal resale, purchase, transportation, and use. Physical properties, consumer perspectives and tariff classifications all contribute to evaluating the "likeness" of products. See *EC-Asbestos*, WT/DS 135/AB/R (2001).

In addition to film distribution quotas (Article IV), two major exceptions apply to Article III: Government procurement policies (see Section 1.14), and authorized subsidization of domestic industries.

The core text of Article III provides:

> The contracting parties recognize that internal taxes and other internal charges, and laws, regulations and requirements affecting the internal sale, offering for sale, purchase, transportation, distribution or use of products, and internal quantitative regulations requiring the mixture, processing, or use of products in specified amounts or proportions, should not be applied to imported or domestic products to afford protection to domestic production.
>
> The products of the territory of any contracting party imported into the territory of any other contracting party shall not be subject, directly or indirectly, to internal taxes or other internal charges of any kind in excess of those applied, directly or indirectly, to like domestic products. Moreover, no contracting party shall otherwise apply internal taxes or other internal charges to imported or domestic products in a manner contrary to the principles set forth in paragraph 1. * * *
>
> The products of the territory of any contracting party imported into the territory of any other contracting party shall be accorded treatment no less favorable than that accorded to like products of national origin in respect of all

laws, regulations and requirements affecting their internal sale, offering for sale, purchase, transportation, distribution, or use. The provisions of this paragraph shall not prevent the application of differential internal transportation charges which are based exclusively on the economic operation of the means of transport and not on the nationality of the product.

Where GATT permits nondiscriminatory "duties, taxes and other charges," the powers of a Contracting Party are limited even as to these devices. First, GATT Article X requires that notice be given of any new or changed national regulations which affect international trade, by requiring the prompt publication of those "laws, regulations, judicial decisions and administrative rulings of general application." Second, the Contracting Parties commit themselves "from time to time" to a continuing series of multilateral tariff negotiations (MTN) to seek further reductions in tariff levels and other barriers to international trade.

Such negotiations are to be "on a reciprocal and mutually advantageous basis." GATT negotiated tariff rates (called "concessions" or "bindings"), which are listed in the "Tariff Schedules", are deposited with GATT by each participating country. These concessions must be granted to imports from any Contracting Party, both because the GATT requires MFN treatment, and because Article II specifically requires use of the negotiated rates.

The 1947 GATT Agreement and its subsequent multinational negotiating rounds were quite successful in reducing tariff duty levels on trade in goods. See Section 1.3 below. This was its original purpose, and the mechanism was well-adapted to accomplishing that goal. However, its effectiveness was also limited to trade in goods, and primarily to reduction of tariffs in such trade. It was not designed to affect trade in services, trade-related intellectual property rights or trade-related investment measures. As tariff duty rates declined, the trade-distorting effects of these other issues became more important. They, along with NTBs, are all addressed in the 1995 package of WTO agreements.

Trade in Goods: General Exceptions

Even within "trade in goods," the 1947 GATT had limitations. It included a Protocol of Provisional Application which allowed numerous grandfathered exceptions to Members' obligations under the GATT Agreement. The Protocol exempted from GATT disciplines the national laws of Member States which were already enacted and in force at the time of adoption of the Protocol. This "grandfather clause" no longer applies under GATT 1994.

Framers of GATT 1947 were aware that a commitment to freer trade could cause serious, adverse economic consequences from time to time within part or all a country's domestic economy, particularly its labor sector. The GATT 1947 and 1994 contains at least seven safety valves (in nine clauses of the Agreement) to permit a country, in appropriate circumstances, to respond to domestic pressures while remaining a participant in GATT. Two safety valves deal with unfair trade practices: Antidumping tariff duties (AD) and countervailing duties (CVD) applied against select government subsidies. AD and CVD apply to specific countries in addition to normal WTO-negotiated tariffs. Another important safety valve concerns "safeguard procedures", a temporary time out from import surges, invoked by Presidents Trump to impose additional tariffs against solar panel and clothes washers from anywhere in the world.

General omnibus exceptions to the GATT are established in Chapter XX, notably for measures "necessary" to protect public morals, and human, animal and plant life or health. See *U.S.—Shrimp*, WT/DS 58/AB/R (1998) (protection of endangered sea turtles). Evaluating whether measures are "necessary" requires consideration of reasonably available alternative approaches to achieve public policy goals. See *Brazil—Tyres*, WT/DS332/AB/R (2007) (ban on imports of retreaded tires upheld) and EC-Asbestos, WT/DS/AB/R (2001) (ban on asbestos imports upheld). Another general exception concerns measures "relating to" the conservation of exhaustible natural resources. See *China—Raw Materials*, WT/DS 394, 395, 398 (Panel, 2011) (export quota on bauxite and export duty on fluorspar did not relate to conservation). Other general exceptions concern trade in gold and silver, prison labor, protection of national treasures, commodity agreements, government stabilization plans and products in general or local short supply.

All these general exceptions are subject to the qualifying language of Article XX "chapeau": They may not be applied in an arbitrary or unjustifiably discriminatory manner or constitute a disguised restriction on international trade. See *U.S.—Shrimp*, 21.5, WT/DS58/AB/RW (2001) (unjustifiable and arbitrary discrimination found in U.S. shrimp import restraints intended to conserve endangered sea turtles). For additional examples of the application of these exceptions and its chapeau, see my Concise Hornbook on *International Trade Law*, Chapter 1.

WTO members, in accordance with GATT Articles XII, XV and XVIII, may generally undertake trade and monetary exchange restraints necessary to deal with their balance of payments needs.

Chapter XXI of the GATT preserves the right of states to act in ways each member considers necessary for the protection of its "essential security interests" relating to fissionable materials, traffic in arms, or taken in time of war or an international relations emergency. President Trump in 2018 placed "national security" tariffs on U.S. steel and aluminum imports, triggering retaliatory "re-balancing tariffs" around the globe and WTO dispute complaints. President Biden has removed some of these tariffs primarily in favor of tariff rate quotas on steel and aluminum.

THE WORLD TRADE ORGANIZATION

§ 1.3 The GATT 1947 Multinational Trade Negotiations (Rounds)

Under the auspices of GATT 1947 Article XXVIII, the Contracting Parties committed themselves to hold periodic multinational trade negotiations (MTN or "Rounds"). They completed seven such Rounds with the GATT membership steadily increasing:

- Geneva (1947) with 21 countries
- Annecy (1948) with 27 countries
- Torquay (1950) with 33 countries
- "Dillon Round" Geneva (1960–62) with 36 countries
- "Kennedy Round" Geneva (1964–67) with 74 countries
- "Tokyo Round" Geneva (1973–79) with 85 countries
- "Uruguay Round" Geneva (1986–94) with 128 countries
- The WTO Doha Round (2001–15) with 164 countries is dead

The largest exporters by volume of goods generally take the lead on tariff reduction negotiations. While the first five Rounds concentrated on item-by-item tariff reductions, the "Kennedy Round" (1964–1967) was noted for its achievement of across-the-board tariff reductions. In 1961, GATT began to consider how to approach the increasing trade disparity with the developing world. In 1964, GATT adopted Part IV, which introduced a principle of "diminished expectations of reciprocity." Reciprocity remained a goal but developed nations would not expect concessions from developing nations which were inconsistent with developmental needs. For the developing nations, non-reciprocity meant freedom to protect domestic markets from import competition. Import substitution was a major focus of developmental theory in the 1960s, and developing nations saw keeping their markets closed as saving these domestic industries.

Part IV of GATT 1947 resulted in a substantial growth in developing nation Contracting Parties. Although they also sought preferential treatment of their exports, that was a demand which would remain unsatisfied for another decade and longer when GATT approved "generalized system of tariff preference" (GSP) schemes for developing members.

Nearly a dozen major agreements on nontariff barrier issues were produced in the Tokyo Round. Not all nations participated in the GATT 1947 or are members of its replacement, the WTO. The "Tokyo Round" (1973–1979) engendered agreements about several areas of nontariff barrier (NTB) trade restraints, including agreements designed to lessen NTBs such as complex customs valuation procedures, import licensing systems, and product health, safety, and environmental standards. But the Tokyo NTB agreements were optional, and most of the developing world membership opted out. By the 1990s international trade was once again at a crossroad.

In 1986, the "Uruguay Round" of multilateral trade negotiations began at a Special Session of the GATT Contracting States. This Uruguay Round included separate negotiations on trade in goods and on trade in services, with separate groups of negotiators dealing with each topic. Subtopics for negotiation by subgroups included nontariff barriers, agriculture, subsidies and countervailing duties, intellectual property rights and counterfeit goods, safeguards, tropical products, textiles, investment policies, and dispute resolution. The negotiating sessions were extraordinarily complex but were able to achieve a successful conclusion at the end of 1993, giving birth to the World Trade Organization (WTO) in 1995.

WTO Negotiating Rounds

In 1999 an attempt at launching a "Seattle Round" led by President Clinton failed with violence in the streets. Two years later, the "Doha Round" was successfully launched in Qatar covering all existing WTO fields as well as E-commerce, trade and the environment, debt and finance, and special and differential treatment and assistance for developing countries. Developed WTO countries pushed foreign investment, competition policy, transparency in procurement, and trade facilitation topics. At Cancun in 2003, the WTO developing nations rejected these topics, focusing on agricultural trade barriers to their exports.

Scheduled for completion in 2005, the Doha Round of WTO negotiations collapsed in July 2008 after marathon sessions. India and China insisted upon Special Safeguard Mechanisms against surges in agricultural imports, provisions the U.S. and EU did not accept. The members agreed on nearly all other areas of the Doha Round negotiations. WTO trade initiatives since Doha have been principally limited to *optional* trade facilitation, information technology and agricultural export subsidy agreements.

The Doha Round formally died in 2015. This caused many nations to accelerate their participation in bilateral and regional free trade agreements.

§ 1.4 The World Trade Organization (WTO 1995)

Directory of Agreements

Creating the rules-based World Trade Organization, despite the leading role of the United States, was not easy. Eight years in negotiation, the major issue was trade in agricultural goods, with the EU maintaining a strongly protective position and the Cairns Group led by the USA seeking to reduce agricultural trade barriers and subsidies. In the end, a modest compromise was achieved in the WTO Agreement on Agriculture, discussed below.

What drove that compromise? In this author's opinion, the United States played two critical cards: First, it aggressively undertook unilateral, totally unauthorized trade actions against "foreign country practices" under Section 301 of the Trade Act of 1974, revitalized by President Trump against China in 2018. Under considerable pressure, these actions primarily opened foreign markets to U.S. exports. Second, the United States played the NAFTA card, commencing negotiations and reaching an extensive free trade and foreign investment agreement with Mexico and Canada. NAFTA 1994 negotiations ran about one year ahead of the Uruguay Round, influencing the content of and pushing forward the creation of the WTO and its package of agreements.

That said, significant differences between the WTO Agreements and NAFTA existed. For example, NAFTA covered business visas, state trading, competition policy, and had an entire chapter dedicated to energy, all of which are absent from the WTO package. The WTO Agreements cover customs valuation and pre-shipment inspection, which NAFTA did not. Nothing in the WTO package of agreements touched on labor or the environment, nor NAFTA's two side agreements.

On market access, procurement, investment and most services, NAFTA went further and faster than the Uruguay Round WTO agreements. There was significant overlap on intellectual property where NAFTA's leading edge was particularly influential. The WTO Agreement on Agriculture, on the other hand, exceeded NAFTA's trade opening initiatives. The WTO package also addressed basic telecommunications, which was mostly omitted from NAFTA. The WTO has (since 1997) fostered an information technology tariff reduction agreement, but Mexico does not participate.

These differences may help explain why the basic rule of NAFTA dispute settlement was that the complaining country normally had the prerogative of choosing between NAFTA and WTO procedures. This rule continues to operate as between USMCA and WTO dispute procedures. For details and examples, see my Concise Hornbook on *International Litigation and Arbitration*, Chapter 10.

The WTO Package Deal

The WTO is the product of the Uruguay Round of GATT negotiations, which was successfully completed in 1994. The Uruguay Round produced a package of agreements, the Agreement Establishing the World Trade Organization, and its Annexes, which include the General Agreement on Tariffs and Trade 1994 (GATT 1994) and a series of Multilateral Trade Agreements (the Covered Agreements). These agreements extend way beyond trade in goods to trade in services, trade-related intellectual property rights, trade-related investment measures, and a binding system of dispute settlement.

All the Covered Agreements are non-negotiable; they are mandatory. Four Plurilateral Trade Agreements are optional, though two of these Agreements (Dairy and Bovine Meat) have been rescinded. In addition to the WTO package, new members typically make specific additional trade and trade law commitments in their "Accession Agreements."

GATT 1947 and GATT 1994 are two distinct agreements. GATT 1994 incorporates the provisions of GATT 1947, except for the Protocol of Provisional Application, which is expressly excluded. The problems created by exempting the existing national laws at the time of the adoption of the Protocol were avoided by this exclusion. Otherwise, in cases involving a conflict between GATT 1947 and GATT 1994, GATT 1947 controls. The WTO is guided by the decisions, procedures, and customary practices under GATT. The WTO package of agreements has been routinely construed by reference to the Vienna Convention on the Interpretation of Treaties. See, e.g., *EC—Chicken*, WT/DS269/AB/R (2005).

Annexed to the WTO Agreement are several Multilateral Trade Agreements. As to trade in goods, they include Agreements on Agriculture, Textiles, Antidumping, Subsidies and Countervailing Measures, Safeguards, Technical Barriers to Trade, Sanitary and Phytosanitary Measures, Pre-shipment Inspection, Rules of Origin, and Import License Procedures. In addition to trade in goods, they include a General Agreement on Trade in Services and Agreements on Trade-Related Aspects of Intellectual Property Rights and Trade-Related Investment Measures.

Affecting all these agreements is the Understanding on Rules and Procedures Governing the Settlement of Disputes (DSU). All the Multilateral Trade Agreements are generally binding on all members of the World Trade Organization. Moreover, should a conflict arise between GATT 1994 and one of these Agreements, the latter prevails. Hence in WTO dispute proceedings where a conflict may exist, panels are required to first examine the specific Multilateral Agreement before taking up the GATT 1994 issue. See *EC—Sardines*, WTO/DS231/AB/R (2002) and U.S.—Internet Gambling, WT/DS 285/AB/R (2005).

Existing WTO members may declare "non-application" of all these Agreements vis-a-vis new members, thus opting out of their application to them. The United States, for example, declared non-application of the WTO Agreements to Armenia, Moldova, Georgia, Mongolia, and the Kyrgyz Republic when those nations joined the WTO, although these declarations were subsequently revoked for all but Moldova. The U.S. still has not accepted application of the WTO to Kazakhstan, a WTO member.

In addition to the Multilateral Trade Agreements, there are also Plurilateral Trade Agreements, which are annexed to the WTO Agreement. These agreements, however, are not binding on all WTO members, and states can choose to adhere to them or not. They include Agreements on Government Procurement, Trade in Civil Aircraft, International Dairy (rescinded), and an Arrangement Regarding Bovine Meat (rescinded). Member states which do not join the plurilateral trade agreements do not receive reciprocal benefits under them. Participating members agree to utilize the DSU to settle Plurilateral Trade Agreement disputes.

WORLD TRADE ORGANIZATION AGREEMENTS

AGREEMENT ESTABLISHING THE WORLD TRADE ORGANIZATION

ANNEX 1A: AGREEMENTS ON TRADE IN GOODS

1 General Agreement on Tariffs and Trade 1994

(a) Understanding on the Interpretation of Article II:1(b) (tariff concessions)

(b) Understanding on the Interpretation of Article XVII (state trading enterprises)

(c) Understanding on Balance-of-Payments Provisions

(d) Understanding on the Interpretation of Article XXIV (free trade areas and customs unions) (see Chapter 2)

(e) Understanding on the Interpretation of Article XXV (waivers)

(f) Understanding on the Interpretation of Article XXVIII (modification of tariff schedules)

(g) Understanding on the Interpretation of Article XXXV (non-application of GATT)

2 GATT 1994

3 Agreement on Agriculture

4 Agreement on Sanitary and Phytosanitary Measures

5 Agreement on Textiles and Clothing

6 Agreement on Technical Barriers to Trade

7 Agreement on Trade-Related Investment Measures

8 Agreement on Implementation of Article VI (antidumping and countervailing duties)

9 Agreement on Implementation of Article VII (customs valuation)

10 Agreement on Pre-Shipment Inspection

11 Agreement on Rules of Origin

12 Agreement on Import Licensing Procedures

13 Agreement on Subsidies and Countervailing Measures

14 Agreement on Safeguards

ANNEX 1B: General Agreement on Trade in Services and Annexes

ANNEX 1C: Agreement on Trade-Related Aspects of Intellectual Property Rights, Including Trade in Counterfeit Goods

ANNEX 2: Understanding on Rules and Procedures Governing the Settlement of Disputes

ANNEX 3: Trade Policy Review Mechanism

ANNEX 4: Plurilateral Trade Agreements

ANNEX 4(a) Agreement on Trade in Civil Aircraft

ANNEX 4(b) Agreement on Government Procurement

ANNEX 4(c) International Dairy Arrangement (rescinded)

ANNEX 4(d) Arrangement Regarding Bovine Meat (rescinded)

Accession Agreements undertaken by new members may add to or subtract from the WTO package of mandatory multilateral agreements. China, for example, agreed to the application of special "safeguard" rules against its exports for a limited period after its WTO admission in 2001 and to specific restraints on export taxes.

The duties of the World Trade Organization are to facilitate the implementation, administer the operations and further the objectives of all these agreements. Its duties also include the resolution of disputes under the agreements, reviews of trade policy and cooperation with the International Monetary Fund (IMF) and the World Bank. To achieve these goals, the WTO Agreement provides a charter for the new organization, but for only minimalist institutional and procedural capabilities, and no substantive competence. There is a unified administration of pre-existing and new obligations under all agreements concerning trade in goods, including the Uruguay Round Agreements. In addition, the administration of the new obligations on trade in services, intellectual property and foreign investment were brought under the same roof.

The WTO as an institution has no power to bring actions on its own initiative. Under the provisions of the WTO Agreement, only the members of WTO can initiate actions under the Dispute Settlement Understanding. Enforcement of WTO obligations is primarily through permitting members to retaliate or cross retaliate against other members, rather than by execution of WTO institutional orders. See Section 1.15. As Article 3.2 of the DSU suggests, many panel and Appellate Body decisions utilize the Vienna Convention on Interpretation of Treaties to clarify the meaning of the WTO package of agreements.

Admission to and Exit from the WTO

The existing 130 or so members of GATT 1947 became the WTO's founding member states. Admission to the World Trade Organization is in common practice by "consensus." In theory, this gives each member a veto over applicant countries, though a formal two-thirds affirmative vote could be employed. No nation wishing to join has ever formally been vetoed, though many have been long delayed. Iran's desire to join has basically been frustrated by U.S. refusal to negotiate on WTO entry. It took, for example, well over a decade to negotiate acceptable terms of entry for the People's Republic of China in 2001, Vietnam in 2007 and Russia in 2012.

Such negotiations are handled individually by member states, not by the WTO as an organization. United States negotiations with China were particularly lengthy and difficult, one principal issue being whether China should be admitted as a developing or developed nation, which is normally a self-selected choice. The issue was fudged, with China treated differently within the WTO mandatory package of agreements. The issue remains controversial. China's admission also brought in Chinese Taipei (Taiwan). Hong Kong, admitted under British rule, remains a separate WTO member.

Essentially, applicant countries make an offer of trade liberalization commitments and compliance with the mandatory Covered Agreements to join the WTO. This offer is renegotiated with interested member states, some 40 nations regarding China, including the European Union which negotiates as a unit (NAFTA does not). Regarding China, the last member to reach agreement on WTO admission was Mexico, which extracted stiff promises against the dumping of Chinese goods. The various trade commitments made by the applicant in these bilateral negotiations are consolidated into a final accession protocol, which is then approved by "consensus." At this writing there are approximately 165 WTO member states.

Any member may withdraw with six months' notice. Although this has never happened, there was speculation that the Trump Administration might do so.

§ 1.5 WTO Decision-Making

The World Trade Organization is structured in three tiers. One tier is the Ministerial Conference, which meets biennially and is composed of representatives of all WTO members. Each member state has an equal voting weight. This is unlike the representation in the IMF and World Bank where there is weighted voting, and financially powerful states have more power over the decision-making process.

The Ministerial Conference is responsible for all WTO functions and can make any decisions necessary. It has the power to authorize new multilateral negotiations and to adopt the results of such negotiations. The Ministerial Conference, by a three-fourths vote, is authorized to grant waivers of obligations to members in exceptional circumstances. It also has the power to adopt interpretations of Covered Agreements. When the Ministerial Conference is in recess, its functions are performed by the General Council.

The second tier is the General Council which has executive authority over the day-to-day operations and functions of the WTO. It is composed of representatives of all WTO Members, and each member has an equal voting weight. It meets whenever it is appropriate. The General Council also has the power to adopt interpretations of Covered Agreements.

The third tier comprises the councils, bodies and committees which are accountable to the Ministerial Conference or General Council. Ministerial Conference committees include Committees on Trade and Development, Balance of Payment Restrictions, Budget, Finance and Administration. General Council bodies include the Dispute Settlement Body, the Trade Policy Review Body, and Councils for Trade in Goods, Trade in Services and Trade-Related Intellectual Property Rights. The Councils are all created by the WTO Agreement and are open to representatives of all member states. The Councils also have the authority to create subordinate organizations. Other committees, such as the Committee on Subsidies and Countervailing Measures are created by specific individual agreements.

Trade Policy Review Mechanism

Of the General Council bodies, the two which are most important are the Dispute Settlement Body (DSB) and the Trade Policy Review Body (TPRB). The DSB is a special meeting of the General Council, and therefore includes all WTO members. It has responsibility for resolution of disputes under all the Covered Agreements, discussed in more detail in Section 1.15 under Dispute Resolution.

The purpose of the Trade Policy Review Mechanism (TPRM) is to improve adherence to the WTO agreements and obligations, and to obtain greater transparency. In that regard, the TPRM supplements the general trade law transparency requirements of Chapter X of the GATT. Individual Members of WTO each prepare a "Country Report" on their trade policies and perceived adherence to the WTO Covered Agreements. The WTO Secretariat also prepares a report on each Member, but from the perspective of the Secretariat.

The Trade Policy Review Body (TPRB) then reviews the trade policies of each member based on these two reports. At the end of the review, the TPRB issues its own report concerning the adherence of the member's trade policy to the WTO Covered Agreements. The TPRB has no enforcement capability, but the report is sent to the next meeting of the WTO Ministerial Conference. It is then up to the Ministerial Conference to evaluate the trade practices and policies of the member state.

Consensus Rules

The process of decision-making in the WTO Ministerial Conference and General Council relies upon "consensus" as the norm, just as it did for decision-making under GATT 1947. "Consensus", in this context means that no member formally objects to a proposed decision. Thus, consensus is not obtained if any one member formally objects, and has often been very difficult to obtain, which proved to be a weakness in the operation of GATT. However, there are many exceptions to the consensus formula under WTO, and some new concepts (such as "inverted consensus") which are designed to ease the process of decision-making under WTO.

Article IX (1) of the WTO Agreement first provides that "the practice of decision-making by consensus" followed under GATT shall be continued. The next sentence of that provision, however, states that "where a decision cannot be arrived at by consensus, the matter at issue shall be decided by voting", except where otherwise provided. The ultimate resolution of the conflict between these two sentences is not completely clear.

There are exceptions to the requirement for consensus that are expressly created under the WTO Agreement. One such exception is decisions by the Dispute Settlement Body, which has its own rules (see Section 1.15). Another set of exceptions concerns decisions on waivers, interpretations, and amendments of the Covered Agreements. Waivers of obligations may be granted, and amendments adopted to Covered Agreements only by the Ministerial Conference. Amendments of Multilateral Trade Agreements usually require a consensus, but where a decision on a proposed amendment cannot obtain consensus, the decision on that amendment is to be made in certain circumstances by a two-thirds majority vote.

In "exceptional circumstances", the Ministerial Conference is authorized to grant waivers of obligations under a Covered Agreement by a three-fourths vote. Another exception to the consensus requirement allows procedural rules in both the Ministerial Conference and the General Council to be decided by a majority vote of the members, unless otherwise provided.

Operationally speaking, the WTO membership rarely meets in its entirety. Alliances and groups within the membership meet to undertake WTO decisions. For example, the "Cairns Group" of 18 member-states has focused on agricultural trade issues and endured as a group for some time. Groups and alliances often shift depending upon the subject matter.

§ 1.6 WTO Agreements and U.S. Law

The WTO Covered Agreements concern not only trade in goods, but also trade in services (GATS), trade-related aspects of intellectual property (TRIPs) and trade-related investment measures (TRIMs). The basic MFN and national treatment concepts that GATT 1947 and GATT 1994 apply to trade in goods are now applied to these areas through GATS and TRIPs. These concepts are elaborated and clarified through interpretive "understandings." In addition, there is an attempt to transform all protectionist measures relating to agriculture (such as import bans and quotas, etc.) into tariff barriers, which can then be lowered in subsequent MTN Rounds (a process known as "tariffication"). Some of the WTO provisions, particularly those concerning trade in goods, are discussed in more detail below in relation to United States trade law.

GATT 1947, GATT 1994, the WTO Agreement, and the other Covered Agreements have not been ratified as treaties. They therefore comprise international obligations of the United States only to the extent that they are incorporated in United States' implementing legislation. GATT 1947 was not considered controlling by the courts of the United States, which have always held themselves bound only to the U.S. implementation legislation. The WTO Covered Agreements standing on their own are considered to have a non-self-executed status, and therefore are likely to be regarded in the same manner as GATT 1947.

Fast-Track

The United States enacted legislation to implement WTO and the Covered Agreements on December 3, 1994. The implementing legislation was submitted to Congress under the "fast-track" procedures of 19 U.S.C.A. § 2112. The statutory authority for "fast-track" procedures also required that the President give 90 days' notice of his intention to enter into such an agreement. Fast-track required that the WTO Agreements be considered by Congress as negotiated by the President, with *no* Congressional amendments via the implementing legislation. The Uruguay Round Agreements Act of 1994 was adopted with relatively little controversy. Similar fast-track procedures were in place for the Doha Round of WTO negotiations under the Trade Promotion Authority Act of 2002 but expired in July of 2007.

Fast-track was renewed in 2014 under Presidents Obama and Trump. It remained in effect until July 2021. Nearly all U.S. FTAs, including the USMCA, have been negotiated and implemented under fast-track procedures. President Biden did not seek renewal of fast-track trade promotion authority. See Chapter 4.

§ 1.7 Import/Export Quotas and Licensing, Textiles and Clothing

In addition to requiring MFN and national treatment, GATT 1947 and 1994 prohibits use of certain kinds of quantitative restrictions. Subject to exceptions such as balance of payment crises, Article XI prohibits "prohibitions or restrictions" on imports and it specifically prohibits the use of "quotas, import or export licenses or other measures" to restrict imports from a Contracting Party. Quotas include voluntary export restrain agreements. *See* Japan-Semiconductors, GATT Panel Report (1988). If utilized, Article XIII requires non-discrimination in quantitative trade restrictions, by barring an importing Contracting State from applying any prohibition or restriction to the products of another Contracting State, "unless the importation of the like product of *all* third countries. . . is similarly prohibited or restricted." (emphasis added).

The WTO has significantly reduced the number of trade quotas. By 2005, the Agreement on Textiles eliminated quotas long maintained under the Multi-Fiber Arrangement. See Section 1.7. Voluntary export restraints (quotas) are severely limited by the Safeguards Agreement. In addition, the WTO removes trade quotas by advancing "tariffication," replacing quotas with tariffs—sometimes even at extraordinarily high tariff rates. Tariffication is the approach adopted in the WTO Agricultural Agreement.

Quantity restrictions, such as numerical quotas on the importation or exportation of goods continue to exist, despite GATT Article XI which calls for their elimination, subject to broadly worded exceptions to relieve critical shortages, to ensure domestic price controls, and to remediate short supply conditions. "Tariff-rate quotas" admit a specified quantity of goods at a preferential rate of duty. Once imports reach that quantity, tariffs are normally increased. WTO disputes concerning quotas have resulted in panel and Appellate Body decisions that largely treat import rules that can create de facto quantitative restraint effects as prohibited by Article XI. For example, in *India-Autos* (WTO/DS16/AB/R (2002)) "trade balancing" rules requiring producers to export to import were held to breach Article XI.

The Agreement on Textiles eliminated in 2005 the quotas long maintained under the Multi-Fibre Arrangement (MFA). The demise of MFA textile quotas in 2005, as widely expected, accelerated Chinese and other Asian textile exports to the United States. Responding to domestic pressures, the United States repeatedly invoked special safeguard protections against textile and clothing imports during the ten-year phase-out period that ended in 2005.

Since then, the average U.S. bound and applied tariff on textile products has been around 8 percent.

Import (but not export) licensing schemes are allowed when quotas are permitted. See Section 1.7. International concern about delays which result from cumbersome import licensing procedures was manifested in the 1979 Tokyo Round MTN Import Licensing Code (which most developing countries refused to sign). The United States adhered to this Code, as did a reasonable number of other developed nations.

The Uruguay Round made the Agreement on Import Licensing Procedures (1994) binding on all World Trade Organization members. The Agreement's objectives include facilitating the simplification and harmonization of import licensing and licensing renewal procedures, ensuring adequate publication of rules governing licensing procedures, and reducing the practice of refusing importation because of minor variations in quantity, value, or weight of the import item under license.

§ 1.8 GATT/WTO Nontariff Trade Barrier Codes

TBT and SPS Codes

There are numerous nontariff trade barriers applicable to imports. Many of these barriers arise out of safety and health regulations. Others concern the environment, consumer protection, product standards and government procurement. Many of the relevant rules were created for legitimate consumer and public protection reasons. They were often created without extensive consideration of their international impact as potential nontariff trade barriers. Nevertheless, the practical impact of legislation of this type is to ban the importation of nonconforming products. Thus, unlike tariffs which can always be paid, and unlike quotas which permit a certain amount of goods to enter the market, nontariff trade barriers have the potential to totally exclude foreign exports.

Multilateral GATT negotiations since the end of World War II have led to a significant decline in world tariff levels, particularly on trade with developed nations. As steadily as tariff barriers have disappeared, nontariff trade barriers (NTBs) have emerged. Health and safety regulations, environmental laws, rules regulating products standards, procurement legislation and customs procedures are often said to present NTB problems.

Negotiations over nontariff trade barriers dominated the Tokyo Round of the GATT negotiations during the late 1970s. Optional NTB "codes" (sometimes called "side agreements") emerged from the Tokyo Round. These concerned subsidies, dumping, government procurement, technical barriers (products standards), customs valuation and import licensing. In addition, specific agreements regarding trade in bovine meats, dairy products, and civil aircraft, as well as government procurement, were also reached. The United States accepted all these NTB codes and agreements except the one on dairy products. Most of the necessary implementation of these agreements was accomplished in the Trade Agreements Act of 1979. Nearly all developing world members of GATT opted out of these NTB codes.

Additional NTB codes were agreed upon under the Uruguay Round ending in late 1994 and became part of the WTO legal regime. All the NTB areas covered by the Tokyo Round Codes were revisited, and new codes created for sanitary and phytosanitary measures (SPS), trade-related investment measures (TRIMs), pre-shipment inspection, rules of origin, escape clause safeguards and trade-related intellectual property rights (TRIPs). Unlike the Tokyo Round Codes, the WTO nontariff barrier codes (save a few plurilateral codes) are *mandatory* for all members. The United States Congress approved and implemented these Codes, along with the optional WTO Procurement Code, in December of 1994 under the Uruguay Round Agreements Act.

One problem with nontariff trade barriers is that they are so numerous. Intergovernmental negotiations intended to reduce their trade restricting impact are both tedious and difficult. There are continuing attempts through the World Trade Organization to come to grips with additional specific NTB problems. Furthermore, various trade agreements of the United States have been undertaken in this field. For example, the Canada-United States Free Trade Area Agreement and the NAFTA built upon the existing GATT agreements in attempting to further reduce NTB problems between the United States, Canada, and Mexico.

SPS Code

The SPS Code strongly encourages the use of international SPS standards, such as the Codex Alimentarius Commission. But member states may proceed to enact their own nondiscriminatory SPS rules, subject to the Code's mandates, notably that they be based upon risk assessments and scientific evidence. There is some suggestion in the decisions of the WTO Appellate Body that SPS measures must be "proportional" to the risks involved. See *Japan-Apples*, WT/DS245/AB/R (2003).

Some of the difficulties of these NTBs are illustrated in the *EU Beef Hormones* case (WT/DS 26/AB/R (1998)). The Sanitary and Phytosanitary Code (SPS Code) basically requires adherence to international food standards, or a scientific basis for regulatory rules governing food products. The EU, adhering to "precautionary principles," banned imports of growth-enhancing hormone-treated beef from the U.S. and Canada as a health hazard. The Appellate Body ruled in 1997 under the SPS Code that, since the ban was stricter than international standards, the EU needed scientific evidence to back it up. The Appellate Body noted the EU had failed to undertake a scientific risk assessment, and the EU's scientific reports did not provide any rational basis to uphold the ban. In fact, the primary EU study had found no evidence of harm to humans from the growth-enhancing-hormones. If the "relevant scientific evidence is insufficient", there is limited recognition of precautionary principles in Article 5.7 of the SPS Code.

The Appellate Body concluded that the ban violated the EU's SPS obligations and required the EU to produce scientific evidence to justify the ban within a reasonable time, or to revoke the ban. Arbitrators later determined that 15 months was a reasonable time. But the EU failed to produce such evidence, and the U.S. retaliated (as authorized) by imposing substantial tariffs on EU imports.

Late in 2004, the EU commenced WTO proceedings asserting that new scientific studies and precaution justified its ban and required removal of U.S. retaliation. This WTO proceeding also went against the EU, again in the absence of adequate proof of scientific basis. See *U.S.—Continued Suspension in EC-Hormones*, WT/320/AB/R (2008). Finally, in 2009, a phased four-year settlement of the *Beef Hormones* dispute was reached. The U.S. got a higher quota to export hormone-free beef to the EU in return for phasing out its retaliatory tariffs on EU goods.

TBT Code

Widespread use of "standards" requirements as NTB import restraints resulted in 1979 in the GATT Agreement on Technical Barriers to Trade (called the "Standards Code"). This Code was made operative in the United States by the Trade Agreements Act of 1979 and was followed by a reasonable number of other developed nations.

Its successor is the WTO Agreement on Technical Barriers to Trade (1994) (TBT Code). By explicit provision in Article 1.5 of the TBT Code, the SPS Code takes precedence over the TBT Code. The Appellate Body has held that both Codes take precedence over GATT 1994 issues. The TBT Code is binding on all WTO members. It strongly favors conforming use of international product standards, such as those of the International Standards Organization. See *EC—Sardines*, WT/DS231/AB/R (2002) (EC marketing rule not based on Codex Alimentarius standard).

In general, the TBT Code deals with the problem of manipulation of product standards and labels, product testing procedures, and product certifications to slow or stop imported goods. To this end, the TBT Code requires NTBs to be not more trade restrictive than necessary to effectuate legitimate governmental objectives.

The TBT Code provides, in part and subject to some exceptions, that imported products shall be accorded treatment (including testing treatment and certification) no less favorable than that accorded to like products of national origin or those originating in any other country. It also requires that WTO members establish a central office for standards inquiries, publish advance and reasonable notice of requirements that are applicable to imported goods, and provide an opportunity for commentary by those who may be affected adversely. The TBT Code establishes an international committee to deal with alleged instances of noncompliance. Various United States TBT, notably dolphin-safe and imported meat origin labels as well as flavored cigarette standards, have been challenged in WTO dispute settlement proceedings.

§ 1.9 The WTO Agreement on Agriculture

Agricultural issues played a central role in the Uruguay Round negotiations and are critical to the Doha Round as well. More than any other issue, they delayed completion of the Uruguay Round from 1990 to 1993. The agreement reached in December of 1993 is a trade liberalizing, market-oriented effort. Each country has made commitments on market access, reduced domestic agricultural support levels and export subsidies. The United States Congress approved these commitments in December of 1994 by adopting the Uruguay Round Agreements Act.

Broadly speaking nontariff barriers (NTBs) to international agricultural trade are replaced by tariffs that provide substantially the same level of protection. This is known as "tariffication." It applies to virtually all NTBs, including variable levies, import bans, voluntary export restraints and import quotas. See *Chile—Price Band System*, WT/DS207/AB/R (2002). Tariffication applies specifically to U.S. agricultural quotas adopted under Section 22 of the Agricultural Adjustment Act. All agricultural tariffs, including those converted from NTBs, are to be reduced by 36 and 24 percent by developed and developing countries, respectively, over six and ten-year periods. Certain minimum access tariff quotas apply when imports amount to less than 3 to 5 percent of domestic consumption. An escape clause exists for tariffed imports at low prices or upon a surge of importation depending upon the existing degree of import penetration.

Regarding domestic support for agriculture, some programs with minimal impact on trade are exempt from change. These programs are known as "green box policies." They include governmental support for agricultural research, disease control, infrastructure, and food security. Green box policies were also exempt from GATT/WTO challenge or countervailing duties for 9 years. Direct payments to producers that are not linked to production are also generally exempt. This will include income support, adjustment assistance, and environmental and regional assistance payments. Furthermore, direct payments to support crop reductions and *de minimis* payments are exempted in most cases.

After removing all the exempted domestic agricultural support programs, the agreement on agriculture arrives at a calculation known as the Total Aggregate Measurement of Support (Total AMS). This measure is the basis for agricultural support reductions under the agreement. Developed nations reduced their Total AMS by 20 percent over 6 years, developing nations by 13.3 percent over 10 years. United States reductions undertaken in 1985 and 1990 meant that little or no U.S. action was required to meet this obligation. Agricultural export subsidies of developed nations were reduced by 36 percent below 1986–1990 levels over 6 years and the quantity of subsidized agricultural exports by 21 percent. Developing nations had corresponding 24 and 14 percent reductions over 10 years.

All conforming tariffications, reductions in domestic support for agriculture and export subsidy alterations were essentially exempt from challenge for nine years within the GATT/WTO on grounds such as serious prejudice in export markets or nullification and impairment of agreement benefits. However, countervailing duties could be levied against all unlawfully subsidized exports of agricultural goods except for subsidies derived from so-called national "green box policies." In *U.S.—Upland Cotton* (WTO/DS267/AB/R (2005)), the Appellate Body affirmed that member states must not only conform to the Agreement on Agriculture, but also the SCM Agreement. In that decision, U.S. compliance with the Agriculture Agreement was acknowledged, but its "Step-2" payments to cotton users favoring domestic over imported cotton (local content subsidies) were held to violate the SCM Agreement.

§ 1.10 The General Agreement on Trade in Services (GATS)

Because protectionist barriers to international trade in services were stifling, the United States and other developed countries insisted that there should be a General Agreement on Trade in Services (GATS). In the United States, services account for over two-thirds of the nation's GDP and provide jobs for nearly two-thirds of the work force. Services account for almost one-third of U.S. exports in sectors such as tourism, education, construction, telecommunications, transport, and health. In contrast, most developing nations are minimal exporters of services, save by means of exporting their people, but migration was not included as a subject under the GATS.

Market access for services is a major focus of the General Agreement on Trade in Services (GATS), a product of the Uruguay Round of Negotiations. The GATS defines the supply of services broadly to include providing services across borders or inside member states with or without a commercial presence therein. Apart from ensuring transparency of national regulatory controls over services, the core GATS Article XVII commitment is to afford most-favored-nation treatment to service providers, subject to country-specific, preferential trade agreement or labor market integration agreement exemptions, such as audio-visual services in the EU.

In addition, each WTO member state made under GATS XVI specific schedule of commitments (concessions) on opening their markets in services' sectors negotiated using the WTO Services Sectoral Classification List. They further agreed under Article XVI to provide national treatment to their services' commitment schedule. For example, to what degree may foreign banks or foreign economic consultants provide services, and are they entitled to national treatment? The answers to those questions will be found in the GATS specific commitments of each member.

Much to its consternation, the United States was found to have failed to exclude Internet gambling services under its GATS commitments' schedule. This caused Antigua-Barbuda to prevail in a dispute that alleged U.S. gambling laws discriminatorily prohibited its right to export such services to the U.S. market. See *U.S.—Gambling*, WT/DS285/AB/R (2007). The United States also lost the argument that its Internet gambling services' restraints were justifiable on public morals' grounds. This argument failed as discriminatory under the "chapeau" of the GATS Article XIV general exceptions that are like GATT Article XX general exceptions discussed in Section 1.2.

Special "GATS Rules" govern use of safeguards against surges of services' imports, subsidies applicable to services' exports, and government procurement of services. General GATS exceptions apply (for example, government supplied services), as do national security GATS exceptions.

National laws that restrict the number of firms in a market, that are dependent upon local "needs tests", or that mandate local incorporation are regulated by the GATS. Various "transparency" rules require disclosure of all relevant laws and regulations, and these must be administered reasonably, objectively, and impartially. Specific service market access and national treatment commitments are made by various governments in schedules attached to the agreement. These commitments may be modified or withdrawn after 3 years, subject to a right of compensation that can be arbitrated. Certain mutual recognition of education and training for service-sector licensing occurs. State monopolies or exclusive service providers may continue but must not abuse their positions.

Detailed rules are created in annexes to the GATS on financial, telecommunications and air transport services. Under the Telecommunications Reference Paper (TRP), for example, the United States successfully argued that Telmex had abused its monopoly position in Mexico by charging discriminatory, non-cost-oriented connection fees for foreign calls. See *Mexico—Telecoms*, WT/DS204/AB/R (2004).

The U.S. Congress approved and implemented the GATS agreement in December of 1994 under the Uruguay Round Agreements Act. Subsequently, early in 1995, the United States refused to extend most-favored-nation treatment to financial services. The European Union, Japan and other GATS nations then entered into an interim 2-year agreement which operated on MFN principles. Financial services were revisited in 1996–97 with further negotiations aimed at bringing the United States into the fold. These negotiations bore fruit late in 1997 with 70 nations (including the United States) joining in an agreement that covers 95 percent of trade in banking, insurance, securities, and financial information. This agreement took effect March 1, 1999.

The GATS has reduced unilateral U.S. action under Section 301 to gain access to foreign markets for U.S. service providers. This reduction flows from U.S. adherence to the Dispute Settlement Understanding (DSU) that accompanies the WTO accords. The DSU obligates its signatories to follow streamlined dispute settlement procedures under which unilateral retaliation is restrained until the offending nation has failed to conform to a World Trade Organization ruling.

GATS Disputes

GATS, and the 1996 Protocol on Telecommunications and 1997 Protocol on Financial Services, have generated only a handful of WTO disputes. Here is a sampling of them:

1. *EC—Regime for the Importation, Sale and Distribution of Bananas*, WT/DS27/AB/R (1997) (traders of goods may also be traders of services, such as wholesaling or retailing, GATS Articles II and XVII apply to de jure and de facto discrimination).

2. *Canada—Certain Measures Concerning Periodicals*, WT/DS31/AB/R (1997) (GATT and GATS co-exist, no override).

3. *Canada—Certain Measures Affecting the Automotive Industry*, WT/DS139,142/R (2000) (coverage under GATS must be determined before assessment of consistency with GATS obligations).

4. *Mexico—Measures Affecting Telecommunication Services*, WT/DS204/R(2004) (Mexican cross-border interconnection rates not cost-oriented and unreasonable in breach of Telecoms Annex, failure to allow access to private leased-circuits also violated commitments) (settled with rate reductions and increased access).

5. *United States—Measures Affecting The Cross-Border Supply of Gambling and Betting Services*, WT/DS 285/AB/R (2005) (gambling included in U.S. recreational services' commitments, U.S. import ban amounted to "zero quota" in breach of GATS Article XVI, necessary to protect public morals under Article XIV defense but discriminatory enforcement regarding Interstate Horseracing Act fails to meet "chapeau" requirements) (U.S. pays compensation to all GATS signatories except Antigua and Barbuda, the complaining party. . . . $21 million retaliation authorized in 2008).

6. *China—Certain Measures Affecting Electronic Payment Systems*, WT/DS413/R (2012) (discriminatory restraints on foreign electronics payment services' suppliers violate GATS commitments).

§ 1.11 The WTO and Rules of Origin

The Uruguay Round accord on rules of origin is an agreement to agree. A negotiations schedule was established along with a WTO Committee to work with the Customs Cooperation Council on harmonized rules of origin. Certain broad guiding principles for the negotiations are given and considered binding until agreement is reached. These principles are:

- Rules of origin applied to foreign trade must not be more stringent than applied to domestic goods.
- Rules of origin must be administered consistently, uniformly, impartially, and reasonably.
- Origin assessments must be issued within 150 days of a request and remain valid for three years.
- New or modified rules or origin may not be applied retroactively.
- Strict confidentiality rules apply to information submitted confidentially for rule of origin determinations.

To date, no WTO agreement on rules of origin has been reached. As a result, diverse national, free trade and customs union rules of origin predominate. For NAFTA rules of origin, see Chapter 4. For USMCA rules of origin, see Chapter 6.

§ 1.12 The Trade-Related Aspects of Intellectual Property Rights Agreement (TRIPs)

The Uruguay Round accords of late 1993 include an agreement on trade-related intellectual property rights (TRIPs). This agreement is binding upon the roughly 165 nations that are members of the World Trade Organization. In the United States, the TRIPs agreement has been ratified and implemented by Congress under the Uruguay Round Agreements Act. There is a general requirement of national and most-favored-nation treatment among the parties.

Many developed nations had been trying unsuccessfully to promote expanded intellectual property rights through the U.N.-created World Intellectual Property Rights Organization (WIPO). WIPO agreements are not mandatory, and much of the developing world had declined to opt into their terms. Much to the benefit of private parties in the developed world, the TRIPs Code covers the gamut of intellectual property. It has de facto become a near-global IP Code.

On copyrights, there is protection for computer programs and databases, rental authorization controls for owners of computer software and sound recordings, a 50-year motion picture and sound recording copyright term, and a general obligation to comply with the Berne Convention (1971 version) (except for its provisions on moral rights).

On patents, the Paris Convention (1967 version) prevails, 20-year product and process patents are available "in all fields of technology", including pharmaceuticals and agricultural chemicals. However, patents can be denied when necessary to protect public morals or order, to protect human, animal or plant life or health, and to avoid serious environmental prejudice. The TRIPs provisions did not stop the Indian Supreme Court in 2013 from denying Novartis a patent on its cancer drug, Gleevac. The court took the view that Novartis was engaged in "evergreening", *i.e.*, making small, inconsequential changes to existing patents and that Indian law could require proof of "improved therapeutic efficacy" before a patent grant.

Article 31 of the TRIPs permits compulsory licensing of patents in national emergencies or other circumstances of extreme urgency, subject to a duty to reasonably compensate the patent owner. Thailand has issued compulsory licenses on a range of cancer, heart disease and AIDS drugs. There is considerable controversy over pharmaceutical patents based on traditional medicines of indigenous peoples, which some see as bio-piracy. Proposals have been made to amend TRIPs to require disclosure of the origins of bio-patents, obtain informed consent from the indigenous communities involved, and share the benefits of such patents.

Note that by incorporating the Berne and Paris conventions, TRIPs and the WTO DSU become an enforcement mechanism for those longstanding treaties. For trademarks, the Paris Convention also rules, service marks become registrable, internationally prominent marks receive enhanced protection, the linking of local marks with foreign trademarks is prohibited, and compulsory licensing is banned. But gray market trading and related IP issues are explicitly not covered by TRIPs, allowing each WTO member state to differ on such law.

In addition, trade secret protection is assisted by TRIPs rules enabling owners to prevent unauthorized use or disclosure. These rules closely parallel those of NAFTA. Integrated circuits are covered by rules intended to improve upon the Washington Treaty. Lastly, protection of industrial designs and geographic indicators of product origin (*e.g.*, Canadian Whiskey) are also part of the TRIPs regime.

Mandatory IP infringement and anti-counterfeiting remedies are included in the TRIPs, for both domestic and international trade protection. There are specific provisions governing injunctions, damages, judicial and customs seizures, and discovery of evidence. Willful trademark counterfeiting and copyright piracy on a commercial scale must be criminalized. Counterfeit goods may not be re-exported by customs authorities in an unaltered state.

The Medicines Agreement

Late in 2001, the Doha Round of WTO negotiations were launched. These negotiations have reconsidered the TRIPs agreement, particularly as it applies to developing nations. Their compliance deadline for the TRIPs rules on patents for pharmaceuticals was extended to 2016, thereby allowing a continuation of cheaper, local generics. In addition, a Declaration on the TRIPs Agreement and Public Health was issued at the Qatar Ministerial Conference. This 2001 Declaration includes the following statement:

> We agree that the TRIPs Agreement does not prevent Members from taking measures to protect public health. Accordingly, while reiterating our commitment to the TRIPs Agreement, we affirm that the Agreement can and should be interpreted and implemented in a manner supportive of WTO Members' right to protect public health and, in particular, to promote access to medicines for all.

A "Medicines Agreement" waiver (2003) and amendment to TRIPs (2005) implement this Declaration. Compulsory licensing and/or importation of generic copies of patented medicines needed to address developing nation public health problems are authorized. Such activities may not pursue industrial or commercial policy objectives, and different packaging and labeling must be used in an effort at minimizing the risk of diversion of the generics to developed country markets.

Under pressure from the United States, more advanced developing nations (such as Mexico, Singapore, and Qatar) agreed not to employ compulsory licensing except in situations of national emergency or extreme urgency. Canada, China, the EU, India, South Korea, and other members, on the other hand, have licensed production of drugs for nations incapable of pharmaceutical production. Royalty-free licensing of COVID vaccines has been discussed, but at this writing not implemented.

Special 301—Prioritization of U.S. Intellectual Property Rights Disputes

The Special 301 procedures established by the 1988 Omnibus Trade and Competitiveness Act are permanent features of United States trade legislation. *See* Section 182 of the Trade Act of 1974. Under these procedures the United States Trade Representative is required to identify foreign countries that deny adequate and effective protection of intellectual property rights or deny fair and equitable access to United States persons that rely upon intellectual property protection. The USTR is given discretion to determine whether to designate certain of these countries to be "priority countries."

If so designated, a mandatory Section 301 investigation must follow in the absence of a determination that this would be detrimental to U.S. economic interests or a negotiated settlement of the intellectual property dispute. Once designated, Special 301 investigations and retaliations against priority countries must ordinarily be decided within 6 months by the USTR. Whether to retaliate or not is discretionary with the USTR, but retaliation is not authorized if the country in question enters good faith negotiations or makes "significant progress" in bilateral or multilateral negotiations towards increased protection for intellectual property rights.

Many commentators have observed that unilateral use of Section 301 prior to creation of the WTO helped push the U.S. agenda in the TRIPs negotiations. Since 1994, if the dispute is covered by the WTO TRIPs agreement, the United States should avoid using unilateral Section 301 trade sanctions and pursue WTO dispute settlement. President Trump seemingly ignored this obligation in applying Section 301 tariffs on Chinese goods.

In identifying priority foreign countries in the intellectual property field, Section 182 indicates that the USTR is to prioritize only those countries that have the most "onerous or egregious" practices, whose practices have the greatest adverse impact on United States products and are not entering into good faith negotiations bilaterally or multilaterally to provide adequate and effective protection of intellectual property rights. For these purposes, the term "persons that rely on intellectual protection" covers those involved in copyrighted works of authorship or those involved in the manufacture of products that are patented or subject to process patents. Interestingly, this definition does not include those who rely on United States trademarks.

However, the relevant definitions include trademarks in connection with the denial by foreign countries of adequate and effective protection of intellectual property rights. The definition of practices that deny fair and equitable market access in connection with intellectual property rights appear to be limited to copyrights and patents. This denial must constitute a violation of provisions of international law or international agreements to which both the United States and that country are parties or otherwise constitute a discriminatory nontariff trade barrier.

Regular reports to Congress are required of the USTR by Section 182. The USTR has chiefly placed foreign country intellectual property practices on watch lists rather than formally designating priority countries. These watch lists are divided as between "priority watch lists" and "secondary watch lists." Many nations have been listed by the USTR since 1989 in this fashion. This has the practical effect of placing pressure on those nations to enter negotiations with the United States that will improve their protection of intellectual property rights.

The use of these lists gives the USTR more room to negotiate settlements with the countries concerned. For example, the USTR formally named China, India, and Thailand as the first "priority countries" for Special 301 purposes. The formal process of negotiation backed up by a mandatory Section 301 investigation and potential sanctions was begun. Thailand was cited for its failure to enforce copyrights and for the absence of patent protection for pharmaceuticals. India was named because its patent laws are deficient from the U.S. perspective, particularly on compulsory licensing and the absence of pharmaceutical protection. Extensive book, video, sound recording and computer software piracy in India was also cited.

United States Special 301 investigations and watch lists, now including "Out-of-Cycle Reviews of Notorious Markets", have continued relentlessly despite the WTO TRIPs agreement. The USTR has filed numerous TRIPs complaints with the WTO. Filings have been made, for example, against Denmark, Sweden, Ireland, Ecuador, Greece, Portugal, India, Russia, Pakistan, Turkey and, not surprisingly, China.

TRIPs Disputes

Dozens of TRIPs complaints have been initiated under WTO dispute settlement procedures. Most have been settled, but a few have resulted in WTO Panel and Appellate Body Reports. Here is a sampling of those disputes:

1. *India—Patent Protection for Pharmaceutical and Agricultural Chemical Products*, WT/DS50/AB/R (1998) ("mailbox rule" patent applications for subjects not patentable in India until 2005 inadequate, denial of exclusive marketing rights in breach of TRIPs Article 70.9).

2. *Canada—Term of Patent Protection*, WT/DS170/AB/R (2000) (pre-TRIPs Canadian patents must receive 20-year term).

3. *U.S.—Section 110 (5) Copyright Act*, WT/DS160/R (2000) (copyright exemption for "homestyle" dramatic musical works consistent with Berne Convention, "business use"

exemption inconsistent with Berne and therefore in breach of TRIPs) (settled by payment).

4. *Canada—Pharmaceutical Patents*, WT/DS114/R (2000) (Canadian generic pharmaceutical regulatory review and stockpiling patent rights' exceptions not sufficiently "limited").

5. *U.S.—Section 211 Appropriations Act*, WT/DS176/AB/R (2002) (prohibition against registering marks confiscated by Cuban government, *e.g.*, HAVANA CLUB rum, without original owner's consent violates Paris Convention and TRIPs, trade names covered by TRIPs).

6. *EC—Trademarks and Geographical Indications*, WT/DS 174,290/R (2005) (EC regulation violates national treatment and most-favored treatment obligations to non-EC nationals, procedural violations also found).

7. *China—Measures Affecting Protection and Enforcement of Intellectual Property Rights*, WT/DS362/R (2009) (China's implementation of TRIPs upheld as to criminal law thresholds and disposal of confiscated, infringing goods by customs authorities, rejected as to denial of copyright protection for works not authorized for release in China).

8. *China—Measures Affecting Trading Rights and Distribution Services for Certain Publications and Audiovisuals Entertainment Products*, WT/DS363/AB/R (2009) (China's ADV restrictions limited to state-owned or approved channels violate WTO Accession Protocol, GATT 1994, and GATS; Restraints not necessary to protect public morals).

9. *European Communities—Information Technology Tariffs*, WT/DS375–377 (2010) (EU tariffs on cable converter boxes with Net capacity, flat panel computer screens and printers that also scan, fax, or copy violated 1996 Information Technology Agreement zero tariff rules).

§ 1.13 The Trade-Related Investment Measures Agreement (TRIMs)

The WTO package of mandatory agreements includes TRIMs, Trade-Related Investment Measures. This is the only WTO agreement concerning foreign investment law, an area which is almost devoid of common international rules. The WTO is a trade law organization. Hence its coverage of foreign investment is only "trade-related." In practice, this means that TRIMs is almost exclusively concerned with "performance requirements", *i.e.*, national rules requiring designated performances by foreign investors.

There are 14 performance requirements enumerated in and broadly prohibited by TRIMs. They fall into three general categories: (1) Local content rules; (2) Trade balancing rules; and (3) Export requirements.

Regarding performance requirements, TRIMs tracks the GATT Article III rule of "national treatment" and Article XI proscription against quotas. But member states may "deviate temporarily" from these principles, thus undermining their impact. Trade-related investment practices which are deemed inconsistent with TRIMs are listed illustratively in an Annex. These include minimum domestic content rules (say 50% of the value of the foreign investor's products must be sourced locally), limitations on imports used in production, the linkage of allowable imports to export requirements, export quotas or percentage of production requirements, and restrictions on foreign exchange designed to limit imports.

Perhaps because of their limited scope and soft prohibition, there have been very few TRIMs disputes. The United States and others did succeed in challenging Indonesia's local content requirements for autos. See *Indonesia—Certain Measures Affecting the Automobile Industry*, WT/DS/AB/R 54, 55, 59 & 64 (1998).

§ 1.14 The Optional WTO Public Procurement Code

Where public procurement is involved, and the taxpayer's money is at issue, virtually every nation has some form of legislation or tradition that favors buying from domestic suppliers. The Tokyo Round GATT Procurement Code was not particularly successful at opening government purchasing. Relatively few GATT members and the United States adhered to that Procurement Code. This was also partly the result of the 1979 Code's many exceptions. For example, the Code did not apply to contracts below its threshold amount of $150,000 SDR (about $171,000 since 1988), service contracts, and procurement by entities on each country's reserve list (including most national defense items).

Because procurement in the European Union and Japan is often decentralized, many contracts fell below the SDR threshold and were therefore GATT exempt. By dividing up procurement into smaller contracts national preferences were retained. United States government procurement tends to be more centralized and thus more likely to be covered by the GATT Code. This pattern may help explain why Congress restrictively amended the Buy American Act in 1988.

The Uruguay Round WTO Procurement Code took effect in 1995 and replaced the 1979 Tokyo Round GATT Procurement Code. The WTO Code expanded the coverage of the prior GATT Code to include procurement of services, construction, government-owned utilities, and some state and local (sub-central) contracts. The U.S. and the European Union applied the new Code's provisions on government-owned utilities and sub-central contracts as early as April 15, 1994. Other participants include Armenia, Aruba, Chinese Taipei (Taiwan), Iceland, Japan, Korea, Israel, Lichtenstein, Norway, Singapore, and Switzerland. Nearly all developing nations have opted out of the WTO Procurement Code, though China has expressed interest in it.

Various improvements to the procedural rules surrounding procurement practices and dispute settlement under the WTO Code attempt to reduce tensions in this difficult area. For example, an elaborate system for bid protests is established. Bidders who believe the Code's procedural rules have been abused will be able to lodge, litigate and appeal their protests. The WTO Procurement Code became part of U.S. law in December of 1994 under the Uruguay Round Agreements Act.

The United States has made, with few exceptions, all procurement by executive agencies subject to the Federal Acquisition Regulations under the Code's coverage (*i.e.*, to suspend application of the normal Buy American preferences to such procurement). Thirteen U.S. states have not ratified the WTO Procurement Code. The economic stimulus and auto bail-out legislation of the Obama administration raised questions of U.S. compliance with the Code.

Chapter 13 of the North American Free Trade Area Agreement opened government procurement to U.S., Canadian and Mexican suppliers on contracts as small as $25,000. However, the goods supplied must have at least 50 percent North American content. These special procurement rules effectively created an exception to the GATT Procurement Code, which otherwise applied. The thresholds are $50,000 for goods and services provided to federal agencies and $250,000 for government-owned enterprises (notably PEMEX and CFE). These regulations are particularly important because Mexico, unlike Canada, has not traditionally joined in GATT/WTO procurement codes.

In December 2011 Canada-U.S. procurement provisions were incorporated in a long-awaited agreement to expand the WTO Procurement Code. This expansion selectively brought more types of procurement contracts, notably service contracts, and more subcentral government entities within the Code's coverage. Contract value thresholds were also selectively lowered.

Under the USMCA 2020 agreement, Canada and the United States fall back exclusively on the WTO Procurement Code, while Mexico and the U.S. will utilize bilateral procurement USMCA rules. See Chapter 6.

§ 1.15 WTO Dispute Settlement

GATT 1947 did not have an institutional charter and was not intended to become an international organization on trade. It did later develop institutional structures and acquired quasi-organizational status, but there was always a lack of structure. This lack was most often perceived in the somewhat over-stated inability of GATT to resolve disputes which were brought to it. Indeed, GATT 1947 members could block the formation of a panel to hear a dispute. Moreover, GATT panel decisions could be blocked by the losing state! Hence most GATT 1947 dispute settlement panel reports were un-adopted, and as such "the GATT acquis" is said to merely provide guidance in the context of WTO dispute settlement. See *Japan—Alcoholic Beverages II*, WTO/DS/R 8, 10, 11 (1996).

The WTO provides a unified, mandatory, and exclusive intergovernmental system for settling trade disputes governed by WTO law through the Dispute Settlement Understanding (DSU) using the Dispute Settlement Body (DSB). There are no private remedies, though private sector interests are often motivating elements. In the United States, private parties and their attorneys can attempt to trigger WTO dispute settlement proceedings by filing complaints with the U.S. Trade Representative (USTR), a presidential appointee. Whether to pursue WTO trade law complaints is entirely discretionary for the USTR. Under the terms of the DSU, the USTR can pursue complaints of breach of WTO agreement obligations, or nullification or impairment of benefits accruing under WTO agreements.

The DSB is a special assembly of the WTO General Council and includes all WTO members. There are six stages in the resolution of disputes under WTO:

1) Consultation;
2) Panel establishment, investigation and report;
3) Appellate review of the WTO panel report;
4) Adoption of the panel or Appellate Body decision;
5) Implementation of the decision adopted; and
6) Compensation or authorized retaliation.

There is also a parallel process for binding arbitration, if both parties agree to submit this dispute to arbitration, rather than to a DSB panel. In addition, the party subject to an adverse decision may seek arbitration as a matter of right on issues of compliance and authorized retaliation.

Although the DSU offers a unified dispute resolution system that is applicable across all sectors and all WTO Covered Agreements, there are many specialized rules for disputes which arise under them. Such specialized rules appear in the Agreements on Textiles, Antidumping, Subsidies and Countervailing Measures, Technical Barriers to Trade, Sanitary and Phytosanitary Measures, Customs Valuation, General Agreement on Trade in Services, Financial Services and Air Transport Services. The special provisions in these individual Covered Agreements govern, where applicable, and prevail in any conflict with the general provisions of the DSU.

Under WTO, unlike under GATT 1947, the DSU practically assures that panels will be established upon request by a member state. Further, under WTO, unlike GATT 1947, the DSU virtually ensures the adoption of unmodified panel and appellate body decisions. It accomplishes this by requiring the DSB to adopt panel reports and appellate body decisions automatically and without amendment unless they are rejected by a consensus of all members. This "inverted consensus" requires that all members of the DSB, including the state that prevailed in the dispute, decide to reject the dispute resolution decision. Not surprisingly, this has never happened because if any member formally favors that decision (the winner in the dispute for example), it becomes binding. This inverted consensus requirement is imposed on both the adoption of panel reports or appellate body decisions and on the decision to establish a panel.

The potential resolutions of a dispute under DSU range from a "mutually satisfactory solution" agreed to by the parties under the first, or consultation phase, to authorized retaliation under the last, or implementation phase. The preferred solution is always any resolution that is mutually satisfactory to the parties. After a panel decision, there are three types of remedies available to the prevailing party, if a mutually satisfactory solution cannot be obtained. One is for the respondent to bring the measure found to violate a Covered Agreement into conformity with the Agreement. A second is for the prevailing Member to receive monetary or tariff concession compensation from the respondent, if both parties agree the compensation is sufficient for any injury caused by the measure found to violate a Covered Agreement.

Finally, if no such agreement can be reached, a prevailing party can be authorized to suspend some of its concessions under the Covered Agreements to the respondent. These suspended concessions, called "retaliation," can be authorized within the same trade sector and agreement; or, if that will not create sufficient compensation, can be authorized across trade sectors and agreements.

The entire WTO dispute resolution process, from filing a complaint to authorized retaliation, can take roughly three years. One perspective on WTO dispute settlement seeks a rule-oriented use of the "rule of law." The other seeks a power-oriented use of diplomacy. The United States and less developed countries have traditionally sought to develop a rule-oriented approach to international trade disputes. The European Union and Japan have traditionally sought to use the GATT/WTO primarily as a forum for diplomatic negotiations, although the EU now ranks second in number of WTO dispute proceedings.

These different views created part of the conflict at the December 1999 Seattle WTO meeting (which failed to launch the Millennium Round) and subsequent failure of the Doha Round. If the DSB is a court, its proceedings should be open and "transparent." However, if it is just another form of government-to-government diplomacy, that has always been held in secret.

Phase 1, Consultation

Any WTO Member who believes that the Measures of another Member are not in conformity with the Covered Agreements may call for consultations on those measures. The respondent has ten days to reply and must agree to enter consultation within 30 days. If the respondent does not enter consultations within the 30-day period, the party seeking consultations can immediately request the establishment of a panel under DSU, which puts the dispute into Phase 2.

Once consultations begin, the parties have 60 days to achieve a settlement. The goal is to seek a positive solution to the dispute, and the preferred resolution is to reach whatever solution is mutually satisfactory to the parties. If such a settlement cannot be obtained after 60 days, the party seeking consultations may request the establishment of a panel under DSU, which moves the dispute into Phase 2.

WTO member third parties with an interest in the subject matter of the consultations may seek to be included in them. If such inclusion is rejected, they may seek their own consultations with the other member state. Alternatives to consultations may be provided through conciliation, mediation, or good offices, where all parties agree to use the alternative process. Any party can terminate the use of conciliation, mediation or good offices and then seek the establishment of a panel under DSU, which also will move the dispute into Phase 2.

Phase 2, Panel Establishment, Investigation and Report

If consultations between the parties fail, the party seeking the consultation (the complainant) may request the DSB to establish a panel to investigate, report and resolve the dispute. The DSB must establish such a panel upon request, unless the DSB expressly decides by consensus not to establish the panel. Since an "inverted consensus" is required to reject the establishment of the panel and the complainant member must be part of that consensus, it is almost guaranteed that a panel will be established. Roughly 100 panels were established in the first five years of operation of the DSU, and many more since then.

Almost any WTO member state may intervene in the dispute. No specific legal or trade interest in the dispute is required since every WTO member has a legal interest in seeing that WTO rules are observed. Hence, for example, the United States intervened in the *Bananas* dispute between Latin American exporters and the European Union. One measure of the significance of the dispute is how many and which WTO members join either side of the dispute, resulting in say seven states against ten.

The WTO Secretariat maintains a list of well-qualified persons who are available to serve as panelists, mainly international trade law specialists drawn from the world of law practice, the academe and government service. The panels are usually composed of three individuals from that list who are not citizens of either party. If the parties agree, a panel can be composed of five such individuals. The parties can also agree to appoint citizens of a party to a panel. Panelists may be either nongovernmental individuals or governmental officials, but they are to be selected to ensure their independence. There is a bias towards independent individuals who are not citizens of any party. If a citizen of a party is appointed, his or her government may not instruct that citizen how to vote, for the panelist must be independent. By the same reasoning, a governmental official of a non-party member state who is subject to instructions from a home government would not seem to fit the profile of an independent panelist.

The WTO Secretariat proposes nominations of the panelists. Parties may not normally oppose the nominations, except for "compelling reasons." The parties are given twenty days to agree on the panelists and the composition of the panel. If such an agreement is not forthcoming, the WTO Director-General is authorized to appoint the panelists, in consultation with other persons in the Secretariat.

Complaints brought to DSB panels can involve either violations of Covered Agreements, or non-violation nullification and impairment of benefits under the Covered Agreements. A prima facie case of nullification impairment arises when one member infringes upon the "obligations assumed under a Covered Agreement." Such infringement creates a presumption against the infringing member, but the presumption can be rebutted by showing that the complaining member state has suffered no adverse effect from the infringement. A classic nullification and impairment complaint concerns the use of government subsidies after tariff reductions cause increased imports. See the *Australian Subsidy* case, 2 GATT Panel B.I.S.D. 188 (1950).

The panels receive pleadings and rebuttals and hear oral arguments. Panels can also engage in fact development from sources outside those presented by the parties. Thus, the procedure has aspects familiar to civil law courts. A panel can, on its own initiative, request information, including from experts selected by the panel. It can also obtain confidential information in some circumstances from an administrative body which is part of the government of a member state, without any prior consent from that state. A panel can establish its own group of experts to provide reports on factual or scientific issues. In a series of rulings commencing with the *Shrimp-Turtles* decision in 1998, the WTO Appellate Body has affirmed the right of panels and itself to elect to receive unsolicited informational and argumentative briefs or letters from non-governmental organizations (NGOs), business groups and law firms representing persons interested in the dispute.

A panel is obligated to produce two objectively assessed written reports—an interim and a final report. These reports are normally drafted by the WTO Secretariat, subject to review by the panelists. A panel is supposed to submit a final written report to the DSB within six months of its establishment. The report will contain its findings of fact, findings of law, a decision, and the rationale for its decision. Before the final report is issued, the panel is supposed to provide an interim report to the parties. The purpose of this interim report is to apprize the parties of the panel's current analysis of the issues and to permit the parties to comment on that analysis. The final report of the panel need not change any of the findings or conclusions in its interim report, unless the panel is persuaded to do so by a party's comments. However, if it is not so persuaded, it is obligated to explain in its final report why not. At this writing, well over 200 WTO panel reports have been issued.

The decisions in panel reports are final as to issues of fact. The decisions in panel reports are not necessarily final as to issues of law. Panel decisions on issues of law are subject to review by the Appellate Body, which is Phase 3, and explained below. Any party can appeal a panel report, and appeals are usually taken.

Phase 3, Appellate Review of the Panel Report

Appellate review of panel reports is available at the request of any party, unless the DSB rejects that request by an "inverted consensus." There is no threshold requirement for an appellant to present a substantial substantive legal issue. Thus, most panel decisions are appealed as a matter of course. However, the Appellate Body can only review the panel reports on questions of law or legal interpretation.

The Appellate Body (AB) is a unique institution in the international trade organization and its process. GATT 1947 had nothing comparable to it. The Appellate Body is composed of seven members (or judges) who are appointed by the DSB acting by consensus to four-year terms. Each judge may be reappointed, but only once, to a second four-year term. Each judge is to be a recognized authority on international trade law and the Covered Agreements. To date, Appellate Body members have been drawn mostly from the academy and retired justices. They have come from Germany, Japan, Egypt, India, New Zealand, the Philippines, Argentina, China, the United States, and other WTO member nations.

The review of any panel decision must be performed by three judges out of the seven. The Trump Administration vetoed appointments to the Appellate Body. With only one AB member since late 2019, and none since 2020, it could not function. Many considered this to be a "stealth war" by the United States against the rules-based multilateral WTO system and a way to avoid WTO review of highly debatable Trump tariffs. President Biden has continued to refuse to support Appellate Body appointments.

The EU, China, Japan, Australia, New Zealand, and Canada along with about other WTO members created in mid-2020 an alternative appellate mechanism, the Multi-Party Interim Appeal Arbitration Arrangement. The United States has declined to participate in such arbitrations.

When in operation, the parties do not have any influence over which judges are selected to review a particular panel report. There is a schedule, created by the Appellate Body, for the rotation for sitting of each of the judges. Thus, a party might try to appear before a favored judge by timing the start of the dispute settlement process to arrive at the Appellate Body at the right moment on the rotation schedule, but this limited approach has major difficulties.

The Appellate Body receives written submissions from the parties and has 60, or in some cases 90, days in which to render its decision. The Appellate Body review is limited to issues of law and legal interpretation. The panel decision may be upheld, modified, or reversed by the Appellate Body decision. Appellate Body decisions are anonymous, and *ex parte* communications are not permitted. Appellate Body decisions do not represent binding precedent. That said, many have observed a desire on the part of the Appellate Body to achieve consistency and a willingness to discuss its prior rulings when rendering decisions.

Phase 4, Adoption of the Panel or Appellate Body Decision

Appellate Body determinations are submitted to the DSB. Panel decisions which are not appealed are also submitted to the DSB. Once either type of decision is submitted, the DSB must automatically adopt them without modification or amendment at its next meeting unless the decision is rejected by all members of the DSB acting by "inverted consensus", which has never happened.

An alternative to Phases 2 through 4 is arbitration if both parties agree. The arbitration must be binding on the parties, and there is no appeal from the arbitral tribunal's decision to the DSB or Appellate Body.

Phase 5, Implementation of the WTO Decision

Once a panel or Appellate Body decision is adopted by the DSB, implementation is a three-step process. In the first step, the member found to have a measure which violates its WTO obligations has "a reasonable time" (usually 15 months) to bring those measures into conformity with its WTO obligations. That remedy is the preferred one, and this form of implementation is the principal goal of the WTO dispute settlement system. To date, most disputes have resulted in compliance in this manner.

If the adequacy of compliance is disputed, such disputes typically return to the WTO panel that rendered decision on the merits. The panel then determines, acting as an arbitrator, the amount (if any) of authorized retaliation. The retaliation process is discussed below.

Phase 6, Compensation or Authorized Retaliation

Both "compensation" and "retaliation" provide only for indirect enforcement of DSB decisions. There is no mechanism for direct enforcement by the WTO of its decisions through WTO orders to suspend trade obligations.

Compensation

If the violating measures are not brought into WTO conformity within a reasonable time, the parties proceed to attempt to negotiate an agreement on monetary or tariff compensation granted by the party in violation to the injured party. Such compensation could comprise tariff concessions over and above those already available under the WTO Covered Agreements. See Section 1.4. The nature, scope, amount, and duration of these additional tariff concessions is at the negotiating parties' discretion, but each side must agree that the final compensation package is fair and is properly related to the injury caused by the violating measures.

Arguably, tariff concessions might need to be extended under MFN principles to all WTO members. That is perhaps why few such compensation agreements have ever been achieved. By making cash payments, the United States compensated most of the WTO membership after losing a dispute to Antigua about whether it had "reserved" (excepted) Internet gambling from coverage under the GATS. See Section 1.10. The United States also financially compensated the EU in a copyright dispute involving small business use of music, and Brazil after losing a significant subsidies dispute concerning cotton. See Section 1.16.

Authorized Retaliation

If the parties cannot agree on an appropriate amount of compensation within twenty days, the party injured by the violating measures typically seeks authority from the DSB to retaliate against the party whose measures violated its WTO obligations. In other words, the complainant seeks authority to suspend some of its WTO obligations to the respondent. The retaliation must ordinarily be within the same sector and agreement as the violating measure. "Sector" is sometimes broadly defined, as all trade in goods, and sometimes narrowly defined, as in individual services in the Services Sectoral Classification List. "Agreement" is also broadly defined. All the agreements listed in Annex IA to the WTO Agreement are considered a single agreement.

If retaliation within the sector and agreement of the violating measure is considered insufficient compensation, the complainant may seek suspension of its obligations across sectors and agreements. This is known as "cross-sector retaliation, arguably the "nuclear option" in WTO dispute settlement (see below).

The DSB must grant the complainant's request to retaliate within 30 days unless all WTO members reject it through an "inverted consensus." (Article 22.6, DSU) However, the respondent may object to the level or scope of the retaliation. The issues raised by the objection will be examined by either the Appellate Body or by an arbitrator. The respondent has a right, even if arbitration was not used in Phases 2 through 4, to have an arbitrator review in Phase 5 the appropriateness of the complainant's proposed level and scope of retaliation. The arbitrator will also examine whether the proper procedures and criteria to establish retaliation have been followed. The Phase 5 arbitration is final and binding, and the arbitrator's decision is not subject to DSB review.

In addition to objecting to the level of authorized retaliation, the responding WTO member may simultaneously challenge the assertion of noncompliance (Article 21.5, DSU). This challenge will ordinarily be heard by the original panel and must be resolved within 90 days. The request for authorized retaliation and objections thereto could conceivably be accomplished before noncompliance is formally determined. In practice, WTO dispute settlement has melded these conflicting procedures such that compliance and retaliation issues are decided together, typically by the original panel.

Retaliation in Action

WTO retaliation has rarely been authorized and even less rarely imposed. The amount of a U.S. retaliation permitted against the EU after the WTO *Bananas* and *Beef Hormones* decisions were not implemented by the EU was contested. The arbitration tribunals for this issue were the original WTO panels, which did not allow the entire amount of the almost $700 million in retaliatory tariffs proposed by the United States. The U.S. was authorized and levied retaliatory tariffs amounting to about $300 million against European goods because of the EU failure to implement those WTO decisions.

Since 2000, Congress has authorized rotating WTO retaliatory tariffs in "carousel" fashion upon different goods. The threat of carousel retaliation contributed to an April 2001 settlement of the *Bananas* dispute. In 2009, a four-year settlement of the *Beef Hormones* dispute was reached. The U.S. gets a higher quota to export hormone-free beef to the EU in return for phasing out its retaliatory tariffs on EU goods. The U.S. threat of carousel sanctions was again instrumental to this settlement.

Perhaps the most dramatic use of retaliation occurred in a tax subsidy dispute. The amount of EU retaliation permissible after the U.S. lost (for the second time) under WTO subsidy rules concerning Internal Revenue Code extraterritorial export tax preferences

(FISCs) was disputed. A WTO panel, serving as an arbitrator, authorized approximately $4 *billion* in EU retaliation against U.S. exports. This retaliation commenced in March of 2004 and escalated monthly until the U.S. capitulated by amending the I.R.C. late in 2004.

Cross-Sector Retaliation

In a landmark ruling, a WTO panel acting as an arbitrator authorized Ecuador to remove protection of intellectual property rights regarding geographical indicators, copyrights, and industrial designs on European Union goods for sale in Ecuador. This authorization was part of Ecuador's $200 million compensation in the *Bananas* dispute. The WTO panel acknowledged that Ecuador imports mostly capital goods and raw materials from the European Union and that imposing retaliatory tariffs on them would adversely harm its manufacturing industries. This risk supported "cross-retaliation" under Article 22.3 of the DSU outside the sector of the EU trade violation.

Allowance of cross-sector IP retaliation was probably the most critical driver behind the 2001 settlement of the *Bananas* dispute. Cross-sector retaliation was also authorized against the U.S. after losing a GATS dispute to Antigua on Internet gambling restraints. The United States settled this dispute with nearly all WTO members save Antigua via compensation. At this writing, Antigua is still debating whether and how to retaliate.

§ 1.16 U.S. Involvement in WTO Disputes

The WTO dispute resolution process has been invoked more frequently than many expected. The United States has been a complainant or a respondent in hundreds of disputes since 1995. It has won about 86% of the disputes when filing complaints and has lost about 75% when responding to WTO complaints. The U.S. track record on compliance with WTO decisions is generally good, though not always with alacrity despite repeated losses, notably regarding zeroing in antidumping proceedings. See my Concise Hornbook on *International Trade Law*, Chapter 4. The U.S. has on occasion only complied after authorized retaliation by the complaining party. Sometimes the U.S. avoided compliance via compensation.

The U.S. and the EU have been involved as the complainant or respondent in roughly 80% of all WTO disputes since it became operational in 1995, with China disputes on the rise since 2001.

The United States has settled disputes prior to WTO panel decisions and remains in consultation on other disputes that may be decided by a WTO panel. For the latest summary of all WTO disputes, including many not involving the United States, see www.wto.org.

The sampling of disputes summarized below illustrates the WTO dispute settlement process in action.

United States WTO Disputes

The WTO dispute resolution process has been invoked more frequently than many expected. The United States has been a complainant or a respondent in hundreds of disputes since 1995. It has won about 86% of the disputes when filing complaints and has lost about 75% when responding to WTO complaints. The U.S. track record on compliance with WTO decisions is generally good, though not always with alacrity despite repeated losses (notably regarding zeroing in antidumping proceedings). The U.S. has on occasion only complied after authorized retaliation by the complaining party. Sometimes the U.S. has avoided compliance via compensation.

The U.S. and the EU have been involved as the complainant or respondent in roughly 80% of all WTO disputes since it became operational in 1995, with China disputes on the rise since 2001.

The United States lost a dispute initiated by Venezuela and Brazil concerning U.S. standards for reformulated and conventional gasoline. The offending U.S. law was amended to conform to the WTO ruling. It won on a complaint initiated jointly with Canada and the European Union regarding Japanese taxes on alcoholic beverages. Japan subsequently changed its law. When Costa Rica complained about U.S. restraints on imports of underwear, the U.S. let the restraints expire prior to any formal DSB ruling at the WTO. Similar results were reached when India complained of U.S. restraints on wool shirts and blouses. The United States won a major dispute with Canada concerning trade and subsidies for periodicals This celebrated *Sports Illustrated* dispute proved that WTO remedies could be used to avoid Canada's cultural industries exclusion under NAFTA. See Section 4.2.

In the longstanding *Bananas* dispute noted above, the United States joined Ecuador, Guatemala, Honduras, and Mexico in successfully challenging EU import restraints against so-called "dollar bananas." The EU failed to comply with the Appellate Body's ruling. Retaliatory measures were authorized and imposed on EU goods by the United States, along with cross-sector IP retaliation by Ecuador and others. In April 2001, the *Bananas* dispute was settled on terms that generally converted EU quotas to tariffs by 2006, though limited preferential quotas for ACP exporters were retained. A patent law complaint by the U.S. against India prevailed in the

DSB and ultimately brought changes in Indian law regarding pharmaceuticals and agricultural chemicals.

In *Beef Hormones*, also noted above, the European Union lost twice before the Appellate Body for want of proof of a "scientific basis" for its ban on hormone beef. It refused to alter its import restraints and absorbed $200 million in retaliatory tariffs on selected exports to Canada and the United States. In 2009, an arguably pro-European settlement was reached. The U.S. effectively got a higher quota to export hormone-free beef to the EU, in return for phasing out over four years its retaliatory tariffs on EU goods. The U.S. threat of carousel sanctions, *i.e.*, rotating goods subject to retaliation, was instrumental to this settlement. Meanwhile, because the U.S. beef industry failed to timely ask for a continuation of the retaliatory tariffs, the Federal Circuit ruled in 2010 that they expired in 2007. Refunds were given to importers of EU products who paid those tariffs.

The United States prevailed against Argentina regarding tariffs and taxes on footwear, textiles, and apparel. It lost a challenge (strongly supported by Kodak) to Japan's distribution rules regarding photo film and paper. In this dispute the U.S. elected *not* to appeal the adverse WTO panel ruling to the Appellate Body. In contrast, the European Union took an appeal which reversed an adverse panel ruling on its customs classification of computer equipment. The U.S. had commenced this proceeding. Opponents in many disputes, Japan, the United States, and the European Union united to complain that Indonesia's National Car Program was discriminatory and in breach of several WTO agreements. They prevailed and Indonesia altered its program.

India, Malaysia, Pakistan, and Thailand teamed up to challenge U.S. shrimp import restraints enacted to protect endangered sea turtles. The WTO Appellate Body generally upheld their complaint, and the U.S. moved to comply. The adequacy of U.S. compliance is being challenged by Malaysia. The European Union and the United States jointly opposed Korea's discriminatory taxes on alcoholic beverages. This challenge was successful, and Korea now imposes flat non-discriminatory taxes. The United States also complained of Japan's quarantine, testing and other agricultural import rules. The U.S. won at the WTO and Japan has changed its procedures.

In a semiconductor dumping dispute, Korea successfully argued that the U.S. was not in compliance with the WTO Antidumping Agreement. The United States amended its law, but Korea has instituted further proceedings alleging that these amendments are inadequate. The United States did likewise after Australia lost a subsidies dispute relating to auto leather. The reconvened WTO panel ruled that Australia had indeed failed to conform to the original adverse DSB decision. A U.S. challenge concerning India's quotas on imports of agricultural, textile and industrial products was upheld. India and the United States subsequently reached agreement on a timeline for removal of these restraints.

Closer to home, New Zealand and the United States complained of Canada's import/export rules regarding milk. Losing at the WTO, Canada agreed to a phased removal of the offending measures. The United States also won against Mexico in an antidumping dispute involving corn syrup but lost a "big one" when the Appellate Body determined that export tax preferences granted to "Foreign Sales Corporations" of U.S. companies were illegal.

Another "big one" went in favor of the United States. The European Union challenged the validity under the DSU of unilateral retaliation under Section 301 of the Trade Act of 1974. Section 301 has been something of a *bete noire* in U.S. trade law, but the WTO panel affirmed its legality referencing Presidential undertakings to administer it in accordance with U.S. obligations to adhere to multilateral WTO dispute settlement. This ruling was successfully cited in WTO challenges (noted above) by China against President Trump's Section 301 tariffs.

U.S. involvement in WTO dispute settlement continues to be extensive. The Appellate Body ruled that U.S. countervailing duties against British steel based upon pre-privatization subsidies were unlawful. The European Union prevailed before a WTO panel in its challenge of the U.S. Antidumping Act of 1916, since repealed. U.S. complaints against Korean beef import restraints and procurement practices were upheld. Canada's patent protection term was also invalidated by the WTO under a U.S. complaint. European Union complaints concerning U.S. wheat gluten quotas, and the royalty free small business provisions of the Fairness in Music Licensing Act of 1998 have been sustained. The *Wheat Gluten* dispute questions the legality of U.S. "causation" rules in escape clause proceedings under Section 201 of the Trade Act of 1974.

A WTO Panel ruled that the Byrd Amendment violated the WTO antidumping and subsidy codes. The Byrd Amendment (Continued Dumping and Subsidy Act of 2000) authorizes the Customs Service to forward AD and CVD duties to affected domestic producers for qualified expenses. Eleven WTO members including the EU, Canada and Mexico challenged the Amendment. This ruling was affirmed by the WTO Appellate Body and retaliation was authorized. Late in 2005, the U.S. repealed the Byrd Amendment, subject to a contested two-year phase out. The Appellate Body also ruled against Section 211 of the Omnibus Appropriations Act of 1998 denying trademark protection in connection with confiscated assets (the "HAVANA CLUB" dispute). U.S. compliance with these rulings has been slow in forthcoming. The United States and other complainants prevailed in a WTO proceeding against Indian local content and trade balancing requirements for foreign auto manufacturers. These requirements violated the TRIMs agreement.

The European Union commenced raising tariffs against U.S. goods under the WTO retaliation authorized out of the FSC/export tax subsidy dispute. Monthly increments were planned until either the U.S. complied, or the EU reached the maximum of roughly $4 billion annually it was authorized to retaliate. In the Fall of 2004, the United States repealed the extraterritorial income exclusion, and the EU subsequently removed its retaliatory tariffs. Antigua-Barbuda won a WTO panel ruling under the GATS against certain U.S. Internet gambling restraints. Retaliation was authorized, and the U.S. settled with nearly all members by offering compensation. The U.S. won a panel decision against Mexico's exorbitant telecom interconnection rates but lost a 2004 cotton subsidy challenge by Brazil. Retaliation by Brazil was authorized.

The United States also lost a second dispute with the EU about pre-privatization countervailable subsidies, in particular the legality of the U.S. "same person" methodology. The U.S. won a SPS dispute against Japanese quarantine of U.S. apples, while losing an important softwood lumber "zeroing" methodology complaint brought by Canada. The U.S. repeatedly lost on zeroing disputes brought by other WTO members before grudgingly amending its antidumping rules. The Mexico-United States "sugar war" came to a head before the Appellate Body. Mexico's 20% soft drink tax on beverages not using cane sugar, its 20% distribution tax on those beverages, and related bookkeeping requirements were found to violate GATT Article III and not exempt under Article XX(d).

Subsequently, the two countries settled their dispute by agreeing, effective in 2008, to free trade in sugar and high fructose corn syrup. Sugar remains one of the most highly protected sectors of the U.S. economy sheltered behind quotas dating back to the 1930s. Commonly triple the world commodity price of sugar, U.S. sugar quotas drove Hershey Chocolates among others to move its factories abroad. The CIA reports that sugar producers in Jamaica switched to marijuana because of U.S. sugar import quotas.

The U.S. failed to persuade the Appellate Body to require the European Union under GATT Article X (3) to undertake a major overhaul of its customs law system targeting inconsistencies therein among the 28 member states. The United States lost a cotton subsidy challenge by Brazil. The United States agreed to pay $147 million annually to provide technical assistance to Brazilian cotton farmers. In return, Brazil has suspended retaliatory tariffs and cross-sector IP sanctions authorized by the WTO because of U.S. cotton subsidy violations.

In 2009, a WTO Panel ruled that Airbus had received $20 billion in illegal EU "launch" subsidies. In 2010, that same panel found Boeing the recipient of $5 billion in federal research contract subsidies that violated the WTO Subsidies Code. In 2019, a WTO Panel authorized $7.5 billion in retaliatory U.S. duties on EU goods, which were rapidly adopted at 25% on Airbus planes, Irish and Scotch whiskeys, wine (but not Italian wine, sparkling wines, or wines over 14 degrees alcohol), olives, cheese as well as certain EU dairy and pork products.

In 2020, a WTO Panel authorized $4 billion in retaliatory EU duties on U.S. goods, which it applied to Boeing aircraft and other U.S. goods. Challenging the calculations behind the EU tariffs, the U.S. increased its tariffs on French wine and cognacs late in 2020. None of these actions could be appealed to the WTO Appellate Body for want of sufficient members, a blocking maneuver adopted by the Trump administration (below). However, under a technicality, U.S. buyers (notably Delta) of Airbus aircraft flown first to other countries (say Canada or in Central America) were able to escape retaliatory U.S. import duties.

The EU-U.S. longstanding civil aircraft disputes remained ongoing and were frequently cited by Trump administration critics of the WTO dispute settlement process. Settlement of these disputes was finally achieved under the Biden administration.

§ 1.17 U.S. Blockage of WTO Dispute Settlement

The Trump Administration launched an extensive review and report on U.S. participation in the World Trade Organization (WTO), the ultimate rules-based multilateral agreement embraced by approximately 165 countries and customs territories. Special attention was given to WTO "most-favored-nation" trade principles, trade remedies and dispute resolution. That report was also highly critical of WTO procedures, specific trade remedy decisions, and especially "activism" and "overreach" on the part of the WTO Appellate Body.

President Obama blocked the reappointment of an Appellate Body member accused of "judicial overreach." In what amounts to a hostile act, the United States under Presidents Trump *and Biden* has refused to allow any renewal or new appointments to the WTO Appellate Body (AB), first shrinking its membership from seven to four. What was normally a 90-day process took many months. By the Fall of 2018, there were only three AB members, the minimum quorum necessary for it to conduct proceedings.

Late in 2019, the Appellate Body ceased to function with only one member. Work-around alternatives that would result in voluntary arbitrations by disputing members as an alternative to Appellate Body were adopted, but little used in practice. President Biden continued the blockage in the face of a 2020 WTO Panel ruling against U.S. unilateral Section 301 tariffs on Chinese exports, potential challenges to U.S. national security tariffs on steel and aluminum, and broader concerns about the viability of the WTO to move forward on any trade front (notably subsidies and state-owned enterprises) using consensus decision-making. See Section 1.4.

The WTO rule of international trade law so actively sought by the United States in the early 1990s is endangered. *WTO disputes have been suspended into a legal void.* This has increased the interest in regional and bilateral free trade agreements and the use of their dispute settlement procedures. For more on this theme, see my Concise Hornbook on *International Trade Law*, Chapter 18.

§ 1.18 China Involvement in WTO Disputes

China, a member since 2001, has been involved in several WTO disputes. Here is a sampling of those disputes.

Canada, the European Union, and the United States complained against Chinese duties on imported auto parts (10 percent) that rose to those on complete autos (25 percent) if the imported parts exceeded a fixed percentage of the final vehicle content or price, or if specific combinations of imported auto parts were used in the final vehicle. In addition, extensive record keeping, reporting and verification requirements were imposed when Chinese auto companies used imported parts. In July of 2008, a WTO Panel ruled that these "internal charges" violated Articles III (2) and III (4) of the GATT and China's accession commitments.

The core Panel ruling, affirmed by the Appellate Body, found China's auto parts measures discriminatory in favor of domestic producers, a violation of the national treatment standard for taxes and regulations. This ruling marked the first time since China's admission in 2001 that it was held in breach of its WTO commitments and obligations.

Less than one month after losing this dispute, China enacted a clever "green tax" on gas-guzzling autos, most of which just happen to be imported. The sales tax on cars with engine capacities over 4.1 liters has been doubled to 40%. Autos with engines between 3 and 4.1

liters are taxed at 25%, up from 15%. Most Chinese-made cars have engines with 2.5 liters or less. Autos with engines between 1 and 3 liters remain taxed at 8% and 10%. The smallest cars with engines below 1 liter have their sales tax reduced from 3 to 1 percent. This green tax seemingly was intended to achieve protective results like China's Auto Parts tariff structure.

Other disputes challenging China's compliance with WTO law have been undertaken. They concern China's auto export subsidies and CVDs on auto imports, protection and enforcement of intellectual property rights (2009 WTO Panel ruled against China), trade and distribution of publications and audiovisual entertainment products and services (2009 Appellate Body ruled against China), commodity export tariffs and restrictions (2012 WTO Appellate Body ruled against China), application of Chinese AD to U.S. grain-oriented flat rolled steel (GOES) (2012 WTO Appellate Body ruled against China) and discriminatory treatment of foreign electronic payment services (2012 WTO Panel ruled against China). China's record of compliance with these WTO rulings resembles that of the U.S., somewhat spotty and not always prompt.

China, in turn, challenged U.S. safeguard measures applied to Chinese steel exports (2010 WTO Panel rejected challenge) and tires (2011 WTO Panel rejected challenge). It challenged U.S. antidumping and countervailing duties on paper products from China (2011 WTO Panel ruled against U.S. dual assessment of AD and CVD duties), as well as U.S. AD on Chinese solar panels. China has also applied AD duties to U.S. exports, *e.g.*, chicken.

In a major dispute, China challenged in 2017 continued U.S. and EU application of nonmarket economy rules in antidumping disputes. Losing before WTO panel in 2020, China withdrew this complaint. China has also challenged President Trump's solar panel and clothes washers safeguard tariffs, as well as Trump's "national security" steel and aluminum tariffs. Numerous U.S. CVDs against a range of Chinese goods were successfully challenged in 2018 on procedural grounds by China before a WTO Panel.

By 2024, China's participation in WTO adjudications had greatly surpassed those of the United States. More generally, in the absence of U.S. WTO leadership under Trump and Biden, China has sought to assume that role.

The Trump Administration notably filed in 2018 a WTO complaint, joined by Japan and the European Union, against alleged patent violations of Articles 3 and 28 of TRIPs. These allegations asserted that foreign patent holders are unable to stop Chinese licensees from continuing to use patented technology after licenses expire. They also asserted Chinese discrimination against and less favorable mandatory adverse contract terms for imported foreign technology. The U.S. specifically cited four Chinese laws as the source of these TRIPs violations: The PRC Foreign Trade Law, Contract Law, Chinese-Foreign Equity Joint Venture Law, and the PRC Regulations on the Administration of the Import and Export of Technologies. By agreement, this dispute has been suspended since 2019.

Chapter 2

REGULATING "FREE" TRADE AGREEMENTS

Table of Sections

§ 2.1 One-Way Free Trade: GSP, CBI, AGOA and More

Some goods may enter the United States at less than most-favored-nation tariff levels or duty free. This occurs because of special tariff preferences incorporated into United States law (outlined below). It is important to realize that these preferences create valuable trading opportunities for U.S. importers and exporters located in qualified nations. These people are the clients for whom lawyers work to secure duty-free entry into the United States market. Duty free entry is, of course, the goal of all exporters and importers involved in United States trade. Various free trade and customs union agreements (including USMCA and other FTAs of the

United States) achieving duty free outcomes are discussed below and in Chapter 5.

The widest and most significant of the U.S. duty-free programs is known as the Generalized System of Preferences (GSP) adopted through the GATT. The European Union (see Chapter 3) and Japan have their own versions of GSP. The U.S. GSP is a complex system of duty-free tariff preferences benefiting selected goods originating in developing nations and intended to foster their economic improvement. Irregularly and often retroactively renewed, the U.S. GSP was operative through 2020. Its major beneficiaries at that time were India, Thailand, and Brazil, but President Trump "graduated" India and Turkey from the GSP program. Brazil suggested it may voluntarily give up "developing country" WTO status. At this writing, the U.S. GSP has not been renewed.

Another U.S. program is the Caribbean Basin Economic Recovery Act of 1983 (also known as the Caribbean Basin Initiative, CBI), which permits certain goods to enter the United States market duty free. To a significant degree, the CBI duty free program was duplicated in the Andean Trade Preference Act of 1991 initially benefiting Colombian, Ecuadorian, Bolivian and Peruvian goods. In 2010, the Africa Growth and Opportunity Act (AGOA) granted duty and quota free entry to the U.S. market for apparel made from U.S. fabric and yarn. AGOA, expanded in scope and applicable until 2025, covers much of sub-Saharan Africa. It is now the second most significant source of one-way duty-free entry of goods into the USA. Exports from Nigeria, Angola and South Africa top the list of source countries.

In addition, an important "duty-free" category allows fabricated U.S.-made components shipped abroad for assembly to return to the U.S. without tariffs on the value of the components. Authorization for this importation is found in Section 9802.00.80 of the Harmonized Tariff Schedule. Goods of this type are subject to a United States Customs duty limited in amount to the value added by foreign assembly operations. This provision is perhaps best known in connection with Latin American maquiladoras.

The least restrictive rules of origin for duty free entry of goods into the United States apply to its insular possessions. These include American Samoa, Guam, Johnson Island, Kingman Reef, Midway Islands, Puerto Rico, the U.S. Virgin Islands and Wake Island. Goods from such possessions may contain up to 70 percent foreign value and still be admitted duty-free.

Some of these duty-free programs overlap and effectively compete. It might be helpful to think of them in terms of concentric geographic circles. The widest circle is Section 9802.00.80 which applies to the entire globe. The next circle represents the GSP system and most developing nations. Inside that circle is the Caribbean Basin Initiative, the Andean Initiative, and U.S. insular possessions followed by NAFTA and other U.S. free trade agreements. A manufacturer based in the Caribbean may seek duty free entry into the United States market under Section 9802.00.80, the GSP program or the CBI, but not U.S. free trade agreements, save the Dominican Republic. To most developing nations, these are selectively discriminatory duty-free programs that undermine their GSP benefits.

Unusual trade opportunities can arise by linking U.S. duty free entry programs with those of the European Union (EU). For example, the Union has its own complicated and different GSP program, its equivalent of Section 9802.00.80, and two selective duty-free programs for developing nations. The latter are known as its Mediterranean Policy and Cotonou Conventions. See Chapter 3. A producer in Israel can quite possibly gain duty free access to the EU (under its Mediterranean Policy) and to the United States (under the Israeli-U.S. FTA). A producer in Jamaica might achieve similar results under the Cotonou Conventions, the CBI and/or the GSP programs of the EU and the United States.

For more extensive coverage of global one-way free trade opportunities, see my Concise Hornbooks on *International Trade Law* and *The European Union Beyond BREXIT*.

§ 2.2 The Diverse Content of "Free" Trade Agreements

A word about nomenclature: Not all "free trade agreements" (FTAs) are titled as such and none of them are completely free. In Asia, many FTAs are often called "Cooperation Agreements" or "Economic Cooperation Agreements." See Chapter 5. Canada likes to title its FTAs "Comprehensive" and/or "Progressive." The re-negotiated version of NAFTA initially had several titles, some of which do not even use the word "Trade." See Chapter 6.

Hereafter, this book will stick with FTAs as a generic title, noting that the *CONTENT* of these agreements differs widely around the globe. See *Free Trade Choices* below.

There is continued movement towards free trade agreements (FTAs) and customs unions (CUs) throughout the world, though not often of the consequence of that occurring in Europe and North America. Every country has at least one FTA, some have dozens. These developments are partly a competitive by-product of European and North American integration. Others simply reflect the desire (but not always the political will) to capture the economic gains and international negotiating strength that such economic relations can bring. This is particularly true of attempts at free trade and customs unions in the developing world. Another important element is geo-political. In the wake of China's rise as a global power and its "lifetime friendship" with Russia and Iran regarding war in Ukraine and Gaza/Israel, cultivating friendly trade relations elsewhere has become an imperative for the many other countries in the world.

The growth of such agreements creates systemic risks for the World Trade Organization (WTO), which reports that all its members are partners in one or more regional or bilateral trade agreements. Several studies indicate that the EU and the USA have offered less trade liberalization in WTO talks in product areas they had previously granted preferential tariffs under their FTAs.

Here is a sampling of FTA agreements around the globe: Hong Kong-China, Japan-Singapore, Russia-CIS states, New Zealand-China, Mexico-Israel, Canada-Peru, EU-South Africa, Chile-South Korea, the South Asian Free Trade Area (India, Pakistan, Bangladesh, Nepal, Bhutan, Sri Lanka), and the list goes on. See below the Linked Lists of Operational Multilateral and Bilateral Free Trade Agreements in Sections 2.11 and 2.12.

Prof. Bhagwati of Columbia University cleverly calls these developments the trade "spaghetti bowl." As Prof. Bhala of the University of Kansas has observed, whether this amounts to competitive trade liberalization or competitive trade imperialism are provocative questions.

The Spaghetti Bowl

A variety of factors help explain why FTAs have become a leading edge of international trade law and policy. Difficulties encountered in the GATT/WTO Uruguay, "Seattle" and Doha Rounds of multilateral trade negotiations are certainly crucial. GATT/WTO regulatory failures regarding free trade agreements have also fueled this reality (see below).

Yet these "negatives" do not fully explain the "free" trade feeding frenzy. A range of attractions are also at work. For example, free trade agreements often extend to subject matters beyond WTO competence. Foreign investment law is a prime example, and many FTAs and CUs serve as investment magnets. Government procurement, optional at the WTO level, is also often included. Competition policy and labor and environmental matters absent from the WTO are sometimes covered. In addition, free trade agreements can reach beyond the scope of existing WTO agreements. Services is one "WTO-plus" area where this is clearly true. Intellectual property rights are also being "WTO-plussed" in free trade agreements.

FTAs and CUs are politically and economically selective. In other words, they avoid not only global most-favored-nation principles, but also domestically "sensitive" national politics and economics. For example, Singapore's absence of farm exports helped make it an ideal U.S., EU, and Japanese free trade partner. The micro-sized economy of Chile contributed to its attraction as a free trade partner with Mexico, China, the European Union, the United States, and others. U.S. free trade deals with Jordan, Bahrain and Oman fit economically in a similar fashion, not to mention national security objectives.

Like it or not, the "spaghetti-bowl" maze of FTAs and CUs is driven by powerful negative and positive forces. It is not only the preferred trade medium of today, but also the future. President Trump drove other countries into FTAs faster than he withdrew the United States from them. President Biden declined to initiate any U.S. free trade negotiations, not even with longtime ally Britain. See Chapters 5 and 6.

Already more than half of world trade is conducted under FTAs and CUs. While international trade lawyers may celebrate full employment, it bears remembering that FTAs and CUs are discriminatory. They could render the WTO's MFN tariffs and trade rules (see Chapter 1) the least favored status in world trade. Such an outcome would be especially harmful to the world's poorest nations, those with whom few partners seek a preferential trade agreement. See especially the multilateral and bilateral Linked Lists of operational FTAs in Sections 2.11 and 2.12.

Free Trade Choices

There is a continuum of sorts, a range of options to be considered when nations contemplate economic integration. In "*free trade areas*" (FTAs), tariffs, quotas, and other barriers to trade among participating states are reduced or removed while individual national trade barriers vis-à-vis third-party states are retained. Each FTA partner retains its own external tariff and customs controls, including the right to negotiate FTA with other nations. This was true of NAFTA in 1994 and the hundreds of FTAs now prevalent around the globe.

But there are many varieties of FTAs. Some are limited to trade in goods, which tends to be the case in Asia. See ASEAN in Chapter 5. Others cover only industrial goods, removing the always touchy area of agricultural trade. See EFTA in Chapter 3. Many retain the use internally of countervailing, antidumping, safeguard or national security tariffs under appropriate circumstances, thus diminishing the concept of "free trade."

Some move beyond mere removal of tariff barriers, taking on much more difficult nontariff regulatory barriers (NTBs) governing *health, safety, environmental and other rules.* One reason to do this is that the WTO package does not cover the environment. Another is to achieve a depth not found in the WTO TBT and SPS agreements. See Section 1.8. For *WTO-plus* NTB approaches, see EU legislation in Section 3.4. Compare the WTO-minus coverage of NTBs under NAFTA/USMCA presented in Section 4.3.

FTAs may also cover trade in services, especially those of major traders, for example NAFTA and the USMCA (Chapters 4 and 6), CETA 2017 (Chapter 3), TPP-12 and TPP-11 (Chapter 5), and the Japan-EU Economic Partnership Agreement of 2018 (Chapter 5). Once again, *FTA coverage of services frequently exceeds that of the GATS agreement.* In addition, intellectual property and technology transfers are sometimes included in FTAs in ways that go well *beyond the WTO TRIPs* agreement discussed in Section 1.12. See the TPP-12 and USMCA agreements covered in Chapters 5 and 6.

United States FTAs almost always extensively cover *foreign investment and related dispute settlement.* See Chapters 4 and 6. This topic is largely absent from the WTO package, which focuses only on performance requirements under the TRIMs agreement. Foreign investment is also frequently absent from Pacific Rim FTAs. See Chapter 5.

An increasingly wide range of labor (notably ILO) and environmental rules (covering fishing, timbering, climate change, marine debris, sea life, flora and fauna, ozone layer, endangered and invasive species, and more) have been included in post-NAFTA FTAs. Furthermore, gender, rule of law, human rights, indigenous peoples, cultural industries, anti-corruption, currency manipulation, state-owned enterprises, procurement (optional in the WTO package), maritime transport, business visas, competition (antitrust) law, data localization and privacy, corporate social responsibility and governance, fraud, biologics, digital trade, e-commerce, and other areas of law not at all found in the mandatory WTO package of agreements have been incorporated into more recent FTAs. See Chapters 5 and 6.

Note that the absence of coverage under WTO rules removes the possibility of invoking WTO remedies, an option for example under NAFTA and the USMCA. See Chapters 4 and 6. For such areas, the only remedies available will be those found in bilateral or multilateral FTAs.

Customs Unions and Beyond

Economic integration under FTAs is sometimes surpassed in customs union, common market, economic community, or economic union agreements. All such agreements are built around internal free trade rules.

"Customs unions" (CUs) remove internal trade barriers among participating states and create common trade barriers as regards third-party states. Customs unions have a common external tariff and common customs code. Only the union, not its member states, may negotiate trade agreements with other nations, including FTAs and customs union agreements. The EU customs union is preeminent, see Chapter 3. Another notable CU is that of MERCOSUR, see Section 2.6.

"Common markets" go further than customs unions by providing for the free movement of factors of production (goods, services, capital, people) among participating states. In the European Union, this body of law is known as the fundamental "Four Freedoms." NAFTA and the USMCA notably omit general free movement rights for individuals, limiting movement to business and professional persons under special visas. See Section 6.8.

"Economic communities" build on common markets by introducing some harmonization of basic national policies related to the economy of the community, *e.g.*, transport, taxation, securities, insurance, the environment, employment law and regional growth. The EU started as the European Economic Community (EEC) in 1957.

Finally, *"economic unions"* may embrace a nearly complete harmonization of national policies related to the economy of the union, *e.g.*, company laws, E-commerce, consumer protection, intellectual property and technology, currencies, and government subsidies and procurement. The difference between an economic community and an economic union relates only to the number and importance of harmonized national policies. Such unions may also integrate politically, and on foreign affairs, security, defense, and human rights.

The United States, moving from the Articles of Confederation to the U.S. Constitution of 1789, arguably was the first economic union of note. The USA has a common external tariff, enjoys widespread internal free trade under the Commerce Clause, and has numerous federal common market and economic community policies, along with unity in foreign affairs.

The EEC of 1957 evolved first into the European Community, dropping the word Economic from its title in 1993. By 2009, it renamed itself the European Union.

Trade Creation and Trade Diversion, Rules of Origin

All economic integration agreements are inherently discriminatory in their international trade impact. As non-universalized trade preferences, they tend to simultaneously *create trade* among participating states and *divert trade* between those states and the rest of the world. Thus, while trade creation may represent an improvement in the allocation of scarce world resources, trade diversion may generate an opposite result.

With free trade agreements, diversionary trade effects are usually not distinct because of the absence of a common trade wall against outsiders. Trade diversion nonetheless occurs. "Rules of origin" in free trade area agreements keep third-party imports from seeking the lowest tariff or highest quota state and then exploiting the trade advantages within a free trade area. Under rules of origin, free trade areas are "free" only for goods substantially originating therein. This causes member state goods to be preferred over goods from other states. Rules of origin under a free trade agreement can be as trade diversionary as common external tariffs in customs unions.

Understanding FTA and CU rules of origin is an essential task for lawyers around the world. For different rule of origin approaches, *see* CUSFTA and NAFTA in Chapter 4, and the USMCA rules of origin in Chapter 6.

§ 2.3 GATT Article 24 Rules on FTAs and CUs for Goods

Article 24 of the General Agreement on Tariffs and Trade (GATT) (1947 and 1994) attempts to manage the internal trade-creating and external trade-diverting effects of FTAs, Customs unions and similar arrangements. Proposals for free trade areas and custom unions must be submitted to a formal GATT/WTO review procedure during which "binding" recommendations are possible to bring the proposals into conformity. Such recommendations might deal with Article 24 requirements for the elimination of internal tariffs and other restrictive regulations of commerce on "substantially all" products originating in a customs union or free trade area. Or they might deal with Article 24 requirements that common external tariffs not be "on the whole higher or more restrictive" in effect than the general incidence of prior existing national tariffs. The broad purpose of Article 24, acknowledged therein, is to facilitate trade among the GATT/WTO contracting parties and not to raise trade barriers.

Most free trade and customs union agreements have passed through this review mechanism *without* substantial modification. The GATT, not economic agreements, most often has given way. For example, during GATT review of the 1957 Treaty of Rome creating what is now the European Union, many "violations" of the letter and spirit of Article 24 were cited. The derivation of the common external tariff by arithmetically averaging existing national tariffs was challenged as more restrictive of trade than previous arrangements. Such averaging for a given product fails to take account of differing national import volumes. If a product was faced originally with a below average national tariff and a larger than average national demand, the new average tariff is clearly more "restrictive" of imports than before. Averaging in high tariffs of countries of low demand quite plausibly created more restrictions on third-party trade. If so, the letter and spirit of Article 24 were breached.

Despite these and other arguments, the Treaty of Rome passed through GATT study and review committees without final resolution of its legal status under Article 24. Postponement of these issues became permanent. GATT attempts—through the lawyer-like conditions of Article 24 to maximize trade creation and minimize trade diversion—must be seen as generally inadequate. Treaty terms became negotiable demands that were not accepted. Decades later, the ineffectiveness of GATT/WTO supervision of free trade and customs union agreements continues. At best Article 24 exerts a marginal influence over their contents. Whether the extraordinary proliferation of preferential agreements undermines or supports WTO trade policies is hotly debated.

GATT Regulatory Reform Attempts

The Uruguay Round, which created the World Trade Organization, presented an opportunity to come to grips with the regulatory failure of Article 24. Agreement was reached in 1994 on an "Understanding on the Interpretation of Article 24," which presently binds the roughly 165 member nations of the WTO. This Interpretation reaffirms that free trade area and customs union agreements *must* satisfy the provisions of Article 24, clarifies how before and after evaluations of common external tariffs are to be undertaken, limits in most cases interim agreements to 10 years, and details Article 24 notification, report and recommendation duties and processes.

Most importantly, the 1994 Understanding on Interpretation expressly permits invocation of standard WTO dispute settlement procedures (DSU) regarding any Article 24 matters. All that said, the 1994 Understanding did not come to grips with the systemic ambiguities that led to Article 24's early and ongoing regulatory failure.

The failure to launch a new round of WTO negotiations in Seattle (1999), followed by delays and failure of the Doha Round that commenced in 2001, has contributed to the feeding frenzy of CU and FTA agreements. Supported by provisional application of a 2006 Doha Round WTO Transparency Mechanism, hundreds of agreements have been notified to the WTO. A large additional number are believed *not* to have been notified. In general, most of the notified agreements are bilateral, not regional in character.

Meanwhile, the WTO Regional Trade Agreements Committee, working by consensus, has been unable since 1995 to complete even one assessment of a FTA or CU agreement's conformity to GATT Article 24 or GATS Article 5 (Section 2.3 and 2.4). The same is true for WTO Committee on Trade and Development "review" of Enabling Clause arrangements (Section 2.5).

It has been suggested that this record can be explained by the ambiguous relationship between Committee reports and WTO dispute settlement proceedings. For example, can such reports be used in evidence in WTO dispute proceedings? Can fact-finding by the WTO Secretariat and information gathered for WTO regulatory purposes be similarly used? This "dispute settlement awareness" makes WTO members reluctant to provide information or agree on conclusions that could later be used or interpreted in DSU proceedings.

Decades later, the ineffectiveness of GATT/WTO supervision of free trade and customs union agreements continues. At best Article 24 exerts a marginal influence. The extraordinary proliferation of preferential agreements undermines core WTO trade policies (see Chapter 1).

FTAs and CUs, intended under GATT to be exceptions to nondiscriminatory MFN trade principles (see Section 1.2), represent an exception that has become the rule.

§ 2.4 GATS Integrated Services Agreements

Since 1995, "economic integration agreements" (EIAs) covering services are permitted under Article 5 of the General Agreement on Trade in Services (GATS). Such agreements, which can be staged, must have "substantial sectoral coverage," eliminate "substantially" all discrimination in sectors subject to multilateral commitments, and not raise the "overall" level of barriers to trade in GATS services compared to before the EIA. EIAs involving developing nations are to be accorded "flexibility." Like GATT Article 24 customs unions, there is an Article 5 duty to compensate EIA nonparticipants.

Review of GATS Article 5 notifications is undertaken, when requested by the WTO Council for Trade in Services, by the Committee on Regional Trade Agreements (CRTA). Thus, whereas CRTA examinations of GATT Article 24 agreements are required, such examinations are optional under GATS. Nevertheless, numerous Article 5 examinations have been conducted, including notably the services components of the North American Free Trade Agreement (NAFTA 1994), the EEC Treaty (1957) and EU Enlargement (2004), Japan's FTAs with Singapore, Mexico and Malaysia, China's FTAs with Hong Kong and Macau, and various U.S. free trade agreements.

None of these examinations has resulted in a final report on consistency with GATS Article 5. This pattern continues the GATT/WTO record of regulatory failure regarding economic integration agreements.

§ 2.5 Developing World Free Trade, the Enabling Clause

Developing nations in Africa, the Caribbean, Central America, South America, and Southeast Asia (among others) began adopting free trade and customs union agreements as early as the 1960s. In 1979, under what is commonly called the Enabling Clause, the GATT parties decided to permit developing nations to enter differential and more favorable bilateral, regional, or global arrangements among themselves to reduce or eliminate tariffs and nontariff barriers applicable to trade in goods.

Like Article 24 of GATT, noted above, the Enabling Clause constitutes an exception to most-favored nation trade principles. It has generally been construed to authorize developing world free trade area and customs union agreements. Whether the Enabling Clause was intended to take such agreements out of Article 24 and its requirements, or be construed in conjunction therewith, is unclear. However, the creation of alternative notification and review procedures for Enabling Clause arrangements suggests Article 24 is inapplicable.

Notification to GATT of Enabling Clause arrangements is mandatory. Since 1995, the WTO Committee on Trade and Development (CTD) has been the forum where such notifications are reviewed, but in practice not examined in depth. Enabling Clause arrangements should be designed to promote the trade of developing countries and not raise external trade barriers or undue trade difficulties. Consultations with individual GATT members experiencing such difficulties must be undertaken, and these consultations may be expanded to all GATT members if requested.

Unlike GATT Article 24 and GATS Article 5, neither compensation to nonparticipants nor formal reporting on the consistency with the Enabling Clause of developing nation arrangements is anticipated. The ASEAN-China (2004), India-Sri Lanka (2002), and "revived" Economic Community of West African States (ECOWAS 2005) agreements illustrate notified but unexamined preferential arrangements sheltered by the Enabling Clause.

§ 2.6 African, Islamic World, Caribbean, Latin American, and Southeast Asian FTAs

Africa

Several groups, sometimes overlapping and often poorly implemented, have been formed in Africa, a continent with little internal trade. In 1966 the central African countries of Cameroon, Central African Republic, Chad, Congo (Brazzaville) and Gabon formed the Economic and Customs Union of Central Africa (Union Douaniere et Économique de l'Afrique Centrale: UDEAC) to establish a common customs and tariff approach toward the rest of the world and to formulate a common foreign investment code.

In 1967 Kenya, Tanzania and Uganda created the East African Community (EAC) attempting to harmonize customs and tariff practices among themselves and in relation to other countries. The practical effect of that Community has frequently been negated by political strife, but of late it has enjoyed a comeback and, combined with Rwanda, Burundi, and South Sudan, has tried to develop a customs union.

In 1974 six French-speaking West African nations formed the West African Economic Community (known by its French initials CEAO), which expanded to become the Economic Community of West African States (ECOWAS), encompassing 15 nations. ECOWAS was initially created by treaty in 1975 to coordinate economic development and cooperation, with a revised treaty signed in 1993. Some progress on liberalized industrial trade has been made and a Cooperation, Compensation and Development Fund established. ECOWAS is also involved in peacekeeping missions in West Africa, and has established an active court, the ECOWAS Community Court of Justice. A subset of French-speaking ECOWAS countries formed the West African Economic and Monetary Union (WAEMU or

UEMOA) in 1994 as a customs and monetary union, with Portuguese-speaking Guinea-Bissau joining later. In recent years, some ECOWAS participants have withdrawn amidst strife centered on growing Islamic terror in the region.

In 1991, the Organization of African Unity (OAU) member states agreed to a Treaty Establishing the African Economic Community. This wide-ranging Treaty embraces 51 African nations, and includes a regional Court of Justice, although its practical prospects remain uncertain. In 1995, 12 southern African countries, with post-apartheid South Africa participating for the first time, targeted free trade under the Southern African Development Community. A more limited grouping of South Africa, Botswana, Namibia, Lesotho, and Swaziland comprise the Southern African Customs Union (SACU), created in 2002 and focused primarily of trade in goods. SACU was created after the South Africa-EU FTA of 1999, which remains in force.

A 20-member Common Market for Eastern and Southern Africa (COMESA) has also been created. In 2015, COMESA, SADC and the EAC agreed to work toward a 26-member free trade area. In 2018, 45 African nations signed the *African Continental Free Trade Area* agreement with South Africa, the largest African economy, abstaining. This agreement took effect in 2022 but may prove more aspirational than operational.

Islamic World

Bahrain, Kuwait, Oman, Qatar, Saudi Arabia, and United Arab Emirates formed the Gulf Cooperation Council (GCC) in 1981 with objectives to establish freedom of movement, a regional armaments industry, common banking and financial systems, a unified currency policy, a customs union, a common foreign aid program, and a joint, international investment company, the Gulf Investment Corporation. The Council has implemented trade and investment rules concerning tariffs on regional and imported goods, government contracts, communications, transportation, real estate investment, and freedom of movement of professionals. Progress has been made on a Uniform Commercial Code and a Commission for Commercial Arbitration of the Gulf States.

The GCC also has a major 1990 trade and cooperation agreement with the EU. The GCC has FTAs with Middle East and North African (MENA) countries, and notably with Singapore since 2013. In 2003, the non-Arab states of Iran, Pakistan, Turkey, Afghanistan and six Central Asian nations signed an Economic Cooperation Organization Trade Agreement (ECOTA). In 2004, Jordan, Egypt, Tunisia, and Morocco signed the Agadir free trade agreement. There is also a Greater Arab Free Trade Area (GAFTA), now encompassing 18 Arab nations.

In 2017, a broad economic boycott led by Saudi Arabia of "progressive" Qatar, home to Al Jazeera media and Iranian links, emerged in the Gulf. Qatar, hosting a major U.S. military base, seems to have taken the boycott in stride. Nevertheless, the Qatar boycott clearly undermined GCC goals. Signs of reconciliation emerged in 2021.

Caribbean

Established in 1973, the Caribbean Community (CARICOM) now includes 15 Caribbean states. The 1989 Grand Anse Declaration commits CARICOM to establishment of its own common market. Nine CARICOM members are also members of the Organization of Eastern Caribbean States (OECS), including a 2010 agreement on economic union. Some 37 nations signed the Association of Caribbean States agreement in 1994 with long-term economic integration goals.

The longstanding United States economic boycott of *Cuba* under Fidel Castro has isolated that nation. U.S. policy has not stopped Canada and Mexico from actively trading and investing (tourism especially) in Cuba. And it certainly propelled post-Soviet Cuba into a close relationship with Venezuela under Chavez and Maduro, including a well-known "doctors for oil" agreement. Cuba's larger problem is its regime's isolationist tendencies, fear of "capitalist pollution" and dogmatic ideology. But the winds of change are blowing in Havana, and a dollarized economy is emerging from the underground. In 2015, the U.S. and Cuba commenced "normalization" of their relations, but a softer embargo remains in place, tightened under President Trump, relaxed somewhat under President Biden.

Latin America

Numerous countries in Latin America were members of the Latin American Free Trade Association (LAFTA) (1961) which had small success in reducing tariffs and developing the region through cooperative industrial sector programs. These programs allocated industrial production among the participating states. The Latin American Integration Association (LAIA) (1981), the eleven-member successor to LAFTA, is continuing arrangements for intra-community tariff concessions. They agreed to a 50 percent tariff cut on LAIA goods.

Latin America became a central focus in the 1990s of economic integration. Mexico not only signed a free trade agreement with the United States and Canada, it also agreed to free trade with Colombia,

Venezuela, Chile, Bolivia, Costa Rica, Nicaragua, Guatemala, Honduras, El Salvador, Peru and Uruguay. Furthermore, Mexico has negotiated free trade agreements with Japan, the European Union, EFTA (European Free Trade Assn) and entered in 2013 into The Pacific Alliance with Peru, Chile, and Colombia.

Argentina, Brazil, Paraguay, and Uruguay signed a treaty establishing the MERCOSUR (Southern Cone) common market in 1991 and Chile and Bolivia joined them as Associates in 1996. Modeled on the EU, MERCOSUR is not a well-functioning customs union. Nationally restrictive trade and investment rules dominate. Venezuela under Chavez created the Peoples' Trade Treaty in 2007 aligned with Cuba, Bolivia, Nicaragua, Ecuador, and others. Venezuela obtained membership in MERCOSUR in 2012, only to be evicted on human rights grounds a few years later.

ANCOM ("The Cartagena Agreement") was founded by Bolivia, Chile, Colombia, Ecuador, and Peru in 1969 primarily to counter the economic power of Argentina, Brazil, and Mexico and to reduce dependency upon foreign capital and technology. Its Decision No. 24 regulating foreign investment and technology transfers was widely copied during the 1970s. A major boost came in 1973 with the addition of Venezuela, but some of the fragile dynamics of the regional grouping are illustrated by Chile's withdrawal in 1977, Bolivia's withdrawal in 1981 and resumption of membership barely four months later, and Peru's economic (but not political) withdrawal in 1991 and return in 1996.

In 1958 Costa Rica, El Salvador, Guatemala, Honduras, and Nicaragua formed the Central American Common Market (CACM), another victim of political strife, but still functioning in a limited way, primarily resulting from the 2005 Central American Free Trade Agreement (CAFTA-DR) with the United States. CAFTA-DR also incorporates the Dominican Republic from the Caribbean. See Section 5.2.

All this activity occurred against the background of the Free Trade Area of the Americas (FTAA) initiative of the United States (below). In 2003 the ANCOM and MERCOSUR groups nominally agreed upon free trade, at least partly to counterbalance United States power in the FTAA negotiations. The United States, pursuing in turn a divide and conquer strategy, has attempted bilateral free trade agreements with all ANCOM members save Venezuela. The U.S. now has FTAs with Chile, Peru, and Colombia.

The Free Trade Area of the Americas (FTAA)

The U.S. "Enterprise for the Americas Initiative" (EAI) under elder President Bush raised hopes of economic integration throughout the Americas against a background of competitive regionalism in trade relations, especially between the European Union and North America. At the Americas Summit in Miami, President Clinton and 33 Latin American heads of state (only Fidel Castro was absent) renewed this hope by agreeing to commence negotiations on a Free Trade Area of the Americas (FTAA). The year 2005 was targeted at the Summit for creation of the FTAA.

Preparatory working groups met to discuss the following topics: (1) Market Access; (2) Customs Procedures and Rules of Origin; (3) Investment; (4) Standards and Technical Barriers to Trade; (5) Sanitary and Phytosanitary Measures; (6) Subsidies, Antidumping and Countervailing Duties; (7) Smaller Economies; (8) Government Procurement; (9) Intellectual Property Rights; (10) Services; (11) Competition Policy; and (12) Dispute Settlement. It is expected that each of these areas would be covered in any FTAA agreement. Formal FTAA negotiations were delayed several times, particularly because of differences between Brazil-led MERCOSUR and U.S.-led NAFTA.

Divisions were particularly evident during the November 2003 FTAA ministerial meeting in Miami. Lowered expectations, known as FTAA-Lite, reflect U.S. refusal to budge on agricultural protection and trade remedies, and Brazilian refusal to fully embrace investment, intellectual property, services, and procurement "free trade." Given unsuccessful resolution of these issues in the WTO Doha Round negotiations, FTAA-Lite with different levels of country commitments failed to move forward.

The absence of U.S. fast-track authority and the general perception that political support for free trade in the United States is weak clearly slowed FTAA developments. MERCOSUR and Brazil tried to seize the opportunity to move towards South American free trade. At this point, MERCOSUR's trade associates nominally include every South American nation. This put it in a much better position to negotiate terms and conditions with the NAFTA/USMCA bloc than individual countries or sub-groups within South America. That said, there are presently no ongoing FTAA negotiations in progress.

Southeast Asian Free Trade

Some interesting moves toward developing world free trade and rulemaking have been taken by the Association of Southeast Asian Nations (ASEAN). Its problems, failures and successes are representative of developing world attempts at legal and economic integration. ASEAN has its genesis in the 1967 Bangkok Declaration, with common trade rules in various states of growth, implementation, and retrenchment. ASEAN has internal tariff preferences, industrial development projects, "complementation schemes," and regional joint ventures.

An important juncture in the integration process is the point in time at which member countries of a regional group accept a supranational mechanism for enforcing the regime's law irrespective of national feelings and domestic law within a member country. The ASEAN Secretary-General once remarked that ASEAN's Secretariat was "a postman collecting and distributing letters." The surrender of national sovereignty to ASEAN institutions has been a painfully slow process.

ASEAN was formed in 1967 by Indonesia, Malaysia, the Philippines, Singapore, and Thailand. Brunei joined in 1984, Vietnam in 1995. Laos and Myanmar (Burma) joined in 1997, and Cambodia in 1999. Rarely have such culturally, linguistically, and geographically diverse nations attempted integration. The Bangkok Declaration establishing ASEAN as a cooperative association is a broadly worded document. Later proposals were made for a formal ASEAN treaty or convention but were rejected as unnecessary. The Bangkok Declaration sets forth numerous regional, economic, cultural, and social goals, including acceleration of economic growth, trade expansion and industrial collaboration.

The Bangkok Declaration establishes several mechanisms, but little supranational legal machinery, to implement its stated goals. An annual ASEAN Meeting of Foreign Ministers is scheduled on a rotational basis among the Member States. Special meetings are held "as required." The Declaration provides for a Standing Committee composed of the Foreign Minister of the state in which the next annual Ministerial Meeting is to be held and includes the ambassadors of other ASEAN States accredited to that state. The Declaration also provides for "Ad Hoc Committees and Permanent Committees of specialists and officials on specific subjects." Each member state is charged to set up a National Secretariat to administer ASEAN affairs within that Member State and to work with the Ministerial Meeting and the Standing Committee.

There have been relatively infrequent meetings of the ASEAN heads of government. This contrasts with the semiannual European "summits" that have kept that group moving forward along the path of integration. The third ASEAN summit was held in Manila in 1987. This summit produced an agreement for the promotion and protection of investments by ASEAN investors (national and most-favored-nation treatment rights are created), revised the basic ASEAN joint venture agreement, and continued the gradual extension of regional tariff and nontariff trade preferences. Goods already covered by the ASEAN tariff scheme were given a 50 percent margin of preference. New items received a 25 percent preferential margin. The nontariff preferences generally co-opt GATT rules, *e.g.*, regarding technical standards and customs valuation.

The fourth ASEAN summit in 1992 committed the parties to the creation of a free trade area within 15 years. Five years were cut from this schedule by agreement in 1994, but operational reality has eluded ASEAN free trade (AFTA). In 2003, a "watershed" date for complete integration in an ASEAN Economic Community targeted 2020. In 2007, this target date was changed to 2015, a reflection of the fear that ASEAN risks being overwhelmed by the powerhouse economies of China, India, Korea, and Japan. In 2016, the ASEAN common market was officially launched. Despite the fanfare, its prospects remain limited.

All that said, ASEAN as a group has limited free trade in goods agreements with China, Japan, Korea, and India. ASEAN was the originator of the Regional Cooperation and Economic Partnership (RCEP, effective Jan. 2022) agreement that China encouraged after President Trump refused to implement the Trans-Pacific Partnership (TPP-12, see Section 5.3) that President Obama negotiated as part of his Pivot to Asia China-containment policy. It is not at all clear to what degree ASEAN exports have increased under these agreements other than by becoming more active suppliers of natural resources and components to major-economy Pacific trade partners. For more on Pacific Rim FTAs, see Chapters 4 and 5.

APPENDICES

§ 2.7 Text of GATT 1947/1994 Article 24

Article XXIV: Territorial Application—Frontier Traffic—Customs Unions and Free-trade Areas

1. The provisions of this Agreement shall apply to the metropolitan customs territories of the contracting parties and to any other customs territories in respect of which this Agreement has been accepted under Article XXVI or is being applied under Article XXXIII or pursuant to the Protocol of Provisional Application. Each such customs territory shall, exclusively for the purposes of the territorial application of this Agreement, be treated as though it were a contracting party; *Provided* that the provisions of this paragraph shall not be construed to create any rights or obligations as between two or more customs territories in respect of which this Agreement has been accepted under Article XXVI or is being applied under Article XXXIII or pursuant to the Protocol of Provisional Application by a single contracting party.

2. For the purposes of this Agreement a customs territory shall be understood to mean any territory with respect to which separate tariffs or other regulations of commerce are maintained for a substantial part of the trade of such territory with other territories.

3. The provisions of this Agreement shall not be construed to prevent:

(*a*) Advantages accorded by any contracting party to adjacent countries in order to facilitate frontier traffic;

(*b*) Advantages accorded to the trade with the Free Territory of Trieste by countries contiguous to that territory, provided that such advantages are not in conflict with the Treaties of Peace arising out of the Second World War.

4. The contracting parties recognize the desirability of increasing freedom of trade by the development, through voluntary agreements, of closer integration between the economies of the countries parties to such agreements. They also recognize that the purpose of a customs union or of a free-trade area should be to facilitate trade between the constituent territories and not to raise barriers to the trade of other contracting parties with such territories.

5. Accordingly, the provisions of this Agreement shall not prevent, as between the territories of contracting parties, the formation of a customs union or of a free-trade area or the adoption of an interim agreement necessary for the formation of a customs union or of a free-trade area; *Provided* that:

(*a*) with respect to a customs union, or an interim agreement leading to a formation of a customs union, the duties and other regulations of commerce imposed at the institution of any such union or interim agreement in respect of trade with contracting parties not parties to such union or agreement shall not on the whole be higher or more restrictive than the general incidence of the duties and regulations of commerce applicable in the constituent territories prior to the formation of such union or the adoption of such interim agreement, as the case may be;

(*b*) with respect to a free-trade area, or an interim agreement leading to the formation of a free trade area, the duties and other regulations of commerce maintained in each of the constituent territories and applicable at the formation of such free-trade area or the adoption of such interim agreement to the trade of contracting parties not included in such area or not parties to such agreement shall not be higher or more restrictive than the corresponding duties and other regulations of commerce existing in the same constituent territories prior to the formation of the free-trade area, or interim agreement as the case may be; and

(*c*) any interim agreement referred to in subparagraphs (a) and (b) shall include a plan and schedule for the formation of such a customs union or of such a free-trade area within a reasonable length of time.

6. If, in fulfilling the requirements of subparagraph 5(a), a contracting party proposes to increase any rate of duty inconsistently with the provisions of Article II, the procedure set forth in Article XXVIII shall apply. In providing for compensatory adjustment, due account shall be taken of the compensation already afforded by the reduction brought about in the corresponding duty of the other constituents of the union.

7. (*a*) Any contracting party deciding to enter into a customs union or free-trade area, or an interim agreement leading to the formation of such a union or area, shall promptly notify the CONTRACTING PARTIES and shall make available to them such information regarding the proposed union or area as will enable them to make such reports and recommendations to contracting parties as they may deem appropriate.

(*b*) If, after having studied the plan and schedule included in an interim agreement referred to in paragraph 5 in consultation with the parties to that agreement and taking due account of the information made available in accordance with the provisions of subparagraph (a), the CONTRACTING PARTIES find that such agreement is not likely to result in the formation of a customs union or of a free-trade area within the period contemplated by the parties to the agreement or that such period is not a reasonable one, the CONTRACTING PARTIES shall make recommendations to the parties to the agreement. The parties shall not maintain or put into force, as the case may be, such agreement if they are not prepared to modify it in accordance with these recommendations.

(*c*) Any substantial change in the plan or schedule referred to in paragraph 5(c) shall be communicated to the CONTRACTING PARTIES, which may request the contracting parties concerned to consult with them if the change seems likely to jeopardize or delay unduly the formation of the customs union or of the free-trade area.

8. For the purposes of this Agreement:

(*a*) A customs union shall be understood to mean the substitution of a single customs territory for two or more customs territories, so that

(i) duties and other restrictive regulations of commerce (except, where necessary, those permitted under Articles XI, XII, XIII, XIV, XV and XX) are eliminated with respect to substantially all the trade between the constituent territories of the union or at least with respect to substantially all the trade in products originating in such territories, and,

(ii) subject to the provisions of paragraph 9, substantially the same duties and other regulations of commerce are applied by each of the members of the union to the trade of territories not included in the union;

(*b*) A free-trade area shall be understood to mean a group of two or more customs territories in which the duties and other restrictive regulations of commerce (except, where necessary, those permitted under Articles XI, XII, XIII, XIV, XV and XX) are eliminated on substantially all the trade between the constituent territories in products originating in such territories.

9. The preferences referred to in paragraph 2 of Article I shall not be affected by the formation of a customs union or of a free-trade area but may be eliminated or adjusted by means of negotiations with contracting parties affected.* This procedure of negotiations with affected contracting parties shall, in particular, apply to the elimination of preferences required to conform with the provisions of paragraph 8(a)(i) and paragraph 8(b).

Ad Article XXIV: Paragraph 9

It is understood that the provisions of Article I would require that, when a product which has been imported into the territory of a member of a customs union or free-trade area at a preferential rate of duty is re-exported to the territory of another member of such union or area, the latter member should collect a duty equal to the difference between the duty already paid and any higher duty that would be payable if the product were being imported directly into its territory.

10. The CONTRACTING PARTIES may by a two-thirds majority approve proposals which do not fully comply with the requirements of paragraphs 5 to 9 inclusive, provided that such proposals lead to

the formation of a customs union or a free-trade area in the sense of this Article.

11. Taking into account the exceptional circumstances arising out of the establishment of India and Pakistan as independent States and recognizing the fact that they have long constituted an economic unit, the contracting parties agree that the provisions of this Agreement shall not prevent the two countries from entering into special arrangements with respect to the trade between them, pending the establishment of their mutual trade relations on a definitive basis.

Ad Paragraph 11: Measures adopted by India and Pakistan in order to carry out definitive trade arrangements between them, once they have been agreed upon, might depart from particular provisions of this Agreement, but these measures would in general be consistent with the objectives of the Agreement.

12. Each contracting party shall take such reasonable measures as may be available to it to ensure observance of the provisions of this Agreement by the regional and local governments and authorities within its territories.

§ 2.8 Text of the 1994 Uruguay Round Understanding on the Interpretation of GATT Article 24

Members,

Having regard to the provisions of Article XXIV of GATT 1994;

Recognizing that customs unions and free trade areas have greatly increased in number and importance since the establishment of GATT 1947 and today cover a significant proportion of world trade;

Recognizing the contribution to the expansion of world trade that may be made by closer integration between the economies of the parties to such agreements;

Recognizing also that such contribution is increased if the elimination between the constituent territories of duties and other restrictive regulations of commerce extends to all trade, and diminished if any major sector of trade is excluded;

Reaffirming that the purpose of such agreements should be to facilitate trade between the constituent territories and not to raise barriers to the trade of other Members with such territories; and that in their formation or enlargement the parties to them should to the greatest possible extent avoid creating adverse effects on the trade of other Members;

Convinced also of the need to reinforce the effectiveness of the role of the Council for Trade in Goods in reviewing agreements notified under Article XXIV, by clarifying the criteria and procedures for the assessment of new or enlarged agreements, and improving the transparency of all Article XXIV agreements;

Recognizing the need for a common understanding of the obligations of Members under paragraph 12 of Article XXIV;

Hereby *agree* as follows:

1. Customs unions, free-trade areas, and interim agreements leading to the formation of a customs union or free-trade area, to be consistent with Article XXIV, must satisfy, *inter alia*, the provisions of paragraphs 5, 6, 7 and 8 of that Article.

Article XXIV:5

2. The evaluation under paragraph 5(a) of Article XXIV of the general incidence of the duties and other regulations of commerce applicable before and after the formation of a customs union shall in respect of duties and charges be based upon an overall assessment of weighted average tariff rates and of customs duties collected. This assessment shall be based on import statistics for a previous representative period to be supplied by the customs union, on a tariff-line basis and in values and quantities, broken down by WTO country of origin. The Secretariat shall compute the weighted average tariff rates and customs duties collected in accordance with the methodology used in the assessment of tariff offers in the Uruguay Round of Multilateral Trade Negotiations. For this purpose, the duties and charges to be taken into consideration shall be the applied rates of duty. It is recognized that for the purpose of the overall assessment of the incidence of other regulations of commerce for which quantification and aggregation are difficult, the examination of individual measures, regulations, products covered and trade flows affected may be required.

3. The "reasonable length of time" referred to in paragraph 5(c) of Article XXIV should exceed 10 years only in exceptional cases. In cases where Members parties to an interim agreement believe that 10 years would be insufficient they shall provide a full explanation to the Council for Trade in Goods of the need for a longer period.

Article XXIV:6

4. Paragraph 6 of Article XXIV establishes the procedure to be followed when a Member forming a customs union proposes to increase a bound rate of duty. In this regard Members reaffirm that the procedure set forth in Article XXVIII, as elaborated in the guidelines adopted on 10 November 1980 (BISD 27S/26–28) and in

the Understanding on the Interpretation of Article XXVIII of GATT 1994, must be commenced before tariff concessions are modified or withdrawn upon the formation of a customs union or an interim agreement leading to the formation of a customs union.

5. These negotiations will be entered into in good faith with a view to achieving mutually satisfactory compensatory adjustment. In such negotiations, as required by paragraph 6 of Article XXIV, due account shall be taken of reductions of duties on the same tariff line made by other constituents of the customs union upon its formation. Should such reductions not be sufficient to provide the necessary compensatory adjustment, the customs union would offer compensation, which may take the form of reductions of duties on other tariff lines. Such an offer shall be taken into consideration by the Members having negotiating rights in the binding being modified or withdrawn. Should the compensatory adjustment remain unacceptable, negotiations should be continued. Where, despite such efforts, agreement in negotiations on compensatory adjustment under Article XXVIII as elaborated by the Understanding on the Interpretation of Article XXVIII of GATT 1994 cannot be reached within a reasonable period from the initiation of negotiations, the customs union shall, nevertheless, be free to modify or withdraw the concessions; affected Members shall then be free to withdraw substantially equivalent concessions in accordance with Article XXVIII.

6. GATT 1994 imposes no obligation on Members benefiting from a reduction of duties consequent upon the formation of a customs union, or an interim agreement leading to the formation of a customs union, to provide compensatory adjustment to its constituents.

Review of Customs Unions and Free-Trade Areas

7. All notifications made under paragraph 7(a) of Article XXIV shall be examined by a working party in the light of the relevant provisions of GATT 1994 and of paragraph 1 of this Understanding. The working party shall submit a report to the Council for Trade in Goods on its findings in this regard. The Council for Trade in Goods may make such recommendations to Members as it deems appropriate.

8. In regard to interim agreements, the working party may in its report make appropriate recommendations on the proposed time-frame and on measures required to complete the formation of the customs union or free-trade area. It may if necessary provide for further review of the agreement.

9. Members parties to an interim agreement shall notify substantial changes in the plan and schedule included in that

agreement to the Council for Trade in Goods and, if so requested, the Council shall examine the changes.

10. Should an interim agreement notified under paragraph 7(a) of Article XXIV not include a plan and schedule, contrary to paragraph 5(c) of Article XXIV, the working party shall in its report recommend such a plan and schedule. The parties shall not maintain or put into force, as the case may be, such agreement if they are not prepared to modify it in accordance with these recommendations. Provision shall be made for subsequent review of the implementation of the recommendations.

11. Customs unions and constituents of free-trade areas shall report periodically to the Council for Trade in Goods, as envisaged by the CONTRACTING PARTIES to GATT 1947 in their instruction to the GATT 1947 Council concerning reports on regional agreements (BISD 18S/38), on the operation of the relevant agreement. Any significant changes and/or developments in the agreements should be reported as they occur.

Dispute Settlement

12. The provisions of Articles XXII and XXIII of GATT 1994 as elaborated and applied by the Dispute Settlement Understanding may be invoked with respect to any matters arising from the application of those provisions of Article XXIV relating to customs unions, free-trade areas or interim agreements leading to the formation of a customs union or free-trade area.

Article XXIV:12

13. Each Member is fully responsible under GATT 1994 for the observance of all provisions of GATT 1994, and shall take such reasonable measures as may be available to it to ensure such observance by regional and local governments and authorities within its territory.

14. The provisions of Articles XXII and XXIII of GATT 1994 as elaborated and applied by the Dispute Settlement Understanding may be invoked in respect of measures affecting its observance taken by regional or local governments or authorities within the territory of a Member. When the Dispute Settlement Body has ruled that a provision of GATT 1994 has not been observed, the responsible Member shall take such reasonable measures as may be available to it to ensure its observance. The provisions relating to compensation and suspension of concessions or other obligations apply in cases where it has not been possible to secure such observance.

15. Each Member undertakes to accord sympathetic consideration to and afford adequate opportunity for consultation regarding any

representations made by another Member concerning measures affecting the operation of GATT 1994 taken within the territory of the former.

§ 2.9 Text of WTO Transparency Mechanism for Regional Trade Agreements

(Provisionally Adopted Dec. 14, 2006)

The General Council,

Having regard to paragraph 1 of Article IX of the Marrakesh Agreement Establishing the World Trade Organization ("WTO Agreement");

Conducting the functions of the Ministerial Conference in the interval between meetings pursuant to paragraph 2 of Article IV of the WTO Agreement;

Noting that trade agreements of a mutually preferential nature ("regional trade agreements" or "RTAs") have greatly increased in number and have become an important element in Members' trade policies and developmental strategies;

Convinced that enhancing transparency in, and understanding of, RTAs and their effects is of systemic interest and will be of benefit to all Members;

Having regard also to the transparency provisions of Article XXIV of GATT 1994, the Understanding on the Interpretation of Article XXIV of GATT 1994 ("GATT Understanding"), Article V of GATS and the 1979 Decision on Differential and More Favorable Treatment, Reciprocity and Fuller Participation of Developing Countries ("Enabling Clause");

Recognizing the resource and technical constraints of developing country Members;

Recalling that in the negotiations pursued under the terms of the Doha Ministerial Declaration, in accordance with paragraph 47 of that Declaration, agreements reached at an early stage may be implemented on a provisional basis;

Decides:

A. Early Announcement

1. Without prejudging the substance and the timing of the notification required under Article XXIV of the GATT 1994, Article V of the GATS or the Enabling Clause, nor affecting Members' rights and obligations under the WTO agreements in any way:

(a) Members participating in new negotiations aimed at the conclusion of an RTA shall endeavor to so inform the WTO.

(b) Members parties to a newly signed RTA shall convey to the WTO, in so far as and when it is publicly available, information on the RTA, including its official name, scope and date of signature, any foreseen timetable for its entry into force or provisional application, relevant contact points and/or website addresses, and any other relevant unrestricted information.

2. The information referred to in paragraph 1 above is to be forwarded to the WTO Secretariat, which will post it on the WTO website and will periodically provide Members with a synopsis of the communications received.

B. Notification

3. The required notification of an RTA by Members that are party to it shall take place as early as possible. As a rule, it will occur no later than directly following the parties' ratification of the RTA or any party's decision on application of the relevant parts of an agreement, and before the application of preferential treatment between the parties.

4. In notifying their RTA, the parties shall specify under which provision(s) of the WTO agreements it is notified. They will also provide the full text of the RTA (or those parts they have decided to apply) and any related schedules, annexes and protocols, in one of the WTO official languages; if available, these shall also be submitted in an electronically exploitable format. Reference to related official Internet links shall also be supplied.

C. Procedures to Enhance Transparency

5. Upon notification, and without affecting Members' rights and obligations under the WTO agreements under which it has been notified, the RTA shall be considered by Members under the procedures established in paragraphs 6 to 13 below.

6. The consideration by Members of a notified RTA shall be normally concluded in a period not exceeding one year after the date of notification. A precise timetable for the consideration of the RTA shall be drawn by the WTO Secretariat in consultation with the parties at the time of the notification.

7. To assist Members in their consideration of a notified RTA:

(a) the parties shall make available to the WTO Secretariat data as specified in the Annex, if possible in an electronically exploitable format; and

(b) the WTO Secretariat, on its own responsibility and in full consultation with the parties, shall prepare a factual presentation of the RTA.

8. The data referred to in paragraph 7(a) shall be made available as soon as possible. Normally, the timing of the data submission shall not exceed ten weeks—or 20 weeks in the case of RTAs involving only developing countries—after the date of notification of the agreement.

9. The factual presentation provided for in paragraph 7(b) shall be primarily based on the information provided by the parties; if necessary, the WTO Secretariat may also use data available from other sources, taking into account the views of the parties in furtherance of factual accuracy. In preparing the factual presentation, the WTO Secretariat shall refrain from any value judgement.

10. The WTO Secretariat's factual presentation shall not be used as a basis for dispute settlement procedures or to create new rights and obligations for Members.

11. As a rule, a single formal meeting will be devoted to consider each notified RTA; any additional exchange of information should take place in written form.

12. The WTO Secretariat's factual presentation, as well as any additional information submitted by the parties, shall be circulated in all WTO official languages not less than eight weeks in advance of the meeting devoted to the consideration of the RTA. Members' written questions or comments on the RTA under consideration shall be transmitted to the parties through the WTO Secretariat at least four weeks before the corresponding meeting; they shall be distributed, together with replies, to all Members at least three working days before the corresponding meeting.

13. All written material submitted, as well as the minutes of the meeting devoted to the consideration of a notified agreement will be promptly circulated in all WTO official languages and made available on the WTO website.

D. Subsequent Notification and Reporting

14. The required notification of changes affecting the implementation of an RTA, or the operation of an already implemented RTA, shall take place as soon as possible after the changes occur. Changes to be notified include, inter alia, modifications to the preferential treatment between the parties and to the RTA's disciplines. The parties shall provide a summary of the changes made, as well as any related texts, schedules, annexes and

protocols, in one of the WTO official languages and, if available, in electronically exploitable format.

15. At the end of the RTA's implementation period, the parties shall submit to the WTO a short written report on the realization of the liberalization commitments in the RTA as originally notified.

16. Upon request, the relevant WTO body shall provide an adequate opportunity for an exchange of views on the communications submitted under paragraphs 14 and 15.

17. The communications submitted under paragraphs 14 and 15 will be promptly made available on the WTO website and a synopsis will be periodically circulated by the WTO Secretariat to Members.

E. Bodies Entrusted with the Implementation of the Mechanism

18. The Committee on Regional Trade Agreements ("CRTA") and the Committee on Trade and Development ("CTD") are instructed to implement this Transparency Mechanism. The CRTA shall do so for RTAs falling under Article XXIV of GATT 1994 and Article V of GATS, while the CTD shall do so for RTAs falling under paragraph 2(c) of the Enabling Clause. For purposes of performing the functions established under this Mechanism, the CTD shall convene in dedicated session.

F. Technical Support for Developing Countries

19. Upon request, the WTO Secretariat shall provide technical support to developing country Members, and especially least-developed countries, in the implementation of this Transparency Mechanism, in particular—but not limited to—with respect to the preparation of RTA-related data and other information to be submitted to the WTO Secretariat.

G. Other Provisions

20. Any Member may, at any time, bring to the attention of the relevant WTO body information on any RTA that it considers ought to have been submitted to Members in the framework of this Transparency Mechanism.

21. The WTO Secretariat shall establish and maintain an updated electronic database on individual RTAs. This database shall include relevant tariff and trade-related information and give access to all written material related to announced or notified RTAs available at the WTO. The RTA database should be structured so as to be easily accessible to the public.

H. Provisional Application of the Transparency Mechanism 22.

22. This Decision shall apply, on a provisional basis, to all RTAs. With respect to RTAs already notified under the relevant WTO transparency provisions and in force, this Decision shall apply as follows:

(a) RTAs for which a working party report has been adopted by the GATT Council and those RTAs notified to the GATT under the Enabling Clause will be subject to the procedures under Sections D to G above.

(b) RTAs for which the CRTA has concluded the "factual examination" prior to the adoption of this Decision and those for which the "factual examination" will have been concluded by 31 December 2006, and RTAs notified to the WTO under the Enabling Clause will be subject to the procedures under Sections D to G above. In addition, for each of these RTAs, the WTO Secretariat shall prepare a factual abstract presenting the features of the agreement.

(c) Any RTA notified prior to the adoption of this Decision and not referred to in subparagraphs (a) or (b) will be subject to the procedures under Sections C to G above.

I. Reappraisal of the Mechanism

23. Members will review, and if necessary modify, this Decision, in light of the experience gained from its provisional operation, and replace it by a permanent mechanism adopted as part of the overall results of the Round, in accordance with paragraph 47 of the Doha Declaration. Members will also review the legal relationship between this Mechanism and relevant WTO provisions related to RTAs.

ANNEX
Submission of Data by RTA Parties

1. RTA parties shall not be expected to make available the information required below if the corresponding data has already been submitted to the Integrated Data Base (IDB), or has otherwise been provided to the Secretariat in an adequate format.

2. For the goods aspects in RTAs, the parties shall submit the following data, at the tariff-line level:

(a) Tariff concessions under the agreement:

(i) a full listing of each party's preferential duties applied in the year of entry into force of the agreement; and

(ii) when the agreement is to be implemented by stages, a full listing of each party's preferential duties to be applied over the transition period.

(b) MFN duty rates:

(i) a full tariff listing of each RTA party's MFN duties applied on the year of entry into force of the agreement; and

(ii) a full tariff listing of each RTA party's MFN duties applied on the year preceding the entry into force of the agreement.

(c) Where applicable, other data (*e.g.*, preferential margins, tariff-rate quotas, seasonal restrictions, special safeguards and, if available, ad valorem equivalents for non-ad valorem duties).

(d) Product-specific preferential rules of origin as defined in the agreement.

(e) Import statistics, for the most recent three years preceding the notification for which they are available:

(i) each party's imports from each of the other parties, in value; and

(ii) each party's imports from the rest of the world, broken down by country of origin, in value.

3. For the services aspects in RTAs, the parties shall submit the following data, if available, for the three most recent years preceding the notification: trade or balance of payments statistics (by services sector/subsector and partner), gross domestic product data or production statistics (by services sector/subsector), and relevant statistics on foreign direct investment and on movement of natural persons (by country and, if possible, by services sector/subsector).

4. For RTAs involving only developing countries, in particular when these comprise least developed countries, the data requirements specified above will take into account the technical constraints of the parties to the agreement.

§ 2.10 Text of GATS Article V: Economic Integration Agreements

1. This Agreement shall not prevent any of its Members from being a party to or entering into an agreement liberalizing trade in services between or among the parties to such an agreement, provided that such an agreement:

(a) has substantial sectoral coverage; and

(b) provides for the absence or elimination of substantially all discrimination, in the sense of Article XVII, between or among the parties, in the sectors covered under subparagraph (a), through:

(i) elimination of existing discriminatory measures, and/or

(ii) prohibition of new or more discriminatory measures, either at the entry into force of that agreement or on the basis of a reasonable time-frame, except for measures permitted under Articles XI, XII, XIV and XIV bis.

2. In evaluating whether the conditions under paragraph 1(b) are met, consideration may be given to the relationship of the agreement to a wider process of economic integration or trade liberalization among the countries concerned.

3. (a) Where developing countries are parties to an agreement of the type referred to in paragraph 1, flexibility shall be provided for regarding the conditions set out in paragraph 1, particularly with reference to subparagraph (b) thereof, in accordance with the level of development of the countries concerned, both overall and in individual sectors and subsectors.

(b) Notwithstanding paragraph 6, in the case of an agreement of the type referred to in paragraph 1 involving only developing countries, more favorable treatment may be granted to juridical persons owned or controlled by natural persons of the parties to such an agreement.

4. Any agreement referred to in paragraph 1 shall be designed to facilitate trade between the parties to the agreement and shall not in respect of any Member outside the agreement raise the overall level of barriers to trade in services within the respective sectors or subsectors compared to the level applicable prior to such an agreement.

5. If, in the conclusion, enlargement or any significant modification of any agreement under paragraph 1, a Member intends to withdraw or modify a specific commitment inconsistently with the terms and conditions set out in its Schedule, it shall provide at least 90-days advance notice of such modification or withdrawal and the procedure set forth in paragraphs 2, 3 and 4 of Article XXI shall apply.

6. A service supplier of any other Member that is a juridical person constituted under the laws of a party to an agreement referred

to in paragraph 1 shall be entitled to treatment granted under such agreement, provided that it engages in substantive business operations in the territory of the parties to such agreement.

7. (a) Members which are parties to any agreement referred to in paragraph 1 shall promptly notify any such agreement and any enlargement or any significant modification of that agreement to the Council for Trade in Services. They shall also make available to the Council such relevant information as may be requested by it. The Council may establish a working party to examine such an agreement or enlargement or modification of that agreement and to report to the Council on its consistency with this Article.

(b) Members which are parties to any agreement referred to in paragraph 1 which is implemented on the basis of a time-frame shall report periodically to the Council for Trade in Services on its implementation. The Council may establish a working party to examine such reports if it deems such a working party necessary.

(c) Based on the reports of the working parties referred to in subparagraphs (a) and (b), the Council may make recommendations to the parties as it deems appropriate.

8. A Member which is a party to any agreement referred to in paragraph 1 may not seek compensation for trade benefits that may accrue to any other Member from such agreement.

§ 2.11 Linked List of Operational Multilateral Free Trade Agreements (2021)

- Andean Community—1969
- ASEAN-Australia-New Zealand Free Trade Area (AANZFTA)—2010
- ASEAN Free Trade Area (AFTA)—1992
- Asia-Pacific Trade Agreement (APTA)—1975
- Central American Integration System (SICA)—1993
- Central European Free Trade Agreement (CEFTA)—1992
- Common Market for Eastern and Southern Africa (COMESA)—1994
- Commonwealth of Independent States Free Trade Area (CISFTA)—2011
- Comprehensive and Progressive Agreement for Trans-Pacific Partnership (CPTPP)—2018
- Dominican Republic-Central America Free Trade Agreement (DR-CAFTA)—2004
- East African Community (EAC)—2005

- Eurasian Economic Union (EAEU)—2015
- European Economic Area (EEA; European Union-Norway-Iceland-Liechtenstein)—1994
- European Free Trade Association (EFTA)—1960
- European Union Customs Union (EUCU; European Union-Turkey-Monaco-San Marino-Andorra)—1958
- G-3 Free Trade Agreement (G-3)—1995
- Greater Arab Free Trade Area (GAFTA)—1997
- Gulf Cooperation Council (GCC)—1981
- International Grains Agreement—1995 Comprising a Grains Trade Convention (GTC) and a Food Aid Convention (FAC)
- Pacific Alliance Free Trade Area (PAFTA)—2012
- South Asian Free Trade Area (SAFTA)—2004
- Southern African Development Community Free Trade Area (SADCFTA)—1980
- Southern Common Market (MERCOSUR)—1991
- United States, Mexico, Canada (USMCA) Agreement—2020

Source: Wikipedia 2021

§ 2.12 Linked List of Operational Bilateral Free Trade Agreements (2021)

Armenia has bilateral agreements with the following countries and blocs:

- Commonwealth of Independent States
  - Belarus
  - Kazakhstan
  - Kyrgyzstan
  - Moldova
  - Russia
  - Turkmenistan
  - Tajikistan
  - Uzbekistan
- Eurasian Economic Union
  - Eurasian Customs Union members
    - Vietnam free trade agreement
- European Union Armenia qualifies to export its products under the EU's Generalized System of Preferences (GSP)
- Georgia
- Ukraine

- United States Armenia qualifies to export its products under the U.S. Generalized System of Preferences (GSP) program

ASEAN has bilateral agreements with the following countries and blocs:

- ASEAN-China Free Trade Area (ACFTA), in effect as of 1 January 2010
- ASEAN-India Free Trade Area (AIFTA), in effect as of 1 January 2010
- ASEAN-Japan Comprehensive Economic Partnership (AJCEP), in effect as of 1 December 2008
- ASEAN-Korea Free Trade Area (AKFTA), in effect as of 1 January 2010
- ASEAN-Australia-New Zealand Free Trade Area (AANZFTA), in effect as of 1 January 2010

Caribbean Community (CARICOM) has bilateral agreements with the following countries:

- Costa Rica
- Dominican Republic
- Chile
- Australia
- Bolivia
- Canada
- Central America (Costa Rica, El Salvador, Honduras, Guatemala and Nicaragua)
- China
- Colombia
- Cuba
- Ecuador
- EFTA (Iceland, Liechtenstein, Norway and Switzerland)
- European Union
- Hong Kong SAR
- India
- Japan
- Malaysia
- MERCOSUR (Argentina, Brazil, Paraguay, Uruguay and Venezuela)
- Mexico
- Panama
- Peru

- Trans-Pacific Strategic Economic Partnership (Brunei, Chile, New Zealand and Singapore)
- Turkey
- South Korea
- United States
- Vietnam

The **People's Republic of China** has bilateral agreements with the following blocs, countries, and its two special administrative regions:

- ASEAN, China-ASEAN Free Trade Area (2010)
- Australia, China-Australia Free Trade Agreement (2015)
- Chile, China-Chile Free Trade Agreement (2006)
- Costa Rica, China-Costa Rica Free Trade Agreement (2011)
- Georgia, China-Georgia Free Trade Agreement (2017)
- Hong Kong, Mainland and Hong Kong Closer Economic Partnership Arrangement (CEPA) (2003)
- Iceland, China-Iceland Free Trade Agreement (2014)
- Macau, Mainland and Macau Closer Economic Partnership Arrangement (CEPA) (2003)
- Maldives, China-Maldives Free Trade Agreement (2017)
- New Zealand, China-New Zealand Free Trade Agreement (2008)
- Pakistan, China-Pakistan Free Trade Agreement (2006)
- Peru, China-Peru Free Trade Agreement (2010)
- Republic of China (Taiwan), Economic Cooperation Framework Agreement (2010)
- Singapore, China-Singapore Free Trade Agreement (2009)
- South Korea, China-South Korea Free Trade Agreement (2015)
- Switzerland, China-Switzerland free trade agreement (2014)

Costa Rica has bilateral agreements with the following countries and blocs (date it took effect):

- Canada (1 November 2002)
- Chile (15 February 2002)
- People's Republic of China (1 August 2011)
- Caribbean Community (CARICOM) (15 November 2005)
    - Trinidad & Tobago (15 November 2005)
    - Guyana (30 April 2006)
    - Barbados (1 August 2006)
    - Belize (10 March 2011)

    - Jamaica (1 June 2015)
    - Still awaiting approval from:
        - Suriname
        - Antigua and Barbuda
        - Dominica
        - Grenada
        - Saint Kitts and Nevis
        - Saint Lucia
        - Saint Vincent and the Grenadines
- Colombia (1 August 2016)
- Dominican Republic (7 March 2002)
- EFTA (2 May 2014)
    - Norway (20 August 2014)
    - Switzerland (29 August 2014)
    - Liechtenstein (29 August 2014)
    - Iceland (5 September 2014)
- El Salvador Customs union, (1963, re-launched on 29 October 1993)
- European Union (1 October 2013)
- Guatemala Customs union, (1963, re-launched on 29 October 1993)
- Honduras Customs union, (1963, re-launched on 29 October 1993)
- Mexico (1 January 1995)
- Nicaragua Customs union, (1963, re-launched on 29 October 1993)
- Panama (31 July 1973, renegotiated and expanded for (1 January 2009)
- Peru (1 June 2013)
- Singapore (16 May 2013)
- United States (1 January 2009)

EFTA has bilateral agreements with the following countries—including dependent territories—and blocs:

- Albania
- Canada: Canada-European Free Trade Association Free Trade Agreement
- Chile
- Colombia
- Gulf Cooperation Council (GCC)
- Faroe Islands (autonomous entity of Denmark)

- Egypt
- Hong Kong
- Israel
- Jordan
- Lebanon
- Macedonia
- Mexico
- Morocco
- Palestinian Authority
- Serbia
- Singapore
- Southern African Customs Union
- Tunisia
- Singapore
- South Korea
- Turkey
- Ukraine

The **Eurasian Economic Union** consisting of Russia, Belarus, Kazakhstan, Armenia, and Kyrgyzstan has following free trade agreements, see further here:

- Moldova (2013)
- Uzbekistan (2014)
- Egypt (2015)
- Tajikistan (2016)
- Vietnam (2016)
- China (2019)
- Iran (2021)

The **European Union** has bilateral agreements with the following countries and blocs:

- Albania SAA (2009)
- Algeria AA (2005)
- Andorra CU (1991)
- Bosnia and Herzegovina SAA (signed 2008, entry into force pending)
- Canada: Comprehensive Economic and Trade Agreement (provisionally applied)
- Chile AA (2003)
- Egypt AA (2004)
- Faroe Islands, autonomous entity of Denmark (1997)
- Israel AA (2000)

- Jordan AA (2002)
- Lebanon AA (2006)
- Macedonia SAA (2004)
- Mexico AA (2000)
- Montenegro SAA (2010)
- Monaco CU (1958, Franco-Monegasque Treaties)
- Morocco AA (2000)
- Palestinian Authority interim AA (1997)
- San Marino CU (2002)
- Serbia SAA (signed 2008, entry into force pending)
- South Africa AA (2000)
- South Korea: European Union-South Korea Free Trade Agreement (Entry into force: 13 December 2015)
- Switzerland FTA (1973)
- Tunisia AA (1998)
- Turkey CU (1996)
- EU Overseas Countries and Territories
- EU-Japan Economic Partnership Agreement (2018)

The **Faroe Islands** have bilateral agreements with the following countries and blocs:

- Switzerland
- Norway
- Iceland (The Hoyvík Agreement)
- The European Union

The **Gulf Cooperation Council (GCC)** has bilateral agreements with the following countries:

- EFTA (Entry into force: 1 July 2014)
- Singapore (Entry into force: 1 September 2013)

Hong Kong has bilateral free trade agreements with the following countries and blocs:

- Australia
- Chile
- China
- EFTA (Iceland, Lichtenstein, Norway, Switzerland)
- Georgia
- ASEAN
- Macau
- New Zealand

India has bilateral agreements with the following countries and blocs:

- Afghanistan
- ASEAN (Brunei, Cambodia, Indonesia, Laos, Malaysia, Myanmar, Philippines, Singapore, Thailand, Vietnam)
- Bhutan
- Chile
- Japan
- Malaysia
- Mercosur (Argentina, Brazil, Paraguay, Uruguay, and Venezuela) Note: Venezuela was suspended from the grouping in 2016.
- Nepal
- Singapore
- Sri Lanka
- South Korea

Indonesia has bilateral agreements with the following countries and blocs:

- Australia (Indonesia-Australia Comprehensive Economic Partnership Agreement, signed in 2019)
- Chile (Chile-Indonesia Comprehensive Economic Partnership Agreement, signed in 2017)
- EFTA (Indonesia-EFTA Comprehensive Economic Partnership, signed in 2018)
- Japan (Indonesia-Japan Economic Partnership Agreement, signed in 2007)
- Mozambique (Indonesia-Mozambique Preferential Trade Agreement, signed in 2019 but not yet in force as of 2020)
- Pakistan (Indonesia-Pakistan Preferential Trade Agreement, signed in 2012)
- Palestine (Indonesia-Palestine Trade Facilitation for Certain Products)
- South Korea (Indonesia-Korea Comprehensive Economic Partnership Agreement, signed in 2020)

Japan has bilateral agreements with the following countries and blocs:

- ASEAN (Entry into force: 2009)
- Australia (Entry into force: 2015)
- European Union (EU-Japan Economic Partnership Agreement) (Entry into force: 2019)
- India (Entry into force: 2011)

- Indonesia (Japan-Indonesia Economic Partnership Agreement) (Entry into force: 2008)
- Malaysia (Entry into force: 2006)
- Mexico (Entry into force: 2005)
- Mongolia(Entry into force: 2016)
- Peru (Entry into force: 2012)
- Philippines (Entry into force: 2008)
- Singapore (Entry into force: 2002)
- Switzerland (Entry into force: 2009)
- Thailand (Japan-Thailand Economic Partnership Agreement) (Entry into force: 2007)
- Vietnam (Entry into force: 2009)
- United Kingdom (Signed: 2020)

Jordan has bilateral agreements with the following countries and blocs:

- Canada
- Algeria
- Libya
- Syria
- Kuwait
- Bahrain
- Peru
- United States (United States-Jordan Free Trade Agreement)
- The European Free Trade Association
- The European Union

Kazakhstan has bilateral agreements with the following countries and blocs:

- Russia
- Ukraine
- Uzbekistan

The **Kyrgyz Republic** has bilateral agreements with the following countries:

- Kazakhstan (Entry into force: 11 November 1995)
- Moldova (Entry into force: 21 November 1996)
- Russian Federation (Entry into force: 24 April 1993)
- Ukraine (Entry into force: 19 January 1998)
- Uzbekistan (Entry into force: 20 March 1998)

Laos has bilateral agreements with the following countries and blocs:

- Thailand

Lebanon has bilateral agreements with the following countries and blocs:

- Gulf Cooperation Council (GCC)
- Iraq
- The European Union

Malaysia has bilateral agreements with the following countries:

- India
- Australia

Maldives has bilateral agreements with the following countries:

- China, (China-Maldives Free Trade Agreement) (2017)
- South Asian Free Trade Area

Mercosur:

- Israel
- Egypt
- Lebanon
- Palestine
- European Union (in principle)

Mexico has bilateral agreements with the following countries and blocs:

- Chile-Mexico Free Trade Agreement
- Colombia-Mexico Free Trade Agreement
- Costa Rica-Mexico Free Trade Agreement
- EFTA-Mexico Free Trade Agreement (Iceland, Liechtenstein, Norway, Switzerland)
- European Union-Mexico Economic Partnership
- Israel-Mexico Free Trade Agreement
- Japan-Mexico Economic Association Agreement
- Nicaragua-Mexico Free Trade Agreement
- Northern Triangle (El Salvador, Honduras, and Guatemala)
- Panama
- Uruguay-Mexico Free Trade Agreement

Morocco has bilateral agreements with the following countries and blocs:

- The European Union
- The European Free Trade Association
- Jordan

- Egypt
- Tunisia
- State of Palestine
- United Arab Emirates
- Turkey
- United States

New Zealand free trade agreements:

- Australia (as Closer Economic Relations)
- Malaysia
- Singapore
- Thailand
- Chile
- People's Republic of China (*see* China-New Zealand Free Trade Agreement)
- Brunei (*see* Trans-Pacific Strategic Economic Partnership)
- Hong Kong (*see* Hong Kong-New Zealand Closer Economic Partnership Agreement)
- Republic of China (Taiwan)

Panama has bilateral agreements with the following countries:

- Chile
- Costa Rica
- El Salvador
- Guatemala
- Honduras
- Mexico
- Nicaragua
- Republic of China (Taiwan)
- Singapore
- United States

Peru has bilateral agreements with the following countries:

- Canada
- EFTA
- People's Republic of China
- Japan
- Mexico
- Singapore
- Thailand
- United States
- EU

Serbia has bilateral agreements with the following countries and blocs:

- EU (SAA)
- EFTA
- CEFTA
- Russia
- Belarus
- Turkey
- Kazakhstan
- United States (GSP)

Singapore has bilateral agreements with the following countries and blocs:

- Australia
- Brunei
- Chile
- Republic of China (Taiwan)
- European Free Trade Association
- Gulf Cooperation Council (GCC)
- India
- Japan
- Jordan
- New Zealand (separate from the Trans-Pacific Strategic Economic Partnership (see above) and is still in force)
- Panama
- Peru
- South Korea
- Sri Lanka
- People's Republic of China
- United States
- European Union

South Korea has bilateral agreements with the following countries and blocs:

- ASEAN
- Australia (Korea-Australia Free Trade Agreement KAFTA)
- Canada (Canada-South Korea Free Trade Agreement)
- China
- Chile
- Colombia
- EFTA

- European Union (European Union-South Korea Free Trade Agreement) (Entry into force: 13 December 2015)
- India (Comprehensive Economic Partnership Agreement)
- New Zealand
- Peru
- Singapore
- Turkey
- United States (US)
- Vietnam

Switzerland (which has a customs union with Liechtenstein, sometimes included in agreements) has bilateral agreements with the following countries and blocs:

- Albania (Signed: 17.12.2009. Entry into force: 01.11.2010)
- Canada (Entry into force: 01.07.2009)
- Chile (Entry into force: 01.12.2004)
- People's Republic of China (Entry into force: 01.07.2014)
- Colombia (Signed: 25.11.2008. Entry into force: 01.07.2011)
- Egypt (Entry into force: 01.09.2008)
- European Union (Entry into force: 01.01.1973. Bilateral CH-EU)
- Faeroe Islands (Entry into force: 01.03.1995. Bilateral CH-Faeroe)
- Israel (Entry into force: 01.07.1993)
- Japan (Entry into force: 01.09.2009. Bilateral CH-Japan)
- Jordan (Entry into force: 01.09.2002)
- Republic of Korea (Entry into force: 01.09.2006)
- Lebanon (Entry into force: 01.01.2007)
- Macedonia (Entry into force: 01.05.2002)
- Mexico (Entry into force: 01.07.2001)
- Morocco (Entry into force: 01.12.1999)
- Palestinian Authority (Entry into force: 01.07.1999)
- Peru (Signed: 24.06.2010 (EFTA) and 14.07.2010 (Peru). Entry into force on 01.07.2011)
- Serbia (Signed: 17.12.2009. Entry into force: 01.10.2010)
- Singapore (Entry into force: 01.01.2003)
- SACU (Entry into force: 01.05.2008)
- Tunisia (Entry into force: 01.06.2006)
- Turkey (Entry into force: 01.04.1992)
- Ukraine (Signed 24.06.2010. Entry into force 01.06.2012)

Republic of China (Taiwan) has bilateral agreements with the following countries:

- People's Republic of China, Economic Cooperation Framework Agreement
- El Salvador
- Guatemala
- Honduras
- Nicaragua
- New Zealand
- Singapore
- Panama

Thailand has bilateral agreements with the following countries:

- Australia
- India
- Japan (Japan-Thailand Economic Partnership Agreement signed in 2007)
- New Zealand
- Peru
- Chile

Tunisia has bilateral agreements with the following countries and blocs:

- Morocco
- The European Free Trade Association
- Jordan
- Senegal
- Egypt
- Algeria
- Libya
- Mauritania
- Turkey
- The European Union

United States has bilateral agreements with the following countries and blocs:

- Australia
- Bahrain
- Chile
- Colombia
- Costa Rica
- the Dominican Republic

- Dominican Republic-Central America Free Trade Agreement
- El Salvador
- Guatemala
- Honduras
- Israel
- Jordan
- Korea
- Nicaragua
- Oman
- Panama
- Peru
- Morocco
- Singapore

Source: Wikipedia 2021

Chapter 3

THE EU CUSTOMS UNION, TRADE RELATIONS AND BREXIT

Table of Sections

NOTE: What follows is an extremely abbreviated summary of the creation and evolution of the European Union (EU), its legal system, customs union, free trade agreements, and policies affecting international trade. For much more extensive coverage, and copies of governing EU treaties referenced below, see my Concise Hornbook on *The European Union Beyond BREXIT*.

THE EU AND ITS CUSTOMS UNION

§ 3.1 The European Economic Community (EEC 1957)

In 1957, the European Economic Community was created under the Treaty of Rome by Italy, France, West Germany, Luxembourg, Belgium, and the Netherlands. Over time, additional members were added: Britain, Eire, and Denmark in 1973, Greece in 1981, Spain and Portugal in 1986, Austria, Sweden, and Finland in 1995, Poland, Hungary, The Czech Republic, Slovakia, Estonia, Lithuania, Latvia, Slovenia, Malta, and Cyprus in 2004, and Romania and Bulgaria in 2007. In 2007 the Reform Treaty (Treaty of Lisbon) was signed, eventually going into effect on December 1, 2009, among 28 now 27, nations. Under the latter treaty, the amended Treaty of Rome became the Treaty on the Functioning of the European Union (TFEU).

With Croatia joining in 2013, the EU had 28 member states, but in June 2016 voters in the United Kingdom approved a referendum calling for that country to leave the EU, which happened in 2020. Apart from the United Kingdom, the only major nonmember nations in Western and Central Europe are Switzerland, Norway, and Iceland.

§ 3.2 The European Free Trade Area (EFTA 1959) and Beyond

The EEC Treaty as drafted in 1957 was much less "dirigiste" than its predecessor, the 1951 European Coal and Steel Treaty. Nevertheless, Britain once again abstained from membership because of the nature and extent of the European control over the economy. Britain, too, was still preoccupied with its empire-based trade relations. Europe was important, but it had not yet become critical to British trading interests.

The fragmentation of Europe's economy during the 1950s became even more accentuated by the emergence of another competing organization. Led by Britain, many of the fringe or traditionally neutral nations of Western Europe organized themselves into the European Free Trade Association (EFTA) in 1959. Austria, Denmark, Iceland, Norway, Portugal, Sweden, and Switzerland joined this undertaking. With eight nations, essentially surrounding the core six nations who created the EEC in 1957, Britain felt that it had contained French influence and ideas in the economic sphere.

True to British philosophy, the EFTA Treaty was very limited in scope. It applied only to free trade in industrial goods, omitting coverage of agriculture, transport, labor, capital, technology, and services to mention only a few areas fully incorporated into the EEC Treaty. Moreover, the British view on the nature of the governmental institutions required to achieve industrial free trade prevailed. A single institution, the EFTA Council, was created. Since it normally followed a unanimous voting principle, each of the member states retained a veto over new policy developments within the EFTA group. The surrender of national sovereignties to EFTA was minimized, a theme that was to return decades later with BREXIT.

Thus, by 1960, Europe was economically allied in three major trade groups. France and an increasingly powerful West Germany led Italy and the Benelux states in the European Coal and Steel and Economic Communities. Britain and its partners were loosely integrated through the European Free Trade Association. And the whole of Eastern Europe came under the sway of Soviet dominance through COMECON. In addition, Finland became associated with EFTA and Greece and Turkey were associated with the EEC. Only Spain under Franco remained an economic outcast. More than a decade passed before major shifts in these alliances occurred.

EFTA and the EEC Reconciled (1973)

During the 1960s, Britain began to come to grips with the loss of its empire. Although special trading relations were often preserved with former colonies through the Commonwealth network, it became increasingly apparent that Britain's economic future lay more in Europe than Africa, Asia, or the Caribbean. Moreover, the EEC had helped to spur a phenomenal economic recovery on the Continent at a time when many were questioning the competitiveness of British industry.

For these reasons, and others, Britain began to seek membership as early as 1961 (only two years after the formation of EFTA). France under the leadership of Charles De Gaulle would have none of it. Since the Treaty of Rome provided (as the Treaty on European Union still does) that all new memberships require a unanimous Council vote, France was effectively able to veto the British application. It was not until the resignation of De Gaulle in 1969 that the British were able in due course to secure membership in the EEC. New Members (1973) Agreement on the terms of British accession (including withdrawal from EFTA and the elimination of trade preferences with major Commonwealth nations) was reached in 1971, with an effective date of January 1973.

The switch from EFTA to the EEC by Britain under Conservative Party leadership was undertaken with an ambivalence that continued to be evident. It was only with reluctance that the British accepted the surrenders of sovereignty inherent in the EEC Treaty. From 1973 onwards, more and more of the economic life of the United Kingdom would be governed by the four institutions of the European Community (now Union). British reluctance to join the Common Market was replayed in a 1975 national referendum under a Labor Party government. Approximately 60 percent of the populace voted to remain a member of the Community.

Denmark also switched sides in 1973. Norway was scheduled to become a member of the EEC at that time, and the terms of its membership had been negotiated, but the people of Norway rejected the Community in a national referendum. Ireland also joined the EEC in 1973.

In addition to the expansion of the EEC to nine members, 1973 brought an even greater degree of European economic integration. Although EFTA remained intact, each of the remaining EFTA nations signed bilateral trade treaties with the expanded Community. These treaties governed trade relations between all EFTA nations and the Community until 1994. They essentially provide for industrial free trade. Thus the 1973 enlargement of the European Economic Community was the catalyst for an initial effort at Western European integration, a reconciliation of the EFTA and EEC trading alliances. This was an historic watershed in European economic integration.

European Economic Area (1994)

Relations between the Union and the EFTA states—excepting Switzerland—were put on a new footing with the entry into force of the Agreement on the European Economic Area (EEA) in 1994. The EEA establishes a free trade area larger than NAFTA and, in addition, provides that the four fundamental freedoms of the internal market of the Union (free movement of goods, persons, services and capital) as well as the competition rules and certain horizontal policies (social policy, consumer protection, environment, statistics and company law) are applied throughout the EEA area. The EFTA states had to adopt the "acquis communautaire", *i.e.*, the established EU law in all these areas.

A special EFTA Surveillance Authority was set up with powers like those of the Commission, and an EFTA Court, resembling the European Court of Justice. However, the EEA Agreement did not create a customs union, thus there is no common external customs tariff nor application of EU free trade agreements. Excluded are also such sensitive subjects like agriculture, fisheries, and economic and monetary policy. The lasting importance of the EEA Agreement is difficult to assess since several EFTA countries joined the EU in 1995, and *it now applies only to Norway, Iceland, and Lichtenstein. These countries make contributions to the EU budget.*

§ 3.3 The EU Legal System

The Europeans have been creating law at dazzling though sometimes irregular speed. Without an understanding of these areas, it is almost impossible to function as a lawyer on EU matters.

The two founding treaties of the European Union, the Treaty on the Functioning of the European Union (TFEU) and the Maastricht Treaty on European Union (TEU), are the "primary" sources of regional law. They are "quasi-constitutional." The treaties have a common set of core institutions, as described below. These are the Council, the Commission, the Parliament, and the Court of Justice. These institutions, supplemented by the European Council, European Central Bank, and other EU bodies, and by national legislatures, courts and tribunals, have been busy generating a remarkably vast and complex body of "secondary" law.

Some law is adopted directly at the regional level, but much of it is enacted by national governments under regional "direction." Similarly, some (and the most important) of the case law is created by decisions in the European Court of Justice and its companion General Court (see below), but much development also occurs in the national courts, acting in many instances with "advisory rulings" from the Court of Justice. European secondary law also includes international obligations, sometimes undertaken through "mixed" regional and national negotiations and ratifications.

There are two main types of legislative acts, directives, and regulations (see below). These acts should be distinguished from declarations, resolutions, guidelines, notices, policy statements, recommendations, opinions, and individual decisions, all of which rarely involve legislative acts and are sometimes referred to as "soft law."

The Reform Treaty of 2009, in new TFEU provisions, enumerates categories and areas of exclusive, shared, and supportive EU competences or powers. These enumerations determine when and to what degree the EU and/or the member states may legislate. Exclusive EU competences include the customs union, internal market competition rules, marine conservation, and the Common Commercial Policy (external trade and investment relations). The Union also has exclusive competence over international agreements provided for in EU legislative acts, necessary to enable the exercise of its internal powers, or those agreements whose conclusion may affect common rules or alter their scope. In all these areas, member states may legislate only if empowered by the Union to do so, or to implement EU acts.

When the TFEU enumerates a shared competence, the Union may legislate. Member states may legislate only to the extent the EU has not done so or ceased to exercise a shared competence. Shared competences include the internal market, social policy, cohesion, agriculture and fisheries, the environment, consumer protection, transport, trans-European networks, energy, the area of freedom, security and justice, and common public health safety concerns. Special more-permissive rules allow member states greater latitude in the areas of research, technology development, space, third world development and humanitarian aid.

Lastly, the Union is authorized to legislate in support of, to coordinate with, or to supplement (but not supersede) member state competence in areas designated in Article 6 of the TFEU. These include human health, industry, culture, tourism, education and training, youth, sport, civil protection, and administrative cooperation. EU acts in these areas may not entail harmonization of member state laws or regulations.

EU Legislation

Article 288 of the TFEU clarifies the powers of the Council and the Commission to make regulations and issue directives. EU regulations are similar in form to administrative regulations commonly found in North America. EU directives, on the other hand, have no obvious parallel. A directive establishes regional policy. It is then left to the member states to implement the directive in whatever way is appropriate to their national legal system. This may require a new statute, a Presidential decree, an administrative act or even a constitutional amendment. Sometimes it may require no action at all. As Article 288 indicates, a directive is "binding as to the result to be achieved" but "leave[s] to the national authorities the choice of form and methods."

Most of the legislative acts of the 1980s single market campaign were directives. Regulations have since become more common. All directives contain time limits for national implementation. The more controversial the policy, the longer the likely allotment of time. The Reform Treaty of 2009 makes it clear member states must adopt all measures necessary to implement legally binding Union acts.

The Commission initiates the process of legislation by drafting proposals, which the Council (comprised of ministers from the governments of the member states) has the power to adopt into law. Although the Council and Parliament may request the Commission to submit legislative proposals, neither can force the Commission to do so except through litigation before the Court of Justice. Only the Commission can draft legislative proposals. This makes the Commission the focal point of lobbying activities, a point not lost on U.S. companies with stakes in EU legislative outcomes, such as the banking, biotech and software directives.

The Commission's legislative proposals are always influenced by what it believes the Council and Parliament will accept. The Council, however, has the right to amend legislative proposals by unanimous vote. Parliament's role was traditionally consultative. Over time, it became and remains the source of *proposed* amendments. Note that Parliament does not have the power to enact law! This absence of legislative power is so fundamental that many observers decry a "democratic deficit" in Europe. This deficit has been partially "remedied" by conveying "co-decision" powers to Parliament. These powers amount to a Parliamentary right, in the absence of conciliation with the Council, to veto selected legislative proposals.

EU Council

The foregoing analysis of legislative process illustrates the dominant role of the Council in regional affairs. The Council, also known since 1993 as the Council of the European Union (EU Council), consists of representatives of the governments of the member states. There are presently 27 Council members. However, the people who comprise the Council change according to the topic at hand. The national ministers of foreign affairs, agriculture, economy and finance (ecofin), social affairs, environment, etc. are sent to Brussels to confer and vote on matters within their competence. Some refer to the Ecofin Council, the Environment Council, the Agriculture Council and so forth to differentiate the various Councils. Several different Council meetings can take place at once.

Most of the voting in the Council now takes place on a qualified majority basis. The rules that define this procedure are given in Article 238 of the TFEU. Since November 1, 2014, a qualified majority is defined as at least 55% of the members of the Council (with a minimum number of 15) who represent member states comprising 65% of the population of the Union. Any blocking minority must include at least 4 Council members. A relatively simplified "double majority" voting system was undertaken in 2014.

EU Commission

The pivotal role of the European Commission in the law-making process should be evident. Apart from administrative cooperation on criminal and police matters, where a quarter of the member states can initiate EU acts, the Commission alone drafts legislative proposals. The Commission can also prosecute when proper legislative procedures are not followed. Furthermore, in certain areas, notably agricultural and competition law, the Council has delegated to the Commission the authority to issue implementing regulations and decisions that establish law. These acts detail administrative rules rather than create new or broad policies. The Council establishes the "target prices" for agriculture, but the Commission issues thousands of regulations aimed at realizing these goals.

The Commission has also promulgated an important series of "group exemption" regulations for business competition law. These cover franchising, technology transfers, distribution, and a variety of other business agreements. Lastly, the Commission is authorized by Article 106 of the TFEU to issue (on its own initiative) *directives* addressed to member states regarding public enterprises. This authority avoids the usual legislative process. The Reform Treaty of 2009 added a citizen's initiative procedure. One million EU citizens from a significant number of member states may "invite" the Commission to submit proposals in areas of regional concern.

The Commission performs other functions in addition to those concerning law-making. The most important of these include its prosecutorial powers against individuals and enterprises for breach of selected laws, and against member states for failure to adhere to their treaty obligations. The Commission negotiates international trade and other agreements. It also administers the EU budget and publishes a general and a series of specific annual reports (*e.g.*, on competition policy), all of which are a good way to survey regional affairs.

Unlike the ministers of the Council, Commissioners are not supposed to function as representatives of their nations. Commissioners are appointed by a qualified majority of the Council subject to Parliament's approval for five-year renewable terms. The President of the Commission is similarly appointed by the European Council and Parliament. Great pains are taken to ensure the independence of Commissioners from their home governments. Article 245 of the TFEU stipulates that Commissioners must be chosen based on competence and their independence must be "beyond doubt." Any breach of this trust by Commissioners could lead to compulsory retirement or dismissal by the President of the Commission.

Court of Justice of the European Union

The EU is unique among regional economic organizations in having a powerful and active court to enforce its laws and treaties. The Court of Justice of the European Union (CJEU) rules on disputes involving EU laws and treaties. Its decisions are binding on EU institutions and the member nations' governments.

The CJEU consists of three courts, the Court of Justice (informally called the European Court of Justice or ECJ), the General Court, and the Civil Service Tribunal. The Court of Justice hears referrals from national courts regarding the proper interpretation of EU law, claims brought by the Commission against member states for failure to comply with EU obligations, claims brought by member states against EU institutions and appeals from decisions of the General Court. The General Court hears claims by individuals and corporations (and in some cases by member states) against EU institutions. The Civil Service Tribunal hears disputes between EU institutions and their staff.

Article 267 TFEU vests jurisdiction in the European Court to give "preliminary rulings" (sometimes called "advisory rulings") on the interpretation of the Treaty, the validity and interpretation of acts by the Union's institutions and other matters. These rulings occur when national courts or tribunals (faced with an issue of Union law) request them. Article 267 requests or "references" are discretionary with the judges of the lower-level courts and tribunals of the member states. They cannot be initiated as a matter of right by litigants, nor by arbitrators designated by contract to resolve a dispute when those arbitrators are not functioning as a court or tribunal of a member state. This is a particularly notable decision because ever increasing numbers of business and trade disputes are being taken to binding arbitration.

Whenever a national court considers a reference necessary to enable judgment, it may seek the advice of the European Court by posing questions to it. It may do so even when the European Court or a higher national court has already ruled on the question of EU law at hand. In other words, the common law doctrine of binding precedent does not remove the discretion of lower courts to invoke Article 267. Similarly, the fact that appeals are mandatory under national law does not block utilization of Article 267 references to the ECJ if the lower court believes such a reference is necessary to enable it to give judgment.

In practice, lower courts refer EU law issues to the ECJ quite regularly. Assuming the request comes from a proper national court or tribunal, the European Court of Justice cannot refuse the reference, even when it has already ruled on the EU legal issue. Once underway, the Commission almost always files a written brief expressing its opinion in Article 267 proceedings. The government of the member state whose court or tribunal is the source of the reference typically does so as well. Private parties "interested" in the questions being referred may not intervene. After a preliminary ruling of the European Court is secured, the national court is obliged to implement that ruling in its final judgment. The ruling is also binding on appeal of that judgment, and (at a minimum) persuasive in courts of other nations.

Decisions of the EU courts are binding on EU institutions, member states, and perhaps most importantly, the national courts of the member states. Over time, the EU courts have issued key decisions on a wide range of issues affecting trade and investment, including tariff policies, nontariff trade barriers, competition law and intellectual property.

§ 3.4 The EU Customs Union and Common Market

The free movement of goods within Europe is based upon the creation of a customs union. Under this union, the member states have eliminated customs duties among themselves, *including* antidumping and countervailing duties. They have established a common customs tariff and customs code for their trade with the rest of the world. *The EU, not individual member states, has exclusive authority to negotiate trade agreements and treaties, including EU free trade and customs union agreements.*

Quantitative restrictions (quotas) on trade between member states are also prohibited, except in emergencies and other limited situations. The right of free movement applies to goods that originate in the Common Market and to those that have lawfully entered it and are said to be in "free circulation." U.S. exports to the EU, having cleared customs into its Common Market, can be moved across internal EU borders at will.

The establishment of the customs union has been a major accomplishment, though not without difficulties. The member states committed themselves not only to the elimination of tariffs and quotas on internal trade, but also to the elimination of "measures of equivalent effect." The elastic legal concept of measures of equivalent effect has been interpreted broadly by the European Court of Justice and the European Commission to prohibit a wide range of trade restraints, such as administrative fees charged at borders which are the equivalent of import or export tariffs. Charges of equivalent effect to a tariff must be distinguished from internal taxes that are applicable to imported and domestic goods. The latter must be levied in a nondiscriminatory and non-protective manner, while the former are prohibited entirely, there has been a considerable amount of litigation over this distinction.

Common Customs Code

Articles 206–207 of the Treaty on the Functioning of the European Union (TFEU) concern trade between the European Union and third countries. These articles vest in the European Union control over external commercial relations, a power completely absent from the NAFTA/USMCA agreement. This is referred to as the Union's "common commercial policy," and it covers both imports and exports. Article 207 provides some illustrative examples of the wide scope of this policy, including tariffs, quotas, trade agreements, export controls, dumping and subsidies. For example, its common rules on exports generally authorize free exportation of Union products, subject to security (oil and defense) and environmental exceptions. The Common Commercial Policy can also involve the application of international boycott sanctions. The 1993 Treaty on European Union added provisions intended to promote cooperation among the member states and the Union on aid to developing nations.

The European Court of Justice has ruled that the member states cannot enact external commercial policy laws without "specific authorization." In this field, the Union should be supreme. Operationally speaking, however, this is not always the case. This is illustrated by the following discussion of national import quotas, voluntary export restraints and "mixed" trade agreements. Surrendering national sovereignty over external commercial relations is a most sensitive area.

Customs Union

As regards customs law, which is invariably involved in any trade transaction with the Union, the relevant provisions are Articles 28–32 TFEU. The basic principle is that the EU is a customs union, with a directly applicable prohibition of national customs duties and measures having an equivalent effect on internal trade. The EU also has a common customs tariff. Once goods have cleared customs in any member state they are released for "free circulation", moving throughout the Union without incurring any further tariffs or any other equivalent charges. Equivalent charges are understood to comprise any pecuniary charge, however small and whatever its designation and mode of application, which is imposed unilaterally on domestic or foreign goods by reason of the fact that they cross a frontier, and which is not a customs duty in the strict sense. Hence products originating in third countries enjoy the same status as goods originating in a member state for purposes of internal trade.

In addition, U.S. exporters to any of the member states will pay the same customs duties, regardless of the port of entry. This is different from NAFTA/USMCA arrangements, which establish a free trade area exclusively for products originating in North America, with no common external tariff. Canada, Mexico, and the U.S. have retained different tariff levels and law, and the right to pursue their own international trade agreements.

Customs Code

The customs law of the EU had been dispersed and shattered in some 25 individual directives and regulations. In a major codification effort, all these texts were consolidated and further developed in a Common Customs Code which entered into force on Jan. 1, 1994. This Code includes coverage of customs clearance procedures, customs warehouses and free trade zones, duty free entry for processing and re-export (inward processing arrangement), duty free entry of components of Union origin that have been processed abroad (outward processing arrangement), classification, valuation, origin, payment and customs' bonds. Judicial review of decisions of the national customs authorities must be allowed by a national court capable of referring questions of EU law to the European Court of Justice under Article 267 TFEU.

Nontariff Trade Barriers

Nontariff trade barriers (NTBs) were the principal focus of the 1980s Europe without Internal Frontiers campaign for a fully integrated Common "Single Market." Many legislative acts were adopted which target NTBs. When possible, a common European standard is adopted. For example, legislation on auto pollution requirements adopts this methodology. Products meeting these standards may be freely traded inside the Common Market. Traditionally, this approach (called "harmonization") has required the formation of a consensus as to the appropriate level of protection.

Once adopted, harmonized standards must be followed. This approach can be deceptive, however. Some harmonization directives contain a list of options from which member states may choose when implementing those directives. In practice, this leads to differentiated national laws on the same so-called harmonized subject. Furthermore, in certain areas (notably the environment and occupational health and safety), the TFEU expressly indicates that member states may adopt laws that are more demanding. The result is, again, less than complete harmonization.

Many efforts at the harmonization of European environmental, health and safety, standards and certification, and related law have been undertaken. Nearly all of these are supposed to be based upon "high levels of protection." Some have criticized what they see as the "least common denominator" results of harmonization of national laws under the campaign for a Europe without internal frontiers. One example involves the safety of toys. Directive 88/378 permits toys to be sold throughout the Common Market if they satisfy "essential requirements." These requirements are broadly worded in terms of flammability, toxicity, etc. There are two ways to meet these requirements: (1) produce a toy in accordance with CEN standards (drawn up by experts); or (2) produce a toy that otherwise meets the essential safety requirements. Local language labeling requirements necessary for purchaser comprehension have generally, though not always, been upheld.

The least common denominator criticism may be even more appropriate to the second legislative methodology utilized in the internal market campaign. The second approach is based on the *Cassis* principle of mutual reciprocity. Under this "new" minimalist approach, EU legislation requires member states to recognize the laws of other member states and deem them acceptable for purposes of the operation of the Common Market. For example, major legislation has been adopted concerning professional services. By mutual recognition of higher education diplomas based upon at least three years of courses, virtually all professionals have now obtained legal rights to move freely within the Union in pursuit of their careers. This is a remarkable achievement.

Article 36 TFEU

The provisions of the EEC Treaty of Rome (now TFEU) dealing with the establishment of the customs union do not adequately address the problem of nontariff trade barriers (NTBs). As in NAFTA and the world community, the major trade barrier within the European Union has become NTBs. To some extent, in the absence of a harmonizing directive completely occupying the field, this is authorized. Article 36 TFEU permits national restraints on imports and exports justified on the grounds of:

(1) Public morality, public policy ("ordre public") or public security;

(2) The protection of health and life of humans, animals or plants;

(3) The protection of national treasures possessing artistic, historical, or archeological value; and

(4) The protection of industrial or commercial property.

Article 36 amounts, within certain limits, to an authorization of nontariff trade barriers among the EU nations. This "public interest" authorization exists in addition to, but somewhat overlaps with, the Rule of Reason exception formulated under Article 34 in many ECJ decisions. However, in a sentence much construed by the European Court of Justice, Article 36 continues with the following language: "Such prohibitions or restrictions shall not, however, constitute a means of arbitrary discrimination or a disguised restriction on trade between member states."

In a wide range of decisions, the Court of Justice has interpreted Article 36 in a manner which generally limits the ability of member states to impose NTB barriers to internal Union trade. Britain, for example, may use its criminal law under the public morality exception to seize pornographic goods made in Holland that it outlaws, but not inflatable sex dolls from Germany which could be lawfully produced in the United Kingdom. Germany cannot stop the importation of beer (*e.g.*, Heineken's from Holland) which fails to meet its purity standards. This case makes wonderful reading as the Germans, seeking to invoke the public health exception of Article 30, argue all manner of ills that may befall their populace if free trade in beer is allowed. See *Commission v. Germany* (1987) Eur. Comm. Rep. 1227.

Equally interesting are the unsuccessful Italian health protection arguments against free trade in pasta made from common (not durum) wheat, the failure of French standards' arguments against free trade in foie gras, and the rejection of Spain's "chocolate substitutes" labeling rule for chocolate containing vegetable fats.

But a state may obtain whatever information it requires from importers to evaluate public health risks associated with food products containing additives that are freely traded elsewhere in the Common Market. This does not mean that an importer of muesli bars to which vitamins have been added must prove the product healthful, rather that the member state seeking to bar the imports must have an objective reason for keeping them out of its market. Assuming such a reason exists, trade restraint may not be disproportionate to the public health goal. A notable ECJ opinion invalidated a French public health ban on U.K. beef imports maintained after a Commission decision to return to free trade following the "mad cow" outbreak. See *National Farmers Union v. Secretariat General* (2002) Eur. Comm. Rep. I–9079.

Public security measures adopted under Article 36 can include external as well as internal security. In one case, the validity of national restrictions on the export of strategic goods to the U.S.S.R. was noted. An unusual case under the public security exception contained in Article 36 involved Irish petroleum products' restraints. The Irish argued that oil is an exceptional product always triggering national security interests. Less expansively, the Court acknowledged that maintaining minimum oil supplies did fall within the ambit of Article 36. The public policy exception under Article 36 has been construed along French lines ("ordre public"). Only genuine threats to fundamental societal interests are covered. Consumer protection, though a legitimate rationale for trade restraints, does not fall within the public policy exception of Article 36. Permitting environmental protesters to block the Brenner Pass for 30 hours was an acceptable public policy in support of fundamental assembly and expression rights.

Intellectual Property Rights as Trade Barriers

A truly remarkable body of case law has developed around the authority granted national governments in Article 36 TFEU to protect industrial or commercial property ("intellectual property") by restraining imports and exports. These cases run the full gamut from protection of trademarks and copyrights to protection of patents and know-how. There is a close link between this body of case law and that developed under Article 101 TFEU concerning restraints on competition. Trade restraints involving intellectual property arise out of the fact that such rights are nationally granted. Owners of intellectual property rights within the Union are free under most traditional law to block the unauthorized importation of goods into national markets. There is a strong tendency for national infringement lawsuits to serve as vehicles for the division of the Common Market.

Considerable energy has been spent by the Commission on developing Common Market rights that would provide an alternative to national intellectual property rights. Late in 1993, the Council reached agreement on an EU trademark regime and the Council adopted Directive 89/104, which harmonizes member state laws governing trademarks. As a result, for example, the United Kingdom enacted the Trade Marks Act of 1994. The Court of Justice has ruled that goods bearing trademarks registered somewhere in the EU may be freely circulated marked with an "R" in a circle after the trademark. National law on unfair competition cannot be used to impede trade in such goods on the grounds that the mark in question is not registered in the country of sale. In the copyright field, several directives have harmonized European law, perhaps most importantly mandating copyrights for computer software.

A long-proposed EU Patent Convention finally came into force in 2014 as the EU Unitary Patent (UP) regime. It is applicable in all EU member states save Spain and Italy, miffed by the omission of their languages as "official." The UP regime operates in French, German, or English through its headquarters in Paris. It can issue or revoke a Common Market patent valid in any contracting state. Transfers and licenses for part of the Union are possible. The cost saving UP is an alternative to (but not a replacement for) national patent and European Patent Convention rights. However, the UP requires its signatories to harmonize national patent laws to conform to Unitary Patent rules on infringement, litigation procedures, exhaustion of rights and other issues. New Unified Patent Courts of First Instance and Appeal have been created in Luxembourg. Their centralized jurisdiction will govern infringement and validity disputes concerning national patents, European patents, and Unified patents.

The European Court of Justice has addressed IP trade barrier problems and generally resolved against the exercise of national intellectual property rights in ways which inhibit free trade *inside* the Union. In many of these decisions, the Court acknowledges the existence of the right to block trade in infringing goods but holds that the exercise of that right is subordinate to the TFEU. The Court has also fashioned a doctrine which treats national intellectual property rights as having been exhausted once the goods to which they apply are freely sold on the market. One of the few exceptions to this doctrine is broadcast performing rights which the Court considers incapable of exhaustion. Records, CDs, and cassettes embodying such rights are, however, subject to the exhaustion doctrine once released into the market.

Such goods often end up in the hands of third parties who then ship them into another member state. The practical effect of many of the rulings of the Court of Justice is to remove the ability of the owners of the relevant intellectual property rights from successfully pursuing infringement actions in national courts. When intellectual property rights have a single proprietor and have been placed on goods by consent, as when a licensor authorizes their use in other EU countries, then infringement actions to protect against parallel imports of the goods to which the rights apply are usually denied. This may not be the case, however, when voluntary trademark assignments that are not anticompetitive are involved. In such cases, the ECJ has demonstrated some concern for consumer confusion when trade in parallel goods occurs.

It is only when intellectual property rights do not have a single proprietor (thus sharing a "common origin") or the requisite consent is absent that they stand a chance of being upheld so as to stop trade in infringing products. Compulsory licensing of patents, for example, does not involve consensual marketing of products. Patent rights may therefore be used to block trade in goods produced under such a license. But careful repackaging and resale of goods subject to a common or even different trademark may occur against the objections of the owner of the mark. And compulsory licensing cannot be conditioned upon import bans applicable to the beneficiary licensee. Such bans offend the free movement of goods law of the EU and unfairly create investment incentives.

Centrafarm Case, Exhaustion Doctrine

An excellent example of the application of the exhaustion doctrine developed by the Court of Justice in the intellectual property field, as applied to a U.S. company, can be found in the *Centrafarm* case. 1974 Eur. Comm. Rep. 1147. The United States pharmaceutical company, Sterling Drug, owned the British and Dutch patents and trademarks relating to "Negram." Subsidiaries of Sterling Drug in Britain and Holland had been respectively assigned the British and Dutch trademark rights to Negram. Owing in part to price controls in the UK, a substantial difference in cost for Negram emerged as between the two countries. Centrafarm was an independent Dutch importer of Negram from the UK and Germany.

Sterling Drug and its subsidiaries brought infringement actions in the Dutch courts under their national patent and trademark rights seeking an injunction against Centrafarm's importation of Negram into The Netherlands. The Court of Justice held that the intellectual property rights of Sterling Drug and its subsidiaries could not be exercised in a way which blocked EU trade in "parallel goods." In the Court's view, the exception established in Article 36 for the protection of industrial and commercial property covers only those rights that were specifically intended to be conveyed by the grant of national patents and trademarks.

Blocking trade in parallel goods after they have been put on the market with the consent of a common owner, exhausting the IP rights in question, was not intended to be part of the package of IP benefits conveyed. If Sterling Drug succeeded, arbitrary discrimination or disguised restriction on Union trade would be achieved. The European Court of Justice ruled in favor of the free movement of goods within the Common Market even when that negates clearly existing national legal remedies.

While the goal of creation of the Common Market can override national intellectual property rights where internal trade is concerned, these rights apply fully to the importation of goods from *outside* the European Union. North American exporters of goods allegedly subject to rights owned by Europeans may therefore find entry into the EU challenged by infringement actions in national courts. But, in reverse, U.S. owners of EU intellectual property rights may do likewise. This is notably true regarding trade in gray market goods. Levi Strauss, citing its British trademarks, successfully kept low-price (made in the USA) Levi's out of the EU. Monsanto, on the other hand, was unable to invoke its European GMO patent rights to block importation of Argentinian bioengineered soybeans.

EU Agricultural Policy and International Trade Barriers

Here are the basic principles governing what is perhaps the most controversial of all Union policies, the Common Agricultural Program (CAP). The inclusion of agricultural trade was a critical element to the politics of the Union and remains largely without precedent in other regional economic treaties throughout the world. For many reasons, including the desire for self-sufficiency in food and the protection of farmers, free trade in agricultural products is an extremely sensitive issue.

When the Common Market was established in 1957, France and Italy had substantial farming communities, many of which were family based and politically powerful. Both countries envisioned that free trade in agricultural products could threaten the livelihoods of these people. The solution, as outlined in the Treaty, was to set up a "common organization of agricultural markets." The objectives of the CAP include the increase of productivity, the maintenance of a fair standard of living for the agricultural community, the stabilization of markets, and the provision of consumer goods at reasonable prices. It has not proved possible to accommodate all these objectives. Consumer interests have generally lost out to farmers' incomes and trading company profits.

Target prices for some commodities (*e.g.*, sugar, dairy products, and grain) are established and supported through Union market purchases at "intervention levels." "Variable import levies" (tariffs) are periodically changed to ensure that cheaper imports do not disrupt CAP prices. External protection of this type is also extended to meat and eggs. Fruit, vegetables, and wine are subject to quality controls which limit their flow into the market. Wine and agricultural products are subject to regulated designations of origin, Rioja wine from Spain and Feta cheese from Greece, for examples. Such regulations do not extend to generic food names, such as edam, jenerver (gin) and emmenthal, which can be freely traded with proper labels indicating variations in product qualities.

In recent years, perhaps the most controversial "common organization" has been for bananas. The Europeans import bananas under a complex quota system adopted in 1993 that favors former colonies and dependencies. Those affected went bananas over this regulation. Several challenges originating from Germany failed before the European Court of Justice, but in the end the United States, Mexico, Ecuador, Guatemala, and Honduras prevailed in the World Trade Organization. After suffering "authorized retaliation" in the form of tariffs on EU exports, the Europeans adjusted their "common organization" for bananas by replacing its quotas with non-preferential tariffs.

The European Agricultural Guidance and Guarantee Fund (better known by its French initials as FEOGA) channels the Union agricultural budget into export refunds, intervention purchases, storage, and structural adjustment. Agricultural policy regulations cannot discriminate against like or substitute products. But the bias towards producers, not consumers, in the CAP has been consistently upheld by the Court of Justice. Agricultural goods, like industrial products, can trigger free movement litigation.

In one case, for example, the Court of Justice suggested that British animal health regulations were a disguised restraint on Union trade in poultry and eggs. As with industrial goods, if the real aim is to block imports, such regulations are unlawful measures of equivalent effect to a quota. On the other hand, the United Kingdom could establish a Pear and Apple Development Council for purposes of technical advice, promotional campaigns (not intended to discourage competitive imports), and common quality standards for its members. But it could not impose a mandatory fee to finance such activities.

Apart from variable tariff protection, CAP quality control regulations can serve to keep foreign agricultural products from entering the European Union market. For example, the ban on beef hormones adopted by qualified majority vote in the late 1980s stirred opposition internally. In the United States, the beef hormones legislation was vehemently opposed by the White House but accepted by the renegade Texas Department of Agriculture which offered as much hormone-free beef to the Union as it would buy. The Texas offer delighted the EU Commissioner on Agriculture who rarely has a U.S. ally and is said to have wired: "I accept."

A veritable maze of legislation and case law governs the CAP. For many years, special agricultural "monetary compensation amounts" (MCAs) have been collected at national borders, greatly contributing to the failure to achieve a Europe without internal trade frontiers. It was not until 1987 that firm arrangements were made to dismantle the MCA system. In most years, the net effect of the CAP is to raise food prices in the EU substantially above world price levels. CAP has meant that agriculture is heavily subsidized. Indeed, it continues to consume a major share of the Union budget and at times seems like a spending policy that is out of control.

The Common Agricultural Policy does include a variety of "structural" programs intended to reduce the size of the farm population, increase the efficiency of its production, and hold down prices. These programs have involved retirement incentives, land reallocations, and training for other occupations. There has been a gradual reduction in the number of EU farmers over the years. In 1988, the Council adopted rules designed ultimately to reduce agricultural expenditures by linking total expenditures to the Union's rate of economic growth, establishing automatic price cuts when production ceilings are reached, and creating land set-aside and environmental protection incentives for farmers.

France and Italy, in the early years of the EU, became major beneficiaries of CAP subsidies. West Germany, with a minimal agricultural sector, was the primary payor under the program. It, in turn, principally benefitted from the custom union provisions establishing free trade in industrial goods. Hence a basic tradeoff was established in 1957 by the Treaty of Rome. France and Italy would receive substantial agricultural subsidies out of the regional budget while West Germany gained access for its industrial goods to their markets. Germany now holds a 25 percent share of internal EU trade. Britain, like Germany, saw itself as a net payor under the CAP. It repeatedly was able to negotiate special compensatory adjustments.

Greece, Spain, Portugal, and Ireland, on the other hand, looked forward eagerly to membership and CAP subsidies. These countries, along with unified Germany, Austria, Sweden, and Finland (whose agricultural subsidies were reduced upon joining the CAP), are often the least efficient producers of agricultural products. As such, they stand to lose the most if CAP is substantially replaced by market forces.

Each enlargement of the Union plugs more farmers into the extraordinary CAP subsidy system and the ten new members admitted in 2004 gained full payments by 2013. The big cost for CAP followed enlargement of the European Union to include Hungary and Poland, among others. The Amsterdam and Nice Treaties notably failed to resolve ongoing disputes over agricultural reform. A last-minute deal in 2002 capped costs at their 2006 level plus 1 percent a year starting in 2007. In theory this will force a gradual winding down of CAP subsidies. Significant efforts are being made to decouple CAP subsidies from production levels, notably for cotton, tobacco, and olive oil. Production quotas for milk were dismantled in 2015, and for beet (sugar) in 2017. One wonders how much longer European taxpayers will continue to pay for the CAP.

In the main like the United States, the European Union seems unable to stabilize the level of its agricultural subsidies. This results in overproduction ("butter mountains" and "wine lakes") and frequent commodity trade wars. A significant amount of fraud to obtain CAP subsidy payments has occurred. In 1989, the House of Lords Select Committee on the European Community released a scathing report on subsidy abuses entitled "Fraud against the Community." Others legitimately farm marginal land with lots of fertilizer. The excess produce is stored, used in social welfare programs, and frequently "dumped" in cheap sales abroad. Despite its incredible cost, the CAP remains one of the political and economic cornerstones of the Union.

External protests from North America notwithstanding, the CAP is unlikely to disappear. The provocative question much debated in the Uruguay Round of GATT negotiations is whether a mutually satisfactory reduction in the level of North American and European Union subsidies to agriculture can be achieved. In 1992 the Council of Agricultural Ministers agreed as an internal matter to cuts in support prices of 29 percent for cereals, 15 percent for beef and 5 percent for butter. Farmers received direct payments representing the income lost from the price cuts. Further price cuts and direct payments were agreed in 1999. It was hoped that these reductions would reduce EU export subsidies on agricultural goods and international trade tensions.

They also supported the argument that the extraordinary level of European subsidization of agriculture was simply not sustainable in cost or EU politics. European Union agricultural trade restraints are of enormous consequence to North American exporters. Equally significant are EU "export refunds" on agricultural commodities, refunds that affect the opportunities of North American exporters in other parts of the world. The United States has consistently argued (at times successfully) that these refunds violate the GATT rules on subsidies, while at the same time increasing its own export subsidies on agricultural goods. The result has been an agricultural "trade war" between the U.S. and the EU.

Each side has sought to outspend the other on agricultural export subsidies in a market that has been wonderful to buyers. Major attempts at a resolution or at least diminishment of the agricultural trade war was undertaken in the Uruguay Round of GATT negotiations during the late 1980s and early 1990s. Late in

1992, both sides announced the resolution of several longstanding subsidies' disputes (notably on oilseeds) and a compromise on the contested Uruguay Round agricultural trade issues. Agreement was reached on 20 percent mutual reduction in internal farm supports and a 21 percent mutual reduction on export subsidies measured on a volume basis over 6 years using a 1986–90 base period.

After a year of French protests and further negotiations, this agreement was formally incorporated into the WTO accords. Under it, the Union has been gradually switching from production and export subsidies to direct income support for farmers and rural businesses. This decoupling of agricultural subsidies from output has steadily progressed and is crucial to the long-term viability of the CAP. Tensions between Europe and the United States on agricultural trade have of late diminished (though hardly disappeared), but repeated U.S. Farm Bills threaten to reignite them.

The EURO

The EURO is the common currency of 19 of the 28 EU members (collectively called the "Eurozone"). It was initially adopted by 11 nations in 1999, with coins and currency introduced in 2002 and national currencies phased out and eliminated. Of the 15 EU nations in 1999, Britain, Denmark and Sweden refused to adopt the EURO, and Greece initially did not meet the fiscal qualifications (Greece joined in 2001). Since 2001, an additional 7 nations from eastern and southern Europe have adopted the EURO. In addition, a few small countries use the EURO even though they are not part of the agreements creating the monetary union, and several countries have their national currencies fixed to the Euro. Nine countries are currently members of the EU but not the Eurozone (Britain, Denmark, Sweden, Poland, Czech Republic, Hungary, Bulgaria, Romania, and Croatia).

The arrival of the EURO has important implications for the United States and the dollar. For decades, the dollar has been the world's leading currency, although its dominance has been declining since the early 1980s. Use of the Deutsche Mark and Yen in commercial and financial transactions, and in savings and reserves, had been steadily rising. The EURO is likely to continue the dollar's decline in all these markets. It is certainly the hope of many Europeans that they have successfully created a rival to the dollar. NAFTA, in contrast, does not even hint at a common North American currency.

As part of the creation of the EURO, the member nations established the European Central Bank (ECB) and the European System of Central Banks (ESCB). The ECB and ESCB are governed by an executive board of six persons appointed by the member states and the governors of the national central banks. The ECB and the ESCB are independent of any other European institution and in theory free from member state influence. Their primary responsibility is to maintain price stability, specifically keeping price inflation below two percent per year. The main functions of the ECB and ESCB are: (1) defining and implementing regional monetary policy; (2) conducting foreign exchange operations; (3) holding and managing the official foreign reserves of the member states; and (4) supervising the payments systems. The ECB has the exclusive right to authorize the issue of bank notes within the Common Market and must set interest rates to principally achieve price stability.

Regrettably, the fiscal enforcement system established when the EURO was created did not work. Since 1999, many EURO states have been under threat of sanction for failure to comply with the maximum 3 percent budget deficit rule. Yet no Eurozone member state was ever sanctioned, suggesting this system for controlling national deficits was toothless. In a death knell, sanctions for failure to comply with 3 percent rule were held unenforceable by the European Court of Justice. *Commission v. Council* (2004) Eur. Comm. Rep. I–6649 (Case C–27/04). The initial enforcement system was replaced by the 2012 Treaty on Stability, Coordination and Governance discussed below.

The global financial crisis of 2008, high debt and continuing sluggish economic performance have put intense pressure on the weaker Eurozone economies, notably Greece, Cyprus, Spain, Portugal, Ireland, and Italy. Financial rescue packages ("bailouts") of debt-ridden Eurozone members have sometimes been necessary, including three successive bailouts of Greece subject to austerity conditions. In March 2012, with market pressures and threats of a Greek default or exit from the Eurozone escalating, 25 of the then-27 EU members (minus Britain and the Czech Republic) adopted a Treaty on Stability, Coordination and Governance (TSCG) intended to provide a "permanent" solution to the EURO crisis, including a permanent 900 billion Euro loan fund, a Fiscal Compact, and ECB purchases of national government debt ("quantitative easing").

The EURO Crisis Continues

The EURO was conceived as a unifier for Europe. It has become instead a divisive wedge among creditors and austerity weary debtor nations. That said, by 2014 Ireland and Portugal had refinanced and exited their bailouts without credit line safety nets, taken to be "success" stories. Cyprus did likewise in 2016. But Greece, Italy and Spain remained troubled, and the Eurozone crisis was anything but over.

With deflation and economic stagnation apparent, the ECB undertook starting in 2015 a massive, unprecedented, and controversial "quantitative easing (QE)" program to buy up national government debt. This program resembled that which the U.S. Federal Reserve had been pursuing for some time. In 2016, the ECB extended its bond buying program to select corporate debt and reduced bank loans to zero interest for up to four years. These QE policies reduced European government borrowing costs, tended to reinforce European equity prices, and weakened the EURO (thus enhancing exports). But they appear to have had diminishing returns, pushing ECB bank deposit interest rates into negative territory for example. The ECB terminated its QE program in 2019.

Greece elected a government strongly opposed to the austerity conditions attached to its bailouts, lowering the Grexit threshold. There is cause for opposition to the austerity loan conditions. Over the first six years, Greece received over 240 billion Euros in bailout funds, plus the private sector debt restructuring, yet its economy has shrunk by at least 25%, and its debt to GDP ratio has risen dramatically to over 175%. In short, the bailouts and their conditions have proven self-destructive, making it less (not more) likely that Greece can ever repay its debts.

Greek society pays a very heavy price: Unemployment is widespread, poverty is growing, young people and bank deposits are fleeing, property values are speedily descending, and disillusionment is pervasive. Corruption and tax evasion remain entrenched.

Amidst another Greek crisis in 2015, the EURO initially plunged in value, but rallied somewhat by mid-2015, just in time for a third bailout of Greece by the Troika comprised of the ECB, EU Commission, and IMF. This bailout, like its predecessors and over IMF objections, did not reduce the amount of Greek national debt. One year later in 2016, it was déjà vu all over again. Greece needed more financial support to avoid default, and the IMF, after a somewhat scathing internal review of its participation in the second Greek bailout, pushed hard for debt reductions. Germany and the EU limited their support to extending Greek debt maturities, along with interest rate and debt repayment caps. This support was notably contingent upon pension and tax collection reforms in Greece.

By 2024, little had had changed: The IMF was still unwilling to participate in the third bailout, Germany unwilling to write off Greek debt, and the Greek government and its people suffering from austerity fatigue.

An essential question is whether a Greek default can be absorbed without taking down other Eurozone states and the EURO itself? In other words, whether a Greek default would prove contagious is the key systemic question. Portugal and Ireland, the bailout "success" stories, remain deeply indebted. Spain and Italy have survived on cash infusions that make the debt of Greece look miniscule, and major Italian banks appear insolvent.

The 2012 ESM mechanism has yet to be invoked, and Commission review of Fiscal Compact compliance has been "flexible." Hence the "permanent" solution to the EURO crisis created in 2012 is in doubt. Even some of the world's best financial market wizards say there is no clear-cut answer to the question of what happens in Europe or globally if Greece defaults or a EURO member withdraws from the Zone.

§ 3.5 A Timeline of European Integration

1949—COMECON Treaty (Eastern Europe, Soviet Union)

1950—European Convention on Human Rights

1951—European Coal and Steel Community (ECSC) ("Treaty of Paris")

1957—European Economic Community Treaty (EEC) ("Treaty of Rome"), European Atomic Energy Community Treaty (EURATOM)

1959—European Free Trade Area Treaty (EFTA)

1968—EEC Customs Union fully operative

1973—Britain and Denmark switch from EFTA to EEC; Ireland joins EEC; Norway rejects membership; remaining EFTA states sign industrial free trade treaties with EEC

1979—Direct elections to European Parliament

1981—Greece joins EEC

1983—Greenland "withdraws" from EEC

1986—Spain and Portugal join EEC; Portugal leaves EFTA

1987—Single European Act amends EEC Treaty to initiate campaign for a Community without internal frontiers by 1993; qualified majority legislative votes commence

1990—East Germany merged into Community via reunification process

1991—COMECON defunct; trade relations with Central Europe develop rapidly

1993—Maastricht Treaty on European Union (TEU); EEC Treaty renamed EC Treaty

1995—Austria, Finland, and Sweden join EU; Norway votes no again

1999—Amsterdam Treaty

1999—Common currency (EURO) managed by European Central Bank commences with 11 members

2002—ECSC Treaty expires; coverage added to EC Treaty

2003—Treaty of Nice; EU Charter of Fundamental Rights "declared"; draft Constitution for Europe released

2004—Cyprus, Estonia, Slovenia, Poland, Hungary, the Czech Republic, Slovakia, Latvia, Lithuania, Malta join EU

2005—Constitution for Europe overwhelmingly defeated in France and Netherlands

2007—Accession of Bulgaria and Romania; Reform Treaty of Lisbon proposed

2008—Irish voters reject Reform Treaty

2009—Reform Treaty approved in Ireland . . . takes effect Dec. 1; EU Charter of Fundamental Rights becomes binding law; EC Treaty renamed Treaty on the Functioning of the European Union (TFEU)

2010—Greece and Ireland bailed out; 1 trillion EURO financial crisis safety net created

2011—Portugal bailed out; EURO in crisis

2012—Spanish and Italian banks bailed out, Greece bailed out again; EURO in extreme crisis; Treaty on Stability, Coordination and Governance (TSCG) adopted by 25 member states creating a permanent European Stability Mechanism crisis loan fund and a Fiscal Compact with balanced budget rules; ECB agrees to buy unlimited short-term national bonds

2013—Croatia joins EU, Cyprus bailed out

2014—Scotland votes to remain in the UK

2015—Greece bailed out for third time; mass migration to Europe; terrorism inside EU increases

2016—UK votes to leave EU (BREXIT); migrant and terrorist waves escalate

2017—BREXIT negotiations commence

2020—BREXIT effective Jan 31, 2020

2021—EU-UK Trade and Cooperation Agreement governs future relations

2023—Russia invades Ukraine

§ 3.6 Major Amendments of the 1957 EEC Treaty

1987—Single European Act

1993—Maastricht Treaty

1999—Amsterdam Treaty

2002—ECSC Treaty folded into EC Treaty

2003—Treaty of Nice

2005—Defeat of Treaty establishing Constitution for Europe

2009—Reform Treaty of Lisbon

§ 3.7 Chronology of European Union Member Countries (27)

1957—France, Germany, Italy, Belgium, Netherlands, and Luxembourg create EEC (6)

1973—United Kingdom, Eire and Denmark (9)

1981—Greece (10)

1986—Spain and Portugal (12)

1995—Austria, Finland, and Sweden (15)

2005—Cyprus, Estonia, Slovenia, Poland, Hungary, Czech Republic, Slovakia, Latvia, Lithuania, and Malta (25)

2007—Bulgaria and Romania (27)

2013—Croatia (28)

2020—BREXIT (27)

§ 3.8 Chronology of Euro Zone Participants (19)

1999—Germany, France, Ireland, Spain, Portugal, Austria, Italy, Netherlands, Luxembourg, Belgium, Finland

2001—Greece

2007—Slovenia

2008—Cyprus, Malta

2009—Slovakia

2011—Estonia

2014—Latvia

2015—Lithuania

EU TRADE RELATIONS

§ 3.9 EU Trade Relations with North America, Japan, and China

As a rule, trade between the United States and the Common Market is voluminous, roughly in balance and yet fractious. While the focal point in recent years has been agricultural trade, especially the problems of export subsidies and nontariff trade barriers (notably Europe's banana quotas, beef hormone bans and freeze on GMO (genetically modified organism) approvals), there are many contentious issues. For example, Airbus subsidies are said to threaten Boeing and vice versa before the WTO. These longstanding, unresolved disputes resulted in significant U.S. tariffs on EU airplanes, wine, whiskeys and more in 2019 followed by EU tariffs on U.S. aircraft and goods in 2020. European digital industry taxes on Amazon, Google and the like emerged as another flashpoint in 2020. There is continuing concern that both North America and Europe may turn inward and protective.

Europe, for its part, has begun imitating the United States' practice of issuing annual reports voicing *its* objections to U.S. trade barriers and unfair practices. Extraterritorial U.S. jurisdiction has been a constant complaint, including the Helms-Burton Cuban LIBERTAD and the Iran-Libya Sanctions Acts. These reports have also targeted Section 301 of the Trade Act of 1974 (below). The Europeans perceive Section 301 as a unilateral retaliatory mechanism that runs counter to multilateral resolution of trade disputes through the GATT/WTO.

Trade relations between the EU and the U.S. improved in limited ways under the Transatlantic Economic Partnership Program. A 20-year dispute on wine production and labeling practices, for example, was finally resolved, and there is agreement on use of International Financial Reporting Standards, replacing U.S. Generally Accepted Accounting Principles. Common standards for electric vehicles have been agreed. In 2012, faced with recessionary economies and the rising economic tide of Asia, the EU and the United States started negotiations on a Transatlantic Trade and Investment Partnership Agreement (TTIP), subsequently dropped by the Trump administration.

Deep underlying conflicts remain, especially regarding cultural goods (TV shows, films), agriculture, GMOs, airplane subsidies, and procurement. It is this author's view that NAFTA/USMCA, the EU and more recently China are competing with good reason for possession of the world's largest market. Larger markets bring greater leverage in intergovernmental trade negotiations, economies of scale, and improved "terms of trade" (pay less for imports, receive more for exports), as well as enhanced abilities to exercise global economic leadership. The struggle for global market power is likely to continue.

Trump, Biden and Europe

At over $1 trillion a year, the trading relationship between the United States and the European Union is one of the largest in the world, accounting for over one-third of global trade. Europe has typically had a trade in goods surplus, while the U.S. has had a trade in services surplus. Net U.S. goods and services trade with Britain has generated a slight surplus, slight deficit with France, a small deficit with Italy and a notable deficit with Germany. EU and U.S.

job and technology creating investment surpasses $5 trillion in each other.

The U.S.-EU negotiations for a Transatlantic Trade and Investment Partnership (TTIP) initiated by President Obama disappeared under President Trump and failed to re-surface under President Biden. After considerable delay, Canada and the EU implemented their Comprehensive Economic and Trade Partnership (CETA, below) in 2017, and Mexico substantially re-negotiated its year 2000 EU free trade deal. The EU also implemented a major FTA with Japan in 2019 (below).

The EU free trade initiatives with Canada and Mexico were in part driven by the prospect of a NAFTA re-negotiation failure. These agreements allow duty free trade in autos, avoiding an EU tariff of 10%, Canadian tariff of 6.1%, and Mexican tariff of about 7%. American car exporters, including U.S.-based European and Asian firms, must pay these tariffs to their competitive disadvantage.

Subjecting the European Union to U.S. national security tariffs on steel and aluminum under the Trump administration generated equivalent EU retaliation. President Trump's threat to impose 25% national security tariffs on all U.S. auto imports sparked increased dialogue between the EU and the United States aimed, a bit unrealistically, at negotiation of a "no subsidies, no nontariff trade barriers, and no tariffs outside industrial goods" agreement. Limited progress was made toward such an outcome.

For decades, though not without disputes taken to the GATT/WTO, the United States and Europe have maintained a critically important strategic and economic partnership. NATO, for example, counts 26 of the 27 EU states as members. President Trump's rejection of the Paris accord on climate change, the Iran nuclear agreement, the short-range missile treaty with Russia, and his G7 plus Russia goals also signaled the potential for a dramatic shift in European-U.S. relations. Trump's harping on NATO defense contributions by EU member states and threats to remove troops from Germany fueled discord.

U.S. national security sanctions by the Trump administration on the Nordstream and Turkstream gas pipeline projects from Russia to the EU harkened back to similar Reagan era efforts. U.S. 2021 tariff threats against EU and UK tech taxes on Amazon, Google, Facebook, and other tax avoiding tech firms stirred major controversy. All this suggested that America First policies and tariffs of the Trump administration placed much risk on the longstanding allied relationship with Europe.

Biden and Europe

The Biden administration moved smoothly to reduce trade tensions with Europe. The longstanding Airbus/Boeing subsidy dispute was settled, including as regards the UK. A second settlement removed Trump's national security tariffs on EU (but not UK) steel and aluminum in favor of tariff rate quotas based on pre-Trump trade levels. U.S. return to the Paris Accord, an OECD agreement creating a minimum corporate tax of 15%, and joint renewal of a dialogue with Iran on nuclear issues improved relations. But the bumbled U.S. withdrawal from Afghanistan with little or no notice to its NATO allies made Europeans wonder if they can count on U.S. leadership. The Biden administration's role in a revitalized NATO alliance after Putin's 2023 invasion of Ukraine has helped removed those doubts.

For much more on U.S.-EU Trump-era trade policies and disputes, and Biden impacts thereon, see my *International Trade Law* Concise Hornbook.

Japan and China-EU Trade

The European Union's trade relations with Japan and China are less voluminous, less in balance and (at least superficially) less fractious than with the United States. Japan and China run an annual surplus in its trade with the EU, but the amount is much smaller than the huge surplus they accumulate in trading with the States. Many Europeans speak quietly and with determination about their intent to avoid the "United States example" in their trade relations with Japan and China. Less quietly, some national governments imposed rigorous quotas on the importation of Japanese autos and instituted demanding local content requirements for Japanese cars assembled in Europe.

The Union, for its part, has frequently invoked antidumping countervailing duty proceedings against Japanese and especially Chinese goods. It has demonstrated a willingness to create arcane rules of origin that promote its interests at the expense of Japan and China. At the GATT/WTO level, however, Japan and the EU share common concerns about retaining their agricultural support systems. These concerns place them in opposition to the U.S. and others who seek to liberalize world trade in agricultural products.

The meteoric economic rise of China, combined with U.S. withdrawal from the Trans-Pacific Partnership (TPP) under President Trump, pushed Japan and the European Union into an historic free trade agreement in 2018. Each is expected to get greater (but not 100%) access to the other's markets, notably Japanese autos to Europe and EU agricultural goods to Japan. For more coverage and a link to the agreement, see Sections 5.5 and 5.9.

§ 3.10 EU International Trade Governance

Article 218 TFEU establishes the procedures used in the negotiation of most trade agreements with the European Union. Basically, the Commission proposes and then receives authorization from the Council to open negotiations with third countries or within an international organization. When the Commission reaches tentative agreement, conclusion or ratification must take place in the Council. If the Commission alone concludes an agreement, the European Court of Justice will declare void the act whereby the Commission sought to conclude the agreement. The Council votes by qualified majority on Common Commercial Policy agreements. These include most GATT/WTO agreements.

The Council votes unanimously on association agreements and on international agreements undertaken via Article 352 (*e.g.*, environmental conventions prior to 1987). The 1993 Treaty on European Union amended Article 218 to provide that the Council must also vote unanimously on international agreements covering areas where a unanimous vote is required to adopt internal EU rules. Parliament's role in international agreements was expanded by the TEU and the Reform Treaty of 2009. Its assent must now be obtained for virtually all EU trade and foreign investment agreements. The Council is also authorized to take emergency measures to cut off or reduce trading with other nations for common foreign or security policy reasons.

An opinion of the European Court as to the compatibility with the TFEU of the proposed agreement and the procedures used to reach it may be obtained in advance at the request of the Commission, Council, or a member state. There are no public proceedings when such opinions are sought. Use of this advance ruling procedure may forestall judicial review of the compatibility of Union agreements with the Treaty. This lesson was vividly made when the Court of Justice rejected the final draft of the 1991 European Economic Area Agreement between the EU and EFTA because it considered the provisions on judicial control incompatible with the authority of the Union's legal order. This rejection sent the Agreement back for renegotiation and a new set of dispute settlement procedures which subsequently met with ECJ approval.

Trade agreements and other international treaties of the European Union are subject to judicial review by the Court of Justice as "acts" of its institutions. Moreover, such agreements are binding on the member states which must ensure their full implementation.

When the European Court holds international agreements of the Union to be "directly effective" EU law, individuals may rely upon them in national litigation. The direct effects doctrine has led to cases where citizens end up enforcing the trade agreements of the EU despite contrary law of their own or other member state governments.

ERTA and WTO Agreements Cases

Article 220 TFEU gives the Commission the power to represent the Union within the General Agreement on Tariffs and Trade (GATT)/WTO. This representation affords EU nations much more bargaining power over tariffs and other trade issues with Canada, the United States, and Japan than they ever had individually. The exact extent and delimitation of the Union competences and the competences of the member states were disputed. With regard to the many Uruguay Round agreements, therefore, the European Commission requested the European Court of Justice to render an opinion to determine whether the Union was competent to conclude the Agreement establishing the World Trade Organization (WTO), in particular as regards the Agreement on Trade in Services (GATS), the Agreement on Trade-Related Aspects of Intellectual Property Rights, including trade in counterfeit goods (TRIPs), and with respect to products and/or services falling within the ECSC and EURATOM Treaties. This WTO Agreements opinion is discussed below.

Article 207 TFEU conveys the power to enter international commitments to the European Union. This is the case by implication even when there is no express Treaty authorization to enter into international agreements necessary to achieve internal Common Market objectives. A prominent *ERTA* decision of the European Court holds the scope of the Union's trade agreements power to be coextensive with all *effective* surrenders of national sovereignty accomplished under the Treaty. *Commission v. Council*, 1971 Eur. Comm. Rep. 263 Thus, if an internal economic policy matter is governed by existing EU law, the external aspects of that policy are (either expressly or *by implication*) exclusively within the Union's competence.

More recently, the Court of Justice revisited the ERTA doctrine in an opinion reviewing the Uruguay Round trade agreements. The European Community had long represented the member states in the GATT and exclusively negotiated these agreements. But the General Agreement on Trade in Services (GATS) and the Agreement on Trade-Related Aspects of Intellectual Property (TRIPs) raised special concerns since the Treaty and ERTA were ambiguous as to whether the Union or the member states or both had the power to conclude these agreements.

The Court of Justice, in the complex *WTO Agreements* Opinion 1/94, 1994 Eur. Comm. Rep. I–5267, ruled that the Union had exclusive power regarding trade in goods agreements (including agriculture) based on Article 207 authorizing the Common Commercial Policy. While the cross-frontier supply of services not involving movement of persons also fell under Article 207, all other aspects of the GATS did not. Regarding TRIPs, only the provisions dealing with counterfeit goods came under the Community's exclusive Article 207 authority. Noting that the effective surrender of national sovereignty over intellectual property is not (yet) total and that internal trade in services is not "inextricably linked" to external relations, the Court ruled the competence to conclude GATS and TRIPs was jointly shared by the Community and the member states. Likewise, they share a duty to cooperate within the WTO in the administration of these agreements and disputes relating to them.

Subsequently, under the Lisbon Treaty of 2009, trade in services, trade-related intellectual property rights, and notably foreign direct investment became exclusive EU competences. Court of Justice Opinion No. 2/15 issued May 16, 2017, regarding the first of the EU's "new generation" free trade agreements between Singapore and the EU affirmed this exclusivity, excepting portfolio investment and foreign investor-state dispute settlement. The Court also held that air and maritime services, certain government procurement, non-commercial aspects of IP rights, renewable energy, and sustainable development labor and environmental standards fell within the EU's exclusive competence. Since the EU-Singapore agreement goes beyond the EU's exclusive competences, it had to be ratified by all 40 national and regional parliaments of the member states. This resulted in a prolonged and problematic process as Canada (below) has learned.

Member State Involvement

Article 351 TFEU indicates that most treaties the member states reached prior to joining the EU continue to be valid even if they impact on areas now governed by Union law. Many bilateral treaties of Friendship, Commerce and Navigation fall within this category despite their impact on immigration, employment, and investment opportunities. For example, such a dispute between Germany and the Commission concerned the compatibility of the preference-provision in the Utilities Directive for supply contracts with the German American Treaty of Friendship and Commerce of 1953. Member states are required to take all appropriate steps (*e.g.*, upon renewal) to eliminate any incompatibilities between national trade and investment agreements and the Treaty. Whether prior treaties can be invoked to negate or fail to fulfill Treaty obligations is unclear.

As a rule, member states may not negotiate trade treaties in EU-occupied fields. They may do so on a transitional basis in areas where the Union lacks authority or (less clearly) has not effectively implemented its authority. For example, in the early 1970s the EU had not developed an effective overall energy policy, although it clearly had competence in the coal and nuclear fields. Thus, the International Energy Agreement achieved through the Organization for Economic Cooperation and Development (OECD) in 1975 after the first oil shocks is not an EU agreement. In contrast, the Union clearly had competence in the field of export credits. OECD arrangements in this area are exclusively the province of the Union with no residual or parallel authority in the member states.

Likewise, in 2002 the ECJ ruled that bilateral "open skies" aviation agreement between eight individual member states and the United States were illegal incursions into an exclusively EU domain. A United States-European Union open skies agreement followed in 2008.

The *ERTA* and to a lesser degree the *WTO* decisions of the European Court, combined with the expanding competence of the Union, leaves less and less room for national governments to enter into trade agreements. Several ECJ decisions suggest that the Union's external authority parallels its internal powers even if it has not effectively implemented those powers. However, recognizing the sensitivities involved, "mixed agreements" negotiated by the Commission (acting on a Council mandate) and representatives of the member states are frequently used. Both the Union and the member states are signatories to such accords. This has been done with the "association agreements" authorized by Article 217 TFEU, certain of the WTO Codes, the Ozone Layer Convention, and the Law of the Sea Convention.

The Court of Justice has upheld the validity of mixed international agreements and procedures but suggested that absent special circumstances their use should not occur when the Union's exclusive jurisdiction is fully involved. In other words, mixed procedures should be followed only when the competence to enter and implement international agreements is in fact shared between the Union and its member states. The Treaty of Nice (2003) makes it clear that trade agreements relating to cultural and audiovisual services, educational services, and social and human health services are shared competences. The Reform Treaty (2009) contains a lengthy list of shared competences that are found in Article 4(2) TFEU.

New Generation EU Trade Treaty Governance

The Reform Treaty of 2009 also clarified that trade in goods and services, trade-related intellectual property rights, and foreign investment matters are an exclusive EU competence, as are the customs union, business competition rules, EURO zone monetary policy, and marine biology conservation policies. Article 3 TFEU further indicates that the Union has exclusive competence to conclude international agreements provided for by EU legislative act, necessary to enable the EU to exercise its internal powers, or where concluding an international agreement may affect common rules or alter their scope.

In all these areas, trade agreements can only be concluded by the European Union and need only be approved by the European Parliament. Some have referred to this outcome as a "fast-track" compared to mixed agreement ratifications by all national and regional parliaments.

The European Court of Justice ruled in *Opinion 2/15* concerning the EU-Singapore FTA that ratifications by all national and regional parliaments are not needed if there is no coverage of portfolio investments or investor-state dispute settlement in the FTA. Since these matters were part of that FTA, 28 national and 10 regional approvals were necessary. The same holds true for the investment provisions of CETA, otherwise operational in 2017. *Opinion 2/15* suggests that separating EU FTA and investment agreements might make for smoother governance, which is exactly what took place in 2018 as Japan and the EU signed a free trade agreement with no investment coverage. These two agreements are linked in Sections 3.18 and 3.19 below.

§ 3.11 EU Trade Agreements

Free Trade Agreements

By 2024, the EU had over 40 free trade agreements covering some 70 trade partners, including with Algeria, Chile, Egypt, Iceland, Israel, Jordan, Lebanon, Mexico, Morocco, Norway, Serbia, Southern Africa, Vietnam, Peru, Colombia, Central America (six nations), South Korea, Singapore, Japan, Canada, Tunisia, and a customs union agreement with Turkey.

Mexico and the European Union reached a free trade agreement in 2000, much expanded and re-negotiated in 2020. Mexico, with its NAFTA/USMCA membership, thus becomes a production center with duty free access to the world's two largest consumer markets.

Canada and the EU inked an historic Comprehensive Economic and Trade Agreement (CETA, below) in 2013 that, after much debate focusing primarily on investor-state dispute settlement, finally reached fruition in 2017. In 2018, Japan and the EU also reached a major agreement on a free trade which took effect in 2019.

Perhaps even more remarkably, after 20 years of negotiation, the EU and MERCOSUR (Brazil, Argentina, Uruguay, and Paraguay) signed a free trade deal in 2019. Overcoming protective CAP trade barriers, this FTA contains unprecedented provisions allowing expanded export of MERCOSUR agricultural and meat products to the EU. Ratification of this agreement is currently stalled over EU concerns regarding Brazil's environmental degradation of the Amazon.

India, ASEAN, New Zealand, and the Gulf Council may follow. One notable feature of EU free trade agreements is the inclusion of a Human Rights and Democracy Clause backed up by potential trade sanctions.

For coverage of EU foreign investment law and treaties, see Chapter 7.

Duty Free Access to the EU and U.S. Markets

The endgame so far as exporters to the European Union are concerned is unlimited duty-free access. Except for raw materials, few North American exports will qualify for such treatment. However, subsidiaries based in developing nations, free trade or customs union partners or EFTA countries may achieve this goal. This is possible because of the Union's adherence to the GSP program, its Mediterranean basin trade agreements, the Lomé/Cotonou Conventions, and the EEA Agreement with certain EFTA countries, all noted below. There are, of course, exceptions and controls (quotas, NTBs) that may apply under these programs. Nevertheless, the Common Market is so lucrative that careful study of its external trade rules is warranted.

Such studies can realize unusually advantageous trade situations. For example, many developing nations are Lomé Convention participants or GSP beneficiaries. The goods of some of these nations are also entitled to duty free access to the United States market under the U.S. version of the GSP program, the Caribbean Basin Economic Recovery Act, or various U.S. free trade agreements. See Chapter 2. A producer strategically located in such a nation (*e.g.*, Jamaica) can have the best of both worlds, duty free access to the European Union and the United States. The same applies for Israel which not only has a free trade agreement with the Union but also with the United States.

Since 2000, this ideal outcome has been most importantly available via Mexico, which is a member of USMCA and has a free trade agreement with the European Union. In 2017, the EU and Canada implemented a free trade deal that creates duty free access to the EU, and in 2019 a Japan-EU FTA took effect.

EU Generalized Tariff Preferences (GSP)

The European Union participates in the generalized system of tariff preferences (GSP) initiated within the GATT to give one-way duty-free access to industrial markets for selected goods coming from the developing world. This policy is implemented in the common customs tariff regulations. The Central European countries were added to the Union's GSP list for the interim period between the collapse of the Communist regimes and the entry into force of the free trade and economic association agreements concluded with the EU. The countries of the former USSR are GSP beneficiaries until any free-trade agreement with them comes into force, and provided they undertake to open their markets to developing-country exports.

Approximately 150 non-European developing nations now benefit from the GSP trade preferences of the EU, including China. Burma was suspended from the EU program in 1997 for human rights concerns but has since re-qualified. Since 1998, goods from South Korea, Hong Kong and Singapore no longer qualify. Similarly, the Four Dragons were "graduated" (*i.e.*, no longer treated as developing nations) out of the United States' GSP program in 1989. Brazil, Argentina, and Uruguay have also been graduated.

A revised GSP regime entered into force in 1995. A solidarity mechanism was introduced and applicable in exceptional circumstances: Beneficiary countries whose exports of products covered by the GSP exceed 25 percent of all beneficiaries' exports of those products in that sector will be excluded from GSP entitlement for that sector irrespective of their level of development. In addition, sector/country graduation was introduced based on relative specialization (ratio of a beneficiary country's share of total Union imports), coupled with a development weighing (development index, combining a country's per capita income and the level of its exports as compared with those of the Union). Both mechanisms were phased in gradually to keep within the framework of overall neutrality.

In 2001, the EU began phasing in complete duty-free access for the world's poorest 49 countries, a program known as "Everything But Arms." Special duty-free preferences have been granted to developing countries that combat illegal drug production. Pakistan received this status, over strenuous objections by India before the World Trade Organization. The WTO Appellate Body rejected the EU scheme in 2004 as discriminatory, and in breach of the Enabling Clause.

Subsequent EU amendments continued special duty-free tariff status for countries implementing 27 international conventions related to human and labor rights, the environment and good governance (including drug trafficking). Pakistan remains ineligible for special treatment. The WTO Appellate Body upheld the EU scheme in 2004.

The European Union system of generalized tariff preferences is selectively applied when about 130 "sensitive products" are involved. In other words, there are limitations (quotas and tariff ceilings) on duty-free access to the Common Market if the goods compete with Union manufacturers. However, these GSP limitations do not apply to products already receiving duty free access under the Cotonou Convention or the Union's Mediterranean Policy. Thus, nations that are covered by the latter trade rules still obtain some margin of preference over other third world GSP beneficiaries.

Mediterranean Policy

Another type of EU association agreement involves pursuit of what the EU refers to as its "Mediterranean Policy." This policy acknowledges the geographic proximity and importance of Mediterranean basin nations to the Union. The Mediterranean is viewed as a European sphere of influence. Most of these association agreements grant trade preferences (including substantial duty-free EU entry) and economic aid to Mediterranean nations without requiring reciprocal, preferential access for Union goods. Agreements of this type have been concluded with Algeria, Morocco, Tunisia, Egypt, Jordan, Lebanon, Syria, Israel, the former Yugoslavia, Malta, and Cyprus.

These agreements are not at all uniform. They may be asymmetrical free trade agreements with the final goal of a customs union (Malta, Cyprus), or without such goal (Israel, Maghreb countries) or simple cooperation agreements (*e.g.*, Egypt). In 1995, Europe and these partners agreed to create a Mediterranean industrial free trade zone. Since then, EU trade agreements in the Mediterranean basin have moved significantly towards reciprocal trade preferences.

Central and Eastern Europe

Because the former Soviet Union and its European satellites refused for many years to even recognize the European Community (now Union), some bilateral trade and cooperation agreements between those nations and the member states continue in place. It was not until 1988 that official relations between the Union and COMECON were initiated. As more democracy has taken hold, first generation trade and aid ("Partnership and Cooperation") agreements were concluded by the EU with Hungary, Poland, the Czech and Slovak Federal Republic, Bulgaria and nearly every other Central European nation. Similar agreements were concluded with the Baltic states, Slovenia, Albania, Russia, Ukraine, and other former Soviet nations.

The Union advanced to second generation "association agreements" with some of these countries. These are known as "Europe Agreements." They anticipate substantial adoption of EU law on product standards, the environment, competition, telecommunications, financial services, broadcasting, and a host of other areas. Free movement of workers is not provided. Free trading will emerge over a ten-year period with special protocols on sensitive products like steel, textiles, and agricultural goods. More fundamentally, these agreements are clearly focused on the eventual incorporation of these countries into the Union, as many did in 2005 along with Romania and Bulgaria in 2007.

With respect to the former USSR, the basis of the relationship between the EU and the Commonwealth of Independent States initially was the Trade and Cooperation Agreement of 1989 concluded with the Soviet Union. This agreement has been replaced by bilateral Partnership and Cooperation Agreements. The negotiations with Ukraine were concluded in March 1994, with Kazakhstan and Kyrgyzstan in May 1994, with Russia in June 1994, and with Moldova in July 1994.

These new agreements laid down the framework for future commercial and economic cooperation and created a new legal basis for the development of trade and investment links. For example, the agreement with Russia on trade and trade-related issues removed all quotas and other quantitative restrictions on Russian exports to the European Union, excepting certain textile and steel products. In 2004, responding to the admission of 10 new EU member states, Russia and the European Union concluded a Partnership agreement. Customs duties on cargo shipments between Russia its Kaliningrad enclave on the Baltic Sea are dropped, tariffs generally lowered, Russian steel quotas increased, and EU antidumping duties relaxed. The European Union also promised to guarantee language rights for the Russian-speaking minorities in Estonia and Latvia. However, all agreements with Russia have been undermined by the Russian invasion of Ukraine in 2023.

Russia is concerned with the eastern drift of EU and NATO memberships. Sweden and Finland joined NATO in 2023. Russia organized its own Eurasian Economic Union to counterbalance EU expansion. Belarus, Kazakhstan, and Armenia have signed on. Ukraine, Moldova and Georgia, on the other hand, hope to become EU associates and eventually members.

The Lomé/Cotonou Conventions, Economic Partnership Agreements

The 1957 Treaty of Rome, in a section entitled the "association of overseas territories and countries," was intended to preserve the special trading and development preferences that came with "colonial" status. France, Belgium, Italy, and The Netherlands still had a substantial number of these relationships. Article 200 TFEU completely abolished (after a transitional period) tariffs on goods coming from associated overseas territories and countries. There is no duty on the part of these regions to reciprocate with duty-free access to their markets for EU goods. Although some territories continue to exist (*e.g.*, French territories like Polynesia, New Caledonia, Guadeloupe, Martinique, etc.), most of the once associated overseas colonies are now independent nations. This is true as well for most of the former colonies of Britain, Denmark, Portugal, and Spain.

As independence arrived throughout Asia, Africa and elsewhere, new conventions of association were employed by the EU as a form of developmental assistance. The first of these were the Yaoundé Conventions (1964 and 1971) with newly independent French speaking African states. These conventions were in theory free trade agreements, but the African states could block almost any EU export and the Union in turn could protect itself from agricultural imports that threatened its Common Agricultural Policy. A healthy amount of financial and technical aid from the Union was thrown into the bargain.

When Britain joined in 1973, it naturally wished to preserve as many of the Commonwealth trade preferences as it could. The Yaoundé Conventions were already in place favoring former French colonies south of the Sahara. The compromise was the creation of a new convention, the first Lomé Convention (1975), to expand the Yaoundé principles to developing Caribbean and Pacific as well as English-speaking African nations. The fourth Lomé Convention (1990) governed trade and aid between the EU and number of African, Caribbean and Pacific (ACP) states.

Lomé IV was replaced in 2000 by the Cotonou Agreement. The Cotonou nations presently include:

Angola, Antigua & Barbuda, Bahamas, Barbados, Belize, Benin, Botswana, Burkina Faso, Burundi, Cameroon, Cape Verde, Central

African Republic, Chad, Comoros, Congo, Djibouti, Dominica, Dominican Republic, Equatorial Guinea, Eritrea, Ethiopia, Fiji, Gabon, Gambia, Ghana, Grenada, Guinea, Guinea Bissau, Guyana, Haiti, Ivory Coast, Jamaica, Kenya, Kiribati, Lesotho, Liberia, Madagascar, Malawi, Mali, Mauritania, Mauritius, Mozambique, Namibia, Niger, Nigeria, Niue, Palau, Papua New Guinea, Rwanda, St. Christopher & Nevis, St. Lucia, St. Vincent & The Grenadines, Samoa, Sao Tomé & Principe, Senegal, Seychelles, Sierra Leone, Solomon Islands, Somalia, South Africa, Sudan, Suriname, Swaziland, Tanzania, Togo, Tonga, Trinidad & Tobago, Tuvalu, Uganda, Vanuatu, Zambia and Zimbabwe.

Perhaps the most important feature of this lengthy listing is the developing nations that are *not* Cotonou Convention participants. Unless they fall within the Union's Mediterranean Policy, they are apt to perceive the Lomé/Cotonou Conventions as highly discriminatory against their exports and economic interests.

Unlike the Yaoundé Conventions, the Lomé Conventions did not create (even in theory) reciprocal free trading relationships. While the Lomé states retained substantial duty-free access to the Common Market, the Union obtained no comparable benefit. This one-sided relationship was continued temporarily under the Cotonou Agreement through 2008. Under Cotonou, the Lomé nations promised not to discriminate in trading among EU countries and to grant them most-favored-nation benefits

Most significantly, the Cotonou nations now participate in two innovative EU mechanisms designed to stabilize their agricultural and mineral commodity export earnings. These programs are known as STABEX and MINEX (also known as SYSMIN). STABEX covers (inter alia) ground nuts, cocoa, coffee, cotton, coconut, palm, rawhides, leather and wood products, and tea. MINEX deals with copper, phosphates, bauxite, alumina, manganese, iron ore, and tin. These programs are an acknowledgement of the economic dependence of many Lomé nations on commodity exports for very large portions of their hard currency earnings.

Some have argued vigorously that STABEX and MINEX perpetuate rather than relieve this dependence. Both programs provide loans and grants in aid to Lomé nations who have experienced significant declines in export earnings because of falling commodity prices, crop failures and the like. The greater the dependency and decline, the larger the EU financial transfers. These sums are not, for the most part, tied to reinvestment in the commodity sectors causing their payment, nor to the purchase of Union products or technology. In a world where most development aid is tied (*i.e.*, must usually be spent on the donor's products or projects), STABEX and MINEX represent a different approach. Many Latin American nations have lobbied the United States to create similar mechanisms for their commodities.

The Lomé IV Convention (1990) added several new features carried over under the Cotonou Agreement. The European Union now financially supports structural adjustments in ACP states, including remedies for balance of payments difficulties, debt burdens, budget deficits, and public enterprises. Cultural and social cooperation, trade in services, and environmental issues are also addressed. For example, an agreement not to ship toxic and radioactive waste was reached. The Convention builds upon earlier provisions by specifying protected human rights such as equal treatment, civil and political liberty, and economic, social and cultural rights. Financial support from the EU is given to ACP nations that promote human rights and has been withheld after military coups.

The one-way nature of ACP trade benefits is inconsistent with WTO obligations. The EU has therefore undertaken to negotiate two-way "Economic Partnership Agreements (EPA)" with six groupings of ACP states. The first such EPA was finalized in 2008 with 13 Caribbean nations. Duties on nearly all European exports will be phased out by 2033, trade in services is eased, and procurement as well as investment rules are established. A second EPA was completed in 2016 with southern Africa.

§ 3.12 The European Union as a Trade Policy Model

The European Union has served as a model for economic integration elsewhere in the world. For example, the Andean Community (ANCOM) modeled itself on the EEC (as the EU was then called), as did the Southern African Customs Union (SACU), and the Central American Common Market (CACM), all noted in Section 2.6. These regional economic groups have suffered internal discord, economic stress, and limited success. See especially D. Gantz, *Regional Trade Agreements: Law, Policy, and Practice* (2009). Yet, for the most part, they still aspire to become as comprehensive and effective as the European Union. MERCOSUR, established in 1991 by Brazil, Argentina, Paraguay, and Uruguay, at least on paper comes closest to reproducing the EU model.

The EU trade policy model contrasts with the ASEAN (Association of Southeast Asian Nations) and LAFTA (now ALADI, the Latin American Integration Association) groups. See Section 2.6. These groups have targeted more limited goals as free trade areas. Neither rises to the significance or depth of NAFTA or its 2005 sequel, CAFTA-DR (the Central American Free Trade Agreement between the United States, Costa Rica, Guatemala, Nicaragua, El Salvador, Honduras, and the Dominican Republic). Hundreds of bilateral free trade agreements have been negotiated since NAFTA, including some by the European Union, notably with Canada (CETA 2017) and Japan (2018). See Chapter 5.

At this writing, the European Union and the USMCA present competing trade policy models that have each drawn adherents in the developing world. Apart from their core economic differences (customs union vs. free trade area), the EU model embraces a remarkable legal superstructure to achieve economic integration, notably the regional legislative and litigation systems of the Union. In contrast, the USMCA model, legally speaking, is minimalist. Multiple varieties of arbitration are generally used to resolve disputes, and there are no regional legislative or litigation systems. See Chapters 4 and 6.

Which model offers the best way forward? The Transatlantic Trade and Investment Partnership (TTIP) negotiations commenced in 2013 by the United States and the European Union moved along a track that resembled NAFTA. That said, with BREXIT, the collapse of the Doha Round of World Trade Organization (WTO) negotiations (see Section 1.3), along with U.S. withdrawal by President Trump from the Obama Administration's hard won Trans-Pacific Partnership (TPP-12), analysis of this question has taken on added meaning, particularly since the emergence of TPP-11 and China-led RCEP (see Section 5.5).

BREXIT

§ 3.13 COVID and Trade

Just as BREXIT was accomplished late in January 2020, the COVID-19 pandemic virus arrived. COVID made negotiating a UK-EU future relations agreement more difficult.

In the following months, the EU and UK responses varied considerably. Important EU rules were relaxed or overwhelmed. Government subsidies, notably regulated by EU law (see Chapter 6), proliferated as individual countries sought to rescue their economies. For example, France pumped 8 billion Euros into Renault and Germany sent 9 billion Euros into Lufthansa in return for 20% government ownership. Overall, German subsidies cannot be matched by other EU states, threatening to undermine the operation of the EU's Single Market.

Financial controls came under great pressure as Germany for the very first time acquiesced in agreement with France to *collectively backed* "coronabonds." These common EU bonds are intended to raise money for hard-hit Italy, Spain, and southern member states. They are funded in part by new EU taxes on unrecycled plastic waste and digital levies. The EU Central Bank is authorized to buy coronabonds, essentially eliminating risk of default. Resistance by "The Frugals" (Austria, Denmark, the Netherlands, and Sweden) resulted in greater EU budget rebates for them, and possible "emergency brake" limits on COVID bailout funding.

In crisis mode, the ECB resumed substantial purchases of national bonds ("quantitative easing"), even Greek bonds, as the EURO Zone struggled. Border restraints on goods, notably medical equipment, and medicines, emerged. EU export controls over vaccines in 2021 served as prominent reminder to Britain that BREXIT really did alter trade relations.

Structural shifts, such as re-shoring, combined with increased supply chain protectionism, diminished economic activity. EU fiscal controls over national spending were significantly suspended. Different but major national economic contractions emerged as a European recession set in. Doomloop risks rose as shrinking economies made it harder to service national debts.

Perhaps most seriously, extensive border restraints on people essentially negated the Schengen free movement of people regime. Early on in 2020 EU nations adopted entry bans against each other, later relaxed selectively among "travel bubble" partners subject to mandatory COVID testing rules. In July 2020, international controls barred persons coming from COVID heavy countries like the USA, Russia, and Brazil. Note that the USA had previously in the pandemic crisis barred entry to many EU residents, and in 2021 barred entry to the world absent a negative COVID test.

§ 3.14 BREXIT

Since 2009, Article 50 of the Treaty on European Union (TEU) permits member states to commence withdrawal negotiations from the European Union. Prime Minister Cameron, wanting badly to be re-elected in 2015 and seeking to appease the hard-core Euroskeptic wing of his Conservative Party, promised in his campaign to re-negotiate Britain's position in the EU and hold a referendum on remaining an EU member state. He won re-election, and after negotiating modest changes in U.K.-EU relations, put the Remain or Leave issue to a public vote.

In a hotly contested campaign, with free movement of people within the EU a prominent issue, LEAVE supporters made statements that were simply untrue, for example that Britain would save not pay money by leaving and that the National Health Service would directly benefit from these savings. Future Prime Minister Boris Johnson actively participated in promoting this idea. At no point did the leaders of the Leave movement present a clear plan for or picture of its consequences. Critics maintain that the Leave vote was secured by a campaign riddled with falsehoods that often seemed disconnected from reality. Some Brexiteers even suggested a return to nostalgic Empire glory.

Russia actively supported BREXIT, primarily via divisive Facebook accounts, much as it did in the 2016 U.S. elections in supporting Donald Trump.

After approval by 52% of its voters in a high turnout June 2016 national referendum and strong approval by the House of Commons, Britain commenced two-year withdrawal negotiations on March 29, 2017, nearly the same date as the 60th anniversary of the EU. London, Scotland, and Northern Ireland voted heavily to remain, but the rest of England provided the Leave campaign with victory. Theresa May, a Minister in David Cameron's Cabinet and a quiet Remain supporter, became Prime Minister shortly after the referendum in the wake of Cameron's resignation. For a considerable period, she simply said "BREXIT means BREXIT."

Two different BREXIT negotiations occurred. The first concerned "divorce" withdrawal terms finalized in 2019. The second negotiation, commenced in 2020, concerned future relations between the UK and the EU. Absent a future relations agreement, Britain and the EU faced a "no deal" hard exit, expected by many to be very damaging. During these negotiations there was a standstill. EU law governed, with no participation by the British in its supranational development.

Rallying around a cry for sovereignty, Britain under Prime Minister May commenced over two years of withdrawal negotiations on March 29, 2017, nearly the same date as the 60th anniversary of the EU.

Prime Minister May's Divorce Agreement

Seeking to raise her bargaining power with the EU under a clear mandate from the British people, Prime Minister May held a snap election in June of 2017. Much to her surprise and that of the pollsters, the Conservative Party lost majority control of the UK Parliament. Many factors were in play during the snap election, but it appeared that at least some British voters had second thoughts about the wisdom of BREXIT, particularly the "hard" version she espoused.

The Conservatives were consequently forced to govern in coalition with a small Protestant-dominated Northern Ireland party, the DUP. This coalition was fragile. The DUP wanted agricultural subsidies post-BREXIT, continued access to EU development funds for poorer regions, and a "frictionless" border with Ireland. The DUP leaned toward remaining in the EU.

Some Brexiteers suggested pursuing the "soft exit" Norwegian or Swiss models for relations with the EU post-BREXIT. But these complicated models for the most part involved acceptance of free movement of people, the EU customs union, cash contributions to the EU budget, and deference to EU/EFTA Court decisions. To what degree would a soft exit really be an exit?

Prime Minister May indicated she would continue to pursue a "hard" exit. Prime Minister May was quoted as saying that "better no deal, than a bad deal," suggesting Britain might walk out of the negotiations. By 2019, despite repeated efforts, she was unable to secure UK Parliamentary approval for the BREXIT deal she had negotiated with the EU. The core issue was the possibility under "stopgap" provisions, if no future relations agreement was accomplished, that all the UK would remain inside the EU customs union to ensure that the border between Northern Ireland and Ireland would not become "hard." This possibility sparked fears of a return to violence and conflict like that before the Good Friday accords.

Prime Minister Johnson's Divorce Agreement

In July 2019, Prime Minister May resigned and in the ensuing elections Boris Johnson, former mayor of London and a brazen Brexiteer, became Prime Minister. In short order, he re-negotiated the BREXIT divorce deal to remove hard land border risks, essentially creating an internal UK/EU customs and immigration border in the middle of the Irish Sea cooperatively administered by British and EU authorities.

Under this Divorce Agreement, the UK firmly left the EU customs union, thus freeing up Britain to engage in trade agreement negotiations around the world. Northern Ireland remained part of the UK customs regime but obliged to collect VAT taxes and tariffs on goods (but not services) on behalf of the EU. Northern Ireland also remained in the EU's regulated "single market" for goods. It was agreed that new cooperatively run "trusted traveler" rules on goods moving between Britain and Northern Ireland be established in UK ports. These checks are meant to assure regulatory conformity (especially on agricultural goods and meat) and collect taxes/tariffs on goods "at risk" of being transported or smuggled into the EU via Northern Ireland.

Money Matters

As a mandatory prerequisite to withdrawal negotiations, early on in Prime Minister May's tenure, the EU presented Britain with an expensive "divorce bill" for what it perceived the UK would owe the Union upon departure. The demand for cash included Britain's liabilities under the generous, entirely unfunded EU pension scheme. It also covered pre-BREXIT and post-BREXIT EU projects under the British-approved EU budget running from 2013 through 2020.

In the end, the "divorce bill" amounted to approximately 35 billion Euros. This bill no doubt stunned many Leave backers, who were led to believe BREXIT would result in net savings not loss. In addition, Britain lost two well-staffed and well-paid EU agencies, one on Medicines (EMA), the other on banking (EBA). On the flip side, the EU must adapt to the loss of Britain as a net contributor to its budget.

Divorce Deal Done

The Johnson divorce deal (formally titled the Withdrawal Agreement) was subsequently approved by the EU and the UK Parliaments, thereby setting the formal date for BREXIT to occur on Jan. 31, 2020.

Many in the EU felt Britain should "pay a price" to leave. Put another way, to paraphrase one EU leader: "It cannot be the case that Britain ends up better off outside the EU than inside." Overall, the adverse trade consequences of BREXIT for the UK were more significant than for the EU. *The UK, for example, sends nearly 50% of its exports to the EU, while less than 10% of EU exports end up in Britain.* The UK depends on exports to the EU for approximately 13% of its GDP, while the EU depends on exports to the UK for only 3% of its GDP. All that said, Britain is a substantial market for EU exports (notably autos made in Germany) and the fifth biggest economy in the world, considerations which played in the UK's favor.

Bottom line: The independent Bank of England forecasted the British economy would be 4% smaller ten years after the TCA than if Britain had remained in the EU. *This forecast has proved to be closely on target.*

§ 3.15 The EU-UK Trade and Cooperation Agreement (TCA 2021)

Many in the EU felt Britain should "pay a price" to leave. Put another way, to paraphrase one EU leader: "It cannot be the case that

Britain ends up better off outside the EU than inside." Overall, the adverse trade consequences of BREXIT for the UK were more significant than for the EU. The UK, for example, sends nearly 50% of its exports to the EU, while less than 10% of EU exports end up in Britain. The UK depends on exports to the EU for approximately 13% of its GDP, while the EU depends on exports to the UK for only 3% of its GDP. All that said, Britain is a substantial market for EU exports (notably autos made in Germany) and the fifth biggest economy in the world, considerations which played in the UK's favor.

Nevertheless, after much negotiation and threats of failure, a complex 2,000-page UK-EU Trade and Cooperation Agreement (TCA) was finally reached on Christmas eve of 2020. It took effect Jan. 1, 2021. Fundamentally a "thin" free trade in goods (only) agreement, the TCA exits Britain from the EU customs union and the EU single market freedoms for cross-border movement of goods, services, people and capital. *Unlike most trade deals, the TCA creates more trade restraints than it removes.*

The BREXIT future relations deal needed and obtained qualified majority approval by the EU Council, which for these purposes meant 20 out of 27 member states constituting at least 65% of the EU population must affirm the deal. The consent of the European Parliament as well as the UK Parliament was also required and obtained.

Specific Divorce and TCA provisions are noted in the topics below, followed by an outline of the TCA.

Fishing

It may seem a bit strange, but the issue that most held up the Trade and Cooperation Agreement (TCA) was fishing. The EU created a Common Fisheries Policy (CFP) just prior to the entrance of Britain, Ireland, and Denmark in 1973. It allows EU member states considerable rights to fish in traditionally national waters and regulates levels of catch.

Long a thorn in British culture and its economically insignificant fishing industry, the TCA establishes quotas that reduce by 25% over 5.5 years most EU (notably French) rights to fish in UK waters. Thereafter annual negotiations will follow. Swapping of fish quotas is no longer allowed under the TCA. The irony of this focus is that, for reasons of taste, much of the fish caught or raised in UK waters is exported to the Continent. These exports are expected to continue and are not subject to immediate EU retaliation tariffs if in breach of the TCA, a major concession by the EU that essentially closed the future relations deal.

Early signs under the TCA fishing accord suggest cod catches by British boats (the mainstay of British "Fish n' Chips") have declined. Exports of fish to the EU are tied up in new paperwork requirements. Some Scottish trawlers took to running their salmon directly to Denmark where prices were double those of the UK.

Free Movement and Residency Rights

Students, retirees, entrepreneurs and workers and their families and pets (with pet passports!) had long enjoyed free movement residency, health care and no roaming cell phone rights throughout the Union, no work permits or visas needed. See Chapter 5. Existing residency rights (in the UK known as "settled status") were protected under the Divorce Agreement but became subject on both sides after BREXIT to substantial paperwork requirements and fees.

Provocative free movement questions emerged. What was to happen to the nearly 1 million Poles, 350,000 Romanians, 270,000 French citizens, and the other 2 million or so EU nationals working in Britain? What was to happen to the 1.2 million British retirees and others on the continent? What about EU professionals and restaurant owners who had exercised their EU "right of establishment" to set up shop in the UK, and vice-versa? One could argue that Britain obtained a younger, more skilled taxpaying workforce under the EU free movement of people regime. The EU in turn received a goodly number of higher cost UK seniors.

Future "free movement" rights were eliminated. The TCA enacts visa-controlled movement of people across borders from 2021 forward. For example, the extensive EU Erasmus Program facilitating hundreds of thousands of cross-border student studies, work experiences and apprenticeships will not be available to students from England, Wales, and Scotland, but (thanks to underwriting by Ireland) will be open to students from Northern Ireland. Mutual recognition of professional qualifications, such as those of doctors, nurses, and architects, will be more limited than under EU rules.

Apart from liberal UK-Ireland travel rules, tourist visas as between the UK and the Schengen area are good for 90 days of travel during any six-month period. Advance electronic authorizations are required. Travel insurance with health care coverage has become standard. Mutual emergency health care is generally available, but not automatic for kidney dialysis and the like.

Fearing the worst, some British citizens began efforts to obtain other EU passports to preserve free movement and other EU rights. Dual nationality in Ireland, Sweden and Germany ranked high on this list. A small steady flow of EU nationals out of the UK commenced early in BREXIT's evolution, but most remained.

Free Internal Trade

Agreeing to tariff free *and quota* free trade was relatively easy for the UK and EU in their TCA negotiations. This was the first time the EU had ever agreed to quota free trade.

On both sides, hundreds of millions of customs and tax forms, fees, import licenses, security checks and certifications must now be regularly filed, a significant and costly trade barrier, especially to the UK. Facing lengthy back-ups, cross-border trucking fees are noticeably up. Cross-border online sales have been hit with hitherto absent costs and fees. Early signs suggested some UK and EU importers, particularly smaller firms, are reducing and in some cases eliminating cross-border trade. Marks & Spencer, for example, dropped hundreds of products from its Northern Ireland stores.

Complex rules of origin for goods suddenly applied. For example, gas and diesel autos must contain at least 55% UK and EU combined content to be freely traded. For electric and hybrid vehicles, the rule of origin requirement is 40%, but their batteries are limited in the amount of allowable overseas content starting with 70% and running down to 50% by 2026. More red tape has proliferated, particularly as there are no common certification standards on safety, pollution, and the like for autos. For example, dual production runs for EU and UK compliant vehicles may emerge.

For another example, Britain imports about 25% of its food from the EU while 60% of its agricultural exports head to the continent. No tariffs and quotas apply, but the absence of TCA agreement on common sanitary and phytosanitary standards (SPS) for food generates UK and in reverse EU certification and paperwork issues galore. UK exports of seafood quickly ran into EU import SPS barriers. Much the same problem and costs could emerge regarding pharmaceutical testing and safety certifications.

Britain in principle escaped the EU's voluminous "*acquis communautaire*", its vast body of internal trade legislation, regulations, and case law. But many European Union rules seem inescapable since all goods exported from Britain will need to conform to EU law, and extensive cross-border supply chains compel compliance. For example, all auto imports must under the EU End of Life Vehicles Directive be 95% reusable or recyclable.

The EU, recognizing that the two sides will inevitably become competitors, feared that the UK might become a "Singapore-upon-Thames" neighbor with low-cost product standards and taxation. It extracted significant regulatory commitments from the UK not found in its Canada or Japan free trade agreements. The Divorce deal suggested that each side would keep the same standards on state subsidies, competition law, social and employment rules, the environment, climate change and "relevant" tax matters. In addition, the UK agreed to create an independent regulator of government subsidies along the lines of the EU competition authorities.

These "level playing field" regulations were incorporated in the TCA on a "non-regression" basis, meaning the UK promised not to dilute them, but reserved the right to do so subject to possible (but not instant) retaliatory EU trade sanctions. Arbitration procedures were established to resolve disputes in this critical area, notably avoiding the jurisdiction of the European Court of Justice. If the UK retains EU standards and regulations, will not interpretations of those rules by the ECJ come along with them in arbitrations?

Services and Business Passport Rights

The TCA does not retain the core EU freedom to provide services across borders. The British economy relies very heavily on its services sector, including finance, IT, legal, accounting, insurance, consultation, audio-visual, and architecture for examples.

Much of the EU services sector operates on "passport" principles under EU law. Bankers, securities firms, insurance companies and the like need only obtain a license in one EU state, which then basically qualifies them to do business in the other member states. Britain, London and The City comprise the financial center of Europe. Financial firms (including U.S. firms) used British licenses to springboard throughout the EU.

Without passport rights, and if British regulatory rules do not measure up as "equivalent" to those of the EU, British, U.S. and global finance and service companies licensed in the UK could join the BREXIT exodus. Early in the BREXIT saga this started happening, with roughly 7500 financial sector employees and $1.6 trillion in financial assets departing to the benefit of Frankfurt, Paris, Luxembourg, Dublin and even New York.

The EU has made it clear that certain financial operations traditionally done in London will be obliged to be done within its borders. Most clearing house operations, derivatives, EURO bond, carbon cap and trade, and direct client services are expected as a matter of EU law to be undertaken inside the Union. Trading of EU stocks shifted almost immediately from London to EU-based exchanges, including the London Stock Exchange's Turquoise platform in Amsterdam.

Even if some British service sector regulations are deemed "equivalent" to those of the EU, such treatment can be removed by the EU with 30 days' notice.

Foreign Investment

Many foreign, especially Asian and North American, investors have set up manufacturing and service centers in Britain. For example, Japanese car companies were notably invested in the United Kingdom. Japan was sufficiently worried about BREXIT that its government delivered a detailed memo of concern to the U.K. soon after the vote to leave in 2016.

British and foreign manufacturers based in the U.K. were especially nervous about going from zero tariff entry into the EU to paying tariffs to gain entry to what will remain the world's largest common market. Autos, for example, are subject to 10% EU import tariffs, agricultural goods subject to 30–40% tariffs. In addition, nontariff regulatory barriers could emerge if British health, safety, subsidy, and environmental standards differ from those of the EU.

British and foreign investors essentially put a hold on investment or expansion of existing operations in the U.K. after the BREXIT vote while negotiations proceeded over four years. Just before the scheduled BREXIT deadline of March 29, 2019, Honda announced it would exit production in the U.K. in favor of USA and Japanese plants. Honda anticipates free trading autos into the EU under the 2019 EU-Japan Economic Partnership Agreement. See Chapter 7.

Jaguar Land Rover cut UK employment by thousands of jobs. Dyson, of vacuum cleaner fame, moved its headquarters to Singapore prior to inaugurating an electric vehicle. Nissan too will undertake EV auto production outside the UK. BMW pre-emptively moved its engine production back to Germany. It seems fair to say that many investors in the UK perceived that BREXIT in any form represented a clear and present danger. That perspective was not eliminated by the Trade and Cooperation Agreement of 2021.

More broadly, late in 2020 the EU completed a bilateral Cooperation Agreement on Investment (CAI, referred to as a "BIT") with China. See Chapter 7. Will the UK follow that path? BITs *among* EU members have been invalidated by the European Court of Justice. Britain escapes this ruling via BREXIT.

In sum, foreign investment in Britain has dropped considerably. Why so? It is fundamentally a much smaller market than the EU.

International Trade Relations

Britain pre-BREXIT derived its trade relations with the world predominantly via the EU. Absent a post-BREXIT agreement with the EU regarding future relations, it was assumed that Britain would revert to World Trade Organization rules. See my Concise Hornbook on *International Trade Law*. How sound that assumption was, and what were its implications for the UK, the EU and WTO partners like the United States was unclear.

The UK had traded under WTO tariffs negotiated under the EU umbrella. Might it have been needed to start over as an independent WTO member? Would the EU have needed to compensate WTO members because its tariffs were negotiated on the premise that the UK was included? Since 25% of American exports to the EU go to Britain, these issues mattered to the U.S. and incentivized reaching an agreement on future relations.

"Global Britain" after BREXIT hopes for lots of bilateral free trade and foreign investment deals. Initial dialogues commenced in 2020. Most of the over 70 EU free trade partners (including Korea, Canada, Mexico, Tunisia, Kenya, Southern Africa, Central America, Morocco, Egypt, Ukraine, Norway, Iceland, Japan, Vietnam, Turkey, Singapore) agreed at least initially to roll-over their EU deals to maintain "continuity" with the UK. Such free trade agreements raise critical "rules of origin" and costly documentation issues, for example regarding UK-made automobiles such as BMW's Mini-Coopers and Toyota vehicles. Britain's first FTA that was not a rollover came late in 2021 with Australia. The UK (along with China, Taiwan, and South Korea) actively sought to join the TPP-11 free trade agreement. See Section 5.3. Britain succeeded in this effort and is now a TPP-11 member.

Big trade deals for the UK with the likes of the United States, India, MERCOSUR, and China remain outstanding. President Trump favored a U.S.-UK FTA, but President Biden did not embrace that direction, not the least because of his concerns about the future of peace in Northern Ireland. In 2020, the EU proposed a "New Transatlantic Agenda" with the United States focused on digital supply chain security, climate change, product standards, and dealing with COVID.

The interim year 2020 expanded the scope of UK/EU trade relation issues. Britain and France reversed policy in 2020 by removing participation by China's Huawei in their 5G network. Will the UK and the EU agree on digital revenue taxes, which would notably hit Google, Amazon, Microsoft, Facebook, and other U.S. tech companies? What about data privacy concerning which the EU has been a world leader? For more on such issues, see my Concise Hornbook on *The European Union Beyond BREXIT.*

Northern Ireland and Scotland

Every political district in Scotland voted in 2016 to remain in the EU. But the Conservatives won 12 districts in the June 2017 snap election. The Scotch voted against leaving the UK several years prior to BREXIT. A second referendum could achieve Scottish independence in search of EU membership. Scotland, as an alternative to leaving the UK, might fairly ask whether special arrangements like those discussed below for Northern Ireland could be made for it.

Nearly every district in Northern Ireland voted to remain. Peace and border-free transit has been directly linked under the Good Friday Accords to Irish and UK membership in the EU. After BREXIT, the Ireland/Northern Ireland border will be the only land crossing between Britain and the EU.

Under the Divorce Agreement, the UK and the EU promised to cooperatively administer byzantine trade rules between Ireland and Northern Ireland to keep this border crossing free of customs and immigration controls. As a practical matter, this means that Northern Ireland (unlike the UK) is subject to EU single market regulations *and* the jurisdiction of the European Court of Justice. Northern Island will collect VAT and tariffs on behalf of the EU. However, its goods will enter both the EU and the UK duty-free.

These provisions were negatively received by Protestants in Northern Island, leading to a threat by the UK Parliament under the Johnson administration to disavow them. The threat further undermined EU trust in Boris Johnson as a reliable trade partner. It also caused U.S. presidential candidate Joe Biden to warn of his opposition against a return to a hard border.

Critics maintain that BREXIT is toxic in the long run for the future of Northern Ireland as part of the UK. Certainly, the EU-UK Trade and Cooperation Agreement (TCA) pushes Ireland and Northern Ireland towards eventual unification. The EU-UK agreement on Northern Ireland will be reviewed every four years, opening the door for participation by the Northern Ireland Parliament if it is functioning.

Ireland, a low-tax manufacturing center for many U.S. multinationals, typically shipped substantial goods to the EU using Britain as an inexpensive land-bridge running from Wales to Dover to Calais. This has become a rat's nest of customs law after BREXIT. This now costly land-bridge can be avoided by shipping goods between Ireland and France. Ireland's food imports and exports from and to the UK have traditionally been significant. Ireland has a big stake in BREXIT and the TCA.

Immigration and Free Movement of People

Immigration (mostly by EU nationals) was an issue central to the BREXIT vote. Since Britain did not participate in the Schengen Accord (see Chapter 5), the UK has always maintained its own external border controls for non-EU migrants. For EU and non-EU persons, Britain has established a new merit points-based immigration system, subject to considerable fees.

As noted above, apart from residency benefits existing as of 2021, what changed under the TCA are the extensive rights of UK and EU nationals to freely cross borders in pursuit of employment, education, retirement, or creation of a business.

Cooperation on Foreign Affairs and Security Matters

Administering the TCA will require ongoing trust and cooperation, qualities in short supply after the bruising BREXIT negotiations. The TCA provides for continued UK-EU cooperation on aviation, rail, trucking, defense, foreign affairs, climate change, energy, scientific research (Horizon), intelligence, and national security matters.

UK access to key EU databases will be by request. The UK will not be a member of Europol but will have "a presence" at its headquarters. Euro Warrant criminal procedures may apply in or for the UK.

The Future of the EU

Britain having made its exit, whatever the price, why not others? In recent years, anti-EU parties have emerged throughout the Union. Marine Le Pen, leader of the National Rally Party in France, openly ran on a platform promising a national referendum on leaving the EU (FREXIT). She was resoundingly defeated by Emmanuel Macron, a strong pro-EU candidate. But a less strident Le Pen and her associate Jordan Bardella are back as a political force in France after the 2024 EU Parliament elections. They failed however to take power in subsequent 2024 French Parliamentary elections.

Does BREXIT signal a decline or even the end of the Union? Or perhaps expansion of a "multi-speed" Union, built around a core of EURO Zone states? Remarkably, the initial BREXIT impact served to unify and harden the EU's negotiating positions on divorce and future relations. Likewise, Russia' invasion of Ukraine has generally helped solidify the EU.

The Future of the UK

Britain, in leaving the world's largest common market, becomes a lesser economic power. Yes, it is an independent nation, and yes it has considerable military and diplomatic resources, but it will struggle economically playing in the Big Leagues with China, the United States, and the European Union. Even as a more nimble "Free Agent", Britain will ultimately have less power and influence in global affairs, particularly as self-sufficiency, nativist trade policies, and heightened national and cyber security emerge as top priorities in the wake of China's rise to power.

Who Won?

BREXIT, in this author's opinion, harmed and will continue to harm both Britain and the European Union, more so for the former than the latter. Like the Swiss after Switzerland rejected EU membership, and given the endless joint committees and reviews provided for under the TCA, the UK should expect almost perpetual negotiations with the EU. In those negotiations, Britain (like Switzerland) is likely to frequently be the supplicant.

The big BREXIT winner, in this author's opinion, is Vladimir Putin.

§ 3.16 The TCA in Outline

The EU-UK Trade and Cooperation Agreement (TCA, 2021)

The TCA is expressly "based on international law, not EU law" (Article 14). Supervision and strategic guidance will be undertaken via a "Partnership Council." The TCA contains seven Parts.

Part I concerns common and institutional provisions. It creates joint cumulative rules of origin for goods (Chapter 2) and rules on technical barriers to trade building on the WTO TBT agreement (Chapter 3). Chapter 4 affirms the right of both sides to maintain their own Sanitary and Phytosanitary (SPS) measures. No mention is made of the WTO SPS Code. Chapter 5 on trade facilitation is based on WTO and WCO principles.

Part II governs trade in services and investment. It "locks in" market access in substantially all sectors along the lines of the EU and UK Free Trade Agreements with Japan. National treatment is a key principle along with temporary entry rights. Telecommunications, delivery services, international maritime, and financial services are detailed. New ground is broken for the provision of legal services by British attorneys advising clients on UK and public international law anywhere in the EU.

Title 3 liberalizes digital trade. Title 4 promotes capital movements. Title 5 focuses on IP rights, Title 6 public procurement, Title 7 small and medium enterprises, Title 8 energy, Title 9 Transparency and Title 10 on good regulatory practices.

Perhaps the most critical controversial area, Title 11 contains extensive provisions on creation of a "level playing field" for open and fair competition and sustainable development. Subsidies, competition law, SOEs, taxation, labor and social standards, the environment and climate all fall within Title 11.

Separate headings in Part II exist for the rules on aviation, road transport, social security coordination, short-term visas and fisheries.

Part III covers law enforcement and judicial cooperation in criminal matters. Data exchanges, mutual assistance, money laundering, terrorism, and cooperation with Europol and Eurojust are anticipated.

Part IV is titled "Thematic Cooperation." Health security, cyber security and "migration security" are its focus.

Part V anticipates UK participation in EU programs upon payment of appropriate fees. EU programs such as Horizon Europe, Euratom, Copernicus, and Space Surveillance are specifically named.

Part VI creates dispute settlement procedures and safeguard remedies. The opening language provides: "This Agreement includes dispute resolution mechanisms that are appropriate for a relationship between sovereign equals. This means that there is no role for the Court of Justice of the European Union."

Consultations about asserted breaches of the Agreement precede arbitration. No specific arbitration tribunals or procedures are provided. Rectification by the Party in breach or suitable compensation may follow. If the dispute is not resolved, then the Party not in breach can suspend obligations under the Agreement. Cross-suspension may occur, subject to certain conditions and limitations.

In the event of serious economic, societal or environmental difficulties that are likely to persist, the EU or UK may unilaterally undertake strictly proportionate and time-limited remedial safeguard measures.

Part VII indicates that the Agreement is to be reviewed every five years and can be extended to new EU member states. It does not apply to Overseas Territories of the EU or UK. Either Party may terminate the Agreement with 12 months advance notice.

TCA Annexes cover nuclear cooperation and exchanges of classified information.

Chapter 4

CUSFTA 1989 AND NAFTA 1994

Table of Sections

§ 4.1 U.S. Fast-Track Procedures and Free Trade Agreements

Fast-Track

Some U.S. efforts to reduce trade restrictions have been multilateral or regional efforts (*e.g.*, the WTO, NAFTA, and CAFTA-DR). Others have been bilateral, for example U.S. free trade agreements. In both situations, Congress intermittently since 1974 has given quite broad authority to the President, or the President's representative, to reduce or eliminate U.S. tariffs on a reciprocal "fast-track" basis. For U.S. free trade partners, fast-track procedures generally mean that once a deal is reached, Congress cannot alter it.

In other words, fast-track is very desirable to nations seeking FTAs with the United States.

Fast-track procedures originated as a compromise after Congress refused to ratify two major components of the Kennedy Round of GATT negotiations. The first such authorization lasted from 1991 to 1996 and made possible U.S. implementation of NAFTA in 1993 and the WTO package of agreements in 1995. From 1996 onward, Congress refused to grant fast-track authority to President Clinton.

The Trade Act of 2002 authorized President George W. Bush to negotiate international trade agreements on a fast-track basis, a procedure that requires Congress to vote within 90 legislative days up or down, without amendments, on U.S. trade agreements. In return, Congress receives substantial notice and opportunity to influence U.S. trade negotiations conducted by the U.S. Trade Representative (USTR). President Bush and the USTR quickly completed, and Congress approved free trade agreements with Chile and Singapore, and thereafter with Morocco, Australia, Central America/Dominican Republic (CAFTA-DR), Peru, Jordan, Oman, and Bahrain. The President's fast-track authority expired in July 2007 after agreements with Colombia, Panama and South Korea had been signed. Approval of these FTAs by Congress under fast-track was delayed several years into the Obama administration.

Congress granted fast-track trade promotion authority to President Obama in the summer of 2015, lasting beyond his Presidency through June 2018. With all three NAFTA nations participating in the Trans-Pacific Partnership (TPP-12) agreement, NAFTA could have been effectively updated by the TPP-12. President Trump, however, withdrew the U.S. from the agreement almost immediately upon taking office in 2017. The remaining 11 TPP states subsequently signed on to a modified TPP-11 agreement minus the United States in 2018. The TPP-12 and TPP-11 agreements are discussed in Chapters 5 and 6.

In 2018, President Trump requested and obtained, in the absence of Congressional disapproval, a three-year extension of fast-track authority running to July 2021. Thereafter, there was no renewal, nor request for renewal, of fast-track during the Biden Presidency.

U.S. Free Trade Agreements

The United States has negotiated a variety of free trade agreements. The first in 1985 was with Israel. The second was with Canada. This agreement was adopted through the United States-

Canada Free Trade Area Agreement Implementation Act of 1988. The Canada-U.S. Agreement (CUSFTA) is discussed below.

The United States negotiated along with Canada and Mexico a three-way North American Free Trade Area Agreement (NAFTA). NAFTA took effect in 1994 with full implementation in nearly all areas by the year 2003. NAFTA was incorporated into United States law by the North American Free Trade Agreement Implementation Act of 1993.

Late in 2001, Jordan and the United States agreed on free trade. In 2003, the United States reached free trade agreements with Chile and Singapore, notably incorporating coverage of E-Commerce and digital products. Early in 2004, free trade between the United States and five Central American states (CAFTA) plus the Dominican Republic, and with Australia and Morocco, was agreed. More bilateral free trade deals were struck with Bahrain, Oman and Peru, and additional agreements with Panama, Colombia and South Korea took effect in 2012.

These trade agreements provide duty-free import opportunities into the U.S. market. Unlike the one-way U.S. free trade programs (see Section 2.1), these agreements are reciprocal. They open foreign markets to United States exports on a duty-free basis. In addition, they establish detailed rules targeting nontariff trade barriers (NTBs) among the parties.

President Donald Trump repeatedly declared his intention to renegotiate or withdraw from NAFTA. Any NAFTA nation could withdraw from the agreement upon six months' notice. Coverage of NAFTA's re-negotiation and its USMCA outcome is presented in Chapter 6.

§ 4.2 Canada-U.S. Free Trade (CUSFTA)

North American economic integration began in earnest when Canada and the United States concluded a broad free trade and foreign investment agreement in 1989. Without intending to do so, the Canada-United States Free Trade Agreement (CUSFTA) laid the foundations for NAFTA 1994. In the United States, CUSFTA was almost a non-event. In Canada, the agreement was much contested. Special Parliamentary elections focused on CUSFTA kept the Mulroney government in power, which was critical to Canadian ratification of the agreement.

NAFTA did not repeal the Canada-United States Free Trade Agreement. The CUSFTA agreement continued (and continues) to govern selected areas of trade (as specified in NAFTA and the USMCA). Officially, the United States and Canada "suspended" their

1989 agreement. If NAFTA had failed or either Canada or the United States withdrew from it, CUSFTA would have come out of suspended animation and continued to bind the two countries. There was no comparable arrangement for the United States and Mexico under NAFTA.

Understanding the CUSFTA agreement is important because it served as the model upon which NAFTA was built. In some areas, the terms of NAFTA were identical or nearly so. In others, minor or major changes were made which are best understood as attempts at improving upon the early experience of free trade and expanded foreign investment. NAFTA and USMCA insights can still be drawn from CUSFTA even as it lies in suspended animation.

The Canada-United States Free Trade Agreement was limited in its scope and purposes. Nevertheless, the CUSFTA agreement is lengthy and relatively complex. It was comprised of eight Parts divided into a total of twenty-one chapters. Each chapter was comprised of various Articles and accompanying Annexes. Above all CUSFTA was a pragmatic agreement.

Core Commitments—Federalism, Supremacy and Nondiscrimination

Chapter One of the Agreement contains a listing of CUSFTA objectives. Internal trade barriers on goods *and* services are to be eliminated, fair competition facilitated, and investment opportunities liberalized. Effective procedures to administer CUSFTA, to resolve disputes, and cooperation to expand and enhance the benefits of the agreement were also listed as objectives.

In realizing these objectives, Canada and the U.S. promised to "ensure that all necessary measures are taken in order to give effect to [CUSFTA's] provisions, including their observance by state, provincial and local governments" (Article 103). This obligation was a major commitment, particularly for Canada since it has a relatively weak federal system with the provinces retaining considerable power. Binding the two federal governments to free trade was relatively simple. Binding their political subdivisions proved more difficult.

Canada and the United States affirmed their existing 1989 bilateral and multilateral trade agreements. They self-servingly declared their agreement consistent with Article 24 of the original (pre-Uruguay Round) General Agreement on Tariffs and Trade (GATT 1947). Article 24 governs the establishment of free trade areas by GATT signatories (see Chapter 2), and CUSFTA did indeed ultimately pass examination by a GATT working party.

If there had been inconsistencies between CUSFTA and then existing trade agreements, CUSFTA is supreme (Article 104). Under this supremacy rule, for example, conflicts with the GATT 1947 agreement would apparently result in regional rules prevailing. This potential was somewhat minimized via incorporating by reference into CUSFTA various GATT provisions, including the 1979 Procurement Code and Articles III, XI and XX of the GATT 1947.

There were specific exceptions to CUSFTA supremacy, some limited in scope, if conflicts arise with any of the following agreements: (1) The GATT rules on antidumping and countervailing duties; (2) the GATT rules on balance of payments problems; (3) the OECD Code of Liberalization of Capital Movements; (4) the Income Tax Convention between Canada and the U.S.; and (5) the International Monetary Fund Agreement. In addition, it was generally specified that CUSFTA was *not* supreme on agriculture, emergency trade relief, wine and spirits, trade in goods, energy, tariff waivers and investment matters. These exceptions had less impact than their numbers imply.

Canada and the United States broadly promised to grant "national treatment" on investment and trade matters. Each side agreed to treat the other's investors and traders in the same manner as their own, a general promise not to discriminate on the grounds of nationality. In addition, Article III of the GATT 1947 agreement, along with its interpretative notes, was specifically incorporated into CUSFTA. Article III stipulated national treatment for goods on taxation, fees and charges, distribution or sale requirements, transport rules, and domestic sourcing (among other matters). *Id.* Furthermore, the existing GATT interpretations of Article III were to be applied under CUSFTA. Several Article III disputes subsequently went to binding arbitration under Chapter 18 of CUSFTA (below).

A state or provincial treatment rule was also created. Regarding like, directly competitive or substitutable goods, treatment that is no less favorable than the most favorable treatment that the state or province grants to any goods was required. Hence, unlike at the federal level, this rule was not one of identical treatment, but a variation on most-favored-nation (MFN) treatment. The states and provinces were obliged to treat goods from the other country in the best manner they treated goods coming from anywhere, including their own state or province. Arguably, this duty provided greater protection from nondiscrimination than simply national treatment.

Trade in Goods

Part Two of the 1989 Canada-United States Free Trade Agreement, covered in Chapters 3 through 12, governed free trade in goods. This central goal must be measured against a history of substantial free trade in goods prior to 1989. Canada, for example, had been exporting more than 75 percent of its goods to the U.S. on a duty-free basis prior to the CUSFTA agreement. Most goods were entering the United States at an average 5 percent tariff. Hence, tariffs were not really a significant trade relationship.

Both countries were much more concerned with nontariff trade barriers (NTBs), such as health, safety, environmental and technical product regulations. NTBs sometimes excluded goods totally from either market, and each country sometimes applied international trade remedies to limit the cross-border flow of goods. With its commanding dependency on access to the U.S. market, this Part of the CUSFTA agreement was critical to Canada. Conversely, the United States was ready to make concessions on trade in goods to obtain benefits on trade in services, technology, and cross-border investment.

Tariffs and Quotas

Canada and the United States agreed to a phased elimination of the tariffs applicable to their trade in goods. Article 401 created a schedule for import tariff removals starting in 1989 and ending in 1998. This schedule was not subsequently altered by NAFTA. Schedule A goods immediately became duty free on January 1, 1989. Schedule B goods became duty free after 5 years of 20 percent annual reductions on January 1, 1993. Schedule C goods became duty free on January 1, 1998, after 10 years of 10 percent annual reductions. Schedule C goods included the most tariff-sensitive, such as agricultural products, textiles, and clothing.

Export taxes (tariffs) were prohibited at the outset of the CUSFTA agreement. Canada and the U.S. also agreed not to employ "customs user fees" which function like tariffs. The United States phased out its existing fees as applied to Canadian goods. In addition, private sector requests for accelerated tariff reductions ahead of the timelines in the CUSFTA Schedules were allowed. Companies and industries filed a surprising number of petitions for acceleration with their governments. Canadian and United States officials then met and decided which tariffs to reduce on an accelerated basis. Considerable acceleration in tariff removals was achieved under CUSFTA and this innovative process continued under NAFTA.

The CUSFTA agreement, unlike the customs unions of Europe and MERCOSUR, *did not embrace the creation of a common external tariff*. In other words, the United States and Canada retained their own tariffs on goods entering their markets. Goods from the rest of the world are still, even after NAFTA and the USMCA, subject to United States or Canadian (not CUSFTA, NAFTA or USMCA) tariffs.

Nevertheless, certain external tariff tensions were addressed in CUSFTA. These primarily concerned foreign goods that entered Canada or the United States and were subsequently shipped to the other country. The widespread practice of "drawback" under customs law was the main issue. The refunding of tariffs that manufacturers pay on imported goods after they are exported or incorporated or consumed in the production of goods subsequently exported, is the essence of drawback. Drawback can take the form of waivers or reductions in such duties. Either way, manufacturers have lower costs because of the customs refund. Supporters of drawback argue that the imported goods have not come to rest, merely passed through, and therefore should be beneficially tariffed.

Canada and the United States recognized that drawbacks created problems for their free trade agreement. Manufacturers obtaining them could sell at lower costs than competitors not benefiting from drawback. To solve this problem, Canada and the United States agreed to all but eliminate drawbacks on goods they trade and were scheduled have done so by 1996. However, this commitment was notably altered by the NAFTA agreement of 1994.

Another external tariff tension that CUSFTA remedied was waivers of tariffs triggered by "performance requirements." Such requirements were primarily found in Canadian law. Often, a Canadian manufacturer had to incorporate a minimum amount of Canadian content, purchase or substitute Canadian goods, and maintain minimum export percentages. Manufacturers meeting Canadian performance requirements were recipients of drawback or tariff waivers as an investment incentive. This resulted in an unfair advantage for Canadian manufacturers competing under CUSFTA with United States companies that did not obtain comparable benefits. Article 405 of CUSFTA prohibited new or expanded tariff waivers based upon performance requirements (*i.e.*, a "standstill" was stipulated). For all but Auto Pact goods, tariff waivers were eliminated in 1998.

Regarding trade quotas and their equivalents, Canada and the United States agreed to apply Article XI of the GATT 1947. Most quotas were banned, excepting notably agricultural, fishery or marketing quotas. Several Article XI disputes were arbitrated under Chapter 18 of CUSFTA (below).

The Origin of Goods

Free trade agreements like CUSFTA, NAFTA and the USMCA have a critical problem. Since Canada and the United States did not establish a common external tariff, other nations in theory could ship their goods into the country with the lowest tariff and then benefit from free trade. If so, third party goods could "free ride" on CUSFTA. To prevent this, Canada and the United States crafted rules to decide which goods came from their countries and allowed only those goods to be freely traded. All other goods are subject to national tariffs and trade restraints as they cross the border.

The CUSFTA "rules of origin" became one of the most complex and controversial of the agreement's provisions. Canada and the United States, with different legal traditions in this area, undertook a path-breaking set of rules of origin. To start, they agreed that all goods "wholly obtained or produced" within either or both of their nations could be freely traded. Since this rule applies mainly to minerals, agricultural goods, and fish, it was not difficult to fulfill.

Manufactured goods, not so clearly Canadian or United States in origin, were another story. In the global economy, with multinationals producing goods and parts in many nations, it is hard to ascertain which products come from where. In the United States, the origin of goods has typically been decided under the doctrine of "substantial transformation." See *Anheuser-Busch Brewing Assn. v. United States*, 207 U.S. 556 (1908). If in the process of manufacture, a material or part was "substantially transformed" into a new product, then its foreign origin was lost. The material or part so transformed originates as a matter of U.S. law in the country of transformation.

Unfortunately, the doctrine of substantial transformation in U.S. customs law has many imprecisions. Canada and the United States, having adopted the Harmonized Tariff System (HTS) of classification of goods, moved in a different direction.

Under Article 301 of CUSFTA, they agreed that whenever items of third-party origin were transformed to a degree that their tariff classification under the HTS changed, then those items originated in Canada or the United States. But packaging, combining or diluting goods of third-party origin was insufficient. *The core CUSFTA rule of origin was therefore linked to changes in HTS tariff classifications.* This approach embodied the idea but provided more precision than the doctrine of substantial transformation. For more on the HTS system, see my Concise Hornbook on *International Trade Law*, Chapter 3.

Canadian legal traditions and priorities were the primary source of additional CUSFTA "content" rules of origin. The CUSFTA content rules of origin applied only to trade in selected (but quite a large number) goods. These rules generally had to be satisfied *in addition to* the basic rule of change in tariff classification. In a few instances, the content origin of the goods sufficed for free trade.

Canada and the United States agreed, in most circumstances, on a 50 percent CUSFTA content rule. The value of materials originating in Canada or the United States plus the direct cost of processing performed in either or both countries had to exceed 50 percent of the value of the goods crossing the border. Only if this content rule was satisfied could many goods be freely traded under CUSFTA. Companies whose economic contribution to the region was less significant could not participate in free CUSFTA trade.

The 50 percent CUSFTA content rule of origin proved difficult to apply. In one noted case, it became especially controversial regarding Honda automobiles. See Cantin and Lowenfeld, 87 Am. J. Int'l Law 375 (1993). The dispute centered on how to treat third party content that was "rolled up." Honda-U.S. exported auto engines with 10 percent third party content to Honda-Canada. Since the value of the engines was 90 percent United States in origin, when Honda-Canada installed the engines in its automobiles, it "rolled up" (treated as American) the 10 percent third party content when it subsequently shipped the autos to the United States.

Canada took the position that the engines were 100 percent American in origin. But U.S. Customs ruled that the 10 percent third-party engine value could not be rolled up in this manner, which meant that overall, the autos did not meet the 50 percent CUSFTA content rule. They therefore could not be freely traded and were subject to United States tariffs. The *Honda* case reverberated in the NAFTA negotiations. Important changes were later made in the North American rules of origin for automobiles. The "roll-up/roll-down" issue has re-emerged under the USMCA. See Chapter 6.

Special rules of origin for textiles and clothing were created under CUSFTA and then tightened under NAFTA. Demanding "fabric-forward" production requirements were stipulated to exclude third party textile goods from CUSFTA free trade. Certain fabrics (like silk) were exempt from these special CUSFTA origin requirements.

Product Standards

Canada and the United States focused on technical product standards as nontariff trade barriers in Chapter 6 of their agreement. Unusually, and importantly, Chapter 6 did not apply to state, provincial or local governments. The GATT Code on Technical Barriers to Trade of 1979 was affirmed by the two countries. This Code provided that technical standards and product certification systems could not be used to create obstacles to trade, and foreign goods had to be treated no less favorably regarding standards than domestic goods. Coverage of process and production methods (PPMs) was omitted from the 1979 Code.

Under CUSFTA, "standards-related measures" (SRM) (including production processes) and "product approval procedures" were subject to free trade goals (Article 603). If the demonstrable purpose of standards was to achieve legitimate domestic objectives without excluding goods fulfilling those objectives, then CUSFTA's terms were met. Otherwise, a disguised obstacle to Canada-United States trade might occur and breach the treaty. Regarding each other's standards and certification systems, Canada and the United States generally granted mutual recognition. This approach meant that most goods certified as meeting technical standards by Canada, or the United States, could be freely traded.

A separate and detailed Chapter 7 was created for agricultural, food and beverage products. For these goods, a unification or harmonization approach was adopted for both standards and inspection procedures. In further contrast, CUSFTA's harmonized "sanitary and phytosanitary" (SPS) rules were made binding on state, provincial and local governments.

Free Trade Exceptions

Article 1201 of CUSFTA incorporated Article XX of the GATT 1947 agreement. Article XX creates general exceptions to the free movement of goods. These exceptions, however, may not be used in ways constituting "a means of arbitrary or unjustifiable discrimination" or "a disguised restriction on international trade."

The exceptions to international free trade in goods found in Article XX of the GATT include restraints of trade justified on grounds of public morals, protection of human, animal or plant life or health, compliance with laws and regulations which are compatible with the GATT, prison labor, and protection of national historic or artistic treasures. Article XX also exempted international restraints of trade undertaken to conserve natural resources (jointly undertaken with restraints on the domestic sector), to adhere to intergovernmental commodity agreements or domestic price stabilization programs, and in response to supply shortages.

Canada attempted to invoke Article XX to conserve Pacific salmon and herring as exhaustible natural resources by means of "landing" requirements. A CUSFTA dispute settlement panel ruled against Canada, finding that these requirements were enacted to restrain trade as well as conserve the species (CDA–89–1807–01). The panel doubted that the alleged conservation benefits were sufficiently large to justify the commercial inconvenience of landing *all* salmon and herring caught in Canada's Pacific waters. Despite this ruling, and CUSFTA Commission efforts at compromise, Canada has continued to impose limited landing requirements as Canadian fisherman assert excessive catches by U.S. boats.

A second group of CUSFTA general exceptions to free trade, borrowed from GATT 1947, deal with "national security." Article 2003 of CUSFTA was essentially lifted from Article XXI of the GATT 1947 agreement. Under it, restrictions on the flow of security-related information, actions to protect national security interests (such as non-proliferation of nuclear weapons), and United Nations peace and security obligations were recognized exceptions to CUSFTA free trade.

However, there was a special agreement regarding energy goods. Such goods could not be restricted except as necessary to: (1) Supply the Canadian or United States military when facing domestic armed conflicts; (2) fulfill critical defense contracts; (3) implement nuclear non-proliferation agreements; or (4) respond to direct threats of disruption in the supply of nuclear defense materials. This proviso reinforced the general CUSFTA commitments made to free trade in energy discussed below.

The Enduring Canadian Cultural Industries Exclusion

Canada has a long history of supporting cultural industries through investment, financial, tax and other governmental acts. The 1989 free trade and foreign investment agreement between Canada and the United States excluded "cultural industries" from its scope. *This exclusion has been retained under NAFTA* and the *USMCA*. The Canadian cultural industry exclusion covers the entire gamut of the NAFTA and USMCA agreements. It applies to goods, services, investment, intellectual property, and dispute settlement.

The argument for this exclusion is not to keep American culture out of the market, but instead to assure a Canadian presence as well. Indeed, Canada maintains that it has neither attempted nor succeeded in keeping out American cultural products and services. That certainly seems right. Over 90 percent of Canada's movie screens and more than 80 percent of its news and TV broadcasts are U.S. controlled. Books of U.S. origin occupy 60 percent of all Canadian shelf space and U.S. magazines take 80 percent of the English-language market.

Cultural industries are defined those engaged in publishing, distributing, or selling:

- Books, periodicals and newspapers (except their printing or typesetting);
- Films or videos; audio or video music recordings; or printed or machine readable music;
- Public radio communications;
- Radio, television, and cable TV broadcasting; and
- Satellite programming and broadcasting network services (Article 2012).

One practical effect of securing the cultural industries exclusion has been to insulate Canada's broadcasting regulations from regional scrutiny. In Canada, content requirements and airtime rules are an important means by which the Canadian Radio-Television and Telecommunications Commission (CRTC) restricts the amount of foreign broadcast material. Current broadcasting regulations employ a quota system mandating Canadian content for a minimum of 60 percent of all programming and 50 percent of prime time. Comparable quotas apply to films, broadcast TV, cable TV and satellite transmissions. "Canadian content" is calculated under a points system traditionally requiring that the producer be Canadian and that at least 6 of 10 key creative positions be filled by Canadians. In addition, most production and distribution expenses must be paid to Canadians.

The requirements for radio are similar and focus on the nationality of the composer and performer, and the location and performance of the selection. The government also provides subsidies and tax incentives for national broadcasting enterprises which have financial difficulty in complying with content quotas. Furthermore, investment regulations effectively limit U.S. ownership or control of Canadian cultural enterprises. For example, Canada refused to permit Borders to open a super-bookstore in Toronto even after securing a Canadian partner as a majority owner. Ironically, although these economically driven rules ensure a national presence in broadcasting, they do not guarantee Canadian cultural content.

All that said, technology has greatly diminished the effectiveness of Canada's audio-visual content rules. Satellite transmission and Internet streaming have made inroads. There is a thriving gray market for dishes aimed at U.S. satellites receiving services paid via a U.S. billing address. More broadly, the Internet has undermined Canada's cultural industry trade restraints in ways that mostly avoid even the most determined regulator. Canadian limits on access to Netflix titles, for example, have been widely circumvented by obtaining U.S. Internet addresses via virtual private networks (VPN) installed on Canadian computers and other devices.

In contrast, there is no cultural industry exclusion under NAFTA or USMCA applicable to Mexico-United States trade and foreign investment. Integration of U.S.-Mexican cultural industries is occurring. In 1996, for example, the United States and Mexico reached agreement allowing companies in either country to compete for provision of satellite services, including direct-to-home and direct broadcast services. Each country retains the right to impose "reasonable" ownership, content, and advertising regulations, but Mexico (unlike Canada) will not impose local content requirements.

There are exceptions and qualifications to the general exclusion of Canadian cultural industries from CUSFTA, NAFTA and USMCA free trade. Tariff reductions were specified under CUSFTA for film, cassettes, records, cameras, musical instruments, and the like. Additional tariff reductions were agreed to in NAFTA. Responding to a United States complaint about Canadian cable TV "pirates," copyright royalties must be paid when U.S.-sourced free transmissions are retransmitted to the Canadian public by cable. In addition, no alteration or non-simultaneous retransmission of such broadcasts is permitted without the permission of the copyright holder. Likewise, no retransmission of cable or pay TV can occur without such authorization.

Occasionally, United States investors may acquire a Canadian cultural industry company by merger or acquisition. If ordered to divest, the U.S. investor must be paid open market value by Canada. Canada, for example, forced Simon & Shuster to divest a Canadian textbook publisher to a Canadian company, which subsequently went bankrupt. No other parties being interested, the Canadian government was obliged to buy the textbook publisher and sold it back to Simon & Shuster.

Canadian Cultural Industries Exclusion—the Sports Illustrated Dispute

Canada's cultural industry exception comes with a price. The United States can unilaterally implement retaliation for cultural industry protection. The U.S. can undertake "measures of equivalent commercial effect" against acts that would have been "inconsistent" with CUSFTA but for the cultural industries exclusion (Article 2005.2). There is no need to utilize CUSFTA's dispute settlement procedures prior to retaliation, which can be anything except a violation of the free trade agreement. The United States could, for example, pursue "Section 301" investigations and unilateral retaliation under the Trade Act of 1974. See Section 1.1. Each year the United States Trade Representative must identify new Canadian acts, policies and practices affecting cultural industries.

Both Canada and the United States have sought to minimize the potential for cultural industry disputes through negotiations. The "successful" resolution of the Country Music Television (CMT) dispute in 1995 is often cited as an example. CMT of Nashville had, in the absence of a Canadian competitor, been licensed as a Canadian cable TV distributor. When a competitor emerged, CMT's license was revoked by the CRTC. CMT then petitioned the USTR for Section 301 relief, and an investigation commenced. Intergovernmental negotiations resulted in the creation of a partnership of the two competitors, which was then licensed by the CRTC.

Cultural industry disputes have also been diverted from CUSFTA by using the World Trade Organization as an alternative forum. In March of 1997, a WTO Dispute Settlement Panel ruled that Canada's taxes, import regulations and postal subsidies concerning magazines (and advertising) violated the GATT 1994 agreement (*WT/DS31/AB/R (1997)*). This longstanding dispute centered on *Sports Illustrated*. Canada was seeking to protect and ensure "Canadian issues" of periodicals and prevent the export of its advertising revenues. The United States overcame culturally based Canadian policies by electing to pursue WTO remedies, although Canada's compliance was disputed. In May of 1999, a settlement was reached. United States publishers may now wholly own Canadian magazines. In addition, Canada permits U.S. split-run editions without Canadian editorial content. Such editions may contain Canadian advertisements not above 12 percent by lineage (rising to 18 percent).

Professor Oliver Goodenough has thoughtfully analyzed Canada's preoccupation with culture. See 15 Ariz. J. Int'l & Comp. Law 203 (1998). He believes that the cultural industry exclusion reflects a weak national identity and that a principal purpose is to rally Canadians around their flag in a "recurring pageant of threat and defense." Professor Goodenough notes that the "war" against Hollywood is primarily protective of Anglophone Canada. Francophone Canada, with a healthy cultural identity, has already demonstrated resilience to U.S. and Anglophonic Canadian influences.

Reaching into the literature on "culture transmission theory," Professor Goodenough finds that most foreign influences will "bounce off" healthy cultures without government intervention or, at the very least, compartmentalize such influences in ways which separate them from hearth and home. He concludes that Canada is "defending the imaginary to death" and if it continues to press its cultural protection policies: "[I]t will indeed be to the death, a death brought about not by 'invasion' from the south, but by the incomparably better claims to culturally based nationhood possessed by Francophone Quebec and by the First Nation Peoples. Rather than acting as a rallying cry for national preservation, cultural protection provides the intellectual basis for a break-up of Canada."

Procurement

The GATT Procurement Code of 1979, along with past (1986) and future (1995) amendments, was incorporated by reference into CUSFTA. The agreement, however, surpassed the Code as it existed in 1989 in several important ways. The number of goods eligible for free procurement trade was increased, the value of eligible contracts decreased to $25,000 U.S. and its equivalent in Canadian dollars, and a general rule of most-favored-treatment for goods with at least 50 percent cost-based CUSFTA origin was established.

Canada and the United States also agreed to create opportunities to challenge procurement awards before administrative authorities, a remedy followed in NAFTA, the 1995 WTO Procurement Code, and under the USMCA as between Mexico and the United States. See Chapter 6.

Temporary Safeguard Import Restraints

In a step well ahead of the rest of the world, Canada and the United States agreed to dramatically reduce their rights to take unilateral, temporary action against import surges. When such surges cause or threaten serious injury to domestic producers of similar or competing products, Article XIX (the "escape or safeguards clause") of the GATT permits taking relief in the form of tariffs, quotas, voluntary trade restraints or other protection measures. Nations impacted by such relief can retaliate equivalently. Canada and the United States significantly limited each other's right to pursue *bilateral* escape clause relief. After 1997, CUSFTA eliminated bilateral escape clause relief except with the other's unlikely consent. This ban continued in effect under NAFTA but was softened in the USMCA. See Chapter 6.

A different type of escape clause relief (known as "global actions") could be undertaken when the trade involves third parties. If global actions were taken under the GATT, neither Canada nor the United States may restrict imports from the other unless they are "substantial" and "contributing importantly" to injury or its threat (Article 1102). However, several WTO Appellate Body rulings cast doubt on the legality of excluding or favoring Canada or Mexico in global escape clause proceedings. See *U.S.—Lamb Meat from New Zealand*, WT/DS 177/AB/R (May 16, 2001).

While the huge amount of trade between Canada and the United States is not always harmonious, CUSFTA virtually took Canada-United States trade out of escape clause proceedings. In contrast, NAFTA 1994 established escape clauses to insure against the possibility of import surges from Mexico. Temporary import restraints were even subject to a special "understanding" supplementing NAFTA.

Wine, Beer, and Spirits

The barriers to trade in alcoholic beverages between the United States and Canada presented a complex regulatory maze. Beer was so difficult that little agreement was reached, and existing restraints were retained on both sides of the border. Wine and spirits were dissected under Chapter 8 of CUSFTA, and these rules remained in force under NAFTA.

Nondiscriminatory national treatment and most-favored sub-national treatment on licensing the sale of wine and spirits was required. Wine and spirits licensing had to be undertaken using normal commercial considerations without causing disguised barriers to trade. Prompt, fair, and objective appeals from administrative boards were to be made available to applicants from either side of the border. Furthermore, pricing decisions by public distributors had to be nondiscriminatory, but could reflect actual cost-of-service differentials between handling domestic and imported wines or spirits. Canadian price mark-ups above those levels were removed between 1989 and 1995.

Regulations governing the distribution of wine and spirits were also subject to general national and most-favored treatment rules. Certain traditional exceptions continue in force. For example, Ontario and British Columbia obliged private sellers to favor wines originating in their provinces. And Quebec required food stores to sell wine bottled in that province. Canada did eliminate longstanding blending requirements on U.S. bulk distilled spirits, and the exclusive right to sell products labeled Bourbon Whiskey and Canadian Whiskey was recognized. Under NAFTA, exclusivity was also extended to Tennessee Whiskey and Mexican Tequila and Mezcal.

The extensive CUSFTA 1989 dismantling of restrictive trade regulations governing wine and spirits contrasts with the coverage of beer. Restrictive and discriminatory beer practices in effect on October 4, 1987, were retained. Only new restraints had to conform to the national and most-favored treatment obligations. Notably,

Canada and the United States reserved their GATT 1947 rights and obligations for wine, spirits, *and* beer.

The GATT subsequently provided a venue to challenge some of the trade restraints on beer preserved by CUSFTA. See GATT Doc. DS17/R (Oct. 16, 1991); BISD395/206 (June 19, 1991). Ontario, for example, maintained "warehouse charges" and "environmental" taxes that mostly hit U.S. beer. The United States at one point slapped a 50 percent tariff on Ontario beer. By filing GATT complaints and engaging in negotiations, both countries largely succeeded in removing restraints of trade on beer. This was the last of the Canadian-U.S. "beer wars."

Energy

Canada exports large amounts of oil, gas, coal, electricity, and uranium to the United States. This helps meet the energy-hungry needs of the United States. The CUSFTA provisions on trade in energy goods contained in Chapter 9 were unusually significant. Similar provisions were retained under NAFTA, but there was a dispute about their meaning if an energy crisis occurred.

The Canadian National Energy Board (NEB) regulates trade in energy goods by licensing surplus exports. The NEB has the power to regulate the prices of Canadian energy imports and exports, determining whether prices are "just and reasonable." The United States perceived this price regulation as constituting minimum export price controls. Article 902(2) of the CUSFTA agreement banned such price controls. CUSFTA also disallowed charging higher than domestic prices for energy exports. Furthermore, since Canada taxes the export of energy goods, Article 903 prohibited discriminatory taxation. Export taxes and fees were permissible only if they were imposed domestically, and Canada consequently adjusted export taxes.

Perhaps most importantly for the national security of the United States, Canadian law authorizes the NEB to restrain energy exports in times of crisis, as Canada did during the world oil shocks of the 1970s. Article 904(a) of CUSFTA is less than a model of clarity but seems to remove this authorization as it might apply to exports to the United States. Canada appeared instead obliged in a crisis to maintain the prior proportion of exports to domestic production. The standard proportions among the various energy exports to the United States had apparently also to be maintained. The only exception to these duties was if sharing under the International Energy Program is imposed. *The USMCA dropped these controversial provisions.*

Motor Vehicles

Under their bilateral Auto Pact of 1965, Canada and the United States substantially embraced free trade in new automobiles and OEM parts. The Auto Pact was retained under CUSFTA (and NAFTA 1994) subject to some changes. Tariffs on auto parts traded between Canada and the United States were extinguished. Canada's historic blockage of the importation of used vehicles from the United States was also eliminated. The United States adopted the more rigorous 50 percent regional content test of origin found in CUSFTA but permitted manufacturers to average their value content over 12 months.

On the Canadian side, the Auto Pact was limited under CUSFTA to the Big Three and by special exception CAMI (a General Motors-Suzuki joint venture). No other manufacturers (including various Japanese companies) could acquire preferential Auto Pact status. They and other manufacturers had to meet the general CUSFTA rule of origin content requirements. Canada further agreed to abolish tariff refunds and waivers for non-Auto Pact producers. But Canada retained its sales to production performance ratio obligations and various "Canadian value-added" content rules for Auto Pact companies.

Services

The United States, with many highly competitive service providers, sought a general commitment to free trade in services from Canada. Chapters 14 and 17 of CUSFTA made it clear that the U.S. failed to generally obtain free trade in services. Substantial free trade in "covered" services was all that could be agreed upon. Annex 1408 of the CUSFTA agreement listed the services subject to its free provision rules. This list included some glaring omissions, such as transportation, that were not remedied until NAFTA 1994.

Service providers and service seekers acquired benefits under CUSFTA. The "provision" of covered services included the right to locate in one country and service clients in the other. Provision embraced production, distribution, sale, purchase, marketing, delivery, and use of covered services. Provision also included access to and use of domestic distribution systems. Beneficiaries could establish a "commercial presence" to facilitate covered services, such as establishing a sales agency or branch office in the other country. The right to invest to provide covered services was also protected. Indeed, virtually *any* activity associated with the provision of covered services was allowed, including the organization, control, operation, maintenance and disposition of companies, branches, agencies, offices, or other facilities to conduct business as well as borrowing money and handling property.

Who could provide services was clarified in Article 201 of CUSFTA. Canadian and United States nationals *and* enterprises principally carrying on business in either country were the main beneficiaries. Such businesses had to be incorporated or otherwise constituted under Canadian or United States laws. The Agreement's focus on principal place of business meant that Canadian or U.S. businesses owned or controlled by individuals or companies from other nations benefited from free trade in CUSFTA-covered services. Denial of these third-party benefits was possible only if the service was provided "indirectly." This exception functioned like a rule of origin. It ensured that only service providers with substantial businesses in Canada or the United States could partake of free trade.

Cross-border CUSFTA service providers and seekers received "no less favorable" treatment than nationals and enterprises under Canadian and United States laws. For each federal government, national treatment was the general rule. Each state, province or local government was obliged to grant most-favored-nation treatment to service providers and seekers. Ironically, while California could give less than most-favored treatment to New York service providers, it could not do so to Canadians. *Since CUSFTA's beneficiaries included enterprises principally carrying on business in Canada or the United States, third party subsidiaries qualified for national and most-favored-nation services treatment.*

There were significant exceptions to the CUSFTA standards for service providers. Canada and the United States indefinitely retained (in their 1989 form) inconsistent statutes and regulations. Furthermore, Article 1402.3 allowed for deviations in treatment for prudential, fiduciary, health and safety or consumer protection reasons. Any such different treatment had to be "equivalent in effect" to that applied domestically for the same reasons. No deviation could require the establishment of a commercial presence to provide services in the other country. And, borrowing from GATT 1947 language relating to goods, no deviation (including tax laws), could serve as an "arbitrary or unjustifiable discrimination" or a "disguised restriction" on CUSFTA trade in services.

Canada and the United States retained their own licensing and certification systems for services. They agreed that these systems should "relate principally to competence or the ability to provide" covered services. (Article 1403) Licensing and certification could not discriminatorily impair or restrain access. Existing inconsistent statutes and regulations were indefinitely retained, but no new licensing or certification statute or regulation could require a commercial presence, arbitrarily discriminate, or disguise a trade restraint.

Financial Services

The provisions of Chapter 17 of CUSFTA reflected the complexity and sensitivity of the financial services sector. For purposes of Chapter 17, "financial services" were defined to exclude securities underwriting and sales of insurance policies. Insurance services were generally a covered service under Chapter 14 of CUSFTA.

Each country made commitments to alter specific statutes and regulations to benefit the other's financial sector. These commitments were retained under NAFTA. Canada made commitments on financial services in three key sectors:

(1) Greater U.S. ownership of Canadian banks;

(2) Deregulation of U.S.-controlled foreign bank subsidiaries; and

(3) Reduced application of Canada's foreign investment control laws.

The United States also made three major commitments on financial services:

(1) Permission for U.S. banks to underwrite Canadian debt;

(2) Extension of future U.S. Glass-Steagall Act (48 Stat. 162) amendments to Canadian-controlled financial institutions; and

(3) A promise not to restrict interstate branching rules.

The Canadian commitments allowed United States residents and U.S. companies controlled by such persons to acquire Canadian banks and federally regulated trust, loan and life insurance companies. However, no one person could own more than 10 percent of a Schedule A bank class of securities. Limits on the total domestic assets of banking subsidiaries controlled by U.S. citizens or permanent residents were removed, as were restraints on the transfer of loans from subsidiaries to their parent companies. Moreover, new branches of U.S.-controlled banking subsidiaries could be opened without getting the approval the Minister of Finance. More broadly, Canada agreed not to apply its investment review powers over U.S. financial institutions in a manner that would be inconsistent with the "aims" of Chapter 17.

The United States commitments permitted federally regulated U.S. banks to underwrite and market the debt of Canada, its political subdivisions, and the debt of Canadian agencies backed by full faith and credit. This authority was an exception to the general prohibition against U.S. banks dealing in securities contained in the Glass-Steagall Act of 1933. Canadian public debt has since been more readily sold in the United States. If the U.S. amended the Glass-Steagall Act or its regulations at any future time (which it has now done), Canadian-controlled financial institutions had to be given equal treatment. For these limited purposes, a financial institution controlled directly or indirectly by persons who ordinarily reside in Canada sufficed. In the event of federal regulation of interstate branches, the United States agreed not to adopt or apply any laws that would be more restrictive on Canadian banks than those in force at the state level on October 4, 1987.

These commitments notwithstanding, Canada and the United States publicly expressed mutual dissatisfaction with treatment of financial institutions in the other's country. Both promised no reduction in existing rights and privileges, except if the benefits from future deregulation of financial markets were not extended to each other absent "normal regulatory and prudential considerations." Canada and the United States gave each other notice and an opportunity to comment on proposed financial regulations. Consultation between the Canadian Department of Finance and the U.S. Treasury Department was frequent. Such consultations generally displaced regional dispute settlement procedures.

Foreign Investment

Chapter 16 of CUSFTA governed laws, regulations and policies generally affecting cross-border investment by Canadian or United States investors. However, financial services, cultural industries, transportation services, government procurement and services not covered by CUSFTA did not benefit from Chapter 16. CUSFTA created a rule of national treatment at the federal level and most-favored treatment at lower levels of government. Such rules covered establishing new businesses, acquiring, or selling existing ones, and conducting business operations.

The foreign investment rules of CUSFTA applied *only* to United States and Canadian nationals, governments, and enterprises they controlled. This differed from CUSFTA free trade in services which benefited third party providers established or principally doing business in Canada or the United States. Nevertheless, it was forbidden to require that shareholders include nationals of either country. Nor could investors be forced due to nationality to divest a qualified investment.

Perhaps most importantly, Canada undertook to amend its 1985 Investment Canada Act (ICA). The ICA normally applied to foreign acquisitions of Canadian businesses worth more than 5 million Canadian dollars. CUSFTA did not suspend the ICA's application to U.S. acquisitions of existing Canadian businesses, but it did alter the thresholds triggering Canadian review. Only direct acquisitions or sales of Canadian firms subject to CUSFTA that exceeded $150 million Canadian dollars could be reviewed by Canada's investment authorities. Indirect acquisitions of Canadian businesses were not reviewable unless they fell in the economic sectors excluded from CUSFTA. These commitments were continued under NAFTA.

The United States could not trigger dispute settlement about any Canadian decision under the ICA regarding an acquisition by a U.S. investor. Significantly from the point of view of existing U.S. investors in Canada, the $150 million threshold also triggered a "right of exit." Canadian investments below that amount could be sold to non-Canadians without ICA review.

Performance requirements were a central focus of CUSFTA's investment rules. They could not be imposed as a condition to allowing or operating an investment. Article 1603 prohibited (for CUSFTA investors) performance requirements on exports, obligations to substitute or purchase local goods or services, and domestic content minimums. Even so, certain types of performance requirements (notably employment, technology transfer, or research and development obligations) were permissible for CUSFTA investors. With third party investors, any performance requirement could be used, provided this did not have a "significant impact" on trade between Canada and the United States.

Direct or indirect nationalization or expropriation of investments held by each other's investors was banned by CUSFTA 1989. The only exception was for nondiscriminatory public purposes in accordance with due process of law and upon payment of prompt, adequate and effective compensation at fair market value. Cross-border CUSFTA investors were free to transfer their profits, dividends, royalties, fees, interest, and other earnings or proceeds from the sale or liquidation of their investments. Canada or the United States could prevent such transfers (acting equitably, without discrimination and in good faith) under their bankruptcy, insolvency, creditors' rights, securities, criminal, currency transfer reporting, tax withholding or court judgment enforcement laws. New tax or subsidy rules were allowed provided they did not arbitrarily or unjustifiably discriminate between Canadian or U.S. investors, or function as a disguised restriction on the CUSFTA benefits of those investors.

Note that there were no provisions allowing foreign investors to file claims against governments for damages caused by alleged violations of rights created under CUSFTA. Such remedies became a controversial focus of dispute settlement under NAFTA. See Section 4.10.

Temporary Visas for Businesspersons

Chapter 15 of CUSFTA 1989 governed *temporary* entry for businesspersons engaged in trading goods or services, or cross-border investors. Similar provisions were found under NAFTA. Four groups of persons were granted preferential treatment: (1) Business visitors; (2) professionals; (3) traders and (substantial) investors; and (4) intra-company transferees. In the event of disputes concerning the entry of businesspersons, all available appeals in Canada or the United States had to be first pursued. Only if there was a pattern of restrictive practices was dispute settlement under Chapter 18 of CUSFTA an option.

All four categories were exempted from labor certification or employment validation tests demonstrating in advance that a local person could not fulfill the needs that these businesspersons temporarily met. On the other hand, all such businesspersons had to meet the standard national security, public health, and safety requirements for entry. Except for business visitors, employment authorization prior to entering the other country was required. *Tens of thousands of Canadian professionals took advantage of CUSFTA visas to head south for employment in the United States.*

CUSFTA Dispute Settlement

Dispute settlement under NAFTA replaced comparable procedures first established under CUSFTA. Chapter 18 of CUSFTA employed consultations and, if necessary, arbitration to settle most kinds of disputes. Chapter 19 of CUSFTA utilized special binational panels to resolve antidumping and countervailing duty disputes. All the CUSFTA dispute settlement decisions, including those cited in this chapter, can be obtained at www.nafta-sec-alena.org.

None of CUSFTA's dispute settlement procedures were mandatory. For example, disputes that could be resolved under CUSFTA, the GATT 1947 agreement, or the GATT Tokyo Round Codes could be pursued in either forum. Practically speaking, forum shopping as between Chapters 18 and 19 and the GATT (now WTO) was perfectly acceptable. However, once an avenue of relief was chosen by the complaining party, the dispute had to be resolved there exclusively.

One reason behind this legitimization of forum shopping was the sorry state of GATT 1947 and GATT Code dispute settlement procedures in 1989. "Working-Groups" or panels composed of experts who were not from the nations in dispute issued a "report." This report made findings of fact, rendered conclusions of law, and made remedial recommendations which were forwarded to the GATT Council. Lengthy, cumbersome, and subject to a consensus vote in the GATT Council, GATT dispute settlement in 1989 was not really binding as each nation could negate the panel's ruling. Even if the process worked, compliance was essentially voluntary.

The GATT (now WTO) did offer political advantages as a dispute settlement forum. Its membership of about 165 nations frequently means that others will join in the dispute, thus raising visibility and pressure. This was true for CUSFTA in 1989 and remained true under NAFTA. However, NAFTA complicated the forum selection process (see below). The USMCA also provides complainants with a WTO dispute settlement option. See Chapter 6.

Intergovernmental CUSFTA Dispute Settlement

Dispute settlement under Chapter 18 of the CUSFTA agreement applied in most instances, but notably not concerning financial services. The Canada-United States Trade Commission (TC) was the center of the Chapter 18 dispute settlement process. International trade representatives of Canada and the United States or their designees constituted the CUSFTA Trade Commission, which was aided by Secretariats in Ottawa and Washington, D.C. There were three stages to Chapter 18 dispute settlement: (1) Bilateral Consultations; (2) Trade Commission Review; and (3) Binding Arbitration.

The CUSFTA Trade Commission was after 1994 largely supplanted by the NAFTA Trade Commission. The CUSFTA Commission provided a forum to discuss CUSFTA disputes. Consultations always preceded Commission deliberations. Questions of implementation, interpretation, application, allegedly inconsistent action, or "nullification and impairment" of benefits expected under the CUSFTA agreement fell within its jurisdiction. The CUSFTA Commission had the power to delegate its responsibilities to ad hoc committees and working groups. It could also obtain the advice of nongovernmental individuals or groups. The Commission promulgated its own rules and procedures and functioned by cooperative consensus.

Notice as far in advance as possible was required of any proposed law with the potential to materially affect the operation of CUSFTA. With or without notice, Canada and the United States undertook to consult in good faith and "make every attempt" at a mutually satisfactory resolution. A meeting of the CUSFTA Trade Commission became mandatory only if no resolution was made within 30 days. The Commission then sought to resolve the dispute promptly, relying at its discretion on mediators acceptable to both sides.

For most disputes the CUSFTA Commission could refer the matter to binding arbitration only by mutual agreement. If no consensus was reached to refer the dispute to arbitration, the fallback was to appoint a panel of experts. Only in disputes concerning emergency escape clause proceedings was binding arbitration mandatory. The Commission could set the terms for arbitration of CUSFTA disputes, but unless it directed otherwise an arbitration panel was established following the provisions of Article 1807. Under Article 1807, two panelists were chosen by each side with the fifth member (absent agreement) chosen by lot. A list of qualified panelists was established by the Commission. The confidential arbitration panel set its own procedural rules, including a hearing and the right of reply.

An innovative provision of CUSFTA authorized the submission of memoranda by the governments of Canada and the United States acting jointly if possible, or singly if not, to courts or administrative tribunals in either country. Such submissions could only concern issues of interpretation, but they could be requested by a national court or tribunal entertaining CUSFTA issues in litigation. This little used request authority resembled somewhat the advisory ruling procedure followed in Europe as between national courts and the European Court of Justice. Memoranda on interpretative issues could be submitted whenever the governments of Canada or the United States considered it meritorious.

Arbitration Decisions Under CUSFTA Chapter 18

Chapter 18 of CUSFTA resulted in five binding arbitrations. Other trade disputes were taken to the GATT, and some contentious issues resolved during the NAFTA and Uruguay Round negotiations.

In the first Chapter 18 arbitration panel, the United States complained against Canadian landing requirements for fish (mostly salmon) caught in their waters. A prior GATT panel ruling against Canadian fish export controls had led to the landing requirements. The CUSFTA arbitration panel ruled with one dissent in favor of the United States argument that the requirements unfairly increased the burden of exporting Canadian fish in violation of GATT Article XI and were not exceptions under GATT Article XX, discussed above (CDA–89–1807–01). Canada accepted the panel's findings. A mutually satisfactory settlement was then reached, but salmon fishing in the Northwest remains a remarkably divisive issue to this day.

The second arbitration panel under Chapter 18 upheld United States limits on the sale of undersized lobsters. By a split vote, argued under GATT Articles III and XI which were incorporated by reference into the CUSFTA agreement, the panel decided that since both Canadian and United States lobsters were affected there was no unlawful trade restraint (USA–89–1807–01). The third CUSFTA panel upheld, contrary to a U.S. Customs Service ruling, Canada's practice of including certain interest payments in the costs of production of automobiles (USA–92–1807–01). This issue arose when Canada determined CUSFTA content in ascertaining origin under Article 304. The panel followed the Vienna Convention of the Law of Treaties in interpreting CUSFTA even though the United States is not a party to that Convention.

The fourth arbitration panel generally agreed with Canada's interpretation of Article 701.3 of the CUSFTA agreement (CDA–92–1807–01). Minimum pricing of durum wheat for sale to the United States was at issue. This dispute was surrounded by U.S. perceptions of unfair subsidization of Canadian wheat exports. Once again, the Vienna Convention was invoked to interpret CUSFTA. Canadian wheat exports have remained the center of considerable controversy, trade complaints and intergovernmental memoranda of understanding imposing tariff rate quotas.

The fifth and final CUSFTA arbitration panel concerned Puerto Rico's refusal to allow entry of "improperly certified" long-life milk from Quebec (USA–93–1807–01). Articles III and XI of the GATT were at issue. This panel generally supported the U.S. position that it was entitled to enforce its standards against Canadian goods. The panel suggested that if both countries were essentially using the same inspection standards, then entry should have been allowed as a matter of good faith to avoid nullification and impairment of CUSFTA trade benefits. Ongoing equivalency discussions between the two trade partners were recommenced.

Dumping and Subsidy Dispute Settlement

Dispute settlement under CUSFTA Chapter 19 was limited to two types of international trade law actions: Antidumping and subsidy countervailing duty proceedings. Both are GATT-authorized and regulated. See Section 1.1 and for details my Concise Hornbook on *International Trade Law*, Chapters 4 and 5. Antidumping and countervailing duty actions had been frequently used by the United States to impede entry of Canadian goods. Chapter 19 attempted to respond to critical Canadian concerns.

Such proceedings typically commenced at the request of industries that face import competition and can ultimately result in the imposition of special tariffs on imported goods. Antidumping duties apply to imported goods or services sold at below home country prices (price discrimination) that injure or threaten domestic industries. Countervailing duties apply to imported goods that have benefited from export or specific domestic governmental subsidies and have injured or threaten national industries.

Antidumping actions challenge private sector activities while countervailing duty actions question governmental acts. The amount of tariff duties possible is the margin of the dump or the level of subsidy determined to exist. Many antidumping duty proceedings (the most prevalent) are "settled" when the exporter agrees to raise its prices. Countervailing duty disputes may also be settled by intergovernmental accords. *See* the Softwood Lumber Agreement (below).

Canada and the United States had long acknowledged through the GATT the unfairness of dumping and subsidy practices. Unlike the European Union, they were unwilling to eliminate internal utilization of these trade remedies. GATT Codes on antidumping and countervailing duties provided the basic ground rules, but GATT dispute settlement was inadequate in the 1980s. Most importantly, Canada was distrustful of lengthy judicial reviews and law in U.S. courts of administrative antidumping and countervailing duty determinations. Prime Minister Mulroney walked away from the CUSFTA negotiating table to emphasize their concerns. *The result was a unique form of dispute settlement under Chapter 19 of CUSFTA that was largely replicated in NAFTA and the USMCA, procedures which exist nowhere else in the world.*

Under Chapter 19, binational panels of mutually approved experts (mostly international trade lawyers and law professors) ultimately decided antidumping and countervailing duty disputes. Prior to CUSFTA, the final resolution of such disputes had been in the national courts. Each country selected two panelists with an additional panelist chosen by mutual agreement. Each side had four opportunities to reject the other side's proposed panelists. No cause for rejection was required. A majority of the panelists had to be lawyers in good standing.

The administrative proceedings of Canada and the United States determining the existence of dumping or a countervailable subsidy remained in place. These decisions are made by the International Trade Administration (Commerce Dept.) in the United States and by the Deputy Minister of National Revenue for Customs and Excise in Canada. Likewise, the domestic proceedings used to decide if there has been material injury (or its threat) to a domestic industry were also retained. These decisions are made by the U.S. International Trade Commission and the Canadian Import Tribunal.

All Chapter 19 proceedings were pursued under the laws of Canada and the United States, neither of which was substantively changed by CUSFTA 1989. The critical change was the remarkable surrender of judicial sovereignty accomplished by Chapter 19. After CUSFTA, all final national administrative determinations in antidumping or countervailing duty proceedings were only "appealable" by all interested parties to a quasi-judicial binational CUSFTA panel.

When an antidumping or subsidy proceeding came before a CUSFTA panel, the legal principles that would have been used by a court in the importing country controlled. For binational panels reviewing final U.S. determinations this meant that U.S. Supreme Court and Federal Circuit Court of Appeal (but not Court of International Trade) decisions were binding precedent. By its terms, CUSFTA provided that previous panel decisions were not to be treated as precedent. NAFTA and USMCA also retain these rules.

There were no new CUSFTA standards for review. With much controversy, each panel proceeded to apply the different standards of judicial review traditionally found in the law of Canada and the United States. For example, Canada's standards of review under the Federal Court Act § 28(1) are failure to observe principles of natural justice, jurisdictional abuse, errors in law, and pervasive, capricious, or insupportable erroneous findings of fact. The standards of the U.S. Tariff Act of 1930 § 516A(b)(1)(A) and (B) are findings or conclusions unsupported by substantial evidence in the record or otherwise not in accordance with law.

There were over fifty CUSFTA Chapter 19 panel decisions, with more than two-thirds of them reviewing U.S. antidumping and countervailing duty determinations. Not surprisingly, trade in steel products garnered first place in the pursuit of market protection. The U.S. steel industry has a long history of resorting to antidumping and countervailing duties to obtain shelter from import competition. Many observers noted that the mere filing of AD and CVD complaints can produce some breathing room for domestic industries.

Most Chapter 19 panel decisions under CUSFTA were rendered in less than a year. Technically, these decisions either affirmed the final determination under review or, reversing, referred the determination back to the relevant administrative tribunal. It was up to that tribunal to take appropriate action. If it did not, and a second panel review took place, the agency was typically instructed to act in a not inconsistent manner by the second or (infrequently) third panel. The only further review, a final appeal by Canada or the United States (not the interested parties) of a panel decision, could come before an "Extraordinary Challenge Committee" (ECC). Such Committees were composed of three mutually acceptable judges.

ECC review of binational Chapter 19 panel decisions was intended to be truly extraordinary. In fact, there were only three such reviews (see below) between 1989 and 1994. All of them were raised by the United States. Many believe these challenges were politically motivated, in part to persuade Congress to extend fast-track trade agreements authority to the President and in part to assuage key private sector interests.

Challenges to CUSFTA (and NAFTA/USMCA) panel decisions were allowed only in limited circumstances such as if a panel member engaged in gross misconduct, was biased, or had a serious conflict of interest. Challenges could also be raised if the panel departed seriously from a fundamental rule of procedure, or it manifestly exceeded its powers, authority, or jurisdiction. The challenger has the duty to prove that the error alleged materially influenced the panel's decision and threatened the integrity of the review process.

Binational Panel and Extraordinary Challenge Committee Decisions Under Chapter 19

The legal and political controversy surrounding Chapter 19 panel decisions under CUSFTA sometimes blurs their practical consequences for tariffs and trade between the two countries. A careful reconstruction of that impact was undertaken by a leading international trade attorney. See Mercury, 15 N.W. J. Int'l Law & Bus. 525 (1995). This study demonstrates that Canadian exporters were disproportionate beneficiaries in terms of CUSFTA Chapter 19 outcomes.

Chapter 19 dispute settlement under CUSFTA in the five years prior to NAFTA 1994 was voluminous. With a few exceptions, most analyses of these decisions suggest an objective and not terribly politicized process. But the ability of binational panels to expertly rule under Canadian and United States law has been hotly contested. A prominent U.S. judge involved in the infamous *Softwood Lumber* dispute wrote a blistering dissent. See *ECC–94–1904–01–USA* (Wilkey, J.). Some administrative determinations had to be repeatedly reviewed by CUSFTA panels before compliance was achieved. One must wonder whether Chapter 19, which was intended to reduce trade tensions and suspicions, did not instead intensify Canada-U.S. antidumping and countervailing duty disputes.

Appeals to CUSFTA Extraordinary Challenge Committees demonstrated limited opportunities for relief. For example, the first Extraordinary Challenge Committee decision concerned U.S. countervailing duties on Canadian exports of pork (*ECC–91–1904–01–USA*). The initial binational panel decision questioned the substantiality of the evidence supporting the International Trade Commission's domestic injury determination. Upon reconsideration, the ITC found a threat of material injury to the U.S. domestic pork industry for a second time. A second binational panel decision ruled that the ITC had exceeded its notice for the proceedings and issued specific evidentiary instructions to the ITC.

The ITC's next decision bitterly denounced the second binational panel's ruling. The ITC asserted that the panel's decision violated fundamental principles of CUSFTA and contained egregious errors of U.S. law. Nevertheless, the ITC acquiesced. It determined no threat of material injury expressly (and only) because of the binding nature of the CUSFTA panel's decision. The United States Trade Representative alleged gross error and sought review by Extraordinary Challenge Committee of the panel's *Pork* rulings. The Committee unanimously held that there was no gross error even if some of the panel determinations might not have followed U.S. rules of evidence. The Committee did caution panels not to rely on evidence not appearing in the record of the national proceedings.

The second extraordinary challenge concerned exports of live swine from Canada (*ECC–93–1904–01–USA*). Once again, the Committee unanimously ruled against the challenge, although it did acknowledge that the panel may have made errors of law.

The Endless Softwood Lumber Dispute

The bitterly disputed binational panel decisions on U.S. countervailing duty actions against Canadian exports of softwood lumber did not conclude with the third Extraordinary Challenge Committee proceeding in 1994 from which Judge Wilkey so vigorously dissented. Trade tensions and negotiations continued. Canada, the victor before the Challenge Committee, appeared to realize that it might lose the next time around if changes in U.S. countervailing duty law were recognized. Indeed, these changes were undertaken specifically for that purpose. In 1996, a "settlement" was reached.

The 1996 Softwood Lumber Agreement applied to Alberta, British Columbia, Ontario, and Quebec. It committed Quebec, for example, to raising its "stumpage" (timbering) fees. British Columbia (the largest exporter) promised to impose taxes on shipments of lumber to the U.S. above designated levels starting at 9 billion board feet. In addition, the Canadian federal government promised to impose taxes if exports exceed 14.7 billion board feet. The U.S. government and forest industry, in turn, pledged not to commence a countervailing duty action for 5 years so long as the agreement was followed.

In 2001, the 1996 Agreement lapsed and U.S. countervailing duties on Canadian lumber were renewed, followed by Canadian challenges under NAFTA and within the WTO. Billions of dollars in U.S. antidumping and countervailing duties on Canadian lumber were collected. In 2006, a second Softwood Lumber Agreement was achieved. Canada, then with about 34 percent of the U.S. softwood lumber market, agreed to impose rising export taxes if prices fall below specified trigger levels. About 80 percent of the duties previously collected were returned to Canadian producers.

The Second Agreement was to be "dispute-free" for a minimum of three years. Nevertheless, the U.S. commenced arbitration proceedings before the London Court of International Arbitration (LCIA) in 2007 and 2009 challenging the adequacy of Canadian implementation of the Agreement. Several LCIA rulings subsequently found Canada in breach of the 2006 Agreement. The 2006 Agreement was extended to October 2015.

To this day, softwood lumber disputes continue. Indeed, the Trump Administration levied countervailing duties on Canadian lumber in 2017 prior to commencing re-negotiation of NAFTA. Canada promised compensation to its exporters and filed yet another dispute under NAFTA and before the WTO. In 2021, the Biden Administration followed suit with another round of CVD on Canadian softwood lumber imports. As always, such duties raise the cost of new and re-modeled housing in the United States.

NAFTA

The United States is Mexico's largest trading partner, accounting in 1994 for nearly 70 percent of all Mexican trade and more than 60 percent of its foreign direct investment. In contrast, trade with Mexico in 1994 totaled only 7 percent of all U.S. international trade. Those facts help explain why Mexico was the major beneficiary of the NAFTA accord. *Today Mexico is the number one U.S. trade partner (surpassing even China).*

§ 4.3 Getting to NAFTA

NAFTA did not repeal the Canada-United States Free Trade Agreement. The United States and Canada "suspended" their 1989 agreement. If NAFTA failed to be re-negotiated or either Canada or the United States withdrew from it, CUSFTA would have come out of suspended animation and continue to bind the two countries.

The U.S. free trade agreement with Canada in 1989 was nothing less than path breaking, the most sophisticated free trade agreement in the world. For most Canadians and Americans, revising the design to include Mexico required considerably more effort and discomfort. The discomfort came from years of observing protectionist Mexican trade policies, uncontrolled national debt, corruption, and the sense, somehow, that Mexico just did not "fit." In the end, these perspectives were overcome.

Mexico under Presidents de la Madrid, Salinas, Zedillo, and Fox had been unobtrusively breaking down its trade barriers and reducing the role of government in its economy. More than half of the enterprises owned by the Mexican government a decade ago have been sold to private investors, and more are on the auction block. Tariffs have been slashed to a maximum of 20 percent and import licensing requirements widely removed. Export promotion, not import substitution, became the highest priority. Like the U.S. and Canada, Mexico (since 1986) participates in the General Agreement on Tariffs and Trade (GATT) and World Trade Organization (WTO). See Chapter 1. This brought it into the mainstream of the world trading community on a wide range of fronts, including participation in nearly the full range of the Uruguay Round WTO agreements.

Mexican debt, hopefully, promises to become a manageable problem, although the collapse of the peso in 1994 and its slide in 2008/09 cast doubt on this. One party rule has ended, with signs of a more pluralistic democracy on the horizon. Admittedly, political, and economic corruption still runs deep within Mexico, but the winds of change are blowing. Major prosecutions of leading police, union and business leaders have been undertaken. Perhaps most significantly, the rapid privatization of the state-owned sector of the economy combined with increasing tolerance of international competition has reduced not only the need for government subsidies but also to a degree the opportunity for personal enrichment by public officials.

Presidents Bush and Salinas, and Prime Minister Mulroney, pushed hard in 1991 to open "fast-track" negotiations for a free trade agreement. In 1992, these efforts reached fruition when a NAFTA agreement was signed by Canada, the United States and Mexico with a scheduled effective date of Jan. 1, 1994. President Bush submitted the agreement to Congress in December 1992.

President Clinton supported NAFTA generally, but initiated negotiations upon taking office for supplemental agreements on the environment and labor. This delayed consideration of the NAFTA agreement in Congress until the Fall of 1993. Ratification was considered under fast-track procedures which essentially gave Congress 90 session days to either ratify or reject NAFTA without amendments. After a bruising national debate that fractured both Democrats and Republicans with each party doing its best to avoid Ross Perot's strident anti-NAFTA attacks, ratification was achieved in mid-November, just weeks before NAFTA's effective date.

During this same period, Canada's Conservative Party suffered a devastating defeat at the polls. This defeat was partly a rejection by the Canadian people of the earlier ratification of NAFTA under Prime Minister Mulroney.

§ 4.4 Trade in Goods, Rules of Origin

Although each partner affirmed its rights and obligations under the General Agreement on Tariffs and Trade (GATT), NAFTA generally took priority over other international agreements in the event of conflict. NAFTA, for example, prevailed over the former Multi-Fiber Arrangement on trade in textiles. Certain exceptions to this general rule of supremacy applied. The trade provisions of the international agreements on endangered species, ozone-depletion and hazardous wastes notably took precedence over NAFTA (subject to a duty to minimize conflicts). Unlike the GATT/WTO, NAFTA created a general duty of national treatment for goods binding on all states, provinces, and local governments of the three countries.

Prior to NAFTA, Mexican tariffs on U.S. goods averaged about 10 percent. U.S. tariffs on Mexican imports averaged about 5 percent. Under NAFTA, Mexican tariffs were eliminated on all U.S. exports within ten years except for corn and beans which were subject to a fifteen-year transition. United States tariffs on peanuts, sugar and orange juice from Mexico also lasted 15 years. Immediate Mexican tariff removals under the "A" list covered about half the industrial products exported from the United States. Further tariff eliminations were made for the "B" list after 5 years and for the "C" list when the treaty matured in ten years. Accelerated tariff reduction may occur by bilateral accord. The existing Canada-U.S. tariff reduction schedule remained in place.

Safeguard (escape clause) rules and procedures were generally applicable to United States-Mexico trade under the NAFTA. These permitted temporary trade relief against import surges subject to a right of compensation in the exporting nation. During the 10-year transition period, escape clause relief could be undertaken only once per product for a maximum in most cases of 3 years. The relief was the "snap-back" to pre-NAFTA tariffs. After the transition period, escape clause measures could only be undertaken by mutual consent.

If a global escape clause proceeding was pursued by one NAFTA partner, the others had to be excluded unless their exports account for a substantial share of the imports in question (top five suppliers) and contribute importantly to the serious injury or threat thereof (rate of growth of NAFTA imports must not be appreciably lower than total imports).

NAFTA Rules of Origin

Mexico has the highest average tariffs on imported goods, the U.S. has the lowest, and Canada falls in the middle. Since free trade in goods only applies to goods that originate in North America, non-originating goods are subject to the normal tariffs of Canada, Mexico, and the United States. *Origin determinations are thus critical to NAFTA/USMCA traders.* There were Uniform NAFTA Regulations governing rules of origin and customs procedures, including a common Certificate of Origin.

Article 401 of NAFTA starts with the primary rule that all goods wholly obtained or produced entirely inside NAFTA originate there. Canadian lumber, U.S. apples and Mexican oil provide examples. Such goods fell under NAFTA Preference Criterion A. Article 415 authorized free trade in goods made from materials that "originate" exclusively within NAFTA, Preference Criterion C. Agricultural, timber and mining products almost always qualify as such. A laptop computer whose components all come from Mexico, Canada or the United States would qualify under Criterion C.

Article 401 adopted the change of tariff classification rule of origin initiated in CUSFTA (below). Subject to various exceptions, goods produced in one or more of the three countries with non-originating materials could be freely traded when all such materials (excepting a *de minimis* amount) undergo a change in tariff classification based upon the Harmonized Tariff System (HTS). Ordinarily this required a change at the HTS product classification level and was known as Preference Criterion B. This Criterion was the most used of all NAFTA's rules of origin for goods. *See* Example 1 below and *Cummins v. United States*, 454 F.3d 1361 (Fed. Cir. 2006) (crankshafts from Brazil not Mexico, no change in tariff classification).

Meeting the NAFTA change in tariff classification rule of origin was sometimes insufficient to allow free trading. Some goods had *also* to contain a minimum "regional value content" (discussed below) to qualify under Preference Criterion B. For example, footwear, chemicals, and automobiles fell into this category. There were fewer such content requirements under NAFTA than under CUSFTA.

Electronics and machinery are generally exempt. See Example 2 below.

Article 401 also permitted certain assembly goods that do not undergo a change in tariff classification to be freely traded if their regional value content is sufficient. This was NAFTA Preference Criterion D. For goods with very small non-originating content, NAFTA created a "*de minimis*" rule of origin. Article 405 generally permitted free trade in goods whose non-originating value is 7 percent or less. Such goods, in other words, were treated as originating in North America and could be freely traded.

Here are two U.S. Customs Service examples of goods that qualified for free trade under NAFTA Criterion B:

Example 1

Frozen pork meat (HTS heading 0203) is imported into the U.S. from Hungary and combined with spices imported from the Caribbean (HTS subheadings 0907–0910). Then, the spiced meat is mixed with cereals grown and produced in the U.S. to make fresh pork sausage (HTS heading 1601).

The Annex 401 rule of origin for HTS heading 1601 states:

> A change to heading 1601 through 1605 from any other chapter.

Since the frozen meat is classified in Chapter 2 and the spices are classified in Chapter 9, these non-NAFTA-originating materials meet the tariff shift requirement. Note that one does not need to consider whether the cereal meets the applicable tariff shift requirement, as the cereal is itself NAFTA-originating.

In conclusion, fresh pork sausage is originating under NAFTA.

Example 2

A manufacturer purchases inexpensive textile watch straps made in Taiwan (HTS heading 9113), to be assembled with originating mechanical watch movements (HTS heading 9108) and originating cases (HTS heading 9112). The value of the straps is less than seven percent (7%) of the total cost of the final watch (HTS heading 9102).

The rule of origin under Annex 402 for HTS heading 9102 states:

> A change to heading 9101 through 9107 from any other chapter; A change to heading 9101 through 9107 from 9114, whether or not there is also a change from any other chapter, provided there is a regional value content of not less than:

a) 60 percent where the transaction value method is used, or

b) 50 percent where the net cost method is used.

Remember that only non-originating materials need to meet the required tariff shift requirement, and, in this case, the textile straps are the only non-originating component. As the value of the straps is less than seven percent (7%) of the total cost of the finished watch, the *de minimis* rule applies, and the finished watch is originating under NAFTA.

Regional Value Content

Article 402 established NAFTA's "top down" regional content valuation methods. These methods represent a change from CUSFTA's "bottom up" measurement of value for purposes of determining the origin of goods. There were two NAFTA regional content valuation methods: Transaction Value and Net Cost Value.

In most instances, the importer seeking to qualify goods for duty free treatment under NAFTA could elect between the transaction value or net cost methods. The net cost method was generally thought to be the more difficult rule of origin. For most transactions among related parties, the net cost method had to be used. Manipulation of prices in transfers among corporate affiliates could otherwise take advantage of NAFTA's transaction value method. The net cost method had to also be followed if Customs rules the transaction value method "unacceptable."

The NAFTA transaction value method followed the GATT Customs Valuation Code of 1979 to which Canada, Mexico and the United States adhere. This method starts with an analysis of the F.O.B. price paid, including generally commissions, transport costs to the point of direct shipment, royalties on the goods, and manufacturing proceeds upon resale. Profits are included in the transaction value method of establishing the origin of goods as part of the price paid. The value of non-originating materials is then subtracted to arrive at the regional value content of the goods expressed in percentage terms. Normally, this percentage had to be at least 60 percent to free trade the goods under NAFTA.

The NAFTA net cost method started with a product's net cost to determine its regional value content. The value of non-originating materials was then subtracted. For NAFTA purposes, net cost was defined as total cost less expenses of sales promotion, marketing, after-sales service, royalties, shipping and packing, non-allowable interest charges and other "excluded costs." There were three authorized methods of allocating costs in calculating net cost (Article

402.8). The producer could elect among these methods (provided the allocation of all costs was consistent with the Uniform NAFTA Regulations on Rules of Origin and Customs Procedures).

A regional content of 50 percent or more calculated on a net cost basis qualified most goods for free trade under NAFTA. For light duty motor vehicles and their parts, a regional value content rising to 62.5 percent after 2002 was required. Automotive goods had to be valued on a net cost basis.

The value of non-originating materials (VNM) was excluded under both methods when determining the NAFTA origin of goods. This value was usually based on transaction values. If necessary, alternative values as determined under the GATT Customs Valuation Code of 1979 were used. "Intermediate materials" fabricated by producers was generally treated as originating, a rule which benefits vertically integrated producers.

NAFTA embraced an "all or nothing" *roll up* approach to non-originating materials that resolved some of the disputes that emerged under CUSFTA. In sum, the value of non-originating materials in components used to produce a good that is North American in origin was excluded from the VNM calculation in assessing regional content. This means that for both the transaction value and net cost methods, these materials are excluded in the determination of non-originating value. However, a tracing requirement for automobiles was added. The value of non-originating automotive materials had to be traced back through suppliers. In the United States, cumulation provisions allowed free trade partners to use inputs from other countries with which the U.S. free trades and still qualify for preferential treatment.

Components that did not originate in NAFTA but possess some originating materials, on the other hand, were rolled down on the same all or nothing basis. In other words, these originating materials were included in the determination of non-originating value. However, a nonintegrated producer could "accumulate" such originating material when calculating the regional value content of finished goods.

A diagram of the transaction (TV) and net cost (NC) methods of calculating regional value content percentages was provided in Article 402 of the agreement. For these purposes VNM equals the value of non-originating material.

$$\text{Regional Value Content} = \frac{TV-VNM}{TV \times 100}$$

$$\text{Regional Value Content} = \frac{NC-VNM}{NC \times 100}$$

Rules of Origin, Textiles and Apparel

Like automobiles, textiles and apparel had unique NAFTA rules of origin. Special production requirements were created that protect North American manufacturers. There was a "yarn forward" rule. This required: (1) Use of North American spun yarns; (2) to make North American fabrics; (3) that were cut and sewn into clothing in North America. Similarly, cotton and man-made fiber yarns had to be "fiber forwarded" for North American free trade.

These "triple transformation" rules of origin had a substantial impact. Initially, Mexican imports (heavily comprised of U.S. content) displaced East Asian apparel, though less so after 2001 when China joined the World Trade Organization. Furthermore, Mexico raised its tariffs on non-NAFTA textiles in the wake of its 1995 financial crisis, while continuing NAFTA tariff reductions. The margin of preferential access to Mexico for Canadian and United States textiles was thus magnified. Exports of U.S. textile components to Mexico also were enhanced by greater allowance under NAFTA of maquiladora apparel sales inside Mexico. However, since 2005 when international textile and apparel quotas were eliminated by WTO agreement, Mexico has lost substantial market share to China and East Asia.

Silk, linen, and other fabrics that are scarce in North America were exceptions from NAFTA's triple transformation rules, but still had to be cut and sewn in North America. Textile products with less than 7 percent non-originating material measured by weight could also be freely traded. This amount was treated as *de minimis*. Some non-qualifying textiles and clothing could be preferentially traded under quotas within NAFTA. U.S. manufacturers complained about Canadian exports of wool suits under preferential quotas.

Rules of Origin, Electronics

NAFTA created some unique rules of origin for consumer electronics products. These rules were based on changes in tariff classifications that contain components. For example, to qualify for free trade, traditional color television sets with screens over fourteen inches had to contain a North American-made color picture tube. Since 1999, color television sets had also to contain, among other things, North American amplifiers, tuners, and power suppliers.

For a video cassette recorder to qualify for preferential treatment under NAFTA, it had to contain a North American circuit board. For a microwave oven, all the major parts, except the magnetron, had to be made in the North American countries. Computers needed a North American motherboard. Traditional computer monitors, like color television sets, had to contain a North American color picture tube to be considered NAFTA originating.

The initial impact of NAFTA on the electronics and computer industries has been significant. United States, Japanese and Korean investment in electronics production facilities in Mexico grew, especially in the manufacture of those components that convey NAFTA origin. Mexican purchases of U.S. electronic components and finished goods produced in maquiladoras went up substantially. However, since 2001, as with textiles, there has been some disinvestment from Mexico as firms move their electronics plants to China and other low-cost Asian manufacturing centers. More significantly, almost all production of flat screen TVs and monitors is done in Asia, not Mexico. The NAFTA free trade incentives and rules of origin for electronics simply did not overcome Asia's lower production costs.

§ 4.5 Energy

Canada and Mexico are important sources of United States energy imports. With oil embargoes in mind, energy security was a major goal for the United States in negotiating NAFTA in the 1990s. Nevertheless, the United States was unable to obtain the same degree of energy security from Mexico that it secured from Canada. Under CUSFTA, Canada arguably promised in an energy crisis to maintain energy exports to the USA consistent with prior export levels. See Section 4.2. However, Canada unilaterally issued in 1993 a declaration interpreting CUSFTA as *not* requiring Canadian energy crisis exports at any given level or proportion.

Like cultural industries for Canada, energy was non-negotiable for Mexico. Chapter 6 of NAFTA deals with trade in energy and basic petrochemical goods. It opens with a most unusual sentence: "The Parties confirm their full respect for their Constitutions." This is an oblique reference to the revolutionary Mexican Constitution of 1917 that reserved ownership and development of natural resources to the state. Today this constitutional clause is most evident in PEMEX, the state oil, gas, and basic petrochemical monopoly.

CFE, the state electricity monopoly, also embodies revolutionary state ownership principles. In 1992, prior to NAFTA, the private sector was allowed to invest in electrical generation facilities provided the energy produced was self-consumed or sold to CFE. The

PEMEX and CFE monopolies subsequently underwent internal Mexican reforms not obligated under NAFTA.

NAFTA Annex 602.3 demonstrated what "full respect" for the Mexican Constitution means. In it, *Mexico reserved to its state a lengthy list of strategic activities:* Exploration, exploitation, and refining of crude oil and natural gas; production of artificial gas and basic petrochemicals; pipelines; foreign trade in and transport, storage, and distribution of the same; virtually the entire supply of electricity to the public in Mexico; and nuclear energy.

No private Canadian, Mexican or United States investment was permitted in these areas. However, it should be noted that basic petrochemicals include ethane, propane, butanes, pentanes, hexanes, heptanes, carbon black feedstocks and naphthas. Compared to past Mexican law, this was a narrow definition.

NAFTA investors could participate in all secondary and non-reserved basic petrochemicals, but there has been a slowdown in privatization of such opportunities. Transportation, distribution, and storage of natural gas were opened to private investors (including foreigners) in 1995, and several U.S. companies successfully bid on such opportunities. In 1999, Mexico proposed major structural reforms of its electricity sector, including privatization of power companies. Amendments to Mexico's constitutional law would be required. At this writing, reform of Mexico's electricity sector is still pending.

Cross-border trade in energy services was possible only by permit of the Mexican government. Cross-border trade in natural gas and basic petrochemicals was similarly allowed with PEMEX through regulated supply contracts. In some cases, Mexico permitted performance clauses in energy service contracts. Mexico's traditional opposition to sharing oil and gas ownership rights in PEMEX drilling contracts continued.

Mexico allowed 100 percent foreign ownership of new coal mines. Existing joint ventures could become wholly owned by NAFTA investors. Mexican tariffs on coal were completely removed at the outset. NAFTA nationals could own or operate electricity companies when the production was for the owner's use. Excess electricity had to be sold to CFE at rates agreed upon by contract. Co-generation is another possibility when electricity is generated by industrial production. Once again, excess supplies go to CFE at agreed rates. Independent power production plants located in Mexico can be owned and operated by NAFTA nationals, but CFE gets the electricity. This has been done by leasing foreign-owned plants to CFE. In the border region, CFE may contract to sell electricity to United States utilities.

NAFTA incorporated by reference the GATT 1947 provisions relating to quotas and other restraints on trade in energy and petrochemical goods. Presumably, this applied to GATT 1947 Articles XI, XX and XXI. As in other areas, this incorporation permitted utilization of NAFTA dispute settlement.

In addition, other rights and obligations relating to energy goods were established by NAFTA. There was an express prohibition of import or export price controls that applies to all parties. In times of energy crises, Canadian (but not Mexican) restraints had to be proportionate to past export/domestic utilization ratios. Crisis restraints could not push export prices higher than those charged domestically. And the normal channels of supply had to be maintained. Mexico was also exempted from the NAFTA rules on restraining trade in energy goods for reasons of national security but was required to adhere to the general NAFTA rules on national security trade restraints.

Energy export licensing was permissible under NAFTA. Export taxes and other charges can be used only if they apply to energy goods consumed domestically. The regulation of energy was subject to NAFTA's general national and most-favored treatment duties. The more specific rules of Chapter 6 on trade restraints and export taxes also applied. NAFTA nations had also to "seek" to ensure that energy regulation does not disrupt contractual relationships "to the maximum extent practicable." They had to provide for "orderly and equitable" implementation of regulatory measures.

§ 4.6 Services

Cross-border NAFTA trade in services was subject to national treatment, including no less favorable treatment than that most favorably given at federal, state, or local levels. No member state could require that a service provider establish or maintain a residence, local office, or branch in its country as a condition to cross-border provision of services. However, a general standstill on existing discriminatory or limiting laws affecting cross-border services was adopted. Mutual recognition of professional licenses was encouraged (notably for legal consultants and engineers), but not made automatic. All citizenship or permanent residency requirements for professional licensing were eliminated.

Additionally, a NAFTA country could deny the benefits of the rules on cross-border provision of services if their source was a third country without substantial business activities within the free trade area. For transport services, these benefits could be denied if the services were provided with equipment not registered within a NAFTA nation. Most air, maritime, basic telecommunications and social services were not covered by these rules, nor those subject to special treatment elsewhere in the NAFTA agreement (*e.g.*, procurement, financing, and energy). Even so, NAFTA considerably broadened the types of services covered by freer trade principles, including Accounting, advertising, architecture, broadcasting, commercial education, construction, consulting, enhanced telecommunications, engineering, environmental science, health care, land transport, publishing, and tourism.

Whereas the CUSFTA allowed free trade in services only for those sectors that were positively listed in the agreement, NAFTA adopted a broader "negative listing" approach. All services sectors were subject to free trade principles unless the NAFTA agreement specified otherwise.

Foreign Legal Consultants

Mexico has a unified national licensing system for attorneys (Abogados). Canada licenses its attorneys (Barristers and Solicitors) on a provincial basis. The 50 states of the United States and the District of Columbia do likewise. While the traditional perception that business lawyers are not fungible is open to challenge in a regional economy, it is reasonable to conclude that the services of Canadian, Mexican and United States lawyers cannot generally be substituted.

Professor James Smith has argued that United States and Mexican legal traditions, constitutions and political systems are so "markedly different" that legal training and law practice in one country is more likely to "hinder rather than aid" in understanding each other's legal systems. See 1 U.S.—Mexico L.J. 85 (1993). Certainly, the different Civil and Common Law legal traditions and ethical rules found in Quebec, the rest of Canada (ROC), Mexico, and among the states of the United States support this conclusion. On balance the broad exclusion of legal services from NAFTA seems justified, though less so for international business attorneys.

Against this background, NAFTA sought an alternative to mutual licensing of lawyers based on their national certifications. This alternative, the licensing of "foreign legal consultants," proved agreeable. Some U.S. states had already authorized licensing foreign legal consultants primarily to retain opportunities for U.S. lawyers practicing abroad, especially in France. New York, California, Florida, Texas, Alaska, Connecticut, the District of Columbia, Georgia, Hawaii, Illinois, Michigan, New Jersey, Ohio, Oregon, and Washington had done so prior to NAFTA. British Columbia, Ontario and Saskatchewan also licensed foreign legal consultants. Mexico had no experience with such licensure but promised to do so under

NAFTA for jurisdictions granting reciprocal rights to Mexican attorneys.

In Section B of Annex 1210.5, the NAFTA partners agreed to promote the licensing of foreign legal consultants. This, of course, is ultimately a decision for the states and provinces of the U.S. and Canada. It was also agreed that such consultants would be permitted to practice or give advice on the laws of their home jurisdiction. It was unclear whether this includes the right to practice "international law" as a foreign legal consultant. One could argue that since the law of NAFTA is by ratification or implementation part of the law of Canada, Mexico, and the United States that foreign legal consultants should at a minimum be able to counsel on it.

The issue of just what law a foreign legal consultant can practice has split U.S. states. Alaska, California, Connecticut, Florida, Georgia, and Texas only permit foreign legal consultants to advise on the law of their home jurisdictions. Nearly all the other participating states follow the Model Rule of the American Bar Association which permits practice of law except that of the licensing state and the United States.

The Trucking Dispute

Unlike CUSFTA, NAFTA created a timetable for the removal of barriers to cross-border land transport services and the establishment of compatible technical, environmental and safety standards. This extended to bus, trucking, port, and rail services. It was intended to eliminate the historic need to switch trailers to Mexican transporters at the border. Cross-border truck deliveries in the border states were supposed to come online late in 1995, but U.S. concerns about the standards of Mexican carriers and (one suspects) Teamsters Union influence delayed this result. After 6 years, truckers were supposed to be able to move freely anywhere within NAFTA. *In 2001, Mexico unanimously prevailed in a NAFTA arbitration panel on trucking access to the United States.*

President George W. Bush commenced a pilot cross-border trucking program, but funds for it were eliminated in the Obama economic stimulus bill (H.R. 1105). Mexico undertook, as permitted, retaliatory tariffs on selected U.S. goods. Finally, a settlement was reached in 2010 allowing certified Mexican trucks to role on U.S. highways. Mexico removed its retaliatory tariffs. However, the USMCA 2020 Agreement partially reversed this outcome and permits blocking long-distance Mexican trucking in the USA and Canada. See Section 6.8.

Telecommunications

Public telecommunications networks and services were opened on reasonable and nondiscriminatory terms for firms and individuals who need the networks to conduct business, such as intra-corporate communications or enhanced telecommunications and information services. This means that cellular phone, data transmission, earth stations, fax, electronic mail, overlay networks and paging systems are open to Canadian and American investors. Many of them had tried to enter the Mexican market but been largely stymied by Telmex and Carlos Slim.

Each NAFTA country was required to ensure reasonable access and use of leased private lines, terminal equipment attachments, private circuit interconnects, switching, signaling, and processing functions and user-choice of operating protocols. Conditions on access and use may only be imposed to safeguard the public responsibilities of network operators or to protect technical network integrity.

Under NAFTA, rates for public telecommunications transport services should reflect economic costs and flat-rate pricing is required for leased circuits. However, cross-subsidization between public transport services was not prohibited, nor were monopoly providers of public networks or services. Such monopolies could not engage in anticompetitive conduct outside their monopoly areas with adverse effects on NAFTA nationals. Various rights of access to information on public networks and services were established, and NAFTA limited the types of technical standards that could be imposed on the attachment of equipment to public networks.

Financial Services

Financial services provided by banking, insurance, securities, and other firms were separately covered under NAFTA. Trade in such services was generally subject to specific liberalization commitments and transition periods. Financial service providers, including non-NAFTA providers operating through subsidiaries in a NAFTA country, were entitled to establish themselves anywhere within NAFTA and service customers there (the right of "commercial presence"). Existing cross-border restraints on the provision of financial services were frozen and no new restraints could be imposed (subject to designated exceptions).

Providers of financial services in each NAFTA nation received both national and most favored nation treatment. This included equality of competitive opportunity, which was defined as avoidance of measures that disadvantage foreign providers relative to domestic providers. Various procedural transparency rules were established to facilitate the entry and equal opportunity of NAFTA providers of financial services. The host nation could legislate reasonable prudential requirements for such companies and, under limited circumstances, protect their balance of payments in ways which restrain financial providers.

The following are some of the more notable country-specific commitments on financial service made under NAFTA:

> **United States**—A grace period allowed Mexican banks already operating a securities firm in the U.S. to continue to do so until July of 1997.
>
> **Canada**—The exemption granted U.S. companies under the Canada-U.S. FTA to hold more than 25 percent of the shares of a federally regulated Canadian financial institution was extended to Mexican firms, as was the suspension of Canada's 12 percent asset ceiling rules. Multiple branches could be opened in Canada without Ministry of Finance approval.
>
> **Mexico**—Banking, securities and insurance companies from the U.S. and Canada were able to enter the Mexican market through subsidiaries and joint ventures (but not branches) subject to market share limits during a transition period that ended in the year 2000 (insurance) or 2004 (banking and securities). Finance companies were able to establish separate subsidiaries in Mexico to provide consumer, commercial, mortgage lending or credit card services, subject to a 3 percent aggregate asset limitation (which did not apply to lending by affiliates of automotive companies). Existing U.S. and Canadian insurers could expand their ownership rights to 100 percent in 1996. No equity or market share requirements applied for warehousing and bonding, foreign exchange and mutual fund management enterprises.

§ 4.7 Foreign Investment

NAFTA's foreign investment law was extremely controversial and investor-state arbitrations were aggressively pursued. This generally remains a "hot area" of free trade law.

Investing in Mexico

The cross-border investment rules established in 1989 by Canada and the United States were reviewed in Chapter 3. NAFTA placed special emphasis on relaxation of Mexico's foreign investment controls. These controls find their roots in the revolutionary 1917 Mexican Constitution and the nationalization of foreign oil and gas interests in 1937 as well as the widespread adoption of foreign investment control commissions throughout Latin America during the 1970s. Under Mexican regulation of foreign investment since the 1940s, some industries were reserved for state ownership while others could only be owned by Mexicans. Foreigners were ordinarily allowed to invest in less sensitive industries, but often subject to mandatory joint venture requirements with majority Mexican ownership and "Calvo clause" rules limiting foreign investor dispute remedies to those available under Mexican law.

In 1973, Mexico promulgated an Investment Law that mandated more use of joint ventures if approved by the National Foreign Investment Commission. This Law was the most restrictive of its kind in Mexican history. By the 1980s, after years of mismanagement and corruption while awash in petroleum dollars, Mexico had a massive national debt problem. Foreign investment regulations issued by Presidential decree in 1989 shifted significantly towards allowance of wholly owned subsidiaries. However, these regulations conflicted with the 1973 Investment Law. These uncertainties were finally resolved in 1993 as a direct consequence of NAFTA when Mexico adopted a new Law on Foreign Investment.

The 1993 Law is much more permissive of foreign investment without prior approval of by the Mexican Investment Commission. Although adopted on the eve of NAFTA, the 1993 Law opens many of the same doors to all investors, not just those from NAFTA. Investment opportunities based upon the NAFTA agreement that are not generally available include the suspension of many performance requirements, the phased removal of market share caps on financial services, and reduced thresholds triggering Investment Commission review. In addition, NAFTA investors are not subject to Mexico's mandatory joint venture rule, nor its "Calvo clause." Removal of these restrictions represents a major concession on the part of Mexico.

Acquisitions or sales of existing Mexican companies are generally subject to Commission review if exceeding $25 million U.S. This threshold increased to $150 million U.S. for NAFTA investors in 2003. For NAFTA investors, no permission from the National Commission was required to invest on a wholly owned basis or acquire or sell Mexican companies whose values fall below this threshold.

Investment Rights

In an unusual provision, Article 1112 subordinated all of Chapter 11 on investment to the rest of the NAFTA agreement. In other words, if there were inconsistencies between Chapter 11 and other parts of the NAFTA agreement, those other parts were supreme. That said, NAFTA provided investors and their investments with important rights.

Canadian, Mexican and United States citizens, permanently resident aliens, and other designated persons were eligible to benefit from NAFTA's investment rules. In addition, most private and public, profit and nonprofit businesses "constituted or organized" under Canadian, Mexican or United States law also qualified. This coverage specifically included businesses operating as corporations, partnerships, trusts, sole proprietorships, joint ventures, and business associations.

Furthermore, in a notable change from CUSFTA, it was not necessary for such businesses to be owned or controlled by Canadian, Mexican or U.S. nationals or enterprises. As with services, this meant that businesses owned by anyone which were "constituted or organized" inside NAFTA benefited from the agreement *provided* they carried on substantial business activities in North America. *Thus Asians, Europeans, and Latin Americans (for example) could invest in North America and benefit from NAFTA investment rights and remedies.* See the Corn Syrup Sweeteners arbitration dispute below. Exceptions were made for NAFTA businesses owned or controlled by third parties from countries lacking diplomatic relations with or economically embargoed by Canada, Mexico, or the United States.

Beneficiaries of NAFTA rights enjoyed a broad definition of "investment." This definition included most stocks, bonds, loans, and income, profit, or asset interests. Real estate, tangible, or intangible (intellectual) business property, turnkey or construction contracts, concessions, and licensing and franchising contracts were also generally included (Article 1139). However, under Annex III, each member state reserved certain economic activities for its state or domestic investors. Mexico did so under its 1993 Foreign Investment Law. For the purposes of Chapter 11, investment was defined to exclude claims to money arising solely from commercial contracts for the sale of goods or services, or trade financing, and claims for money that do not involve the interests noted above.

Treatment of Foreign Investors and Investments

The NAFTA agreement established a so-called *"minimum standard of treatment"* for NAFTA investors and investments: "Treatment in accordance with international law," including "fair and equitable treatment and full protection and security" (Article 1105.) For example, if losses occurred due to armed conflict or civil strife, NAFTA investors and investments had to be accorded nondiscriminatory treatment in response. An official NAFTA interpretative ruling indicates that Article 1105 embraces treatment in accordance with "customary" international law, a ruling intended to limit the scope of protection afforded to foreign investors. In addition, limiting definitions of "fair and equitable treatment" and "full protection and security" were established in subsequent U.S. free trade agreements. See Section 5.2.

Beyond this minimum, NAFTA investors and their investments were entitled to the better of national or most-favored-nation treatment from federal governments. Such treatment rights extended to establishing, acquiring, expanding, managing, conducting, operating, and selling or disposing of investments. From state or provincial governments, NAFTA investors and their investments were entitled to receive the most-favored treatment those governments grant their own investors and investments. Along these lines, United Parcel Service found Mexico lacking when it was initially limited to using smaller vans than Mexican competitors. UPS persuaded the United States to lodge a complaint under Chapter 20 (below) which led to intergovernmental consultations followed by NAFTA Commission mediation. These efforts lasted many months but eventually UPS got permission to use larger vans.

Article 1102 of NAFTA prohibited requiring minimum levels of equity holdings by nationals of the host government. Hence the historic bias in Mexican law towards mandatory joint ventures was overcome by NAFTA. No investor could be forced on grounds of nationality to sell or dispose of a qualified investment. Mandatory appointment of senior managers based on nationality was also contrary to NAFTA. However, it was permissible to require boards of directors and corporate committees with majorities from one nationality or residence, provided this did not materially impair the investor's ability to exercise control. Canadian law often makes such stipulations. Residency requirements were generally authorized if there was no impairment of the treaty rights of NAFTA investors.

Article 1106 of NAFTA 1994 prohibited various investment performance obligations, including tax-related measures, in a scope that surpasses the WTO Agreement on Trade-Related Investment Measures (TRIMs 1995, see Section 1.13). Requirements relating to exports, domestic content, domestic purchases, trade balancing of foreign exchange inflows or earnings, import/export ratios, technology transfers, and regional or global sales exclusivity ("product mandates") were broadly prohibited. All other types of investment-related performance requirements, such as employment and research and development obligations, were not prohibited and therefore presumably lawful.

Article 1106.3 of NAFTA further prohibited conditioning the receipt or continued receipt of "an advantage" (*e.g.*, a government subsidy or tax benefit) on compliance with requirements relating to domestic content, domestic purchases, domestic sales restraints, or trade balancing. But "advantages" could be given when the requirements concern production location, provision of services, training or employing workers, constructing, or expanding facilities, or carrying out research and development locally. By way of exception, domestic content or purchase requirements *and* advantages could be linked to investor compliance with: (1) Laws and regulations that are consistent with NAFTA; (2) laws necessary to protect human, animal or plant life or health; or (3) laws needed to conserve living or non-living exhaustible natural resources. However, such requirements could not be applied arbitrarily or unjustifiably and could not constitute a disguised restraint on trade or investment.

All monetary transfers relating to NAFTA investments were allowed "freely and without delay." (Article 1109) Such transfers had to be possible in a "freely usable currency" at the market rate of exchange prevailing in spot transactions on the transfer date. For these purposes, monetary transfers specifically included profits, dividends, interest, capital gains, royalties, management, technical assistance, and other fees, returns in kind, and funds derived from the investment. Sale or liquidation proceeds, contract payments, compensatory payments for expropriation and NAFTA dispute settlement payments were also encompassed.

Requiring investment-related monetary transfers or penalizing them was prohibited. However, such transfers could be controlled in an equitable, nondiscriminatory, and good faith application of bankruptcy, insolvency, creditors' rights, securities, criminal, currency reporting and satisfaction of judgment laws. Whereas tax withholding was a justifiable basis for restricting monetary transfers under CUSFTA, this was not the case under NAFTA. Special restraints could arise in connection with balance of payments problems and taxation laws.

Expropriation

Article 1110 of NAFTA generally prohibited direct or indirect nationalization or expropriation of NAFTA investments. Measures "tantamount to" nationalization or expropriation, such as creeping expropriation or confiscatory taxation, were also prohibited. What the unusual words "tantamount to" meant became a major issue in NAFTA investor-state arbitrations. See Section 4.8. Expropriation, nationalization, or tantamount measures could occur for public purposes on a nondiscriminatory basis in accordance with due process of law and NAFTA's "minimum level of treatment" (above).

Post-NAFTA U.S. free trade agreements expressly limited the possibility of succeeding with "indirect" regulatory taking expropriation claims. See Section 5.2.

Any authorized expropriation had to result in payment of compensation without delay. The amount of payment had to be equivalent to the fair market value of the investment immediately prior to expropriation. In valuing the investment, going concern value, asset value (including declared tax values of tangible property) and other appropriate factors had to be considered. Payment had to be made in a manner that is fully realizable, such as in a "G7" currency (U.S. dollars, Canadian dollars, EUROs, British pounds sterling, Japanese yen). Interest at a commercially reasonable rate also had to be included. If payment was made in Mexican pesos, this amount had to be calculated as of the expropriation date in a G7 currency plus interest.

Certain governmental acts were not treated as expropriations. For example, NAFTA specified that nondiscriminatory measures of general application that impose costs on defaulting debtors were not tantamount to expropriation of a bond or loan *solely* for that reason. Compulsory licensing of intellectual property rights was deemed not an expropriation. Revocation, limitation, or creation of IP rights as allowed by Chapter 17 of NAFTA was also deemed not an expropriation.

These provisions embodied an historic change in Mexico's position on expropriation law. Without explicitly saying so, Mexico essentially embraced the U.S. position that under "international law" expropriation of foreign investments requires "prompt, adequate and effective" compensation. Mexico had specifically rejected this standard in negotiating a settlement of its oil and gas (and land) expropriations in the 1930s. Down through the years Mexico adamantly clung to its view that compensation would only be paid according to Mexican law. For investors protected under NAFTA (which were not just Canadian and U.S. investors), Chapter 11 represented the dawn of a new era.

Exceptions and Reservations, the Environment

Annexes I–IV of the NAFTA agreement reveal a host of investment-related reservations and exceptions. Many pre-existing, non-conforming regulations were grandfathered though most (not including basic telecommunications, social services, and maritime services) were subject to a standstill agreement intended to avoid relapses into greater protection. In contrast, regulations promoting investment "sensitive to environmental concerns" were expressly authorized. Mexico's tradition of assessing the environmental impact of foreign investments therefore continued. There was also a formal recognition that creating exceptions to environmental laws to encourage NAFTA investors to establish, acquire, expand, or retain their investments was inappropriate. However, NAFTA's Chapter 20 dispute settlement mechanism could not be invoked concerning this "commitment." Only intergovernmental consultations were mandatory.

Other investment-related exceptions concerned government procurement, subsidies, export promotion, foreign aid and preferential trade arrangements. These exceptions applied mostly to the rules on nondiscriminatory treatment and performance requirements. Most general exceptions to NAFTA 1994, such as for Canadian cultural industries (above), also applied to its investment rules. The general "national security" exception, for example, allowed the United States to block the acquisition of U.S. companies by foreigners (including Canadians and Mexicans) under CFIUS national security regulations (50 U.S.C. App. § 2170). See my Concise Hornbook on *Foreign Investment Law and Disputes*.

§ 4.8 Arbitration of Investment Disputes

NAFTA created a highly innovative and increasingly controversial investment dispute settlement system. This system provided a way for foreign investors to challenge governmental and state enterprise acts and recover damages for violation of rights established in Chapter 11. Remarkably, investors may not only assert claims as individuals, but also on behalf of NAFTA enterprises they own or control directly or indirectly (Article 1117). This authorization avoids one of international law's most famous problems . . . "standing to sue" when the investor's only loss or damage is injury to its investment abroad. See *Belgium v. Spain (the "Barcelona Traction Case")*, 1970 Int'l Court of Justice 3 (preliminary objections).

Intergovernmental NAFTA dispute settlement did not apply to "investor-state disputes." Such disputes were instead subject to binding arbitration, another major concession on the part of Mexico which has always adhered to the "Calvo Doctrine." That doctrine (widely followed in Latin America) requires foreign investors to forego protection by their home governments, be treated as Mexican nationals, and pursue legal remedies exclusively in Mexico. *See* Article 27 of the Mexican Constitution.

Individual investors claiming that a government has breached NAFTA investment or state enterprise obligations, or that one of its monopolies has done so, commence the dispute resolution process. All claims were filed against the federal government even when it is state, provincial, or local government action that was being challenged. This can place Canada, Mexico, and the United States in the awkward position of defending sub-central governmental acts. See the *Metalclad* and *Loewen* arbitrations in Section 4.9.

The investor had to allege that the breach of NAFTA caused loss or damage. Such claims had to be asserted no later than three years after the date when knowledge of the alleged breach and knowledge of the loss or damage was first acquired or should have been first acquired. However, decisions by the Canadian or Mexican foreign investment control commissions, national security actions, and Canadian cultural industry reservations could not be the basis for such a claim. Moreover, a host of reservations and exceptions contained in Chapter 11B denied access to NAFTA's investor-state arbitration remedy. Even so, as outlined below, the number of claims filed was substantial with some claims producing unexpected results. The process itself fell into dispute and was notably altered under the USMCA. See Section 6.7.

Before submitting a claim to arbitration, individual investors had to give 90 days' advance notice to the host country. Such notice included an explanation of the issues, their factual basis, and remedies sought. Claimants also had to consent in writing to arbitrate under the procedures established in the NAFTA agreement. *They had to waive in writing their rights to initiate or continue any other damages proceedings.* See *Commerce Group Corp. v. El Salvador* (ICSID, 2011) (CAFTA-DR tribunal dismisses complaint due to pending litigation). Individual investors did not, however, waive their rights to injunctive, declaratory, or other extraordinary relief (not involving damages). These remedies could not be awarded through NAFTA arbitration of investor-state disputes.

Investment Dispute Arbitration Procedures, Appeals and Remedies

The NAFTA nations consented unconditionally in advance to the submission of investor claims to arbitration under NAFTA procedures. Furthermore, they agreed not to assert insurance payments or other investor indemnification rights as a defense, counterclaim, right of setoff or otherwise. *Arbitration of investor-state disputes continues in a more limited way as between Mexico and the United States under the USMCA Agreement. It is eliminated as between the United States and Canada.* See Section 6.8.

The investor submitting a claim to arbitration against a NAFTA state ordinarily could elect between the following arbitration rules:

(1) The ICSID Convention (detailed in Section 7.5) if both member states adhere. This was impossible initially

since only the United States had ratified ICSID. Canada has now also done so.

(2) The Additional Facility Rules of ICSID provided one-member state (*i.e.*, the United States or more recently Canada) adheres to the ICSID Convention. or

(3) The U.N.-derived UNCITRAL Arbitration Rules.

NAFTA investor-state tribunals have three panelists. The investor and the state each choose one arbitrator. If possible, the third presiding panelist is chosen by agreement. The ICSID Secretary-General selects the presiding arbitrator if agreement is not reached within 90 days. That person is chosen from a consensus roster of acceptable names but may not be a national from either side of the dispute.

Investor-state tribunals must decide the dispute in accordance with the NAFTA agreement and "applicable rules of international law." The responding state could raise defenses based upon reservations or exceptions contained in Annexes I–IV to the NAFTA agreement. In such instances, the NAFTA Commission (not the arbitration panel) generally issued a binding ruling on the validity of such a defense. Defenses based upon permissible regulation of monetary transfers by financial institutions were generally decided by the NAFTA Financial Services Committee.

By agreement of the parties, the investor-state arbitration tribunal could obtain expert reports on factual issues concerning environmental, health, safety, or other scientific matters. The tribunal could also order temporary relief measures to preserve rights or the full effectiveness of its jurisdiction. It could, for example, order the preservation of evidence. The tribunal could not, however, order attachment or enjoin governmental regulations being challenged.

NAFTA investor-state tribunals were authorized to award investors or NAFTA enterprises actual damages and interest, or restitution of property, or both. In the entire history of NAFTA arbitrations, damages were awarded against and paid by Canada and Mexico, but not the United States. See the *Metalclad* and *S.D. Myers* arbitrations in Section 4.9.

If the award went to an enterprise, any person could *also* pursue relief under "applicable domestic law." If restitution was ordered, the responsible member state could provide monetary damages and interest instead. NAFTA tribunals could apportion legal fees between the parties at their discretion. Such fees routinely ran into hundreds of thousands, if not millions, of dollars. The costs of administering

Chapter 11 tribunals, including generous fees for the arbitrators, often exceeded $500,000. The losing party was typically required to pay these costs.

The award of the tribunal was binding on the parties, but subject to revision or annulment in the courts of the arbitration's situs. See *Metalclad* and *S.D. Myers*. Absent agreement, the arbitrators determine situs. Professor Brower and others have argued that a standing appellate body not unlike that of the WTO would have provided greater legitimacy and uniformity to Chapter 11 arbitrations. See 36 Vanderbilt J. Transnational Law 37 (2003).

Awards were specifically not "precedent" in future NAFTA arbitrations (Article 1136), yet routinely cited and argued in Chapter 11 proceedings and decisions. NAFTA investor-state arbitration awards were generally honored. Should this not occur, the investor could seek enforcement of the award. NAFTA nations agreed to provide the means for such enforcement. The NAFTA investor-state dispute settlement system meets the various requirements of the ICSID Convention, its Additional Facility Rules, the New York Convention on Recognition and Enforcement of Foreign Arbitral Awards (1958), and the Inter-American Convention on International Commercial Arbitration (1975).

Should it become necessary to judicially enforce an investor-state arbitration award, the New York Convention provided a likely recourse as all three nations adhere to it. However, U.S. courts have held the grounds for denying enforcement of NAFTA awards under the New York Convention limited strictly to its provisions. The longstanding U.S. doctrine of denying enforcement when arbitrators "manifestly disregard the law", a doctrine not incorporated in the New York Convention, was not applied in a NAFTA award enforcement proceeding. See *In re Arbitration between International Thunderbird Gaming Corp. v. United Mexican States*, 473 F.Supp.2d 80 (D.C. 2007).

If there was no compliance with the award and enforcement proceedings failed, the investor's government could as a last recourse commence intergovernmental dispute settlement under Chapter 20 of NAFTA. This panel rules on whether noncompliance inconsistent with the NAFTA agreement has occurred and can recommend compliance. If compliance still does not follow, benefits granted under NAFTA to the noncomplying nation could be suspended.

§ 4.9 Investor-State Arbitrations Under NAFTA

Arbitrated Investor Claims Against Host States

Investors did not hesitate to invoke the innovative investor-state arbitration procedures authorized under Section B of Chapter 11 of NAFTA. Since 2001, in an official Interpretation, Chapter 11 was construed as not imposing a general duty of confidentiality. The NAFTA governments therefore released all documents submitted to or issued by Chapter 11 arbitration tribunals. Moreover, since late 2003 open Chapter 11 hearings have become the rule, as have permissive procedures for non-party submissions (amicus curiae).

Many investors alleged state action that is "tantamount to expropriation." This is a claim that Article 1110 authorized and one which could be construed to fit many fact patterns. National treatment and the NAFTA minimum standard of treatment (see above) were also commonly disputed. Some examples of these disputes follow.

Metalclad v. Mexico

A prominent dispute involved Metalclad Corp. of California, which had acquired a hazardous waste site operated by a Mexican company in Guadalcazar, San Luis Potosi subject to various federal approvals, all of which were obtained. State and local opposition to opening the site after an expensive clean-up resulted in the denial of a building permit in a newly created "ecological zone." Metalclad claimed these acts were tantamount to expropriation, and denial of national and the NAFTA minimum standards of treatment. It sought $90 million in damages from the Mexican federal government, which despite having supported the Metalclad contract was obliged to defend the hostile local and state actions. Metalclad received an award of $16 million under NAFTA Chapter 11 in 2000. The arbitration was conducted under the ICSID Additional Facility rules.

Mexico instituted judicial proceedings to set aside the award in British Columbia, the arbitration's legal *situs*. Canada intervened in support of Mexico. The arbitrators had found the Mexican regulatory action a breach of NAFTA's minimum standard based on a lack of "transparency," and tantamount to expropriation without adequate compensation.

The British Columbia Supreme Court, ruling under the B.C. International Arbitration Act, agreed that the expropriation decision fell within the scope of the dispute submitted and was therefore valid. It rejected, however, the transparency decision as beyond the scope of the submission. The court found no transparency obligations in Chapter 11, and none as a matter of *customary* international law (which traditionally bars only "egregious," "outrageous" or "shocking" conduct). Mexico subsequently paid Metalclad approximately $16 million U.S., the first payment by a state to an investor under Chapter 11.

Ethyl v. Canada and Methanex v. United States

A second prominent dispute involved Ethyl Corp. of the USA, which claimed $250 million U.S. damages against the Canadian government after 1997 federal legislation banning importation or interprovincial trade of the gasoline additive, MMT. Canada was the first country to ban MMT as a pollution and health hazard, although California has also done so. MMT is a manganese-based octane enhancer alleged to interfere with the proper functioning of catalytic converters. Ethyl Corp. is the sole producer of MMT in North America. Ethyl claimed that the new law was tantamount to expropriation, violated NAFTA's national treatment standards and constituted an unlawful Canadian-content performance requirement (because the ban would favor Canadian ethanol as a substitute for MMT).

A dispute resolution panel under Canada's Agreement on Internal Trade struck down the interprovincial trade ban. In 1998, Canada withdrew its ban on MMT and paid $13 million to Ethyl Corp. Ethyl then withdrew its $250 million arbitration claim. Canada noted the current lack of scientific evidence documenting MMT harm, an apparent abandonment of the "precautionary principle." Environmentalists decried evidence of NAFTA's negative impact, and Europeans cited *Ethyl* as a good reason to reject multilateral investment guarantee agreements in the OECD (Organization for Economic Cooperation and Development). Both groups believed Chapter 11 created a privileged class of "super-citizens" who are a threat to state sovereignty.

Methanex Corp. of Canada submitted a claim that was in some ways the reverse of *Ethyl*. Methanex claimed that California's ban of the MTBE gasoline additive (for which it makes feedstock) amounted to an expropriation of its business interests and violated its minimum treatment rights. It sought $970 million in damages and simultaneously filed a petition under the North American Environmental Cooperation Agreement asserting that California failed to enforce its gasoline storage regulations, which Methanex saw as the source of MTBE water pollution. In 2002, the *Methanex* panel working under the UNCITRAL Rules largely rejected the complaint on jurisdictional grounds, allowing a limited re-filing on the question of intentional injury.

The *Methanex* panel notably ruled that it would accept NGO amicus briefs, in this instance from the International Institute for Sustainable Development. This position was subsequently ratified for all Chapter 11 arbitrations by the NAFTA Free Trade Commission in 2003.

Loewen v. United States

The Loewen Group of Canada was held liable by a jury in 1995 to $500 million in a Mississippi breach of a funeral home contract suit. The case was settled for $150 million after the Mississippi Supreme Court required posting a $625 million bond prior to appealing the jury's verdict, a sum more than Loewen's net worth. In 1998, Loewen filed a claim under NAFTA alleging discrimination, denial of the minimum NAFTA standard of treatment, and uncompensated expropriation. This claim, like that of Ethyl Corp., was destined for controversy. Among other things, it challenged the discretion of American juries in awarding punitive damages. Note that it does so in a forum that does not give the American Trial Lawyers Association an opportunity to respond.

In 2003, the *Loewen* panel, calling the Mississippi decision "a disgrace," nevertheless ruled heavily against the bankrupt funeral home giant because its status as a Canadian (versus U.S.) company entitled to NAFTA investor rights was in doubt.

Pope & Talbot v. Canada

Pope & Talbot, Inc. of Portland, Oregon claimed that the 1996 Softwood Lumber Agreement (see Section 4.1) violated the national treatment, most-favored-nation treatment, minimum treatment and performance requirements rules of NAFTA. The claim asserted that the company's British Columbia subsidiary was the victim of discrimination in that the Canadian export restraints required under that Agreement applied only to four Canadian provinces. Pope & Talbot sought $20 million in compensation from the Canadian government. Rejecting most of the claims, the *Pope and Talbot* panel found Canada did violate the NAFTA minimum standard of treatment in denying export authorization to the company's B.C. subsidiary.

Although the award was only about $460,000 U.S., the panel's reasoning set off fireworks. In its view, Article 1105 demanded something more than the level of treatment commanded by customary international law. "Fair and equitable treatment" and "full protection and security" were seen as "additive;" new and expansive norms created by NAFTA's novel investor protection regime.

The additive reading of *Pope & Talbot* was subsequently rejected by the British Columbia Supreme Court in *Metalclad* (above), and collectively negated by a binding interpretation of Article 1105 issued by the three NAFTA parties in 2001. This controversial, defensive interpretation "clarifies" that Article 1105 corresponds to and thus does not expand the *customary* international law standard of minimum treatment (see *Metalclad*) and that a breach of a NAFTA obligation does not ipso facto constitute a breach of that Article.

S.D. Myers v. Canada

S.D. Myers is an Ohio company specializing in hazardous waste management of PCBs. Its Canadian affiliate imported PCBs from Ontario, to the consternation of the only Canadian PCB remediation company, Chem-Security of Alberta. In 1995, Canada banned PCB exports, intentionally giving Chem-Security a monopoly. S.D. Myers asserted this export ban violated the national treatment, performance requirements, expropriation, and fair and equitable treatment provisions of Chapter 11. The arbitrators found in favor of S.D. Myers on the national treatment and fair and equitable treatment claims, awarding over $6,000,000 CDN in damages. Canada appealed to the courts of Ontario, the situs of the arbitration, and lost. In Ontario, at least, considerable deference is given to arbitral decisions. Compare British Columbia in *Metalclad* above. Subsequently, S.D. Myers and Canada settled the dispute.

Mondev v. United States

Mondev is a Canadian company engaged in commercial real estate development. It pursued various claims against the City of Boston and the Boston Redevelopment Authority in Massachusetts courts, which were denied on sovereign immunity grounds. Mondev then filed a Chapter 11 claim arguing primarily unfair and inequitable treatment in the Massachusetts courts.

In its complaint, Mondev directly challenged the 2001 Interpretation of Article 1105, arguing it was de facto an amendment of the NAFTA agreement. Mondev also argued that customary international law should be construed considering conclusions reached under hundreds of bilateral investment treaties and modern judgments. The tribunal recognized that fair and equitable treatment had evolved by 1994 (NAFTA's effective date) beyond what is "egregious" or "outrageous," and that bad faith on the part of states need not be shown. It then ruled against Mondev's denial of justice claims.

Glamis v. United States

Glamis, a Canadian mining company, alleged that government regulations limiting the impact of open-pit mining and protecting indigenous peoples' religious sites made its *proposed* California gold mine unprofitable. Under Chapter 11, it asserted violations of the NAFTA rules against government acts tantamount to expropriation, and denial of fair and equitable treatment. In June of 2009, a Chapter 11 tribunal accepted, in principle, that "regulatory taking" measures could amount to "creeping expropriation." That said, the tribunal undertook a detailed accounting of Glamis' alleged losses and found the mine project still had a net positive value of $20 million U.S. Hence it concluded Glamis was not impacted sufficiently to support a NAFTA expropriation claim.

While the outcome once again allowed the United States to avoid paying Chapter 11 damages, the willingness of the tribunal to entertain a regulatory taking claim was controversial (to put it mildly) and once again raised concerns that foreign investors may have greater rights under NAFTA than U.S. investors possess under United States law.

Corn Syrup Sweeteners v. Mexico

Late in 2009, a third Chapter 11 tribunal ruled against Mexico concerning its 20% tax from 2002 to 2007 on the production and sale of soft drinks using High Fructose Corn Syrup (HFCS). This tax was imposed in the context of a trade dispute between the U.S. and Mexico over HFCS exports south of the border and Mexican sugar exports headed north. U.S. agribusiness giants Cargill, Corn Products International and Archer Daniels Midlands, along with British Tate and Lyle's U.S. subsidiary, successfully argued that the tax constituted a "performance requirement" in violation of NAFTA Article 1106. The Mexican government was ordered to pay a total of $170 million plus interest.

AbitibiBowater v. Canada

In August 2010, the Canadian federal government agreed to pay $130 million CDN to settle a Chapter 11 claim by a U.S. pulp and paper multinational, AbitibiBowater (AB). In 2008, AB closed a longstanding mill in Newfoundland via bankruptcy, terminating 800 workers without severance. Newfoundland passed a law returning, without compensation, the company's water and timber rights to the crown, and expropriating with compensation AB lands, buildings and dams in the province. AB asserted NAFTA expropriation violations. This settlement, along with the *Glamis* decision (above), has raised concerns that resource-related NAFTA investor claims may increase. For example, a Brazilian company with a U.S. subsidiary received a

$15 million settlement form Canada after alleging permit delays for rock quarrying.

Apotex v. Unites States

Apotex is a Canadian manufacturer of generic pharmaceuticals. It filed at least three Chapter 11 claims against the United States. These filings challenged U.S. federal court decisions denying its efforts to obtain "patent certainty" for drugs (to allow its generic versions to proceed), FDA denial of approval for another Apotex generic drug, and FDA import inspection practices for drugs. All these complaints were rejected by a Chapter 11 arbitration panel in 2014.

Exxon/Mobil v. Canada

Exxon/Mobil developed offshore oil fields in Canadian waters. It first challenged Canadian Petroleum Board rules mandating fees to support R & D in Newfoundland and Labrador in the Canadian courts and lost at trial and on appeal. Exxon subsequently filed a Chapter 11 claim which a panel affirmed in 2012, holding these fees amounted to NAFTA-prohibited "performance requirements." The damages awarded amounted to nearly $15 million.

Bilcon v. Canada

Bilcon of Delaware sought to develop a quarry and marine terminal in Nova Scotia, subject to environmental review. A joint federal/province review denied approval based upon "incompatibility with community core values." Bilcon alleged NAFTA Chapter 11 violations of the national and minimum treatment standards (the latter claim focused on fair and equitable treatment). By agreement of the parties, the UNCITRAL Rules governed before the Permanent Court of Arbitration.

In a split 2015 decision, the arbitrators held in favor of Bilcon, noting particularly an absence of fair notice and treatment in the environmental review process, and a fundamental departure from the "likely significant adverse effects after mitigation" standard of evaluation required by Canadian law.

Eli Lilly v. Canada

Eli Lilly filed a claim for damages under Chapter 11 after Canadian courts invalidated patents on two of its blockbuster drugs on grounds that their utility was not shown. Eli Lilly argued unfair, inequitable, and discriminatory treatment. A 2017 arbitration panel rejected these arguments, noting that the "promise of utility" doctrine developed by Canadian courts was well established, putting Eli Lilly on notice prior to its patent claims.

This dispute was unusual because it asserted violation of NAFTA Chapter 11 by Canadian *courts*, not by Canadian legislation or regulation. Subsequently, in June of 2017, the Canadian Supreme Court overturned the "promise doctrine" under its patent law.

Windstream Energy v. Canada and Mesa Power Group v. Canada

Windstream Energy of the USA sought to participate in Ontario's green energy program and obtained a contract to build an offshore wind farm. Subsequently, Ontario imposed a moratorium on offshore wind projects pending further scientific study. This had the effect of suspending but not terminating the Windstream contract. Other participants in the program were offered alternative opportunities to join the green energy program, but Windstream was not.

Windstream filed a Chapter 11 complaint before the Permanent Court of Arbitration arguing discrimination, indirect expropriation, and unfair and inequitable treatment. A 2017 arbitration panel rejected all but the unfair and inequitable treatment claim, recognizing that Ontario had not within a reasonable time clarified the relevant science or the status of the contract, leaving Windstream in legal limbo. It assessed 21 million Euros damages, minus certain adjustments, based upon the value of comparable transactions in Europe.

Mesa Power challenged Ontario's award of power purchase contracts under its green energy program as discriminatory and unfair under Chapter 11 before the Permanent Court of Arbitration in The Hague. In a split decision, the arbitrators rejected Mesa' claims of unfair bidding rules and procedures for power contracts.

Other Foreign Investor Claims of Note

Several U.S. companies commenced Chapter 11 proceedings against Canada asserting damages based on Quebec's moratorium on "fracking", the use of water and chemicals to release sub-surface oil and gas reserves.

After President Obama's rejection in 2015 of the Keystone Pipeline from Alberta's tar sands to Texas, Trans Canada has filed a Chapter 11 claim against the United States alleging discriminatory (non-national) treatment, breach of the duty of most-favored-nation treatment, U.S. governmental acts tantamount to expropriation, and unfair and inequitable treatment. Trans Canada sought more than $15 billion in damages but withdrew its claim after President Trump approved the pipeline, which in turn was reversed by President Biden.

Summary

These examples of investor-state claims under NAFTA represent only a partial summary of the impact of Chapter 11. Lawyers learned that U.S. FTAs and BITs can be used to challenge or threaten to challenge all sorts of existing or proposed government actions, particularly regulatory decisions. *There is leverage in these broad investor rights, and in its mandatory arbitral procedures. That said, the United States never lost an investment arbitration nor paid damages under NAFTA.*

Mutations on the law of investor-state claims subsequently appeared in the U.S.-Chile, U.S.-CAFTA and U.S.-Panama/Peru/Colombia free trade agreements. See Section 5.2. These mutations are in part a response to Congressional concerns expressed in the Trade Promotion Authority (fast-track) Act of 2002 that Chapter 11 of NAFTA accorded "greater substantive rights" to foreigners with respect to investment protection than enjoyed by U.S. investors in the United States.

§ 4.10 Intellectual Property

NAFTA mandated adequate and effective intellectual property rights in all countries, including national treatment and effective internal and external enforcement rights. Specific commitments were made for virtually all types of intellectual property, including patents, copyrights, trademarks, plant breeds, industrial designs, trade secrets, semiconductor chips (directly and in goods incorporating them) and geographical indicators. NAFTA was the first international agreement to address trade secrets, and many of its IP provisions influenced the content of the WTO TRIPs agreement.

General IP Obligations

Specific commitments on patents, copyrights, trademarks, trade secrets and other intellectual property rights were made in the NAFTA agreement. These are discussed individually below. NAFTA also contained some general intellectual property rights obligations. Many of these obligations have counterparts under the TRIPs agreement. See Section 1.12. Except for secondary use of sound recordings, there is a general rule of national treatment.

There was also a general duty to protect intellectual property adequately and effectively, provided barriers to legitimate trade were not created. At a minimum, this duty necessitated adherence to NAFTA Chapter 17. This general duty also embraced adherence to the substantive provisions of: The Geneva Convention of Phonograms (1971); the Berne Convention for the Protection of Literary and

Artistic Works (1971); the Paris Convention for the Protection of Industrial Property (1967); and the 1978 or 1991 versions of the International Convention for the Protection of New Varieties of Plants. Protecting intellectual property rights more extensively than these Conventions was expressly authorized.

The process of intellectual property rights enforcement is covered in detail under NAFTA. Speaking generally, these provisions required fair, equitable, and not unnecessarily complicated, costly, or time-consuming enforcement procedures. Written notice, independent legal counsel, the opportunity to substantiate claims and present evidence, and protection of confidential information were stipulated for civil enforcement proceedings. Overly burdensome mandatory personal appearances could not be imposed.

Remedies to enjoin infringement (new to Mexico), prevent importation of infringing goods, and order payment for damages and litigation costs had to exist. However, proof of knowing infringement or reasonable grounds for such knowledge was an acceptable criterion. Recovery of profits or liquidated damages became available when copyright or sound recording infringement was involved. Disposition of infringing or counterfeit goods outside the ordinary channels of commerce or even by destruction was anticipated by NAFTA. All administrative intellectual property rights decisions were reviewable by a court of law.

Counterfeiting

Criminal penalties were required under NAFTA for willful trademark counterfeiting or copyright piracy undertaken on a commercial scale. For United States law on point, see the Trademark Counterfeiting Act of 1984 (18 U.S.C. § 2320 et seq.). When counterfeit or pirated goods come from outside the region, those affected must be given the opportunity to bar importation and possibly obtain their destruction or other satisfactory disposal.

Despite strong provisions in NAFTA to fight counterfeiting and promote protection of intellectual property, Mexico is seen by some as still not measuring up. Annual submissions by the International Intellectual Property Alliance to the USTR under Special 301 procedures (19 U.S.C. § 2242) document the ineffectiveness of Mexico's anti-piracy law enforcement. Hundreds of millions of dollars of fake CDs, DVDs, software, and the like can be found in Mexican marketplaces and the amount is increasing. Prosecutions to combat counterfeiting have been limited. For example, some 2500 Mexican government raids in 1998 netted just 35 convictions with no fines above $1,000.

Mexico's Customs Law of 1996 placed border controls in the hands of the Mexican Institute of Industrial Property (IMPI) for the first time. This Institute was created in 1993 specifically for the task of enforcing Mexican intellectual property rights. Unlike the U.S. Patent and Trademark Office, IMPI has the power to enforce patent owners' rights against actual and potential infringers. It can prevent any commercialization of an infringing product, including removal from the stream of commerce. Mexico also has had, since 1993, a multi-departmental Anti-Piracy Commission.

In 1998, the U.S. and Mexico reached agreement on new measures to combat counterfeiting in Mexico. These include a national anti-piracy campaign, tax crimes against counterfeiters, expeditious search and seizure and arrest warrants, and increased administrative enforcement resources. These measures in a limited way have helped to stem counterfeit goods in Mexico.

Gray Market Trading

NAFTA left each member state free to adopt its own rules on gray market trading. The question that gray market trading poses for NAFTA is the same as has been debated for decades in Europe. Should national intellectual property rights be allowed to function as trade barriers inside the region? Europe, especially the European Court of Justice, has by and large said no. See Section 3.4. In the European Union, free trade interests usually trump national intellectual property rights. Under NAFTA, there is no clear answer. Chapter 17 took pains to expand and protect national intellectual property rights, and specifically addressed the issue of counterfeiting, but not gray market trading. The relevant law of each NAFTA nation remained intact.

Patents

Article 1709 of NAFTA assured the availability of patents "in all fields of technology." New products and processes resulting from an inventive step that are capable of industrial application are patentable. Patents for pharmaceuticals, computer software, microorganisms and microbiological processes, plant varieties and agricultural chemicals were specifically included under NAFTA and caused changes in Mexican law. In addition, protection for layout designs of semiconductor integrated circuits was provided by Article 1710. All patent rights had to be granted without discrimination as to field of technology, country of origin, and importation or local production of the relevant products.

NAFTA specifically reserved the right to deny patents for diagnostic, therapeutic and surgical methods, transgenic plants and animals, and for essentially biological processes that produce plants or animals. If commercial exploitation might endanger public morality or "ordre public" (state security) no patents need be granted. Patent denials to protect human, animal or plant life or health, or to avoid serious injury to nature or the environment, were also justifiable under NAFTA.

It was agreed that patents in NAFTA nations would run either for 20 years from the date of the filing of the patent application, or 17 years from the grant of patent rights (the traditional U.S. approach). However, the subsequent TRIPs agreement stipulates a 20-year patent term from the date of filing. Canadian, Mexican and United States patent laws now follow this rule. For pharmaceutical patents, effectively speaking, an additional five years of protection from generic competition is often achieved because NAFTA required five-year exclusivity for product approval test data.

Under NAFTA, patent owners generally possess the right to prevent others from making, using, or selling the invention without their consent. No mention is made of the right to block infringing or unauthorized imports. If the patent covers a process, this includes the right to prevent others from using, selling, or *importing* products obtained directly from that process. Assignment or transfer of patents, and licensing contracts for their use and exploitation, were also expressly protected.

On the touchy subject of compulsory licensing, not authorized under U.S. law, NAFTA governments could allow limited nonexclusive usage without the owner's authorization if the invention has not been used or exploited locally through production or importation. This was generally permissible only after reasonable attempts at securing a license. However, under emergency, competition law or public noncommercial circumstances, no prior attempt at securing a license was required. In all cases of compulsory licensing, a duty to adequately remunerate the patent owner was created. Significant changes in Canadian compulsory licensing of pharmaceuticals were made in 1993. These changes caused some pharmaceutical prices to rise in Canada.

Apart from compulsory licensing, NAFTA authorized "limited exceptions" to exclusive patents rights. Such exceptions could not "unreasonably conflict" with the normal exploitation of the patent. Nor could they "unreasonably prejudice" the owner's "legitimate interests."

Copyrights

The NAFTA provisions on copyrights promoted uniformity in North America. Canada, Mexico, and the United States promised extensive protection of copyrights, sound recordings, program-carrying satellite signals and industrial designs. Copyrights are available on all works of original expression. These include books, articles, choreography, photographs, paintings, sculpture, films, videos, records, tapes, CDs, and other traditionally copyrighted materials. In most instances, copyrights must be granted for at least 50 years. The United States grants 70-year copyrights, which are now required for Mexico and Canada under the USMCA.

Computer programs and data compilations which constitute intellectual creations are subject to copyrights. NAFTA Article 1707 required criminal sanctions for makers and sellers of unauthorized decoding devices, and civil sanctions for unauthorized receivers of satellite signals.

Copyright holders also received under NAFTA the rights enumerated in the Berne Convention for the Protection of Literary and Artistic Works (1971). However, translation and reproduction licenses permitted by the Berne Convention were not allowed if these needs could be fulfilled voluntarily by the copyright holder but for national laws. In addition, NAFTA Article 1704.2 specifically conveyed to copyright holders:

(1) Control over importation of unauthorized copies;

(2) First public distribution rights over the work (whether by sale, rental or otherwise);

(3) Control over communication of the work to the public; and

(4) Control over commercial rental of computer programs.

If the original or a copy of a computer program is put on the market, this does not exhaust rental rights under NAFTA. Despite the specific reference to control over unauthorized imports in NAFTA Article 1704.2, blocking free trade in copyrighted goods after their first sale in the United States, Canada or Mexico was not specified. The traditional U.S. "first sale doctrine" limits an owner's rights to control copyrighted goods to their first sale or transfer. Thereafter, the goods can be freely exchanged.

Licensing and conveyance of copyrights, royalties and the like are freely transferable under NAFTA rules. Assignment of works of creation to employers by employees was also protected. However, Article 1705.5 somewhat vaguely allows limits or exceptions in "special cases" that do not conflict with "normal exploitation" of the work. "Fair use" of copyrighted material presumably fell within this provision. These NAFTA exceptions were not intended to unreasonably prejudice the owner's legitimate interests.

Trademarks

Trademarks are found on most products, and service and other marks are commonly used. The pervasiveness of marks arguably made them the most important of NAFTA's intellectual property provisions. Such marks help make markets work by signaling attributes, qualities, price levels and other relevant information. The NAFTA provisions on marks fostered uniform law. They stopped short, however, of establishing a regional trademark as the Europeans have done.

Canada, Mexico, and the United States agreed to register trademarks, service marks, collective organizational marks, and certification marks. All these marks must be capable of distinguishing goods or services. Internationally "well-known" marks were given special protections against pirates. Whether a mark is "well-known" depends upon knowledge of it in the sector of the public normally dealing with the goods or services, including knowledge in the NAFTA country resulting from promotion of the mark there. A reasonable opportunity to petition to cancel trademark registrations had to be granted. In contrast, a reasonable opportunity to oppose registration applications was not mandatory under NAFTA but the nature of the goods or services *per se* could not justify a refusal to register.

To apply for protection, there was no NAFTA requirement of prior usage on goods or services. However, if actual usage did not occur within 3 years, Chapter 17 provided registration could be denied. Immoral, deceptive, scandalous, and disparaging marks, and those that falsely suggest a connection with, or contempt of persons, institutions, beliefs or national symbols could be denied registration. No registration of words in English, French or Spanish that generically designate goods or services was permitted. Registration of marks indicating geographic origin could be rejected if "deceptively misdescriptive." Under NAFTA, trademark registrations had to be valid for at least 10 years. They could be renewed indefinitely provided use was continuous. If circumstances beyond the owner's control justify non-use, registrations could be continued. For all these purposes, the NAFTA nations agreed that use was continued when undertaken by franchisees or licensees.

NAFTA trademark owners could prevent persons from using identical or "similar" signs on identical or similar goods or services if this would cause a "likelihood of confusion." However, the "fair use" of descriptive terms could be allowed. Mandatory use of a second "local" trademark (as Mexico once required) was banned. Mandatory use that reduces the function of trademarks as source indicators was also prohibited. Furthermore, compulsory licensing of trademarks was contrary to NAFTA, but contractual licensing and assignment of trademarks could be conditioned.

Trade Secrets

NAFTA was the first international agreement on trade secret protection. Its primary impact was on Mexican law. At a minimum, each nation ensured legal means to prevent trade secrets from being disclosed, acquired, or used without consent "in a manner contrary to honest commercial practices" (Article 1711). Breach of contract, breach of confidence, and inducement to breach of contract were specifically listed as examples of dishonest commercial practices. Moreover, persons who acquired trade secrets knowing them to be the product of such practices, or who were grossly negligent in failing to know this, engaged in dishonest commercial practices. This was true even if they did not use the secrets in question.

NAFTA did not mention, however, the practice of "reverse engineering." This practice is thought to be common and has been authoritatively endorsed by the U.S. Supreme Court. See *Kewanee Oil Co. v. Bicron Corp.*, 416 U.S. 470 (1974).

For NAFTA purposes, information was "secret" if it is not generally known or readily accessible to persons who normally deal with it, had commercial value because of its secrecy, and reasonable steps were taken to keep it secret. This definition ought to cover, for example, the secret formula for making Coca-Cola. Nevertheless, trade secret holders could be required to produce evidence documenting the existence of the secret to secure protection. Release of such information to government authorities obviously involves risks that need to be considered.

No NAFTA government could discourage or impede the voluntary licensing of trade secrets (often referred to as "know-how licensing"). Imposing excessive or discriminatory conditions on know-how licenses was prohibited. More specifically, in testing and licensing the sale of pharmaceutical and agricultural chemical products, there was a general duty to protect against disclosure of proprietary data.

U.S. Statutes on Trade Secrets

In 1996, independently of NAFTA, the United States enacted the Economic Espionage Act, 18 U.S.C. § 1831 et seq. This Act creates criminal penalties for misappropriation of trade secrets. For these purposes, a "trade secret" is defined as "financial, business, scientific, technical, economic or engineering information" that the owner has taken reasonable measures to keep secret and whose "independent economic value derives from being closely held." All proceeds from the theft of trade secrets and all property used or intended for use in the misappropriation can be seized and forfeited.

The U.S. Defend Trade Secrets Act of 2016 creates a federal private right of action seeking an *ex parte* order to seize, in extraordinary circumstances, property necessary to prevent the propagation or dissemination of a trade secret. Injunctive and damages relief for actual losses and unjust enrichment may follow. However, the Act does not permit restricting an employee's movement to a competitor merely based on what he or she knows unless an employer has grounds to believe the employee intends to misappropriate a trade secret. Criminal fines of the greater of $5,000,000 or three times the value of the stolen trade secret, including research, design and avoided reproduction costs, are established.

The 2016 Act creates an alternative to state actions under the Uniform Trade Secrets Act, which in some states has been construed to permit barring employee movement if trade secret disclosure is "inevitable" in the performance of their new job.

§ 4.11 Other NAFTA Provisions

The provisions on temporary entry visas for businesspersons found in the CUSFTA were extended under NAFTA. These entry rights covered businesspersons, traders, investors, intra-company transferees and 63 designated professionals. Installers, after-sales repair and maintenance staff and managers performing services under a warranty or other service contract incidental to the sale of equipment or machinery were included, as were sales representatives, buyers, market researchers and financial service providers. White collar businesspersons only needed proof of citizenship and documentation of business purpose to work in another NAFTA country for up to 5 years. Canadian professionals flooded into the United States under NAFTA visas. Apart from these provisions, no common market for the free movement of labor was undertaken.

NAFTA embraced a competition policy principally aimed at state enterprises and governmentally sanctioned monopolies, mostly found in Mexico. State owned or controlled businesses, at all levels of government, were required to act consistently with NAFTA when exercising regulatory, administrative, or governmental authority (*e.g.*, when granting licenses). Governmentally owned and privately owned state-designated monopolies were obliged to follow commercial considerations in their transactions and avoid discrimination against goods or services of other NAFTA nations. Furthermore, each country had to ensure that such monopolies do not use their positions to engage in anticompetitive practices in non-monopoly markets. Each NAFTA nation had to adopt laws against anticompetitive business practices and cooperate in their enforcement. This caused Mexico to revive its historically weak "antitrust" laws. A consultative Trade and Competition Committee reviewed competition policy issues under NAFTA.

Other notable provisions in NAFTA included a general duty of legal transparency, fairness and due process regarding all laws affecting traders and investors with independent administrative or judicial review of government action. Generalized exceptions to the agreement covered action to protect national security and national interests such as public morals, health, national treasures, natural resources, or to enforce laws against deceptive or anticompetitive practices, short of arbitrary discriminations or disguised restraints on trade. Balance of payments trade restraints were governed by the rules of the International Monetary Fund.

Taxation issues were subjected to bilateral double taxation treaties, including a new one between Mexico and the United States. The "cultural industry" reservations secured by the CUSFTA covered Canada and Mexico but were not extended to Mexican-U.S. trade. A right of compensatory retaliation through measures of equivalent commercial effect was granted when invocation of these reservations would have violated the Canada-U.S. FTA but for the cultural industries proviso.

NAFTA was not forever. Any country could withdraw on 6 months' notice, something President Trump repeatedly threatened. See Chapter 6. Other countries or groups of countries could be admitted to the NAFTA if Canada, Mexico, and the United States agreed, and domestic ratification followed. In December of 1994, Chile was invited to become the next member of the NAFTA. Negotiations stalled for want of U.S. Congressional fast-track negotiating authority (see Section 4.1), and subsequent bilateral free trade agreements were reached between Chile and each of the three NAFTA nations.

§ 4.12 Dispute Settlement Under NAFTA

The institutional dispute settlement arrangements accompanying NAFTA were minimal. A trilateral Trade Commission (with Secretariat) comprised of ministerial, or cabinet-level, officials met at least annually to ensure effective joint management of NAFTA was established. Various intergovernmental committees were established for specific areas of NAFTA coverage (*e.g.*, competition policy) to oversee much of the work of making the free trade area function. These committees operated based on consensus, referring contentious issues to the Trade Commission.

Intergovernmental Disputes

Investment, dumping and subsidy, financial services, environmental, labor and standards disputes were subject to special dispute resolution procedures. A general intergovernmental NAFTA dispute settlement procedure was also established (Chapter 20). A right of consultation existed when one country's rights were thought to be affected. If consultations did not resolve the issue within 45 days, the complainant could convene a meeting of the Trade Commission. The Commission had to seek to promptly settle the dispute and could use its good offices, mediation, conciliation, or any other alternative means.

Absent resolution, and assuming the dispute fell under WTO jurisdiction, *the complaining country or countries ordinarily could commence dispute proceedings under GATT/WTO or NAFTA.* Once selected, the chosen forum became exclusive. However, if the dispute concerned environmental, safety, health, or conservation standards, or arose under specific environmental agreements, the responding nation could elect to have the dispute heard by a NAFTA panel. In the tuna labeling dispute, however, the United States was unable to get Mexico to withdraw its WTO complaint. For more on WTO dispute settlement procedures, see Section 1.15.

NAFTA Chapters and WTO Agreements

The right of NAFTA governments to elect as between NAFTA and WTO remedies is limited by the substantive content of the NAFTA and WTO agreements. The NAFTA Chapters chart below indicates the closest parallel WTO agreements.

NAFTA	WTO AGREEMENTS
Chapter 3, Trade in Goods	General Agreement on Tariffs and Trade 1994, Agreement on Textiles and Clothing
Chapter 4, Rules of Origin	Agreement on Rules of Origin
Chapter 5, Customs Procedures	No parallel
Chapter 6, Energy and Basic Petrochemicals	No parallel
Chapter 7, Agriculture and SPS Measures	Agreement on Agriculture, Agreement on SPS Measures
Chapter 8, Emergency Action	Agreement on Safeguards

Chapter 9, Product and Service Standards	Agreement on Technical Barriers to Trade
Chapter 10, Procurement	Agreement on Government Procurement (optional)
Chapter 11, Investment	Agreement on Trade-Related Investment Measures (TRIMs)
Chapter 12, Cross-Border Trade in Services	General Agreement on Trade in Services (GATS)
Chapter 13, Enhanced Telecommunications	See GATS, Basic Telecommunications Covered
Chapter 14, Financial Services	See GATS
Chapter 15, Competition Policy, Monopolies and State Enterprises	No parallel, but see Understanding on Interpretation of GATT Article XVII
Chapter 16, Temporary Entry for Businesspersons	No parallel
Chapter 17, Intellectual Property	Agreement on Trade-Related Aspects of Intellectual Property Rights (TRIPs)
Chapter 18, Administrative Provisions	Not applicable
Chapter 19, Antidumping and Countervailing Duty Dispute Settlement	No parallel, but see DSU and Agreement on Implementation of GATT Article VI
Chapter 20, Dispute Settlement	Understanding on Rules and Procedures Governing the Settlement of Disputes (DSU)
Chapter 21, Exceptions	See GATT Articles XX, XXI and Understanding on GATT Balance of Payments Provisions
Agreement on Environmental Cooperation	No parallel
Agreement on Labor Cooperation	No parallel

Chapter 20 Dispute Settlement Procedures

Dispute settlement procedures under NAFTA Chapter 20 involved nonbinding arbitration by five persons chosen in most cases from a trilaterally agreed roster of experts (not limited to NAFTA citizens), with a special roster established for disputes about financial services. *A "reverse selection" process was used.* The chair of the panel is first chosen by agreement or, failing agreement, by designation of one side selected by lot. The chair could not be a citizen of the selecting side but had to be a NAFTA national. Each side then selected two additional arbitrators who were citizens of the country or countries on the *other* side.

The Commission approved rules of procedure including the opportunity for written submissions, rebuttals and at least one oral hearing. Expert advice on environmental and scientific matters could be given by special procedures accessing science boards. Strict time limits were created to keep the panel on track to a prompt resolution. Within 90 days an initial confidential report was circulated, followed by 14 days for comment by the parties and 16 days for the final panel report to the Commission. There was no "appeal" in Chapter 20 disputes from the arbitrators' decision. In contrast, the WTO has an Appellate Body. See Chapter 1.

Early NAFTA Chapter 20 arbitrations concerned Canadian tariffication of agricultural quotas (upheld), U.S. escape clause relief from Mexican corn broom exports (rejected) and a successful Mexican challenge of the U.S. failure to implement cross-border trucking. Once the Trade Commission received a final arbitration panel report, NAFTA required the disputing nations to agree within 30 days on a resolution (normally by conforming to the panel's recommendations). If a mutually agreed resolution did not occur at this stage, the complaining country could retaliate by suspending the application of equivalent benefits under NAFTA, which Mexico did during the trucking dispute. Any NAFTA country could invoke the arbitration panel process if it perceived that this retaliation was excessive.

If NAFTA interpretational issues were disputed before domestic tribunals or courts, the Trade Commission (if agreed) could submit an interpretation to that body. In the absence of agreement within the Commission, any NAFTA country could intervene and submit its views as to the proper interpretation or application of NAFTA to the national court or tribunal.

Dumping and Subsidy Disputes

The independent binational review panel mechanism established in the CUSFTA (see Section 4.2) for dumping and subsidy duties was carried over at vigorous Canadian insistence into NAFTA *and* the USMCA along with the extraordinary challenge procedure to deal with allegations about the integrity of the panel review process. Chapter 19 panels were substituted for traditional judicial review at the national level of administrative dumping and countervailing duty orders. NAFTA did, however, seek to "professionalize" the process by adding judges and retired judges to the roster of acceptable Chapter 19 panelists. The panelists under CUSFTA were more often lawyers, economists, or academicians.

Each party to the dispute chose two panelists (invariably from their home country). Each party could peremptorily reject without cause four panelist selections. The fifth panelist was chosen by agreement if that was possible, or by lot if not. The panel then selected its chair (who must be a lawyer) by majority vote or failing that by lot. This panel selection procedure differed significantly from the "reverse selection" process used in Chapter 20 disputes (above).

Mexico undertook major developments to its law in this area. The Mexican procedures and rules for such panels generally follow those found in the CUSFTA. They are limited to issues of the consistency of the national decisions with domestic law, and once again have been numerous. United States administrative AD and CVD determinations (mostly annual reviews of prior proceedings) were reviewed by NAFTA Chapter 19 panels more often than Canadian or Mexican determinations. Goods from Mexico were involved in the U.S. determinations more than twice as frequently as Canadian goods.

Leather apparel, porcelain-on-steel cookware, cement, oil country tubular goods and fresh cut flowers provide examples of U.S. imports from Mexico that were the subject of Chapter 19 panel decisions. Live swine, concrete, color picture tubes and carbon steel imports from Canada were also decided under Chapter 19. Nearly all these decisions concerned the imposition of U.S. antidumping duties. U.S. exports of synthetic baler twine, steel sheet, malt beverages and refined sugar to Canada, and flat coated steel, steel plate and polystyrene to Mexico, provide examples of Chapter 19 panel decisions reviewing Canadian and Mexican AD and CVD determinations.

The never ending CUSFTA, NAFTA, and now USMCA *Softwood Lumber* dispute involving repeated U.S. CVD tariffs on Canadian exports allegedly subsidized by unfair "stumpage fees" continues. The second Softwood Lumber Settlement Agreement between the two countries expired in 2015. The U.S. took several disputes under this settlement, as agreed, to the London Court of Arbitration. See Section 4.2. The dispute remains ongoing under the Trump and Biden administrations.

Only three U.S.-requested extraordinary challenges to NAFTA Chapter 19 panel decisions were raised. These challenges concerned *Cement from Mexico* (ECC–2000–1904–01), *Magnesium from Canada* (ECC–2003–1904–01) and *Softwood Lumber from Canada*

(ECC–2004–1904–01). All of them were rejected by the Extraordinary Challenge Committees, and none were as provocative as the ECC under CUSFTA.

AD and CVD disputes could also be taken to the WTO by NAFTA governments. In other words, binational panels were not exclusive. The *Softwood Lumber* dispute, for example, resulted in conflicting WTO and NAFTA panel rulings on domestic injury. While most NAFTA trade remedy disputes were resolved by binational panels, some were settled with controversy. The "tomatoes dispute" provides a ready example.

Tomatoes Dumping Dispute

This dispute concerned Mexican exports of tomatoes at prices that were rapidly taking market share from U.S. growers. After failing to persuade the U.S. International Trade Commission to pursue escape clause relief, Florida growers alleged dumping by Mexican tomato producers early in 1996. This politically high-profile petition eventually led to a "suspension agreement" between the U.S. Commerce Department and Mexican growers. The Department promised to suspend its antidumping probe (dumping at a 17.56 percent margin had been found) in return for a commitment by Mexican growers not to sell at less than a specified "reference price." This price was based on the lowest average import price in a recent period not involving dumping. It amounted in 1996 to 20.68 cents per pound. At that price, there was no limit on the volume of Mexican tomatoes that could be shipped to the U.S. market.

Critics from states like Arizona alleged "political blackmail" as the settlement came just days before the 1996 Presidential election vote. President Clinton carried Florida in 1996, something he had failed to do in 1992. In 2013, bowing to pressure from Florida growers, a revised, more restrictive suspension agreement was reached by the Obama administration shortly after his re-election to office. A suspension agreement remains in force, raising prices and managing trade in a most remarkable manner. It has not, however, significantly slowed Mexico's market penetration. Prior to NAFTA, Mexican tomatoes held about 30 percent of the U.S. market. At this point, Mexican tomatoes enjoy at least a 65 percent U.S. market share.

§ 4.13 The 1994 Side Agreements on Labor and the Environment

The North American side agreements on labor (NAALC) and the environment (NAAEC) did not create additional substantive regional rules. Rather the side agreements basically created law enforcement mechanisms. The side agreements committed each country to the creation of environmental and labor bodies that monitor compliance with the adequacy and the enforcement of *domestic* law. The Commission for Environmental Cooperation (CEC) (Montreal) and three National Administrative Offices (NAO) concerning labor matters were empowered to receive complaints. Negotiations to resolve complaints first ensued.

NAAEC Proceedings Summarized

In the absence of a negotiated solution, the NAAEC established five environmental dispute settlement mechanisms. *First,* the CEC Secretariat may report on almost any environmental matter. *Second,* the Secretariat could develop a factual record in trade-related law enforcement disputes. *Third,* the CEC Council could release that record to the public. *Fourth,* if there was a persistent pattern of failure to enforce environmental law, the Council could mediate and conciliate. *Fifth,* if such efforts failed, the Council could send the matter to arbitration and awards could be enforced by monetary penalties. *No NAAEC dispute ever got beyond Stage Three, release of a Factual Record.*

The Commission for Environmental Cooperation (CEC)

A trilateral Commission for Environmental Cooperation (CEC) was established under the NAAEC side agreement. *This Commission has been retained, in an altered role, under the USMCA.* See Chapter 6. The Commission's Environmental Council of Ministers is comprised of cabinet-level officers from each member state. The Council can discuss, recommend, and settle environmental disputes publicly by consensus. The Commission's Secretariat (located in Montreal) investigates, reviews and reports with recommendations to the Council on environmental matters. The Executive Director of the Secretariat rotates every three years among the NAAEC countries. He or she chooses the staff of the Secretariat based on "competence and integrity." However, "due regard" must be given to recruiting "equitable proportions" from each country (Article 11). The CEC Council of Ministers and Secretariat are advised, especially on technical and scientific matters, by a 15-person Joint Public Advisory Committee.

Under the NAAEC, each member state agreed to maintain "high" levels of environmental protection, but this commitment was not enforceable through NAAEC dispute settlement. Rather, NAAEC focused on enforcement of the individual environmental protection standards of each nation. This focus, politically speaking, targeted Mexico. There was a widespread perception in the United States that Mexican enforcement of its environmental laws states was inadequate. Yet many of the complaints lodged under NAAEC challenged Canadian and U.S. environmental law enforcement.

CEC Article 13 Reports

Article 13 authorized the CEC Secretariat to issue reports on virtually any environmental matter not involving law enforcement. Notice of intent to issue such a report had to be first given to the CEC Council of Ministers. If the Council objected by a two-thirds vote, no report could be undertaken. Nongovernmental organizations (NGOs) and others could and did petition for Article 13 reports by the Secretariat. For example, the two first Article 13 reports concerned long range transport of air pollutants and the death of 40,000 migratory birds at the Silva Reservoir in Guanajuato. The latter report determined that avian botulism was the cause of the deaths and fostered a clean-up and cooperative information exchanges.

A 2004 report on the effects of transgenic maize in Mexico was noticeably high profile. Other reports concerned continental pollutant pathways, electricity and the environment, green building in North America, and sustainable freight transport. An Article 13 report concerned water use in the Fort Huachuca, Arizona region. It was undertaken at the initiative of the CEC Secretariat after an Article 14 complaint (below) concerning riparian areas for migratory birds was dismissed. (The Secretariat determined that preparation of a factual record was not warranted.) Article 13 reports could serve as an alternative to direct challenges raised under NAAEC Article 14.

Article 14 Citizen and NGO Submissions

The NAAEC, under Article 14, contained its own submission, response, and dispute resolution process. "Whistleblower" complaints could be filed with the CEC Secretariat by any person or nongovernmental organization (NGO) concerning workplaces, enterprises or sectors that produce NAAEC—traded or NAAEC—competitive goods or services. Article 14 submissions had to allege that a NAAEC nation was not "effectively enforcing" *its* environmental law. See ***SEM–97–005*** (submission challenging Canada's ratification [but not implementation by statute] of Biodiversity Convention did not concern effective enforcement of *Canadian* law). SEM stands for Submissions on Enforcement Matters. Guidelines for such submissions were issued by the CEC Secretariat. They are found at the Secretariat's excellent website, www.cec.org.

The Secretariat could dismiss Article 14 submissions on a variety of grounds. For example, the NAAEC agreement stipulated that no ineffective enforcement of environmental law exists when the action or inaction reflects a reasonable exercise of official discretion in investigatory, prosecutorial, regulatory or compliance matters. Furthermore, since "environmental law" was defined in NAAEC as excluding occupational safety and health laws, and laws that primarily manage the harvest or exploitation of natural resources, such complaints could also be dismissed. See *SEM–98–002* (submission concerning Mexican commercial forestry dispute dismissed). The submission had to "appear to be aimed at promoting enforcement rather than harassing industry." (Article 14(1)(d)). It also had to be filed in a timely manner. See *SEM–97–004* (submission filed three years after Canadian environmental decision not timely).

The CEC Secretariat determined if the submission merited a response from the nation whose environmental law enforcement practices were being challenged. Private remedies available under national law had to be pursued and pending administrative or judicial proceedings kept the CEC from moving forward on the complaint. See *Canadian Wetlands and Canadian Fisheries Act* (CEC rejects citizen and NGO submissions) SEM–96–002 and 003.

Since the NAAEC required extensive private access to environmental remedies, including the ability to file complaints with administrative authorities, access to administrative, quasi-judicial and judicial proceedings, and the right to sue for damages, mitigating relief and injunctions, exhausting national remedies first was a major prerequisite. In evaluating whether a submission merits a response, the Secretariat had also to be "guided" by whether the submission alleged "harm" to the complaining party. Proof of such harm was not mandatory, merely a relevant issue. Several of the Secretariat's early decisions suggest that it takes a liberal view of this "standing" question. See *Cozumel Pier*, SEM–96–001 (discussed below).

In addition, as the rejection by the Secretariat of the first two Article 14 submissions made clear, legislative actions that diminish environmental law enforcement could not be challenged. *See SEM–95–001 and 002.* Complaints by various NGOs against the suspension of enforcement of the U.S. Endangered Species Act listing provisions and elimination of private remedies for U.S. timber salvage sales (both alleged to have been accomplished in appropriations bills) failed to proceed under Article 14.

CEC Factual Records

With or without a response from the member state alleged to be inadequately enforcing its law, the Secretariat had to decide whether development of a factual record was warranted and inform the Council of its reasons. The Council had to approve development of a factual record by a two-thirds vote. If there were past, pending, or possible national administrative or judicial proceedings, the Secretariat or Council was unlikely to allow this to occur. NAAEC governments were obliged to submit relevant information throughout the factual record process, but the Secretariat could not enforce this obligation.

The third submission under Article 14 was made by Mexican NGOs alleging that the Mexican government had failed to conduct an environmental impact review before authorizing a cruise ship pier at Cozumel Island. See *SEM–96–001*. The CEC Secretariat ruled that this complaint passed muster under Article 14 and compiled the first factual record under NAAEC, *Factual Record No. 1* (1997). After summarizing the submission and Mexican response, the CEC "presented" facts with respect to the "matters raised in the submissions." In this record, the CEC adopted the role of a neutral finder of facts.

The second Factual Record concerned a submission that alleged that the Canadian government failed to enforce the Fisheries Act to ensure protection of fish and fish habitat in connection with hydroelectric dams in British Columbia. See *SEM–97–001*. Subsequent Article 14 Factual Records concerned Canadian enforcement of the Fisheries Act in the Arctic (*Oldman River, SEM–97–006*), logging rules in British Columbia (*SEM–00–004*), and mining in British Columbia (*SEM–98–004*).

Other Factual Records covered U.S. law enforcement regarding migratory birds (*SEM–99–002*), Mexican enforcement of hazardous waste law in Tijuana (*SEM–98–007*), and Mexico City (*SEM–03–004*), shrimp farming regulations in Nayarit (*SEM–98–006*), wastewater river pollution in Sonora (*SEM–97–002*), pulp and paper mill pollution in Canada (*SEM–02–003*), Canadian migratory bird protection from logging (*SEM–02–001*), (*SEM–04–006*), access to environmental justice by Mexican Indigenous communities (Tarahumara, *SEM–00–006*), copper smelting pollution in Sonora, Mexico (Molymex II, *SEM–00–005*) pollution of Lake Chapala in Mexico (*SEM–03–003*), auto pollution in Quebec (*SEM–04–007*) and toxic pollutants in Montreal (*SEM–03–005*). All these Factual Records are available at cec.org.

NAALC Proceedings Summarized

The NAALC labor law enforcement system was a calibrated four-tier series of dispute resolution mechanisms. *First*, the NAOs could review and report on eleven designated labor law enforcement matters that correspond to the NAALC Labor Principles. *Second*, ministerial consultations could follow when recommended by the

NAO. *Third*, an Evaluation Committee of Experts could report on trade-related mutually recognized labor law enforcement patterns of practice concerning eight of the NAALC Labor Principles (excluding strikes, union organizing and collective bargaining). *Fourth*, persistent patterns of failure to enforce occupational health and safety, child labor or minimum wage laws could be arbitrated, and awards enforced by monetary penalties. *No NAALC dispute ever got beyond Stage Two, ministerial consultations. The NAALC labor law system, including NAOs, is not repeated in the USMCA.* See Chapter 6.

Labor Law Enforcement Submissions—Union Organizing

Early U.S. organized labor submissions to the United States NAO alleged the firing by U.S. and Japanese maquiladora subsidiaries of Mexican workers due to union organizing activities, *U.S. NAO Submission Nos. 940001, 2 and 3*. Public hearings were held at which Mexican workers, their attorneys and U.S. union supporters gave testimony. Honeywell, General Electric and SONY boycotted these hearings. The NAO Report in the Honeywell and GE cases was generally uncertain as to the legality of the firings under Mexican law, particularly because some of the dismissed workers accepted severance pay which indemnified the employers. No ministerial consultations were recommended, but some employees were reinstated and both Honeywell and GE made it clear to their managers that they did not want a reoccurrence of these events.

With SONY, the NAO Report cited "serious questions" about the legality of the firings and recommended ministerial consultations. These consultations resulted in a series of workshops, conferences, studies, and meetings (including SONY representatives) on union registration and certification (especially of independent unions) in Mexico. In due course, the U.S. Secretary of Labor requested a follow-up NAO report. This report put a positive spin on developments in Mexico concerning union organizing, a topic that NAALC does not allow to proceed to the next dispute settlement tier (an Evaluation Committee of Experts).

On the other side of the border, the Telephone Workers Union of Mexico (collaborating with the Communications Workers of America) (CWA) filed a submission with the Mexican NAO about worker dismissals and a plant closing at Sprint's La Conexion Familiar in San Francisco, *OAN Mex. Submission No. 9501*. Again, the allegation involved denial of labor's right to organize. The NLRB eventually ruled against Sprint and ordered rehiring of the workers. See 322 NLRB 774 (1996). On appeal, the D.C. Circuit found that the claim that plant was closed because of union organizing activities was not substantiated. See *LCF, Inc. v. NLRB*, 129 F.3d 1276 (1997). The

Mexican NAO accepted submissions challenging U.S. labor law enforcement concerning workers in a solar panel plant in California, the Washington State apple industry, a Maine egg farm, migrant workers in New York, H-2B Visa workers, and the North Carolina ban on public sector collective bargaining, *OAN Mex. Nos. 9801, 9802, 9803, 2001–01, 2003–1, 2005–01.*

In the *Sprint* submission the Mexican NAO found "possible problems" in enforcement of U.S. labor law and recommended ministerial consultations. These consultations resulted in a public forum, a special report by the NAALC Commission on *Plant Closings and Labor Rights* (1997) in all three NAFTA nations and monitoring of the pending NLRB proceeding based upon Sprint's actions. The report highlights widespread use of anti-union plant closing tactics in the United States (but not Canada or Mexico):

> U.S. labor law authorities actively prosecute unfair labor practice cases involving plant closings and threats of plant closing. They demonstrate a high level of success in litigation before the NLRB and the courts. However, despite this effective enforcement, the incidence of anti-union plant closings and threats of plant closing continues with some frequency. There appears to be significant variation in the types of statements employers are permitted to make about plant closings in connection with a union organizing effort.
>
> The Secretariat examined all 89 federal appeals court decisions in cases involving plant closings and threats of plant closing published between 1986 and 1993. Of the cases, 70 arose in the context of a new union organizing campaign. Closings or partial closings prompted 32 cases, and 57 cases involved threats of closing. Courts of appeals upheld NLRB determinations that employers unlawfully closed or threatened to close plants in 84 of the 89 cases.
>
> The Secretariat studied 319 decisions of the NLRB between 1990 and 1995 involving plant closings and the threats of closing. Of the total, 109 cases involved closings or partial closings, and 210 involved threats of closing. New union organizing campaigns in non-union workplaces were involved in 275 of these cases, while 44 involved existing unions. The NLRB found a violation by the employer in 283 of the 319 cases.
>
> The Secretariat also looked at case files in two regional offices of the NLRB to determine the volume and disposition of cases that do not reach the level of a published determination by an adjudicator. Findings suggest that for

> every case that reaches a published decision, 10 cases are initiated at the regional office level. More than half of these are withdrawn or dismissed.
>
> In more than 40 percent of cases where the regional office found merit in the charge, the NLRB General Counsel took the case to trial before an ALJ. This is 10 times the rate of enforcement in other cases of meritorious unfair labor practice charges against employers. These findings indicate that the NLRB takes plant closing cases very seriously and actively pursues them to a litigated conclusion. The General Counsel prevails in nearly 90 percent of such cases.
>
> In the United States, resources were readily available to conduct survey research for information that could not be gleaned from administrative and judicial records. Union representatives surveyed reported what they believed to be plant closing threats occurring in half of the sampled union organizing campaigns during the 3-year period studied, with a higher incidence in industries more susceptible to closing such as manufacturing, trucking, and warehousing. Perceived plant closing threats were the largest single factor identified by respondents who decided to withdraw an election petition they had earlier filed, thus discontinuing the organizing campaign. When unions proceeded to an election, the overall union win rate where plant closing threats were reported to have occurred was 33 percent, compared with 47 percent in elections where no threats were reported to have taken place.

The fourth submission to the U.S. NAO was made by labor and human rights groups and a Mexican lawyers association. They claimed that an independent public sector Mexican union lost its representation rights to a rival union when the government merged the Fisheries Ministry into a larger Ministry of the Environment, Natural Resources and Fisheries, *U.S. NAO Submission No. 9610* ("Pesca Union"). After a public hearing at which many testified, the NAO Report recommended ministerial consultations on the effect of International Labor Organization (ILO) Conventions (No. 87 was cited) on Mexican labor law, particularly the prohibition against more than one union in a governmental entity. The independent union subsequently had its registration restored by Mexican court order.

Another union organizing case came to the U.S. NAO in 1996, *Submission No. 9602*. The Communications Workers of America and its Mexican ally (the STRM) alleged that Taiwan-owned Maxi-Switch had a "protection contract" with a CTM union that was not employee approved. CTM is closely allied with the ruling PRI party. After scheduling public testimony, the complaint was withdrawn when registration was granted to a STRM-affiliated "independent" union in the Maxi-Switch maquiladora plant.

Other submissions accepted by the U.S. NAO concerning union organizing in Mexico have involved the Itapsa export processing plant in Ciudad de los Reyes (also filed with the Canadian NAO), and TAESA flight attendants, *U.S. Submissions 9801 and 9901.* A rare Canadian-oriented submission challenged Quebec law enforcement on union organizing at a McDonald's restaurant in St. Hubert, *U.S. Submission 9803.*

Perhaps the most bitter of all thc union organizing complaints was that filed against Han Young, a Hyundai Corporation maquiladora making truck chassis in Tijuana, Mexico, *U.S. NAO Submission No. 9702.* Unions and labor groups from all three NAFTA nations alleged a brutal and blatant pattern of employer-CTM opposition to an independent union organizing effort. The U.S. NAO report documents threats, bribes, harassment, intimidation, and dismissals. Moreover, the independent union's election victory was inexplicably nullified by the local Mexican labor Conciliation and Arbitration Board (CAB). At this point, with outrage and embarrassment evident in the NAO investigation, the Mexican federal and state governments intervened and negotiated a settlement allowing a second supervised election which the independents also won. The local CAB then delayed notifying the election results to Han Young which in turn refused to collectively bargain. Indeed, Han Young hired new workers just in time for the CTM to petition for a third union representation election.

NAO Submission Strategies

One pattern that emerged in NAALC dispute settlement was the cross-border alliance of U.S. organized labor with Mexican labor groups, particularly those that were part of the "forista" movement for independent unions. Another factor of note was the absence of any need to exhaust national administrative remedies, which was required under the NAAEC. Indeed, there were essentially no "standing to complain" requirements under NAALC. The NAOs can investigate and report at their discretion.

One example of creative use of the NAALC involves double barrel submissions. In at least two instances, organized labor and NGOs filed complaints with both available NAOs. In one case, the U.S. NAO and the Canada NAO received essentially the same submission concerning union organizing and occupational safety at an auto parts plant in Ciudad de los Reyes, Mexico, *U.S. Submission No. 97–03* and *Canada Submission No. 98–1.* Each NAO then proceeded to review and report on inadequate Mexican labor law enforcement. Both NAOs recommended Ministerial Consultations.

Likewise, in the Fall of 1998, a coalition of NGOs headed by a Yale Law School group filed submissions with the Canadian *and* Mexican NAOs alleging ineffective enforcement of U.S. minimum wage and overtime pay laws against employers of foreign nationals, *Submission Nos. Canada 98–2 and Mexico 98–04.* These complaints challenged U.S. Labor Department reporting of suspected immigration violations to the U.S. Immigration and Naturalization Service. They alleged that such practices deter immigrant workers from filing wage and hour complaints under U.S. law. On the same day that the Mexican NAO accepted the submission (Nov. 23, 1998), the U.S. government announced that a Memorandum of Understanding had been signed with the intent of dealing with these issues.

After a flurry of NAO submissions during the first decade of NAALC, the numbers dropped significantly. It appears that NAALC as a labor law enforcement "remedy" was increasingly perceived to be not worth pursuing.

Pregnancy Discrimination in Mexico

As the number, scope and creativity of the submissions and reports continued to grow, NAALC appeared to be more than the toothless tiger many have alleged it to be. For example, the U.S. NAO investigated allegations of widespread state-tolerated sex discrimination against pregnant women in maquiladora plants, *Submission No. 97–01.* This complaint could have resulted (but did not) in a report by an Evaluation Committee of Experts (discussed above).

Human Rights Watch/Americas, the International Labor Rights Fund and the Association Nacional de Abogados Democraticos (the same complainants in the *Pesca Union* case above) filed this submission. They maintained that employers regularly used pregnancy tests to avoid the six weeks paid maternity leave required under Mexican law. The Mexican NAO challenged these complaints as beyond the scope of the NAALC, asserted that Mexican law adequately protects women from gender discrimination, and argued that there is no Mexican law against pre-employment pregnancy screening. The U.S. NAO hired an expert on Mexican labor law and gender issues and held public hearings in Brownsville, Texas at which workers and expert witnesses testified.

The NAO, in its report, reviewed Mexican constitutional and labor law, their enforcement bodies, the Alliance for Equality (the Mexican National Program for Women, 1995–2000), the Mexican Human Rights Commission and relevant international conventions. Post-employment pregnancy discrimination is clearly illegal in Mexico. On pre-employment law, one decision of note that emerged from the investigation was that of the Human Rights Commission for the Federal District which found pre-employment pregnancy screening a violation of Articles 4 and 5 of the Mexican Constitution. Here is the U.S. NAO analysis on point. Note especially its implications concerning the credibility of the Mexican NAO submissions in response to the complaint:

> [T]he Human Rights Commission for the Federal District offers a markedly different interpretation to that of the Mexican NAO on the legality of pre-employment pregnancy screening. The Commission found (1) that the federal agencies it investigated did, in fact, conduct pregnancy screening and, (2) this practice violated Mexico's Constitution.
>
> The Mexican NAO has asserted that the recommendations of the Commission are not binding and do not establish jurisprudence. The enacting legislation for the Commission, however, imposes an obligation on the responding agencies to comply with the recommendations once they accept the findings of the report. Additionally, the Commission was created pursuant to the Mexican Constitution and implemented by Federal law. It is composed of prominent jurists, appointed by the President and confirmed by the legislature, and their recommendation, in this case, was complied with by Federal Government agencies. Further, though the case involved public sector agencies, in its recommendation the Commission made no distinction on the application of the appropriate constitutional guarantees between the public and private sectors.
>
> The position of the Human Rights Commission on the legality of pregnancy screening is markedly different from that expressed by the Mexican NAO. Moreover, the *Alliance for Equality* recognized pregnancy screening as a problem and outlined a plan of action to address such discriminatory practices. That pregnancy screening occurs and is of concern is supported by information from companies conducting business in Mexico, women workers, and the submitters. It also appears that the intrusive nature of the

> questioning described in the submission goes beyond what is necessary to determine if an applicant for employment is pregnant.
>
> An additional question is raised with regard to the lack of any legal procedure by which to bring cases of pre-employment gender discrimination. The Mexican NAO asserted that the FLL [Federal Labor Law] does not provide for the adjudication of cases involving pre-employment discrimination. CAB officials interviewed by HRW [Human Rights Watch] also indicated that the CABs had no jurisdiction over these cases as they involved issues that occurred prior to the establishment of the employment relationship. The Mexican NAO's position appears to go beyond the question of pre-employment pregnancy screening to also include the lack of a legal procedure for bringing any pre-employment discrimination issue. Since Mexican law clearly prohibits employers from discriminating in hiring for a variety of reasons, the Mexican NAO's response creates a question as to what process exists for bringing such pre-employment discrimination claims.

The NAO report issued in Submission No. 97–01 recommended ministerial consultations. These resulted in a U.S.-Mexican agreement on an improved "action plan" to combat pregnancy discrimination in the workplace, though pregnancy discrimination at hiring is said to continue.

§ 4.14 Expanding NAFTA

When Canada and the United States agreed to free trade in 1989, there was no expectation of extension of that agreement to Mexico or any other country. The NAFTA agreement, on the other hand, specifically anticipated growth by accession. Article 2204 invited applications to join NAFTA by countries or groups of countries without regard to their geographic location or cultural background. This is unlike the European Union which only allows "European" nations to join. The NAFTA Free Trade Commission was authorized to negotiate the terms and conditions of any new memberships. The resulting accession agreement had to be approved and ratified by each NAFTA nation. Practically speaking, as in the European Union, this means that current members could veto NAFTA applicants.

In December 1994, at the "Summit of the Americas" in Miami, Canada and Mexico joined the United States formally invited Chile to apply for NAFTA membership. This invitation went nowhere because Congress repeatedly refused to authorize "fast-track" negotiations by President Clinton. Fast-track negotiations provide assurance to all concerned that Congress would not be able to alter the terms and conditions of Chile's accession. Under fast-track, Congress would have to approve or disapprove the agreement by majority vote. See Section 4.1. Apart from partisan politics, one thorny issue was whether there would be side agreements with Chile on labor and the environment.

Absent U.S. fast-track authority, Chile, Canada, and Mexico steered different courses. Mexico and Chile renegotiated and expanded their pre-NAFTA free trade agreement. Canada and Chile reached agreement in 1997 on free trade along with side agreements that are like NAAEC and NAALC. Chile in 1996 became a free trade associate of MERCOSUR, the Southern Cone common market of Brazil, Argentina, Paraguay, and Uruguay.

All these free trade commitments flowed partly from want of U.S. fast-track authority. They had an impact on trade and investment patterns. Some U.S. companies with Canadian subsidiaries, for example, shifted production and exports to Canada to take advantage of Canada-Chile free trade. When fast-track authority was finally renewed in 2002, a U.S.-Chile FTA was the first to be signed. See Section 5.1.

§ 4.15 Quebec and NAFTA/USMCA

In 1987, the "Meech Lake Accord" was reached. This agreement recognized Quebec as a "distinct society" in Canada. What the practical consequences of this recognition would have been will never be known. Quebec's adherence to the Meech Lake Accord was nullified when Manitoba, New Brunswick and ultimately Newfoundland failed to ratify the Accord. A second set of negotiations led in 1992 to the Charlottetown Accord which also acknowledged Quebec as a distinct society with its French language, unique culture, and Civil Law tradition. This time a national referendum was held, and its defeat was overwhelming. Quebec, five English-speaking Canadian provinces, and the Yukon territory voted against the Charlottetown Accord.

The Canadian Constitution of 1982 was adopted by an Act of the British Parliament. As such, the Act and the Constitution are thought to bind all Canadian provinces including Quebec. That province, however, has never formally ratified the Constitution of Canada. Since 1982 a series of negotiations have attempted to secure Quebec's ratification, and all have failed miserably.

The failure of these Accords moved Quebec towards separation from Canada. In 1994 and again in 2012, the Parti Quebecois came to power. It held a provincial referendum on separation in 1995. By the narrowest of margins, the people of Quebec rejected separation from Canada. Just exactly what "separation" would have meant was never entirely clear during the debate, perhaps deliberately so.

In 1998, Canada's Supreme Court ruled that Quebec could not "under the Constitution" withdraw unilaterally. To secede, Quebec would need to negotiate a constitutional amendment with the rest of Canada. The rest of Canada would, likewise, be obliged to enter such negotiations if a "clear majority" of Quebec's voters approved a "clear question" on secession in a referendum. Subsequently, the Canadian Parliament legislated rules which will make it difficult for Quebec to separate, should it ever wish to do so. That prospect now seems more remote, particularly because the Parti Quebecois lost power in 2003, resumed power then lost control again.

If Quebec ever separates from Canada, this will raise fundamental issues about Quebec and NAFTA the USMCA. Would Quebec be forced to negotiate for membership? If so, would English-speaking Canada veto its application? Might Quebec's relationship to Canada continue in some limited manner (such as for defense and international trade purposes) such that the USMCA is not an issue at all?

Might Quebec automatically "succeed" to the USMCA agreement, thus becoming a member without application? Customary international practice maintains existing treaties when nations sub-divide. This practice was applied to the Czech Republic, Slovakia, and various states of the former Yugoslavia. Custom suggests that fears in Quebec about losing USMCA benefits are exaggerated.

LINKS

§ 4.16 Link to Text of CUSFTA

http://www.worldtradelaw.net/nafta/Cusfta.pdf.download

§ 4.17 Link to Text of NAFTA

http://www.sice.oas.org/trade/nafta/naftatce.asp

Chapter 5

THE PROLIFERATION OF FREE TRADE AGREEMENTS AFTER NAFTA

Table of Sections

§ 5.1 Free Trade Agreements (FTAs) and Mini-Trade Deals After NAFTA

NAFTA was a watershed event in 1994. In its wake, hundreds of comprehensive free trade agreements (FTAs) influenced by WTO rules (see Chapter 2) proliferated around the world, including for example the European Union and South Africa, Canada and Costa Rica, China and Chile, and Japan and Singapore. The worldwide array of FTAs includes agreements between developed countries (*e.g.*, the United States and South Korea), agreements between developed and developing countries (*e.g.*, Japan and Vietnam) and agreements between developing nations (*e.g.*, India and Sri Lanka).

Sparked and influenced by NAFTA, leading nations gathered networks of broad free trade agreements:

(1) *Japan* has "Economic Partnership Agreements" (free trade agreements) with Mexico, Chile, Thailand, the Philippines, Malaysia, Vietnam, Switzerland, India, Indonesia, Brunei, Singapore, Peru, Mongolia, and the Association of Southeast Asian Nations (ASEAN, Section 2.6), an extensive 2019 agreement with the European Union (Section 5.5). Japan is a leader in the TPP-11 (Section 5.3). In 2020, Japan joined the 15-nation China-led Regional Comprehensive Economic Partnership (RCEP 2020, Section 5.5).

(2) *China* has free trade agreements with its own Hong Kong and Macau Special Administrative Regions, Chile, Pakistan, Costa Rica, Peru, Singapore, New Zealand, Australia, South Korea, Iceland, Maldives, Mauritius, the United Arab Emirates, ASEAN (Section 2.6) and leads RCEP 2020 (Section 5.5). RCEP is the world's largest regional FTA, notably exceeding the USMCA, the EU customs union, and the EU-Japan FTA in terms of its share of global goods trade and GDP. China is a more important strategic trade and supply chain partner with Japan, Vietnam, Australia, New Zealand, and Malaysia than the United States.

(3) The *European Union* has over 70 free trade partners under roughly 40 FTAs, including Algeria, Chile, Egypt, Iceland, Israel, Jordan, Lebanon, Mexico, Morocco, Norway, Serbia, South Africa, Vietnam, Singapore, Japan, Canada, Tunisia and a customs union agreement with Turkey. The Trump administration once criticized the EU as engaged in a "free trade land grab" effectively resurrecting colonial era trade preferences. *The UK post-BREXIT* rolled over many EU FTAs, added new ones with Australia and New Zealand, and joined TPP-11, the first non-Pacific country to do so. See Chapter 3 and my Concise Hornbook on *The European Union Beyond BREXIT*.

(4) The *United States* has 12 bilateral free trade agreements, with Australia (2004), Bahrain (2006), Chile (2004), Colombia (2012), Israel (1985), Jordan (2001), South Korea (KORUS 2012 and 2018, see Section 6.6), Morocco (2006), Oman (2006), Panama (2012), Peru (2007) and Singapore (2004). It has the NAFTA 1994 (see Chapter 4) and USMCA 2020 multilateral agreements (Section 6.8) with Canada and Mexico. The U.S. also has the Dominican

Republic-Central America Free Trade Agreement (DR-CAFTA 2015) with the Dominican Republic, Guatemala, Honduras, El Salvador, Nicaragua, and Costa Rica.

(5) *India* has free trade agreements with ASEAN (Section 2.6), Sri Lanka, Malaysia, the Gulf Cooperation Council (GCC) (Section 2.6), Singapore, Korea, Japan, Afghanistan, Chile, MERCOSUR (Section 2.6) and leads the 7-nation South Asian FTA. India dropped out of the RCEP negotiations and has a limited FTA with Australia.

(6) *South Korea* has free trade agreements with ASEAN, India, Australia, Canada, the United States (KORUS I and II, Section 6.6), China, Chile, Colombia, EFTA, the European Union (KOREU), Turkey, Vietnam, Peru, Singapore and RCEP. South Korea is seeking to join TPP-11.

(7) *Canada* has free trade agreements with Korea, the EU (CETA 2017, Section 5.1), Chile, Peru, Colombia, Costa Rica, Israel, EFTA, Jordan, Panama, Honduras, Ukraine, and is a leader in the TPP-11 (Section 5.3).

(8) *Mexico* has free trade agreements with Chile, Colombia, Venezuela (dormant), Costa Rica, Bolivia, Nicaragua, Guatemala, Honduras, El Salvador, Peru, Uruguay, the European Union, Japan, and Israel. It also has an enhanced Pacific Alliance with Chile, Peru, and Colombia, and participates in the TPP-11 (Section 5.3).

Specific Mini-Trade Deals

In recent years, COVID, the rise of China, dramatic increases in shipping costs, the Russian invasion of Ukraine, and the war between Hamas and Israel have influenced FTA growth and character. Substantial global supply chain revisions are underway. These factors have impacted the alignment, growth and character of free trade agreements. Regional trade agreements like the USMCA, the EU and RCEP have become more significant, and "mini-trade deals" on select trade topics, for example digital trade and data privacy, have proliferated. With WTO-negotiated tariffs at an all-time low below 10%, mini-deals focused on non-tariff trade barriers and topics the WTO does not address are attractive.

The United States under the Biden administration undertook no new comprehensive FTA negotiations, not even with Britain post-BREXIT. Instead, the U.S. has pursued trade-specific mini-deals. For example, the U.S. Indo-Pacific Economic Framework (an "arrangement") acts as an alternative to TPP-11 (Section 5.3). It is focused on regulatory practices, agriculture, digital trade, labor and environmental standards, trade facilitation, supply chains, infrastructure, decarbonization, taxation and corruption. Australia, Indonesia, Japan, South Korea and Singapore are participating. The U.S. also has mini-trade deals with the EU, for example on mutual recognition of food and drug regulations. Studies suggest that the U.S. has over 1,200, and the EU more than 2,000, such mini-trade deals.

These mini-trade deals do NOT require Congressional approval, a major political asset in a divided America.

§ 5.2 Content Changes in U.S. FTAs from NAFTA to President Trump

The United States negotiated free trade agreements post-NAFTA in 1994 prior to the presidency of Donald Trump. These included FTAs with Australia, Bahrain, Chile, Colombia, Jordan, South Korea (KORUS), Morocco, Oman, Panama, Peru, and Singapore, plus the Dominican Republic-Central America Free Trade Agreement (DR-CAFTA) with the Dominican Republic, Guatemala, Honduras, El Salvador, Nicaragua, and Costa Rica.

United States free trade agreements after NAFTA evolved substantively. Coverage of labor and environmental law enforcement was folded into the trade agreement (compare NAFTA's side agreements) and all remedies are intergovernmental (compare private and NGO "remedies" in the side agreements reviewed in Section 4.13). Coverage of labor law was narrowed to core ILO principles: The rights of association, organization, and collective bargaining; acceptable work conditions regarding minimum wages, hours and occupational health and safety; minimum wages for employment of children and elimination of the worst forms of child labor; and a ban on forced or compulsory labor.

Other NAFTA-plus provisions emerged. These are most evident regarding foreign investment and intellectual property. Regarding investor-state claims, for example, post-NAFTA U.S. free trade agreements insert the word "customary" before international law in defining the minimum standard of treatment to which foreign investors are entitled. This insertion tracks the official Interpretation issued in that regard under NAFTA. Further, the contested terms "fair and equitable treatment" and "full protection and security" do not require treatment in addition to or beyond that customary standard, and do not create additional substantive rights. This language was defined for the first time:

> "fair and equitable treatment" includes the obligation not to deny justice in criminal, civil, or administrative adjudicatory proceedings in accordance with the principle of due process embodied in the principal legal systems of the world; and
>
> "full protection and security" requires each Party to provide the level of police protection required under customary international law.

More significantly perhaps, starting with the U.S.-Chile FTA, these agreements contain an Annex restricting the scope of "indirect expropriation" claims:

> Except in rare circumstances, nondiscriminatory regulatory actions by a Party that are designed and applied to protect legitimate public welfare objectives, such as public health, safety and the environment, do not constitute indirect expropriations.

Hence the potential for succeeding with "regulatory takings" investor-state claims has been reduced. The CAFTA-DR agreement anticipates creating an appellate body of some sort for investor-state arbitration decisions.

Regarding intellectual property, post-NAFTA FTAs moved into the Internet age. Protection of domain names, and adherence to the WIPO Internet treaties, were stipulated. E-commerce and free trade in digital products were embraced, copyrights extended to rights-management (encryption) and anti-circumvention (hacking) technology, protection against web music file sharing enhanced, and potential liability of Internet Service Providers detailed.

Less visibly, pharmaceutical patent owners obtained extensions of their patents to compensate for delays in the approval process, and greater control over their test data, making it harder for generic competition to emerge. They also gained "linkage," meaning local drug regulators must make sure generics are not patent infringing before their release. In addition, adherence to the Patent Law Treaty (2000) and the Trademark Law Treaty (1994) was agreed. Anti-counterfeiting laws were tightened, particularly regarding mandatory destruction of counterfeit goods.

Other changes pushed further along the path of free trade in services and comprehensive customs law administration rules. Antidumping and countervailing duty laws remain applicable but appeals from administrative determinations are taken in national courts, not binational panels. Except for limited provisions in the

Chile-U.S. agreement, business visas drop completely out of U.S. free trade agreements, a NAFTA-minus development.

In sum, post NAFTA, the United States generally used its leverage with smaller trade partners in the Americas, the Middle East, and Pacific Rim to obtain more preferential treatment and expanded protection for its goods, services, technology, and investors. Save for the 2012 KORUS agreement (Section 6.6), the U.S. gave up relatively little in return, for example modest increases in agricultural market openings.

§ 5.3 The Trans-Pacific Partnership (TPP-12 2016) and TPP-11 (2018)

TPP-12

Negotiation of the TPP was led by the United States under President Obama's "pivot to Asia" and a desire to create a "next generation" FTA model. Late in 2015, a Trans-Pacific Partnership (TPP) agreement was reached among the three NAFTA nations plus Peru, Chile, Brunei, Singapore, Malaysia, Vietnam, Japan, Australia, and New Zealand (but notably not China). These Pacific Rim partners comprise roughly 40% of world trade. The TPP contained notable developments on freer agricultural and food trade, trade in automobiles and auto parts, bio-similar pharmaceuticals, protection of foreign investment, a self-judging essential security exception, a bar on forced technology transfers as an investor performance requirement, and a procedural tune up of investor-state arbitrations resembling those of CETA 2017 (Section 5.4).

Coverage of minimum wages and working hours, independent unions, technology protections including a prohibition of data localization requirements, anti-corruption obligations in the public and private sectors, due process and private action rights in competition (antitrust) proceedings, service sector openings, e-commerce, criminal sanctions for counterfeiting and trade secret theft, environmental protection and restraints on subsidies for state-owned enterprises (SOEs) were included in TPP-12. It also contained minimal currency manipulation rules, a debated topic. South Korea, Taiwan and Indonesia expressed interest in joining the TPP, which clearly resembled a containment strategy relative to China's rising economic power.

As signed by President Obama, TPP ratification in the United States would have been under fast-track procedures, discussed in Section 4.1. President Trump's quick withdrawal from the TPP mooted this possibility. This decision has had broad consequences in the world of international trade. See Chapter 6. Perhaps most significantly, China, Japan, the EU, Canada, and others have moved away from U.S. trade policy leadership and pursued other free trade partners.

The TPP-12 agreement in full is linked in Section 5.6. Its Contents, Annexes and Related Instruments are reproduced with links in Section 6.3.

TPP-11

The remaining TPP partners, led by Japan and Canada, signed an altered TPP-11 free trade agreement in 2018 covering roughly 15% of global trade. TPP-11 has been re-named the *Comprehensive and Progressive Trans-Pacific Partnership (CPTPP).* It incorporates most TPP provisions, subject to suspensions and side letters altering TPP-12.

Complete duty-free trade in seafood, wine, sheep meat, cotton wool and most manufactured are anticipated under TPP-11. Autos will be subject to a 45% net cost TPP-11 content rule of origin, an advantage expected to favor Japanese exports. Significant intellectual property provisions secured under U.S. pressure, notably eight-year protection for biologic drugs, 70-year copyrights, five-year patent extensions after unreasonable delays in obtaining patents, and eight-year protection of pharmaceutical test data before generic approvals, were dropped.

Canada obtained a cultural industries exclusion, not unlike that of NAFTA 1994. Innovative TPP-12 rules on SOEs were largely retained, including principles of nondiscrimination, adherence to commercial considerations, and limitations on noncommercial governmental assists causing adverse effects and material injury. These rules were diminished for Malaysia in TPP-11. E-commerce trade coverage and protection for digital products drawn from TPP-12 are in TPP-11, but Vietnam has a five-year exception allowing greater control over and taxation of electronic payments along with a national office requirement.

Australia, New Zealand, and Canada now have reduced trade barriers on agricultural exports to Japan, which may prove harmful to USA exports of wheat, dairy products, rice, and beef. Transparency and anticorruption provisions follow APEC Codes and the UN Convention, with no tax deductions for corrupt payments to public officials. Trader/investor/professional visas resembling those of NAFTA 1994 are created, but in a change from TPP-12 migration of skilled labor is subject to local market need tests.

Labor and the environment are also part of TPP-11, potentially subject to trade sanctions. On labor, International Labor

Organization principles dominate much as under TPP-12, though independent labor union rights have been delayed for Vietnam. Vietnam's labor costs are now roughly half those of China, incentivizing investment out of the PRC in the age of Trump tariffs. Australia now has reduced trade barriers on agricultural exports to Japan, which may prove averse to US. exports of wheat, rice, and beef. Transparency and anticorruption provisions follow APEC Codes and the UN Convention, with no tax deductions for corrupt payments to public officials.

Trader/investor/professional visas resembling those of NAFTA 1994 are created, but in a change from TPP-12 migration of skilled labor is subject to local market need tests. On the environment, separate agreements concern the Ozone, Ship Pollution, Biodiversity, Emissions, Invasive Species, Endangered Species, and Capture Fisheries. There is a public submission procedure that can trigger review of environmental issues.

Creation of state-to-state dispute settlement (SSDS) procedures is anticipated. Investor-state dispute settlement (ISDS) by arbitration and payment of damages is provided for but, as under TPP-12, use of domestic courts is first required. The right of member states to regulate in the public interest is made clear. But, in a deviation from TPP-12, ISDS arbitrations do not apply to investment contracts requiring government approval and contracts between companies and governments. Australia, which refused ISDS under the U.S.-Australian bilateral FTA, joined in TPP-11 ISDS. However, compulsory ISDS between New Zealand and five other TPP-11 nations is not mandatory.

No TPP-11 ISDS arbitrations may concern tobacco regulation, a ban originating in TPP-12 after R.J. Reynolds abused ISDS remedies by purchasing a Hong Kong distributor to challenge Australia's plain packaging cigarette laws under a Hong Kong-Australia bilateral investment treaty (BIT) dating from the British era. This maneuver is a good example of foreign investment "treaty shopping." See Section 7.1.

The TPP-11 agreement is linked in Section 5.7. It took effect Feb. 1, 2019. Brunei and Malaysia have not ratified TPP-11. Malaysia indicated its focus is on the RCEP agreement led by China and ASEAN (Section 5.5). Britain (yes, post-BREXIT Britain), Chile, and Peru have joined TPP-11.

China, Taiwan, South Korea, and Ecuador are seeking to join TPP-11. The U.S. under President Biden did not express interest in doing so, favoring instead its Indo-Pacific Framework Agreement. See Section 5.1.

§ 5.4 The Canada-EU Comprehensive Economic and Trade Agreement (CETA 2017)

Given the withdrawal of the United States from the TPP, the uncertain future of TTIP negotiations between the U.S. and the EU, and the onslaught of FTAs Britain is expected to seek after BREXIT, one free trade agreement that now stands out as a trade policy model in the developed world is CETA, the Comprehensive Economic and Trade Agreement between Canada and the EU, provisionally operational since 2017.

Upon ratification, 98% of the tariffs on trade between the parties were eliminated, with tariffs on autos phasing out over seven years, subject to 50 to 55% Canadian content rules of origin except for a generous 20% content rule applicable to the first 100,000 Canadian auto exports. Considerable agreement on product standards and testing in the country of export was reached, and Canadian firms get to bid on EU contracts on the same footing as EU companies. Free trade in services is based on a "negative list", a first for the EU, and will rachet up if either party grants broader entry in any other subsequent free trade agreement. Mobility for service providers and businesspeople is extensive, and mutual recognition of professional diplomas and licensing is anticipated.

Both parties have a history of protecting their agricultural and fish/seafood markets. After various transition periods, CETA renders nearly 95% of these markets duty-free. There are exceptions for meat quotas on both sides and EU cheese export quotas. The EU obtained greater protection for geographic origin of products (Feta cheese, Parma ham), and increased pharmaceutical patent protection. Healthcare and education, along with cultural industries, are excluded under CETA, and Canada continues to control development of its natural resources.

Foreign investor rights and arbitral protections cover the entire EU, another first. Investor-state dispute settlement procedures, like those of NAFTA (Section 4.8), were tuned up in response to numerous criticisms. Third party amicus briefs are allowed, frivolous complaints may be dismissed, biased arbitrators challenged, and there is considerably more transparency. After much debate and controversy, an Investment Dispute Court comprised of EU and Canadian members, will be created to decide investor-state disputes. Canada still gets to apply its Investment Act to EU nationals, subject to the "net benefit" to Canada test, but EU investments under $1.5 billion CDN escape review.

§ 5.5 Pacific Rim Free Trade: ASEAN, RCEP, China, Hong Kong, Japan, Russia, South Korea, and India

The Pacific Rim has not developed an all-inclusive regional free trade agreement, though the China-led RCEP and ASEAN have taken steps in that direction. Other Pacific Rim free trade agreements are noted below.

Southeast Asian Free Trade (ASEAN)

Some interesting moves toward developing world free trade and rulemaking have been taken by the Association of Southeast Asian Nations (ASEAN). Its problems, failures and successes are representative of developing world attempts at legal and economic integration. ASEAN has its genesis in the 1967 Bangkok Declaration, with common trade rules in various states of growth, implementation, and retrenchment. ASEAN has internal tariff preferences, industrial development projects, "complementation schemes," and regional joint ventures.

An important juncture in the integration process is the point in time at which member countries of a regional group accept a supranational mechanism for enforcing the regime's law irrespective of national feelings and domestic law within a member country. In contrast, the ASEAN Secretary-General once remarked that ASEAN's Secretariat was "a postman collecting and distributing letters." The surrender of national sovereignty to ASEAN institutions has been a painfully slow process.

ASEAN was formed in 1967 by Indonesia, Malaysia, the Philippines, Singapore, and Thailand. Brunei joined in 1984, Vietnam in 1995. Laos and Myanmar (Burma) joined in 1997, and Cambodia in 1999. Rarely have such culturally, linguistically, and geographically diverse nations attempted integration. The Bangkok Declaration establishing ASEAN as a cooperative association is a broadly worded document. Later proposals were made for a formal ASEAN treaty or convention but were rejected as unnecessary. The Bangkok Declaration sets forth numerous regional, economic, cultural, and social goals, including acceleration of economic growth, trade expansion and industrial collaboration.

The Bangkok Declaration establishes several mechanisms, but little supranational legal machinery, to implement its stated goals. An annual ASEAN Meeting of Foreign Ministers is scheduled on a rotational basis among the Member States. Special meetings are held "as required." The Declaration provides for a Standing Committee composed of the Foreign Minister of the state in which the next annual Ministerial Meeting is to be held and includes the ambassadors of other ASEAN States accredited to that state. The Declaration also provides for "Ad Hoc Committees and Permanent Committees of specialists and officials on specific subjects." Each member state is charged to set up a National Secretariat to administer ASEAN affairs within that Member State and to work with the Ministerial Meeting and the Standing Committee.

There have been relatively infrequent meetings of the ASEAN heads of government. This contrasts with the semiannual European "summits" that have kept that group moving forward along the path of integration. The third ASEAN summit was held in Manila in 1987. This summit produced an agreement for the promotion and protection of investments by ASEAN investors (national and most-favored-nation treatment rights are created), revised the basic ASEAN joint venture agreement, and continued the gradual extension of regional tariff and nontariff trade preferences. Goods already covered by the ASEAN tariff scheme were given a 50 percent margin of preference. New items received a 25 percent preferential margin. The nontariff preferences generally co-opt GATT rules, *e.g.*, regarding technical standards and customs valuation.

The fourth ASEAN summit in 1992 committed the parties to the creation of a free trade area within 15 years. Five years were cut from this schedule by agreement in 1994, but operational reality has eluded ASEAN free trade (AFTA). In 2003, a "watershed" date for complete integration in an ASEAN Economic Community targeted 2020. In 2007, this target date was changed to 2015, a reflection of the fear that ASEAN risks being overwhelmed by the powerhouse economies of China, India, Korea, and Japan. In 2016, the ASEAN common market was officially launched. Despite the fanfare, its prospects seem limited.

All that said, ASEAN as a group has limited free trade in goods agreements with China, Japan, Korea, and India. It is not at all clear to what degree ASEAN exports have increased under these agreements other than by becoming more active suppliers of natural resources and components to these major-economy partners.

RCEP 2020

As a counterbalance to the U.S.-led TPP-12 (see Section 5.3), China promoted a Regional Comprehensive Economic Partnership (RCEP) with 15 nations including the 10 ASEAN nations, Australia, Japan, Taiwan, New Zealand, and South Korea, but deliberately not the United States. India withdrew from the RCEP negotiations in 2019. RCEP was originally conceived by ASEAN to unify its individual trade treaties with China, India, Japan, South Korea,

Australia, and New Zealand. Early signs after President Trump withdrew from the TPP-12 suggested China would seek to utilize RCEP to integrate much of the Pacific Basin, minus the United States, with its economy. All totaled, RCEP covers roughly 30% of the world's population and GDP.

RCEP became effective Jan. 1, 2022. Over time it is expected to eliminate tariffs on 91% of trade in goods among its members. Japan noticeably will benefit from dramatic tariff drops on its exports to China, to which it sends $50 billion in auto parts each year. Any agreement reducing trade tensions and tariffs between long-feuding Japan and South Korea is remarkable. Special and differential treatment is reserved for the Least Developed RCEP countries. A party may withdraw from RCEP after six months' notice. China's economic hostility towards Australia after that country expressed negative opinions of the PRC regarding COVID and its policies did not keep Australia from passing implementation legislation late in 2021.

RCEP focuses primarily upon tariff reductions on trade in goods, borrowing national treatment, customs valuation, and quota rules from GATT 1994 discussed in Chapter 1 of this book. (RCEP Chapter 2). Free trade in goods is generally subject to a 40% regional value content (RVC) rule of origin (RCEP Chapter 3). RVC is calculated either directly using a build-up transaction formula or indirectly using a build-down cost-based formula. Changes in tariff classifications following the Harmonized Tariff Code adopted by all RCEP members primarily determine a product's origin. The availability of advance rulings and customs appeals is mandatory in each country (RCEP Chapter 4).

RCEP also includes coverage of non-tariff trade barriers borrowing from the WTO SPS and TBT Codes covered in Chapter 1 of this book. Antidumping, countervailing duty and safeguard trade remedy rules largely track WTO principles, accompanied by special exceptions and transitional rules (RCEP Chapter 7). However, there is a specific prohibition against use of the U.S. practice of "zeroing" in antidumping calculations. See my Concise Hornbook on *International Trade Law,* Chapter 4. There are no special trade remedy dispute procedures such as found in NAFTA and the USMCA. See Sections 4.12 and 6.8.

Negative list services commitments are made in Schedules of Commitments, notably in the financial, telecom and professional arenas (RCEP Chapter 8). Temporary business visitor visas are created (RCEP Chapter 9). Treaty-covered foreign investment rights focus national and MFN treatment and on customary international law, including fair and equitable treatment and full protection and security (RCEP Article 10.5). There is an express prohibition of performance requirements for foreign investors (RCEP Article 10.6). Annex 10B governs direct expropriations and "equivalent in effect" government actions (not including compulsory licensing). Promises made to the investor may be considered. Compensation follows national rules applicable to domestic investors. National investment grants and subsidies are *not* governed by RCEP, leaving each country to devise its own foreign investment incentives. *There are no provisions for investor-state arbitrations (detailed in Chapter 7 of this book) in the RCEP Agreement.*

Broad coverage of intellectual property rights, like that found in TRIPs (see Section 1.12), is specified in Chapter 11. Each country maintains its own rules on enforcement and exhaustion of IP rights. Article 11.52 explicitly authorizes RCEP countries to preserve and protect their genetic resources, traditional knowledge, and folklore. E-commerce is promoted, subject to protection of personal information, cyber-security rules, and a bar against localization of computing facilities (RCEP Chapter 12). There are separate chapters on competition law, small and medium enterprises, economic and technical cooperation, procurement, and general exceptions (RCEP Chapters 13–17). The controlling RCEP Joint Committee operates on consensus principles (RCEP Chapter 18).

State-to-state dispute settlement is to be undertaken by three-member Panel Proceedings subject to detailed RCEP Rules of Procedure broadly governed by customary public international law and focused on the impairment of benefits (RCEP Chapter 19). These procedures do not apply to trade disputes. They resemble those of the WTO Dispute Settlement Understanding, minus an Appellate Body (see Section 1.16).

Consultations come first, followed by good offices, conciliation, or mediation efforts. Absent a settlement, a three person RCEP Panel is chosen with one member from both sides and a third member either agreed upon or (if not) chosen by the Director-General of the WTO. Third party access to these dispute procedures is anticipated. The Panel issues a formal Report on the complaint, which in the absence of compliance can be followed by a Compliance Panel Report. If an offending RCEP country fails ultimately to comply with its RCEP obligations, and no compensation is agreed, the prevailing party may suspend RCEP concessions in the sector of the complaint or possibly in another "cross sector."

When both the complaining and responding countries have substantially equivalent rights and obligations under other international agreements (presumably including the WTO), the complaining party gets to choose where to file its complaint. Trade remedy complaints cannot be filed under RCEP Chapter 19 state-to-state dispute settlement

Coverage of labor, the environment and state-owned enterprises are noticeably absent from the RCEP Agreement. Without doubt, RCEP is a significant trade leadership accomplishment for China. Shortly thereafter, China made it clear that next on its Asian trade agenda was a deeper trilateral agreement with Japan, Korea, and the PRC.

China

China and Japan are clearly rivals for economic leadership of the region. By 2022, China had free trade agreements with its own Hong Kong and Macau Special Administrative Regions, Chile, Pakistan, Costa Rica, Peru, Singapore, New Zealand, Australia, South Korea, Iceland, Maldives, and ASEAN. China's massive Belt and Road Initiative (BRI), while not a free trade agreement, promotes Chinese alliances and economic interests across Eurasia and in Africa.

Some commentators note the emergence of a powerful Southern China coastal economic zone embracing Hong Kong, Shenzhen SEZ, Macau, Zhuhai SEZ, and the Chinese province of Guangdong. The Pearl River delta area already serves as the world's leading electronics center and China's role as a critical supply chain partner became evident in the COVID crisis. Re-shoring and relocation of key medical suppliers and business plans to have at least one other supplier besides China multiplied in many economic sectors.

The role of China in Pacific Rim integration is critical. As RCEP (above) illustrates, China is pushing for dominant influence in the Pacific Rim economic sphere. Hong Kong's return in 1997 and Macau in 1999 moved in this direction. Its last renegade territory, Taipei (Taiwan), is targeted for reunification with the motherland. China is also seeking membership in TPP-11.

Hong Kong

The imposition of severe PRC national security measures applicable in and to Hong Kong in 2020 dramatically undermined Hong Kong's "one, two systems" status (which was supposed to last to 2047). The measures broadly criminalize sedition, subversion, terrorism, collusion and acts undermining China's communist regime. The first arrest was of a man carrying a banner calling for an independent Hong Kong. Life in prison is the ultimate sanction.

All activities anywhere in the world by anyone or any business are subject to PRC national security law. Internet regulation, telecom intercepts, media controls and warrantless searches (including of electronic devices) are authorized. Google, Facebook, and other tech companies refused to honor data requests of the Hong Kong government and VPN providers pulled out of the city.

International traders should take note: Article 29, for example, criminalizes cooperation with a "foreign country or an institution, organization or individual" concerning "imposing sanctions or blockades, or other hostile activities" against Hong Kong. The ultimate power of interpretation of the law rests with the National People's Congress of the PRC, not at all known for independence.

PRC security officers operate secretly inside Hong Kong but outside judicial review by its historically independent court and jury system. Complex or serious national security crimes may be tried on the mainland. The U.S., the UK and others and others responded with Hong Kong trade sanctions and restraints, and a willingness to take in some of its citizens. The U.S. formally revoked Hong Kong's "autonomous" status as a trade partner, placing its role as a global finance center and a major re-exporter of goods to and from China at risk. Hong Kong goods must now be labeled "Made in China." The U.S. annulled its extradition treaty, tax preferences, and its Peace Corps and Fulbright programs, as applied to Hong Kong.

The U.S. also blacklisted Carrie Lam, the Chief Executive of Hong Kong, and other HK officials. The power of such blacklisting caused Carrie Lam to report that no bank in Hong Kong would take her as a client. Under threat of communications' controls, the NY Times moved its digital office from Hong Kong to Seoul. The U.S. also undertook control over Chinese firms raising funds in American financial markets (including NYSE de-listings), as well as denial of U.S. investments in Chinese firms linked to its military. See my Concise Hornbook on *Foreign Investment Law and Disputes*. These efforts have accelerated the growing role of Hong Kong as a Chinese-driven financial center and diminished its traditional global importance as a trading and finance center. Many multinational firms (including law firms) have exited Hong Kong, often to Singapore.

Japan

One provocative trade question is the future of Japan. It is not in the interest of any nation that Japan should feel economically isolated or threatened. To some degree, trade in East Asia is growing along lines that follow Japanese investment and economic aid decisions. By 2024, Japan had "Economic Partnership Agreements" (effectively free trade in goods agreements) with Mexico, Chile, Thailand, the Philippines, Malaysia, Vietnam, Switzerland, India, Indonesia, Brunei, Singapore, Peru, Mongolia, and the Association of

Southeast Asian Nations (ASEAN). These agreements essentially encircle China.

After refusing to negotiate a comprehensive bilateral free trade agreement with President Trump, Japan in 2018 signed a major economic partnership agreement with the EU summarized immediately below. Japan also led the creation of TPP-11 (Section 5.3).

Japan-EU Economic Partnership Agreement (2018)

Like CETA (above), the Japan-EU Economic Partnership Agreement of 2018 is a major example of free trade alternatives to Trump's America First trade policy.

The Japan-EU agreement anticipates nearly full tariff removals on goods, notably reducing the 10% EU auto tariff to zero over 7 years. Honda, which has a large plant in the UK, announced in 2019 will close production in favor exporting from Japan under its new free trade agreement with the EU. The EU expects to export more agricultural, textile, chemicals, wood products and leather goods to Japan. Tariff rate quota limitations will protect Japan from EU wheat, dairy, pork, sugar, soft cheese, and beef. Free trade will not apply to rice, Japan's "sacred" food sector, which is protected by a 777% tariff.

Many Japanese nontariff trade barriers (NTBs) are clarified and relaxed, including those related motor vehicles, medical devices, textile labeling, and beer. In general, technical barriers to trade will be governed by international standards. Trade in services is expanded beyond WTO commitments, notably in the following fields: Postal and courier services, telecommunications, finance, and international maritime transport. Temporary business and professional visas going beyond anything the EU had previously agreed to are adopted.

State-owned enterprises of either country receive national treatment when buying or selling on commercial markets. Mutual procurement opportunities are expanded, especially in allowing EU firms to bid on tenders of 54 "core cities" in Japan.

There are obligations to recognize of the eight "fundamental" ILO Conventions, duty free electronic transmissions, and a bar on forced disclosure of source codes. Each side has acknowledged the "adequacy" of the other's data privacy regimes, a priority for the EU operating under its 2018 General Data Protection Regulation. Geographical indicators from Kobe beef to Feta cheese are protected.

In a first, the parties reaffirmed their commitment to the Paris Accord on Climate Change. Various provisions promote sustainable development and corporate social responsibility. There is a specific chapter on corporate governance derived from G20/OECD Principles. The EU ban on imports of whale products is retained in the face of continued Japanese whaling practices. General state-to-state dispute settlement procedures are established.

Foreign investment rules and related dispute settlement are being negotiated separately. These are particularly sensitive to Japan, which has infrequently had to defend itself in investor-state arbitration proceedings.

Trump and Japan, a Mini-Deal (2019)

Japan has run a major trade surplus with the United States for decades, lowered somewhat by a U.S. trade surplus in services. This deficit collided with President Trump's America First trade policies. The Japanese, post President Trump's withdrawal from TPP-12, rapidly undertook an extensive FTA with the European Union and led the way to the TPP-11 agreement.

During the Presidency of Donald Trump, Japan declined or stalled negotiations on a bilateral FTA with the United States. This refusal helps explain why Japan did not receive a temporary exemption from the Trump national security steel and aluminum tariffs. That said, the threat of U.S. national security tariffs on autos generated greater trade discussions in 2019 that resulted in a mini-deal basically expanding U.S. agricultural exports to Japan to those consistent with TPP-12 (Section 5.3). Japan retained its ability to ship cars into the USA under standard American tariffs.

Russia

By 2024, Russia had an FTA with eight formerly Soviet satellite countries under the Commonwealth of Independent States (CISFTA). The CISFTA members are Russia, Ukraine, Moldova, Tajikistan, Armenia, Kazakhstan, Kyrgyzstan, Uzbekistan, and with Ukraine (suspended after Russian annexation of Crimea and occupation of parts of eastern Ukraine). Since 2015, Russia, Kazakhstan, Belarus, Armenia, and Kyrgyzstan joined together in the Eurasian Economic Union (EAEU), strategically linking China's BRI land bridge program with Europe. The EAEU has an FTA with Vietnam and is exploring others.

Russia, with considerable Siberian energy development finance from China, is busy developing a Northern Sea Route to exploit reduced artic ice. This strategic, cost-saving initiative connects China/Japan/Korea with Europe. Russia's invasion of Ukraine has significantly diminished its trade with North America and Europe, frequently replaced by increased trade with China, India and Iran. See my *International Trade Law* Concise Hornbook.

South Korea

By 2024, hustling Korea had free trade agreements with ASEAN, India, Australia, Canada, the United States, China, Chile, Colombia, EFTA, the European Union (KOREU), Turkey, Vietnam, Peru, and Singapore. South Kore participates in the RCEP Agreement (above). At President Trump's insistence, the 2012 KORUS agreement was re-negotiated via a Protocol in 2018 (KORUS II) (Section 6.6).

India

By 2024, India had free trade agreements with ASEAN, Sri Lanka, Malaysia, the Gulf Cooperation Council (GCC), Singapore, Korea, Japan, Afghanistan, Chile, and led the seven-nation South Asian FTA. India's major trade concern is being surrounded by China, notably via China's BRI links with Bangladesh, Nepal, Pakistan, the Maldives, and Sri Lanka and RCEP. India dropped out of the RCEP negotiations in 2019.

India signed free trade deals with the United Arab Emirates and Australia in 2022. The latter, known as ECTA (Economic Trade and Cooperation Agreement) confirms a strategic relationship vis-a-vis China. Eleven years in the making and focused on trade in goods and services, there is little coverage of foreign investment or intellectual property. Over time, 85% of India's tariffs on Australian goods (notably on coal) will be eliminated, likewise for 96% of Australian tariffs on Indian goods (notably leather and textiles). Mutual recognition of professional licenses is anticipated. Greater access to Australian studies and work-study programs is provided for Indian students. Dispute settlement largely tracks the WTO DSU, with the complaining party allowed to elect as between ECTA and WTO remedies.

§ 5.6 European Union FTAs—BREXIT

The European Union is a customs union, not a free trade area. Its trade relations with the rest of the world are exclusively an EU, not a national, competence. The EU has a customs union agreement with Turkey (services excluded). Its other trade agreements are dominated by FTAs, providing access to the world's largest common market.

By 2024, the EU had over 70 free trade partners, including Morocco, Algeria, Tunisia, Libya, Egypt, Israel, Jordan, Lebanon, Norway, Iceland, Serbia, South Africa, Peru, Mexico, Colombia, Central America (six nations), Chile, Singapore, Vietnam, and South

Korea (KOREU). Canada and the EU agreed in 2013 to an historic Comprehensive Economic and Trade Agreement (CETA, Section 5.4) that provisionally reached fruition in 2017 under mixed EU agreement procedures requiring national and regional parliamentary approvals.

In 2018, Japan and the EU, with $22 trillion combined economies, reached agreement on a free trade deal. This accord is titled the EU-Japan Economic Partnership Agreement (Section 5.5). In 2019, Mexico and the EU, whose economies measure nearly $18 trillion, significantly expanded their existing FTA. In 2019, after 20 years of negotiation, MERCOSUR (Brazil, Argentina, Uruguay, and Paraguay) inked a free trade deal "in principle" with the EU (Section 3.17). Implementation has stalled due to Brazilian deforestation and climate change issues in the Amazon.

Agreements with India, ASEAN, and the Gulf Council may follow. One notable feature of EU FTAs is the inclusion of a Human Rights and Democracy Clause backed up by potential trade sanctions.

The EU agreed that during the BREXIT transition period running to January 2021, Britain benefited from the existing EU FTAs embracing over 70 nations. During that period, the UK could negotiate, sign, and ratify, but not enter into force, FTAs with any partner.

An important BREXIT issue was whether Britain individually after BREXIT could duplicate or substantially retain free trade with current EU partners. Would, for example, Canada or Japan be willing to give Britain the same terms they gave the much larger and more economically significant European Union? Answer: Surprisingly, YES. What about developing countries like Vietnam or Mexico? Answer: YES. What about UK Commonwealth countries like Singapore? YES.

Roughly 65 countries, including South Africa, Turkey, and South Korea, agreed to roll-over their EU FTAs to the UK. An FTA with Australia late in 2021 became the UK's first independently achieved free trade agreement, followed by an FTA with New Zealand.

LINKS

§ 5.7 Link to Trans-Pacific Partnership (TPP-12 2016)

https://ustr.gov/trade-agreements/free-trade-agreements/trans-pacific-partnership/tpp-full-text

§ 5.8 Link to Comprehensive and Progressive Trans-Pacific Partnership (TPP-11 2018)

https://international.gc.ca/trade-commerce/trade-agreements-accords-commerciaux/agr-acc/cptpp-ptpgp/text-texte/cptpp-ptpgp.aspx?lang=eng

§ 5.9 Link to Canada-EU Comprehensive Economic and Trade Agreement (CETA 2017)

https://www.international.gc.ca/trade-commerce/trade-agreements-accords-commerciaux/agr-acc/ceta-aecg/text-texte/toc-tdm.aspx?lang=eng

§ 5.10 Link to Japan-EU Economic Partnership Agreement (2018)

https://trade.ec.europa.eu/access-to-markets/en/content/eu-japan-economic-partnership-agreementhttps://policy.trade.ec.europa.eu/eu-trade-relationships-country-and-region/countries-and-regions/japan/eu-japan-agreement_en

§ 5.11 Link to Regional Comprehensive Economic Partnership Agreement (RCEP) (2020)

https://www.dfat.gov.au/trade/agreements/not-yet-in-force/rcep/rcep-text

Chapter 6

TRUMP AND BIDEN ON FREE TRADE: KORUS II AND USMCA

Table of Sections

§ 6.1 America First Trade Policy

For the first time in many years, international trade was a major issue in a U.S. Presidential election. In 2016, Donald J. Trump made it so. He campaigned and tweeted against trade deficits, currency manipulation, NAFTA 1994 as "the worst trade deal ever", and the signed but not ratified twelve-nation (minus China) Trans-Pacific Partnership (TPP). Rallying the oft-forgotten losers under U.S. trade policy, he swept into office in 2017 as the world took a deep breath and wondered what might come.

Major Trump administration trade initiatives were undertaken in areas governed by WTO agreements. These include CVD tariffs against Canadian lumber, global safeguard tariffs on solar panels and clothes washers, and national security tariffs on steel and aluminum. Completely unilateral U.S. Section 301 tariffs were applied to Chinese goods amidst a tech-driven trade war. All were pursued under an America First mantra that undermined the WTO and encouraged traditional U.S. trade partners to pursue free trade alternatives not involving the USA. See Chapter 5.

President Trump criticized and forced a limited renegotiation by Protocol of KORUS I, the U.S.-Korea 2012 bilateral Free Trade Agreement (see Section 6.6). With lots of bluster, the Trump administration spent over a year re-negotiating NAFTA with Canada and Mexico, two countries highly dependent on U.S. trade relations. The USMCA Agreement of 2020 is reviewed in Section 6.8.

Withdrawal from the Trans-Pacific Partnership (TPP-12)

Negotiation of the Trans-Pacific Partnership (TPP) was led by the United States under President Obama's "pivot to Asia" and a desire to create a "next generation" FTA model. Late in 2015, a Trans-Pacific Partnership (TPP-12) agreement was reached among the three NAFTA nations plus Peru, Chile, Brunei, Singapore, Malaysia, Vietnam, Japan, Australia, and New Zealand (but notably not China). These Pacific Rim partners comprise roughly 40% of world trade. South Korea, Taiwan and Indonesia expressed interest in joining the TPP, which clearly resembled a containment strategy relative to China's rising economic power.

As its Table of Contents (see Section 6.3) reveals, TPP-12 contained notable developments on freer agricultural and food trade, trade in automobiles and auto parts, bio-similar pharmaceuticals, protection of foreign investment, a self-judging essential security exception, a bar on forced technology transfers as an investor performance requirement, and a procedural tune up of investor-state arbitrations.

Coverage of minimum wages and working hours, independent unions, technology protections including a prohibition of data localization requirements, anti-corruption obligations in the public and private sectors, due process and private action rights in competition (antitrust) proceedings, service sector openings, e-commerce, criminal sanctions for counterfeiting and trade secret theft, environmental protection and restraints on subsidies for state-owned enterprises (SOEs) were included in TPP-12. It also contained minimal currency manipulation rules, a debated topic.

For more on the content of TPP-12, see Section 5.3.

Trump and TPP-12

President Trump quickly withdrew from the multilateral Trans-Pacific Partnership (TPP), essentially making a gift of trade leadership in Asia to China. President Xi Jinping at Davos accepted this gift, noting ongoing negotiations for its competing trade alliance, The Regional Cooperation and Economic Partnership (RCEP) comprised of the ASEAN states, South Korea, Japan, China, and India, but not the United States. See Section 5.5.

As signed by President Obama, TPP ratification in the United States would have been under the fast-track procedures, discussed in Section 4.1. President Trump's quick withdrawal from the TPP mooted this possibility. Note, however, that the U.S. already had bilateral FTAs, clearly a Trump preference to maximize bargaining power, with four of the 12 TPP partners (Chile, Peru, Singapore, and Australia), plus free trade relations with Mexico and Canada under NAFTA. The Trump Administration's dislike of multilateral trade agreements is reflected in the insightful words of Secretary of Commerce Wilbur Ross:

> Say you're negotiating with 12 different countries. You go to the first one and you want some concession from them. They say, "Yes, we'll give you that concession, but we want something back." So that takes a little nick out of us. Then you go to the next country and you negotiate with them, they take a little nick. You keep doing that 12 times, you get a lot of nicks, and what happens is the other countries get the benefit of things they didn't even ask for because you had to give them to someone else. So I think that's a fundamental concern.

U.S. withdrawal from TPP has had broad consequences in the world of international trade. Perhaps most significantly, China, Japan, the EU, Canada, and others have moved away from U.S. trade policy leadership and pursued free trade partners elsewhere around the globe. See Chapters 3 and 5.

The full TPP-12 agreement is linked in Section 6.4 and its Contents, Annexes and Related Instruments are linked in Section 6.3.

Trump and Biden on TPP-11

The remaining TPP partners, led notably by Japan and Canada, signed an altered TPP-11 free trade agreement in 2018 covering roughly 15% of global trade. TPP-11 was re-named the *Comprehensive and Progressive Trans-Pacific Partnership (CPTPP).* This agreement borrows substantially from TPP-12, minus provisions closely associated with the United States, and subject to a variety of country-specific alterations. See Section 5.3 for TPP-11 details.

TPP-11 took effect Feb. 1, 2019, with ratification still pending in Brunei and Malaysia. Its full text is linked in Section 6.5. South Korea, Taiwan, Ecuador, and China have expressed interest in joining TPP-11. Britain, Peru and Chile have done so. The Biden administration showed no interest in TPP-11, anticipating instead formulation of a new "Indo-Pacific Economic Framework" covering digital trade, labor standards, and trade facilitation along with supply chains, infrastructure, decarbonization, taxation and corruption. See Section 5.1.

§ 6.2 Linked Contents, Annexes and Related Instruments of TPP-12 (2016)

Preamble

1. **Initial Provisions and General Definitions** | Chapter Summary
2. **National Treatment and Market Access** | Chapter Summary
    - Annex 2-D: Tariff Commitments
        - Australia General Notes to Tariff Schedule
        - Australia Tariff Elimination Schedule
        - Brunei General Notes to Tariff Schedule
        - Brunei Tariff Elimination Schedule
        - Canada General Notes to Tariff Schedule
        - Canada Tariff Elimination Schedule
        - Canada Appendix A Tariff Rate Quotas
        - Canada Appendix D Appendix between Japan and the United States on Motor Vehicle Trade
        - Chile General Notes to Tariff Schedule
        - Chile Tariff Elimination Schedule
        - Japan General Notes to Tariff Schedule
        - Japan Tariff Elimination Schedule
        - Japan Appendix A Tariff Rate Quotas
        - Japan Appendix B-1 Agricultural Safeguard Measures
        - Japan Appendix B-2 Forest Good Safeguard Measure
        - Japan Appendix C Tariff-Differentials
        - Japan Appendix D-1 Appendix between Japan and the United States on Motor Vehicle Trade
        - Japan Appendix D-2 Appendix between Japan and Canada on Motor Vehicle Trade
        - Malaysia General Notes to Tariff-Schedule
        - Malaysia Tariff Elimination-Schedule
        - Malaysia Appendix A Tariff Rate Quotas
        - Mexico General Notes to Tariff Schedule
        - Mexico Tariff Elimination Schedule
        - Mexico Appendix A-1 Tariff Rate Quotas and Appendix A-2 Country Specific Allocation for Sugar of Mexico

- Mexico Appendix C Tariff Differentials
- New Zealand General Notes to Tariff Schedule
- New Zealand Tariff Elimination Schedule
- Peru General Notes to Tariff-Schedule
- Peru Tariff Elimination Schedule
- Singapore General Notes to Tariff Schedule
- Singapore Tariff Elimination Schedule
- US General Notes to Tariff Schedule
- US Tariff Elimination-Schedule
- US Appendix A Tariff Rate Quotas
- US Appendix B Agricultural Safeguard Measures
- US Appendix C Tariff Differentials
- US Appendix D Appendix between Japan and the United States on Motor Vehicle Trade
- US Appendix E Earned Import Allowance Program
- Viet-Nam General Notes to Tariff Schedule
- Viet-Nam Tariff Elimination Schedule
- Viet-Nam Appendix A Tariff Rate Quotas

3. **Rules of Origin and Origin Procedures** | Chapter Summary
    - Annex 3-D: Product Specific Rules
    - Annex 3-D: Appendix 1—Automotive
4. **Textiles and Apparel** | Chapter Summary
    - Annex 4-A: Textiles Product Specific Rule
    - Annex 4-A Appendix 1: Short Supply List
5. **Customs Administration and Trade Facilitation** | Chapter Summary
6. **Trade Remedies** | Chapter Summary
7. **Sanitary and Phytosanitary Measures** | Chapter Summary
8. **Technical Barriers to Trade** | Chapter Summary
9. **Investment** | Chapter Summary
10. **Cross Border Trade in Services** | Chapter Summary
11. **Financial Services** | Chapter Summary
12. **Temporary Entry for Business Persons** | Chapter Summary
    - Annex 12-A: Temporary Entry for Business Persons
        - Australia
        - Brunei
        - Canada
        - Chile

- Japan
- Malaysia
- Mexico
- New Zealand
- Peru
- Singapore
- Viet Nam

13. **Telecommunications** | Chapter Summary
14. **Electronic Commerce** | Chapter Summary
15. **Government Procurement** | Chapter Summary
    - Annex 15-A: Government Procurement
        - Australia
        - Brunei
        - Canada
        - Chile
        - Japan
        - Malaysia
        - Mexico
        - New Zealand
        - Peru
        - Singapore
        - United States
        - Viet Nam
16. **Competition** | Chapter Summary
17. **State-Owned Enterprises** | Chapter Summary
18. **Intellectual Property** | Chapter Summary
19. **Labour** | Chapter Summary
    - US-BN Labour Consistency Plan
    - US-MY Labour Consistency Plan
    - US-VN Plan for Enhancement of Trade and Labour Relations
20. **Environment** | Chapter Summary
21. **Cooperation and Capacity Building** | Chapter Summary
22. **Competitiveness and Business Facilitation** | Chapter Summary
23. **Development** | Chapter Summary
24. **Small and Medium-Sized Enterprises** | Chapter Summary
25. **Regulatory Coherence** | Chapter Summary
26. **Transparency and Anti-Corruption** | Chapter Summary

Annexes

  - Chile
  - Japan
  - Malaysia
  - Mexico
  - New Zealand
  - Peru
  - Singapore
  - United States
  - Viet Nam
- Annex IV: State-Owned Enterprise
  - Australia
  - Brunei
  - Canada
  - Chile
  - Malaysia
  - Mexico
  - New Zealand
  - Peru
  - United States
  - Viet Nam

Related Instruments

- **Market Access Related**
  - US-AU Letter Exchange re Recognition of FTA TRQs in TPP
  - US-AU Letter Exchange on Sugar Review
  - US-CA Letter Exchange on Agricultural Transparency
  - US-CL Letter Exchange on Distinctive Products
  - US-CL Letter Exchange regarding Recognition of FTA TRQs in TPP
  - US-JP Letter Exchange on Distinctive Products
  - JP to US Letter on Safety Regulations for Motor Vehicles
  - US-JP Letter Exchange on Operation of SBS Mechanism
  - US-JP Letter Exchange on Operation of Whey Protein Concentrate Safeguard
  - US-JP Letter Exchange regarding Standards of Fill
  - US-JP Letters related to the PHP
  - US-MY Letter Exchange on Auto Imports
  - US-MY Letter Exchange on Distinctive Products
  - US-NZ Letter Exchange on Distinctive Products

- US-PE Letter Exchange on Distinctive Products
- US-PE Letter Exchange on TRQs and Safeguards
- US-VN Letter Exchange on Distinctive Products of US
- US-VN Letter Exchange on Distinctive Products of VN

- **Textiles and Apparel Related**
  - US-BN Letter Exchange on Textiles and Apparel
  - US-MY Letter Exchange on Registered Textile and Apparel Enterprises
  - US-SG Exchange on Letters on Textiles and US-SG FTA
  - US-VN Letter Exchange on Registered Textile and Apparel Enterprises
- **Sanitary and Phytosanitary Related**
  - US-CL SPS Letter Exchange regarding Salmonid Eggs
  - US-CA Letter Exchange on Milk Equivalence
  - US-VN Letter Exchange on Catfish
  - US-VN Letter Exchange on Offals
- **Intellectual Property Related**
  - US-AU Letter Exchange on Selected IP Provisions
  - US-AU Letter Exchange on Article 17.9.7(b) of AUSFTA
  - US-CA Letter Exchange on IP Border Enforcement
  - US-CL Letter Exchange re Geographical Indications
  - US-CL Letter Exchange re Article 17.10.2 of US Chile FTA
  - US-JP Letter Exchange re Copyright Term
  - US-MY Letter Exchange re Articles 18.41 .50 and .52
  - US-MY Letter Exchange re Geographical Indications
  - US-MX Letter Exchange re Geographical Indications
  - US-MX Letter Exchange re Tequila and Mezcal
  - US-PE Letter Exchange re Article 16.14.3 of US-Peru TPA
  - US-VN Letter Exchange on Biologics
  - US-VN Letter Exchange re Geographical Indications
- **Services/Financial Services/E-Commerce**
  - US-CL Letter Exchange regarding Express Delivery Services
  - US-VN Letter Exchange on Pharmaceutical Distribution
  - US-VN Letter Exchange regarding Electronic Payment Services
  - US-AU Letter Exchange on Privacy
- **Temporary Entry**
  - US-JP Letter Exchange re Temporary Entry

- **Government Procurement**
  - US-AU Letter Exchange on AUSFTA GP Thresholds
  - US-CA Letter Exchange re GP Thresholds
  - Letter Exchange US-CA-MX re GP Procedures
- **SOEs**
  - US-SG Letter Exchange on SOE Transparency
- **Environment**
  - US-CL Understanding regarding Fisheries Subsidies and Natural Disasters
  - US-MY Exchange of Letters on Committee to Coordinate Implementation of Environment Chapters
  - US-PE Understanding regarding Biodiversity and Traditional Knowledge
  - US-PE Understanding regarding Conservation and Trade
- **Annex on Transparency and Procedural Fairness for Pharmaceutical Products and Medical Devices**
  - US-AU Letter Exchange on Transparency and Procedural Fairness for Pharmaceuticals and Medical Devices
  - US-JP Transparency and Procedural Fairness for Pharmaceuticals and Medical Devices
  - US-PE Understanding re Transparency and Procedural Fairness for Pharmaceuticals and Medical Devices

US-Japan Bilateral Outcomes

- **US-Japan Motor Vehicle Trade Non-Tariff Measures** | Summary
  - US-JP Letter Exchange on Certain Auto NTMs
  - JP to US Letter on Motor Vehicle Distribution Survey
- **Japan Parallel Negotiations on Non-Tariff Measures** | Summary
  - US-JP Letter Exchange on Non-Tariff Measures

§ 6.3 Link to Trans-Pacific Partnership (TPP-12 2016)

https://ustr.gov/trade-agreements/free-trade-agreements/trans-pacific-partnership/tpp-full-text

§ 6.4 Link to Comprehensive and Progressive Trans-Pacific Partnership (TPP-11 2018)

https://international.gc.ca/trade-commerce/trade-agreements-accords-commerciaux/agr-acc/cptpp-ptpgp/text-texte/cptpp-ptpgp.aspx?lang=eng

§ 6.5 KORUS Re-Negotiated (2018)

Trump and KORUS I and II

In August of 2017, the Trump Administration commenced re-negotiation of the 2012 U.S.-South Korea free trade agreement (KORUS I), expressing concerns about the modest U.S. trade deficit in goods with Korea, while ignoring a sizeable trade surplus in services for a net deficit in 2017 of about $10 billion. Several major Korean firms announced plans to invest in the United States, and Korea pulled its WTO Appellate Body member back home to negotiate with the Trump Administration. These negotiations were notably NOT undertaken under U.S. fast-track trade promotion procedures (see Section 4.1). They were held instead via the Joint Committee process under KORUS I, thereby avoiding Congressional review and approval.

Then North Korea shot a missile over Japan and exploded a thermonuclear bomb. The United States, at a hefty price, promised South Korea major defense armaments and reduced but did not remove pressure to re-negotiate the KORUS I agreement.

The arrival of U.S. defensive radar and missile systems in South Korea, and the promise of more to come, caused China to organize a painful boycott of South Korean goods and tourism. South Korea and China have a free trade in goods agreement, and prominent Korean companies (Lotte supermarkets, KIA cars) have production and distribution centers in the PRC. Hyundai sales in China dropped 34%. In 2018, having made its point, China lifted the boycott, but its impact lingers.

KORUS I re-negotiations were ongoing at U.S. forceful insistence but moving slowly in early 2018. The main issues were Korean auto exports to the USA under a 55% KORUS I origin rule, resulting in roughly a $15 billion auto trade surplus. Korea's exports were in no way matched by U.S. auto exports, despite a generous Korean 25,000 entry waiver of its strict car safety and pollution rules. U.S. exports of agricultural, meat and food products to Korea were also contentious on both sides. The Trump Administration's unilateral 25% steel tariffs of 2018 threatened to hurt sizeable Korean exports and were hard to explain to such a steadfast U.S. ally.

In the afterglow of the 2018 Winter Olympics held in South Korea, President Trump, and North Korea's Kim Jong Un agreed to meet. KORUS I re-negotiations accelerated. Late in March the two sides announced a deal. The U.S. got a meaningless doubling to 50,000 cars of its quota per automaker to enter Korea without meeting local safety and environmental standards. The U.S., which had promised to lift in 2021 its 25% tariff on Korean pick-up trucks and cargo vans, none ever having been shipped to the USA, obtained an extension to 2041.

Korea got a permanent exemption from the 25% Trump steel tariffs (below), subject to a quota limit of 70% of the average Korean steel exports to the USA in 2015–2017. Korea is expected to easily make up for these lost exports in other markets but pay attention to trade diversion restraints by other "collateral damage" countries like the EU, and WTO challenges to this bilateral voluntary export restraint (VER). The Korean steel industry parcels out the quotas among 54 categories of producers, some of which maxed out almost immediately in 2018.

Both sides agreed not to revise existing, contentious KORUS I agricultural trade rules. Increased transparency revisions on Korean customs procedures, and relaxed Korean pharmaceutical access and pricing rules, were also agreed.

All in all, a largely cosmetic, mutually face-saving revision of KORUS I was achieved. Call it KORUS II. President Trump held back signing this "strong card" pending talks with North Korea. Furthermore, the President's threat to globally impose 25% "national security" tariffs on autos and auto parts placed Korea's duty-free access to the U.S. market at risk. See Section 6.1.

KORUS 2012 and the 2018 U.S.-Korea Protocol amending it are linked in Section 6.7. The Protocol took effect Jan. 1, 2019.

§ 6.6 Links to KORUS I and II

https://ustr.gov/trade-agreements/free-trade-agreements/korus-fta

https://ustr.gov/trade-agreements/free-trade-agreements/korus-fta/final-text/september-2018-korus-amendment-and

§ 6.7 NAFTA Re-Negotiated: The 2020 USMCA Agreement and Its Impacts

The Negotiations

Early in 2017, the Trump administration notified Congress of its intent to re-negotiate NAFTA with Canada and Mexico under "fast-track" as authorized in the Trade Promotion Authority Act of 2015. President Trump's prior tweets called NAFTA the "worst trade deal ever." He threatened to withdraw from NAFTA or impose high tariffs on Mexican goods given that country's sizeable trade surplus ($69 billion in 2017) in goods and services with the United States. The U.S. states most involved in NAFTA trade were Texas, North Dakota,

Michigan, Indiana, Kentucky, and Vermont. They let their views be known vociferously in the re-negotiations.

Including merchandise and services, the U.S. had a small trade surplus with Canada in 2017, but President Trump continued to deny that reality, focusing only on a small goods deficit. This approach is about 100 years out of date: Some 150 million U.S. private sector jobs are in the services/technology sector, with tourism and intellectual property rights payments heading the list, followed by finance, insurance, telecommunications, information technology and professional services. U.S. jobs in manufacturing are dwarfed by comparison.

On balance, the initial Trump Administration NAFTA re-negotiation notice was remarkably moderate, as were the subsequently released U.S. negotiating objectives, which partly borrowed from the Trans-Pacific Partnership (TPP) agreement. NAFTA it seemed at first blush would only undergo a tune-up.

Many attribute this outcome to lobbying by major U.S. exporters to Mexico, especially farm products. Under NAFTA, Mexico had become the largest foreign market for U.S. corn, dairy products, poultry, and wheat. Manufacturers, fearing disruption and added costs, were quick to point out the high degree of supply chain integration among the NAFTA countries. Some components cross NAFTA borders repeatedly before a final product is finished.

When negotiations commenced in August 2017, the fundamental relationships between the three NAFTA partners had changed from 1994. Mexico and Canada were still heavily dependent on the U.S. market for their exports, and for technology and foreign investment capital. The United States, however, had become noticeably less dependent on foreign oil imports, but hardly self-sufficient. Mexico, contrary to its strong reservation of oil and gas rights in NAFTA, at its own initiative had amended its Constitution and significantly opened oil and gas exploration to foreign investors. Meanwhile, Canada was still having trouble accepting the reality that satellite and Internet broadcasts, and WTO remedies, had rendered its cultural industries exclusion almost meaningless. See Section 4.2.

By 2018, principally under WTO negotiations, Mexico's average MFN tariff on manufactured goods had fallen to approximately 8%, Canada to 4% and the U.S. to 3.5%. All three countries maintained generally higher tariffs on agricultural goods, and selectively higher tariffs on manufactured goods such as the 25% U.S. tariff on pick-up trucks, a legacy from a 1960s "chicken war" with Europe.

These national tariffs were, of course, not applicable to "North American goods", those goods meeting the NAFTA rules of origin. See

Section 4.4. But tightening up the existing 62.5% auto rules of origin quickly became a focus in the U.S. approach to re-negotiation. The U.S. sought an 85% North American auto content rule, *plus* a 50% U.S. content rule. Tighter auto rules of origin, however, could cause manufacturers to move elsewhere, then pay U.S. tariffs (2.5% for passenger autos) upon entry. The U.S. also wished to re-think the rules on NAFTA trade remedies, such as safeguards, that could result in tariffs on Mexican and Canadian goods. Removal of the waiver for Buy American preferences enjoyed by Canada and Mexico under NAFTA also surfaced as a goal, along with a "balancing" of procurement opportunities as between the U.S. and Mexico and Canada combined. Stronger labor and environmental provisions than offered through the NAFTA side agreements were also on the negotiating table, with relatively little conflict.

So too, the U.S. sought to open its neighbors' duty-free rules for cross-border online sales, think Amazon. Canada started with an unbelievably low online tariff exemption of only $20 CDN (compared to $200 per day CDN for shopping in the USA and returning to Canada with the goods). Mexico had $50 US online limit, while United States buyers could import online up to $800 in duty free goods from either Canada or Mexico.

Other items on the U.S. agenda included improved protection of intellectual property rights, facilitation of cross-border data flows and a ban on forced localization of computer data on servers, opposition to Canadian dairy "supply management" restraints, better customs clearance procedures, tariffs on seasonal agricultural goods (berries for example), expanded coverage of state-owned enterprises, vague references to policing currency manipulation, and dispute settlement.

The U.S. focused particularly on elimination of NAFTA binational panel arbitration of dumping and subsidy disputes, which would return appeals to national courts. Arguing that it promoted outsourcing, the United States also wanted to make NAFTA's controversial investor-state arbitration of disputes optional, forcing such disputes back into national courts or state-to-state negotiations.

Mexico and Canada also came to the table seeking change. Mexico, for example, emphasized its desire for coverage of security, narcotics, and migration issues. Little attention was given to investor/trader/professional visas created under NAFTA, but many talented Canadians and Mexicans working lawfully in the United States put their immigration lawyers on speed dial.

Canada reiterated that continued binational panel arbitration of trade remedy disputes could again be a deal-breaker, noting it had been involved in over 70 such proceedings since 1994, and that a previous Prime Minister had walked out of negotiations with the United States to obtain this unique appeal system. Canada also indicated it would like to see reduced application of Buy American procurement rules and a more "progressive" trade deal like that it achieved in TPP-11. See Chapter 5.

The NAFTA re-negotiations that commenced in August of 2017 were pushed by critical deadlines: The elections for the U.S. House of Representatives (November 2018) and the election of a new President of Mexico (July 2018). Nevertheless, negotiations proceeded at a slow pace, and deadlines for their conclusion were repeatedly extended. In the end the United States employed a divide and conquer strategy by first agreeing to a deal with Mexico, then inviting Canada to join in, which it did.

After a thorough "legal scrub", the leaders of Canada, Mexico and the United States signed a finalized NAFTA re-negotiated agreement (USMCA) on November 30, 2018, one day before Andres Manuel Lopez Obrador took office as President of Mexico. He had won in a landslide, mostly keeping quiet about his views on the agreement re-negotiated by his predecessor, President Pena Nieto.

The signature date was also important to President Trump. It was the last day he could submit the new agreement for Congressional review under U.S. "fast-track" procedures that mandate a Yes or No approval vote by Congress, no amendments allowed. See Section 4.1.

The USMCA Amendment Protocol

The first issue was what to call the new trilateral agreement. The Trump administration, wishing to disassociate from the NAFTA title, preferred the name "United States-Mexico-Canada" (USMCA) Agreement. Canada preferred New NAFTA and/or CUSMA in English or ACEUM in French. Mexico calls it T-MEC in Spanish. For purposes of this book, I primarily call the NAFTA Re-Negotiated trilateral agreement the USMCA.

A second issue was getting the agreement ratified and implemented. With the Democrats in control of the House of Representatives, internal U.S. negotiations primarily drove the three USMCA parties to adopt an amendment Protocol late in 2019. The amendments addressed dispute settlement concerns by preventing the ability of one partner to block intergovernmental dispute settlement by refusing to participate and by improving procedural rules dispute panels. Most of the amendments focused on reform of labor law and practices in Mexico. Language denying entry of goods produced by forced labor and provisions focused on violence against workers were tightened. A new "Rapid Response Mechanism" for independent panel investigation of suspected denials of association and collective bargaining rights at specific workplace facilities was created. The number of mandatory multilateral environmental agreements were expanded. Motor vehicle rules of origin added a steel and aluminum requirement of 70% North American content after seven years for steel and 10 years for aluminum.

The revised USMCA agreement dropped a required 10-year data exclusivity period for biologics competing with biosimilars and dropped a 3-year exclusivity period for clinical data for new uses of previously approved pharmaceuticals. Furthermore, patents were barred for new uses, methods, or processes of existing products. Extending pharmaceutical patent terms for delays in the approval process were limited, and effective awards for successfully challenging patent validity were encouraged.

The USMCA incorporates a mixture of provisions from CUSTA 1989, NAFTA 1994, and the 2016 Trans-Pacific Partnership (TPP-12) agreement signed by President Obama but denied ratification by President Trump. Overall, as economist Gregory Daco noted: The benefits of the USMCA "are not what [it] brings, but rather what it prevents."

For texts of the individual USMCA chapters, 34 in number, plus individual annexes and side letters, see: https://ustr.gov/trade-agreements. *As revised, the USMCA took effect July 1, 2020.*

USMCA Provisions with Little Change from NAFTA

Trade Remedy (AD and CVD) Dispute Settlement. Replacement of national court review of AD and CVD determinations with binational panels was retained under strident insistence by Canada in USMCA Chapter 10.

Safeguards (Escape Clause Proceedings). Despite considerable controversy and pressure, little change was made in 2018 to the NAFTA provisions on this trade remedy. The exclusion of NAFTA partners from global safeguard actions was retained.

Telecommunications. Expanded to allow regulation of mobile service roaming rates.

Temporary Business Visas. Minor changes to NAFTA coverage are contained in USMCA Chapter 16.

Textiles. Small changes in USMCA Chapter 6 tighten up required North American sources.

Canada's Cultural Industry Exclusion. Fully retained under USMCA Chapter 32.

No Private Legal Challenges. As under NAFTA, no person may challenge USMCA provisions in U.S. courts. All remedies are intergovernmental or arbitral.

Foreign Trade Zones (FTZ). Late in 2020, Congress "fixed" a USMCA error to clarify that U.S. manufacturers in American FTZ are not eligible for USMCA preferential treatment, a repeat of the NAFTA rule.

New or Notably Revised USMCA Provisions Common to All Partners

Intergovernmental Dispute Settlement. The Chapter 20 government dispute settlement provisions of NAFTA 1994, including the option to take most disputes to the WTO, was largely replicated in USMCA Chapter 31. Unlike NAFTA, each side cannot block use of the Chapter 31 process by refusing to name panelists (the roster of panelists was agreed upon in advance) and there are sanctions for attempting to do so. Indeed, a list of acceptable panelists was agreed upon in advance of the USMCA. In addition, for the first time ever in a trade agreement, rules of evidence are created for these proceedings.

Chapter 31 is particularly critical to the USMCA labor and environment provisions (below) and topics not covered by the WTO agreements. The first Chapter 31 panel commenced by the U.S. challenged Canada's tariff-rate quotas on American dairy products that primarily applied to dairy processors versus retailers. Chaired by a Uruguayan diplomat, the Panel ruled in favor of the USA and found Canada in breach of its USMCA dairy commitments.

National Security. The NAFTA "essential security interests" exception (Article 2102), resembling that of the GATT/WTO, references actions member nations consider necessary relating to: (1) Information disclosures; (2) traffic in arms and the supply of foreign militaries or security establishments; (3) war time or international relations' emergencies; (4) nuclear weapons proliferation; or breaches of UN Charter peace and security obligations.

USMCA Article 32.2 provides a more ironclad "national security" exception than found in the GATT/WTO and NAFTA rules:

> Essential Security 1. Nothing in this Agreement shall be construed to: (a) require a Party to furnish or allow access to information the disclosure of which it determines to be contrary to its essential security interests; or (b) preclude a Party from applying measures that it considers necessary for the fulfilment of its obligations with respect to the maintenance or restoration of international peace or

security, or the protection of its own essential security interests.

In May of 2019, President Trump, seeking Congressional ratification of USMCA, lifted application of the U.S. steel and aluminum tariffs to Canadian and Mexican exports. Those two partners in turn removed their retaliatory tariffs on U.S. exports. However, the U.S. reserved the right to re-impose its steel and aluminum tariffs if surges beyond historical U.S. imports occur. Canada and Mexico further agreed to monitor and stop diversions of shipments from other nations seeking to avoid U.S. tariffs on steel and aluminum.

The Trump administration threatened to apply global national security tariffs to U.S. auto and auto parts imports. The USMCA anticipates just such action by creating quotas, noted below, to shelter Mexican and Canadian autos and parts from such tariffs if they should emerge.

Autos and Parts. Arguably, the most notable and contentious changes to NAFTA undertaken in the USMCA concern the rules of origin for vehicles and their parts. To be free traded, passenger vehicles and light trucks after a three-year phase-in must contain 75% regional value content, up from 62.5%, both measured using the net cost method. In addition, 70% of the steel (slab steel to be "melted, smelted and poured" in North America within seven years) and aluminum content of such vehicles must originate in North America. The automotive tracing and "deemed originating" rules of CUSFTA 1989 and NAFTA 1994 were terminated in favor of regional content rules for key vehicle components such as engines, body panels, axles, suspension and steering systems, advanced batteries, and transmissions.

Furthermore, 40% of the value of autos and 45% for trucks must be produced by workers earning an average of $16 or more per hour (not including benefits and not indexed for inflation), well above prevailing Mexican wages. This "labor value content" rule favors U.S. and Canadian sourced parts and components and eliminates the possibility of free trading entirely Mexican sourced vehicles. Note that it requires two calculations: Production line wages and labor value content percentages. A useful figure appearing in the U.S. International Trade Commission 2019 Report on the Likely Impact of the USMCA on the U.S. economy diagrams the rules of origin for vehicles.

The complex, micromanagement rules governing auto rules of origin calculations are detailed in the USMCA and explained by Nebraska Law Professor Matthew Schaefer as follows:

> [T]he value from workers making $16/hour [must] "consist of at least 25 percentage points of high wage material and manufacturing expenditures, no more than 10 percentage points of technology expenditures, and no more than 5 percentage points of assembly expenditures." USMCA, Article 4-B.7(1)(d). The technology expenditures can include software (*i.e.*, may "include expenditures on software development, technology integration, vehicle communications, and information technology support operations"). With autos becoming "smart" vehicles and more and more autonomous, software inputs are rapidly increasing and Canada believes this will help its producers meet the new labor wage content rules in auto rules of origin. * * * The USMCA provides that "the production wage rate is the average hourly base wage rate, not including benefits, of employees directly involved in the production of the part or component used to calculate the LVC, and does not include salaries of management, R&D, engineering, or other workers who are not involved in the direct production of the parts or in the operation of production lines." USMCA, Ch. 4, fn. 104. These new rules will essentially be phased in over three or more years.

All these provisions were driven by the Trump administration's goal of bringing vehicle and parts production back home, which is aligned with the Biden administration's push for greater Made in the USA EV vehicle, battery, and auto chip production. Will Mexico be relegated to production of only gasoline and diesel autos?

A grace period ("alternative staging regime") of up to five years can be applied regarding compliance with the USMCA auto rules of origin. As a practical matter it is estimated they will generate compliance costs estimated at between 3 to 5% and likely favor GM, Ford, and Fiat-Chrysler over foreign rivals. About a third of the autos produced in Mexico were thought unable to comply in 2018 with the USMCA rules of origin.

Studies by the USITC and Federal Reserve Bank concluded that roughly 28,000 auto industry jobs would be created in the USA. But the USMCA rules could also raise the cost of cars to consumers in all three countries and make North American automakers (such as BMW based in South Carolina) less competitive in the global marketplace. An IMF study reached a similar conclusion, anticipating that although the USMCA auto rules of origin would create jobs, the cost increases stemming from those rules would lead to 140,000 fewer vehicles sold, with a corresponding reduction in automotive-related jobs.

An alternative to compliance with the new automobile rules of origin is to pay the U.S. passenger auto import tariff of 2.5%, assuming no new U.S. national security or other U.S. tariffs are applied to autos. This author is surprised there no public plans within the auto industry to engage this seemingly cost-effective alternative. The 2.5% alternative is not an option for manufacturers of pick-up trucks and vans, all of which face a 25% U.S. tariff. These vehicles are consequently produced primarily in the USA.

Side letters to USMCA anticipate that the United States could, as threatened, impose "national security" tariffs on autos from anywhere in the world, including its North American partners. Quotas in the side letters exempt 2.6 million Mexican passenger vehicles and light trucks and $108 billion in Mexican auto parts from any such future tariffs. Canada has an exemption for 2.6 million vehicles and $32.3 billion in auto parts. These quotas are currently well above 2018 Canadian and Mexican export levels.

These quotas are not indexed to inflation, and hence in time are likely to be reached. In a backhanded way, they support the threat of U.S. national security tariffs on autos from Japan, the EU, China, and Korea.

EV Vehicles

NAFTA and the USMCA were negotiated before electric vehicles (EV) significantly arrived in the North American market. Late in 2022, the U.S. adopted a maximum $7500 tax credit for EVs subject to detailed rules of origin. To obtain this credit, EVs must be assembled in North America or other countries with which the U.S. has free trade agreements, notably South Korea but not Japan, the EU, or the UK.

In addition, at least 50% (100% by 2029) of the value of an EV battery must be manufactured or assembled in North America to qualify for the full tax credit. Furthermore, 40% (80% by 2027) of the value of the minerals in an EV battery must come from a country with which the U.S. has a free trade agreement (think Mexico and Canada which have lithium resources) or be recycled in North America. EVs purchased for lease (say rental fleets) escape these exacting rules of origin.

The EV tax credit rules of origin overlay the original USMCA vehicle rules of origin. Manufacturer compliance with both regimes will amount to a competitive home run in the auto world. As this book went to print, most major auto companies, battery makers and mineral suppliers are taking their swing at the plate for this home run by investing in North America. Tesla, for example, has plans to create a factory in Mexico that will be twice the size of its Texas plant. GM, Ford, and other EV car makers are already doing so.

Currency Manipulation. Limited transparency and notification obligations regarding currency manipulation have been added to USMCA. Each country must disclose government foreign-exchange transactions. None of the NAFTA partners have in the past been considered currency manipulators. This provision was included mostly as a model for future U.S. FTAs where currency manipulation may be an issue. Disputes regarding currency manipulation which are not associated with any of the North American partners are not subject to USMCA dispute settlement.

Non-Market Economies. Under USMCA Chapter 32 any party may terminate the agreement if a partner enters into a free trade agreement with a non-market economy (NME). This provision is clearly targeted at Canadian and Mexican relations with China, which the United States continues to treat as a NME for trade law matters, treatment that China has contested before the WTO. It could also apply to Cuba and North Korea, but not Vietnam as a pre-existing partner with Canada and Mexico in the TPP-11 agreement that took effect in 2019.

Labor. Unlike the labor and environment "side agreements" to NAFTA (see Chapter 4), the USMCA incorporates these areas into the core agreement making them "enforceable" thereunder. This follows the pattern of the G. W. Bush administration's U.S. free trade agreements with Korea, Peru, Colombia, and Panama, as well as TPP-12. An "Annex on Worker Representation in Collective Bargaining in Mexico" explicitly requires labor law amendments to better protect independent union organizing rights in Mexico, which did not notably improve under the 1994 side agreement. These amendments were undertaken by Mexico with substantial enforcement funding in May of 2019.

Hundreds of thousands of existing employer-friendly unions "protection contracts" (often unknown to workers and shaped by the powerful CTM labor organization) need to be re-examined and validated by worker votes in Mexico. An early review of union contracts at Cemex, Mexico's multinational cement giant, was not encouraging. Some workers were clueless as to what the vote was all about. Others asserted union officials made false statements that benefits would be lost if the contract was rejected.

All Parties agreed to adopt and maintain in law and in enforcement practice labor rights recognized in the International Labor Organization's Fundamental Principles. Imports of goods from forced labor are banned. Protections for migrant workers and protections against violence targeting workers were included.

USMCA Article 23.9 broadly recognizes the goal of promoting equality in the workplace for women and eliminating employment/ occupation discrimination based on sex, sexual harassment, pregnancy, sexual orientation, gender identity and care giving responsibilities. Footnote 13 states that no additional action is required by the United States to comply this Article, disregarding the fact that no federal statute protects U.S. workers from gender identity and sexual orientation discrimination.

Critics, notably the post-election New Democrat Coalition and AFL-CIO, argued that enforcement of labor and environment commitments under USMCA 2018 was inadequate. In 2019, significant amendments to the 2018 agreement on labor were undertaken. A presumption that labor violations affect trade and investment, a NAFTA requirement retained in the USMCA, was added. U.S. government Dept. of Labor personnel will be based in Mexico to monitor that country's labor practices but will not serve as "inspectors."

The 2019 amendments required creation of a U.S. interagency committee to oversee Mexico's labor reform implementation and compliance with USMCA benchmarks. Benchmark failures can lead to enforcement action. A new *facility-specific "Rapid Response Enforcement Mechanism*" was added in 2019 to the USMCA via Annex 31-A. Biden's USTR, Katherine Tai, played a substantial role in drafting the Rapid Response Mechanism.

Three independent labor experts serve on Panels to evaluate asserted violations covering manufactured goods or services traded between the U.S. and Mexico. Tariffs, fines and possibly embargoes may apply to goods or services not produced in compliance with freedom of association and collective bargaining obligations. Complaints regarding Mexican compliance filed by U.S. labor unions have been piling up, including against a General Motors plant in Mexico. Responding to these complaints, several labor votes at Mexican plants have been rejected, rescheduled by Mexican authorities, and resulted in approval of new more independent unions, notably at the General Motors plant.

Environment. On the environment, USMCA borrowed and expanded upon TPP-12 with coverage banning subsidization of illegal, unreported, and unregulated (IUU) fishing and shark finning. New provisions concern invasive alien species, whales and sea turtles, wild flora and fauna, forest management, ozone depletion, environmental impact assessments, as well as cooperation on air quality and marine debris. A side agreement preserves the Commission for Environmental Cooperation (CEC) created under NAFTA. The CEC can continue to receive environmental compliance complaints from the public.

Unlike the Japan-EU FTA of 2018, no mention of climate change is made in the USMCA. Amendments to the USMCA in 2019 created a presumption that an environmental violation affects trade and investment. Commitments were undertaken to adopt and maintain seven multilateral environment agreements (MEAs, including future amendments thereto) taking priority over the USMCA:

(a) The Convention on International Trade in Endangered Species of Wild Fauna and Flora, done at Washington, March 3, 1973, as amended;

(b) The Montreal Protocol on Substances that Deplete the Ozone Layer, done at Montreal, September 16, 1987, as adjusted and amended;

(c) The Protocol of 1978 Relating to the International Convention for the Prevention of Pollution from Ships, 1973, done at London, February 17, 1 978, as amended;

(d) The Convention on Wetlands of International Importance Especially as Waterfowl Habitat, done at Ramsar, February 2, 1971, as amended;

(e) The Convention on the Conservation of Antarctic Marine Living Resources, done at Canberra, May 20, 1980;

(f) The International Convention for the Regulation of Whaling, done at Washington, December 2, 1946; and

(g) The Convention for the Establishment of an Inter-American Tropical Tuna Commission, done at Washington, May 31, 1949.

Under the 2019 USMCA amendments, a U.S. interagency committee will assess and monitor Canadian and Mexican USMCA environmental obligations. A new U.S. customs service verification mechanism will ensure that only legally harvested and taken flora and fauna are traded through Mexico. Additional funds are authorized for the North American Development Bank, the Trade Enforcement Trust Fund, and EPA grants under the Border Water Infrastructure Program.

Digital Trade/Internet Providers. Digital trade, then in its infancy, was not covered under NAFTA 1994. USMCA Chapter 19 follows TPP-12 in banning data localization requirements (Canada has such rules), disallowing customs duties on digital commerce (think Netflix, social media, search engines, data storage, e-books, and software), limiting cross-border restrictions on data flows, requiring anti-spam rules, and protecting consumer privacy. Source codes and algorithms are protected, as are e-signatures and electronic authentications.

Internet service providers (ISPs) are protected under a "safe harbor" from copyright and criminal liability connected to unauthorized actions of their users, provided the ISPs take down copyright infringing material in a timely manner. Canada retained its "notice-and-notice" system requiring ISPs to notify customers of copyright infringement allegations.

Intellectual Property. Copyright protection is extended to life of the author plus 70 years, which will change Canada's 50-year rule, and 75 years for films and other collective works. Trademarks for sounds and scents must be allowed. Concerning geographic indicators, attempts are made at protecting trade between Mexico and the United States in arguably generic product names such as parmesan, feta, and champagne. IP exceptions to promote medicines for all and compulsory patent licensing in national emergencies were retained. IP enforcement exceptions to protect public health and nutrition, and to promote development are recognized.

For the first time in *any* FTA, USMCA requires:

(1) Ex officio authority for law enforcement to seize suspected counterfeit or pirated goods at any time entering, exiting or transiting USMCA nations;

(2) Enforcement procedures for digital world trademark and copyright rights infringement;

(3) Criminal rules against cam cording of movies;

(4) Civil and criminal rules against satellite and cable signal theft;

(5) Broad protection against trade secret theft, including by state-owned enterprises.

Pharmaceuticals and Biologics. Under the 2018 text, biologic (made from living organisms) medicines were to receive 10 years safety and efficacy test data exclusivity protection, adding two years to Canada's eight-year rules. This provision was *removed* by the 2019 amendments. Such provisions typically delay market entry by generic biosimilar firms.

Pharmaceuticals also lost linkage and patent term extension or delay benefits originally in the 2018 text. Generic and biosimilar firms are to obtain marketing approval on the day after patent expiration. In addition, the 2019 amendments removed provisions requiring patent availability for new uses of known pharma products ("evergreening"). These changes focus on expanding and accelerating the growth of generic pharmaceuticals.

Greater transparency in pharma pricing and reimbursement rules, plus independent review procedures, are required. These provisions target single payer health care systems, such as that of Canada. They were in TPP-12 but dropped completely from TPP-11. Disputes regarding pharma transparency are excluded from USMCA dispute settlement.

Financial Services and Information. The USMCA on financial services generally tracks TPP-12, including a narrowing of national treatment and MFN treatment duties in "like circumstances." In addition, USMCA governments are prohibited from preventing financial institutions from transferring personal and other information across borders by electronic or other means. Also, the governments may not restrict financial institutions from locating computing facilities abroad. In either case, regulatory authorities must have immediate, direct, complete, and ongoing access to information for regulatory and supervisory purposes. Each nation must adopt or maintain "a" legal framework that provides protection for personal data and have online consumer protection and anti-spam laws.

On dispute settlement, financial services obligations are subject to USMCA investor-state arbitrations between Mexico (but not Canada) and the United States.

Trucking and Telecom Services. Cross-border long-haul trucking by Mexican carriers is restricted under a Chapter 15 Annex, altering NAFTA provisions and a unanimous NAFTA dispute panel in Mexico's favor. See Chapter 3. In the event of "material harm" (including to American drivers), the U.S. may limit new Mexican cross-border, long-haul trucking services.

Cross-border NAFTA telecom services' provisions were not significantly effective, notably so in Mexico where Carlos Slim's landline and mobile near-monopolies continued to dominate. The USMCA attempts to substantially expand and improve cross-border telecom rights and services.

Provisions Borrowed from TPP-12. New provisions in the USMCA, not found or heavily augmented compared to NAFTA, were primarily borrowed from TPP-12. These include largely aspirational coverage of "good" regulatory practices (Chapter 28, transparency, notice and the like), advancement and protection of the interests of small and medium businesses (Chapter 25), macroeconomic policies and exchange rates (Chapter 33), competition policy (Chapter 21), and anti-corruption law (Chapter 27). More concrete provisions concern competitive neutrality for state-owned enterprises (Chapters 22 and 26), customs and trade facilitation procedures (Chapter 7), and development of sectoral industry standards (Chapter 12) via Annexes to the USMCA.

"De Minimis" Customs Duty and Tax-Free Shipments. Customs duty free shipments to Canada rise to $150 CDN, and to Mexico to $117 US, with the U.S. remaining at $800. The tax-free thresholds are lower: $50 U.S. for Mexico, $40 CDN for Canada, and $800 U.S. for the United States. In both cases, the U.S. amounts could be reduced to match the Canadian and Mexican sums. These duty free and tax-free shipments, employing "simple" customs forms, are expected to boost cross-border e-commerce and small business trading though hardly a victory for online trading.

Amazon, however, quickly set up a major distribution center in Tijuana opposite San Diego. It is said that bulk shipments from China are imported to Mexico, then broken down to $800 segments shipped into the USA avoiding high U.S. on Chinese and Asian goods.

Investor-State Dispute Settlement has been notably changed by Chapter 14 of the USMCA. *See* the coverage of Canada and Mexico below.

Sunset Clause. The United States withdrew its pressure for a five-year sunset clause. Instead, the USMCA will last for 16 years. It will be reviewed every six years starting in 2026, triggering another 16-year period unless rejected by a partner.

As under NAFTA, any Party may withdraw from the USMCA agreement with six months' notice.

Canada Under the USMCA

Canada has for many years been the largest U.S. trade partner for goods. Before NAFTA, most Canadian exports went to the USA, with significant U.S. trade in services, investment and technology flowing north. By 2018, broadly speaking, Canada's economic dependence on the USA remained substantial, a bargaining lever exploited by U.S. negotiators. In the run-up to the finalization of USMCA, Canada reached out for alternatives. It completed a major free trade agreement with the European Union (CETA 2017) and was a leader in developing TPP-11.

Cultural Industries, AD and CVD Disputes, Progressive Goals, Energy. From the Canadian perspective, on the success side of the ledger, Canada retained from CUSFTA 1989 and NAFTA 1994 its cultural industry exclusion (see Chapter 2). At this writing,

Canada is in the process of adopting Online cultural content rules applicable to the likes of You Tube, Tik-Tok and Netflix. Canada also retained utilization of binational panels (instead of judicial review) to resolve antidumping and subsidy disputes. See Chapters 4 and 5.

Canada also secured recognition of the rights of indigenous peoples. The USMCA agreement further requires policies against employment discrimination based on gender identity, sexual orientation, sexual harassment, pregnancy, and caregiving responsibilities, all reflecting Canada's "progressive" perspectives. Footnote 13 in USMCA Chapter 23 appears to exempt the U.S. from these duties.

Canada's much debated promise under CUSFTA and NAFTA to proportionally share energy resources with the USA in energy crises was removed.

Agricultural Goods, Wine. On the negative side of the ledger, Canada made limited concessions allowing greater entry of U.S. dairy (milk, milk powder, milk protein, cream, butter, and cheese), margarine, whey, chicken, egg, turkey and grain products into its market, concessions broadly like those it had made under TPP-12. The U.S. prevailed in 2021 against Canada's tariff rate dairy quotas in the first USMCA formal dispute resolution challenge.

In return, Canada gained small market openings to increase exports to the U.S. of dairy, peanut and processed peanut, and sugar and sugar containing products. Dairy tariff rate quotas commitments on both sides are to be reciprocal based on tonnage. All sides committed to protecting agricultural biotech, including gene editing.

Canada also agreed to open British Columbia grocery stores to sales of U.S. wines.

Procurement. Canada and the United States have no procurement obligations under the USMCA. Hence procurement as between those countries is governed by the positive list Enhanced WTO Procurement Agreement. See my Concise Hornbook on *International Trade Beyond Trump*, Section 1.13. Mexico (which does not participate in the optional WTO Agreement) and the United States largely retained their NAFTA federal/special entity negative-list procurement obligations under Chapter 13 of the USMCA agreement. Canada and Mexico have complained of increased Buy America rules under President Biden.

Investor-State Dispute Settlement. By agreement in Chapter 14, apart from legacy NAFTA claims (presented no later than three years after the USMCA agreement entered into force), Canada and the United States *completely* removed the availability of arbitrations to resolve investor-state disputes. In the future, such disputes will presumably be resolved by state-to-state dispute settlement or the courts of either nation.

Mexico Under the USMCA

Before NAFTA, about most Mexican exports went to the USA, with significant U.S. trade in services, investment and technology flowing south. By 2018, broadly speaking, Mexico's economic dependence on the USA remained overwhelming, a major bargaining lever exploited by U.S. negotiators. In the run-up to the finalization of the USMCA. Mexico also reached out for alternatives. It completed a much-expanded free trade agreement with the European Union and is a member of TPP-11.

Investor-State Dispute Settlement (ISDS). Investor-state arbitration of disputes for damages continues in full as between Mexico and Canada under TPP-11 effective Jan. 1, 2019. Such arbitrations continue under revised terms as between Mexico and the United States. U.S.-Mexico claims involving *covered government contracts* are limited to specified capital-intensive sectors (oil and gas, telecommunications, power generation, telecommunications, transportation, and ownership or management of infrastructure).

Such government contract disputes need not exhaust domestic remedies and may assert the full range of NAFTA investor rights including indirect expropriation and fair and equitable treatment (minimum standard). *USMCA Article 14.6 provides that "the mere fact that a Party takes or fails to take an action that may be inconsistent with an investor's expectations does not constitute a breach" of fair and equitable treatment "even if there is loss or damage to the covered investment as a result."*

For claims *not* involving government contracts, limitations are placed on investor-state arbitrations by the USMCA. *Such claims can only be pursued after investors have spent at least 30 months seeking domestic relief in host nation courts or administrative tribunals.* This rule does not appear to apply to the select government contract claimants noted above.

Claims not involving government contracts are limited to national and most-favored nation treatment, and direct expropriation grounds, notably dropping out fair and equitable treatment and indirect expropriation claims, the two most common claims asserted under NAFTA. See Section 4.9. In addition, borrowing from post-NAFTA U.S. free trade agreements and the TPP-12, "indirect" expropriation claims are also limited. Indirect expropriations are defined in the USMCA as situations "in which an action or series of actions by a Party has an effect equivalent to direct expropriation without formal transfer of title or outright seizure."

"Non-discriminatory regulatory actions by a Party that are designed and applied to protect legitimate public welfare objectives, such as health, safety and the environment, do *not* constitute indirect expropriations, except in rare circumstances." This USMCA language addresses criticisms of NAFTA investor-state arbitrations challenging environmental measures as regulatory takings and/or indirect expropriations.

Investors owned or controlled by non-market economy states are barred from using arbitration remedies. Establishment claims prior to actual investment are generally excluded. And, significantly, *NAFTA's investment coverage of intangible intellectual property rights and of services was dropped from USMCA.*

Energy. Mexico's top priority in negotiating NAFTA, protection of PEMEX as a state monopoly over oil, gas and most petrochemicals, is obliquely referenced in the USMCA. Explicit reference is made to Mexico's direct, inalienable, and imprescriptible ownership of hydrocarbon resources (which conceivably could facilitate the return of PEMEX as an absolute monopoly).

The numerous major oil companies with new wells and drilling rights in Mexico as of 2019 awaited with some anxiety the policies of its new President López-Obrador (known as AMLO). Prior to taking office, AMLO announced a three-year moratorium on new bidding for oil and gas exploration/exploitation blocs. He forced renegotiation of natural-gas pipeline contracts, directed Pemex to construct a new refinery, and gave Pemex over a billion dollars in tax cuts.

That said, buried in USMCA Article 32.11, is an obligation for MFN treatment in the energy sector. Since Mexico agreed under TPP-11 Annexes to preserve the market opening reforms of its prior administration, Article 32.11 could be construed to bar backtracking on energy rules already in place that benefit U.S. and Canadian parties.

Cultural Industry Exceptions. For the first time, USMCA 2020 creates Mexican broadcasting, newspaper, cinema, and audiovisual free trade exceptions resembling those long established for Canada (noted above).

Ratification

Thirteen "side letters' that accompanied the signing of the USMCA on Nov. 30, 2018, took effect immediately. These include Mexican and Canadian exclusions from any future U.S. tariff-rate quotas on the importation of autos (threatened by the Trump administration as a matter of national security), U.S.-Mexico agreements on biologic drugs, cheese names and auto safety standards, and U.S.-Canada agreements on wine, water and energy.

Approval and implementation of the USMCA by the U.S. Congress was complicated by the takeover in November of the House of Representatives by the Democrats. Apart from not wishing to give the President a "victory", the sizeable New Democrat Coalition and the AFL-CIO quickly let it be known that the USMCA's enforcement provisions on labor and the environment were, in their opinion, inadequate. Additional concerns were expressed about access to biologic medicines under the new agreement, the ability to block intergovernmental USMCA dispute settlement by failure to name panelists, and continuance of U.S. national security steel and aluminum tariffs on Canadian and Mexican exports, subsequently removed in May 2019. Republican conservatives opposed the progressive social provisions (above) secured by Canada in USMCA.

President Trump threatened to withdraw from NAFTA (with six months' notice) to pressure Congress to approve and implement the USMCA. In early June 2019, he commenced U.S. "fast-track" procedures under U.S. trade law that anticipate up or down Congressional votes on USMCA as negotiated. No Congressional amendments are permitted under fast-track procedures, but new side letters or side agreements can emerge.

A few days after commencing fast-track, in the name of national emergency, President Trump announced, effective June 10, 2019, a 5% tariff on ALL Mexican goods absent satisfactory Mexican efforts to reduce the flow of Central American asylum-seeking immigrants into the USA. He further threatened to raise this tariff each month to 25% by the Fall of 2019. All this just as Mexico and Canada surpassed China to become the top trading partners of the USA.

Mexico quickly promised to move its National Guard to its Southern border with Guatemala, accept more immigrants returned from or denied asylum by the USA, and generally cooperate on migration issues. Mexico did not, as the U.S. wished, designate itself as a "safe third country", though apparently promised to do so if its immigrant restraints failed to measure up to U.S. goals. Such a designation would render migrants passing through Mexico ineligible to claim asylum in the USA. President Trump removed his national emergency tariff threats.

Meanwhile, formal ratification of the USMCA was undertaken first in Mexico in June of 2019. Negotiations between the Trump administration and Democrats in Congress generated changes on labor, environment, enforcement procedures, and pharmaceutical

USMCA rules that formed the basis for an amendment protocol discussed above that all three countries signed in December of 2019. Ratification commenced shortly thereafter in the Mexican Senate and with an overwhelming approval vote in the U.S. House of Representatives *where more Democrats than Republicans voted in favor of the revised USMCA.*

USMCA Overview

On balance, especially considering the rhetoric and sometimes vitriolic positions of President Trump, there are relatively few provisions of major consequence in the USMCA. Apart from auto rules of origin, removal of investor-state arbitrations between the U.S. and Canada, restricted entry for long-haul Mexican trucks, and closer scrutiny of Mexican unions, most of the agreement contains predictable updates largely derived from TPP-12. In sum, the USMCA makes relatively modest to minor changes and additions to NAFTA.

In other words, the USMCA is not exactly groundbreaking. It primarily repackages free trade rules found elsewhere. That said, the USMCA constituted an FTA model acceptable to President Trump. Of course, no U.S. trade partner enjoys being "bullied" into a deal with a leader they distrust. President Trump repeatedly seemed to ignore or not understand that how you negotiate trade agreements can have long-term relationship costs. These costs were passed along to President Biden who showed no enthusiasm for free trade agreements, not even (unlike President Trump) with Britain.

Much has changed in global trade law and alliances since the USMCA was negotiated. The WTO has stalled as an engine of trade creation and dispute settlement. U.S. use of unilateral Section 301 tariffs against Chinese goods and the PRC's retaliatory tariffs, combined with Russia's invasion of Ukraine, war in the Middle East, supply chain crises, dramatic increases in maritime shipping costs, and COVID have pushed the world into regional and "friend-shoring" (thank you Janet Yellen) trading blocs.

By 2024, Mexico's labor costs were well below those of China. . . that is important news for the future of the USMCA. Indeed, Chinese investments to produce clothing, furniture, computer components and more in Mexico have been rapidly expanding. EV production in Mexico is exploding. Ford, GM, BMW, Bombardier (electric motorcycles), and others have concluded that USMCA offers very attractive opportunities as trade globalization declines.

All these factors have made understanding the USMCA and its business impacts even more essential and valuable to North Americans and the rest of the world.

Friends of USMCA

With many of the phase-in provisions completed, USMCA was operational with relatively few formal disputes arising. Several environmental (*Vaquita*) and labor (*Tridonex, GM Silao*) disputes concerning Mexican practices were resolved amicably through state-to-state negotiations. Mexico's proposed restraints on GMO corn exports from the U.S. and its threatened expropriation for environmental protection of a U.S. owned stone and gravel site in the Yucatan, along with Canada's 3% digital services tax (hello Meta and Alphabet) remain contentious. But most disputes have been held in check by cross-border dialogues. Likewise, the massive switch to politically elected (versus appointed) judges throughout Mexico adopted in the last month of AMLO's 2024 Presidency raises investor fears for judicial independence. Watch for these disputes to influence negotiations commencing in 2026 on renewal of the USMCA.

The timing of USMCA has been lucky. With global tensions, trade costs and restraints, and wars dramatically increased since 2020, international trade with geopolitical "friends" is strategically in demand. As it was under NAFTA, Mexico is particularly well situated to grow economically and gain from the desire of businesses to profit from free trading inside North America. Most notably, Chinese firms (as Japanese and Korean companies did under NAFTA) have come to appreciate Mexico as a welcome, price competitive portal for manufacturing and selling goods.

Boom! North America's trade in goods and services has quadrupled since NAFTA came online in 1994 to more than $7 trillion (roughly 30% of GDP). U.S. trade with its neighbors now totals much more than with the PRC. If there is a major risk to North American well-being, it is mass migration. Hopefully Mexico's new President Claudia Scheinbaum and the winner of the 2024 U.S. Presidential race can continue to steer North America along its lucky road.

§ 6.8 Linked Contents, Annexes and Side Letters of the 2020 USMCA Agreement

Table of Contents

2. National Treatment and Market Access for Goods
    - US Tariff Schedule
        - US Tariff Schedule Appendix 1
    - MX Tariff Schedule
        - MX Tariff Schedule Appendix 1
    - CA Tariff Schedule
        - CA Tariff Schedule Appendix 1
3. Agriculture
4. Rules of Origin
5. Origin Procedures
6. Textiles and Apparel
7. Customs Administration and Trade Facilitation
8. Recognition of Mexican Ownership of Hydrocarbons
9. Sanitary and Phytosanitary Measures
10. Trade Remedies
11. Technical Barriers to Trade
12. Sectoral Annexes
13. Government Procurement
14. Investment
15. Cross-Border Trade in Services
16. Temporary Entry
17. Financial Services
18. Telecommunications
19. Digital Trade
20. Intellectual Property
21. Competition Policy
22. State-Owned Enterprises
23. Labor
24. Environment
25. Small and Medium-Sized Enterprises
26. Competitiveness
27. Anticorruption
28. Good Regulatory Practices
29. Publication and Administration
30. Administrative and Institutional Provisions
31. Dispute Settlement
32. Exceptions and General Provisions
33. Macroeconomic Policies and Exchange Rate Matters
34. Final Provisions

B. Agreement Annexes

- **Annex I Investment and Services Non-Conforming Measures—Explanatory Note**
- **Annex I Investment and Services Non-Conforming Measures—Mexico**
- **Annex I Investment and Services Non-Conforming Measures—United States**
- **Annex I Investment and Services Non-Conforming Measures—Canada**
- **Annex II Investment and Services Non-Conforming Measures—Explanatory Note**
- **Annex II Investment and Services Non-Conforming Measures—Mexico**
- **Annex II Investment and Services Non-Conforming Measures—United States**
- **Annex II Investment and Services Non-Conforming Measures—Canada**
- **Annex III—Financial Services Non-Conforming Measures—Explanatory Note**
- **Annex III—Financial Services Non-Confirming Measures—Mexico**
- **Annex III—Financial Services Non-Conforming Measures—United States**
- **Annex III—Financial Services Non-Conforming Measures—Canada**
- **Annex IV—SOEs Non-Conforming Activities**

C. Side Letters

1. **MX-US Side Letter on 232 Dispute Settlement**
2. **MX-US Side Letter on 232 Process**
3. **MX-US Side Letter on 232**
4. **MX-US Side Letter on Auto Safety Standards**
5. **MX-US Side Letter on Biologics**
6. **MX-US Side Letter on Cheeses**
7. **MX-US Side Letter on Distilled Spirits**
8. **MX-US Side Letter on Prior Users**
9. **CA-US Side Letter on 232 Process**
10. **CA-US Side Letter on Wine**
11. **CA-US Side Letter on Natural Water Resources**
12. **CA-US Side Letter on Energy**

13. **CA-US Side Letter on Research and Development Expenditures**
14. **Side Letter Text on 232 CA-US Response**

Source: https://ustr.gov/trade-agreements/free-trade-agreements/united-states-mexico-canada-agreement/agreement-between

Chapter 7

THE USMCA: ITS ECONOMIC AND BUSINESS IMPACTS[1]

Table of Sections

Sec.

Given three years of anti-NAFTA rhetoric from the campaign trail and then the White House, there was considerable debate among NAFTA experts and vested interest groups regarding what U.S. trade policy should be and the potential damage if the agreement was terminated. Similarly, in fall 2018, as election deadlines in each country pressed politicians and negotiators to find "a deal", lobbying and bargaining intensified resulting first in a U.S.-Mexico agreement and then the United States-Mexico-Canada Agreement or USMCA.

Notice the word "Free" was not included in the 2020 USMCA agreement. The new agreement included rules and language to address technologies, intellectual property, and other goods and services that were not addressed in NAFTA or did not exist when NAFTA was signed. For autos, the agreement also included increased regional content rules and created a new minimum wage requirement. One commentator questioned whether USMCA should be called a trade agreement or a trade protection act.

At various times, President Trump seemingly contradicted himself, calling for higher tariffs on imports from countries whose trade practices he considered "unfair" but then saying: "I'm absolutely a free trader. I'm for open trade, free trade, but I also want smart trade and fair trade." He indicated he wanted to achieve "fairness and reciprocity." Numerous U.S. presidents have articulated similar goals but interpreted the terms differently. Until

---

1 Written by Distinguished Professor of Economics W. Davis Folsom of USC Beaufort.

USMCA negotiations, U.S. presidents generally attempted to achieve fairness and reciprocity in terms of the rules of the game not specific trade outcomes.

The goal of fair trade goes back to colonial America when one of the grievances in the Declaration of Independence was a complaint about Britain's use of mercantilist policies to ban colonial trade with the rest of the world. Post American Revolution, Britain resisted U.S. attempts to establish free trade and, in 1793, Secretary of State Thomas Jefferson, while supporting free trade doctrine, reported many restrictions imposed by trade partners of the new country. Jefferson unsuccessfully proposed achieving reciprocity through retaliation. For the next hundred years or so, the U.S. set tariffs, often as a source of central government revenue, largely without regard to trade partner policies, culminating in the infamous Smoot-Hawley tariffs of 1930.

The goal of reciprocity in trade did not reappear until the Franklin D. Roosevelt years, when the Reciprocal Trade Agreements Act of 1934 gave the president the authority to negotiate changes in trade agreements with other nations. When Donald Trump won the 2016 election, trade law experts were quickly in demand and confirmed that, yes, the president does have authority to negotiate and terminate trade agreements. Often stunned political and industry leaders delved into the various statements made during the election campaign trying to discover what direction the president would take for future U.S. trade policy.

In response to U.S. demands during USMCA negotiations, Canada pursued a fascinating strategy labeled a "charm offensive" by the *Wall Street Journal*. After the 2017 U.S. inauguration, Canadian officials held nearly 300 meetings with U.S. leaders other than President Trump including governors or lieutenant governors in all fifty states. Ottawa was said to be betting that friends in high places across the U.S. would recognize the damage tearing up NAFTA could do to supply chains and growth. The Canadians pressured the Trump administration to leave the pact alone.

Early into his presidency, Trump withdrew from the Trans-Pacific Partnership (TPP) promising, instead, to negotiate and re-negotiate many bilateral agreements with Asian nations. In Spring of 2018, after authorizing unilateral increases in tariffs on steel, aluminum, and products from China, with little media attention, the U.S. and Korea reached a revision of their free trade agreement (KORUS II), signaling to some NAFTA watchers that the White House could engage in and complete trade agreements. In 2019, Trump suggested that if USMCA was not ratified, he might withdraw from NAFTA. Obviously, that did not happen, but it caused analysts to ponder the possibility.

One NAFTA headline read "Leaving NAFTA Would Cost $50 Billion a Year". The author concluded that NAFTA had increased U.S. GDP by 0.2 to 0.3 percent annually. This did not sound like much of an impact until it is compared to U.S. GDP which was then over $20 trillion.

The U.S. Chamber of Commerce was an early voice critical of withdrawal from NAFTA: "Quitting NAFTA would be an economic, political, and national security disaster." Their experts predicted tariffs on all products would snap back to an average of 3.5 percent for the United States, 4.2 percent for Canada, and 7.5 percent for Mexico. The Chamber noted that existing areas cooperation; anti-terror, anti-narcotics, and Central American immigration, would likely end "overnight." Echoing the U.S. Chamber of Commerce, a Peterson Institute for International Economics analyst concluded: "Repeal of NAFTA would be a damaging economic blow to the United States, but it would be a far more serious threat to U.S. homeland security."

§ 7.1 Business Implications of USMCA

Years ago, a U.S. trade assistant described the 1993 flurry of NAFTA negotiations as the "Watergate 300", referring to the fact that the final negotiations took place on the third floor of the Watergate Hotel and an analogy to a car race frenzy. Similarly, finalizing USMCA could be described as somewhere between hostage negotiations and the final lap at Indianapolis 500.

The Trump administration's imposition of steel and aluminum tariffs on materials from NAFTA partners surprised many people, angered others, and led to a stand-off where Mexico was the first to capitulate and Canada later complied. The process was not pretty and often shuffled to the sidelines as China disputes/negotiations took primacy. Somehow, in spring 2019, a tentative agreement was reached and, later that year, a final accord was agreed upon.

In the end, numerous changes and additions were made to NAFTA. Headlines suggested major "winners" included the three political leaders: President Trump for re-negotiating NAFTA, Prime Minister Trudeau for keeping the Chapter 19 dispute resolution mechanism and largely maintaining the Canadian dairy supply management system, and President López Obrador for avoiding the termination of NAFTA. Other "winners" included organized labor, with the $16 per hour minimum wage requirement in automobile production and language directing Mexico to make it easier to form unions, North American steel and aluminum with new content rules, and online shoppers with higher *de minimis* allowances.

"Losers" were predicted to be car buyers in the United States with higher prices and reduced selection among small cars and big business facing increased compliance costs. Industry groups and analysts began to assess the implications of USMCA.

§ 7.2 USMCA in Context

When the USMCA was being negotiated and ratified (2017–2020), the stock market was near an all-time high, unemployment was at a record low, and the economy was digesting a trillion-dollar tax cut. The word pandemic referred to 1918, and the acronym COVID had not yet entered English vocabulary. In 2020, the USMCA languished in Washington as quarantines and supply chain quagmires became a reality.

When finally ratified, the agreement did reduce uncertainty and, as such, facilitate trade and investment decision-making. Numerous North American CEOs were reported as "breathing easier" when passage was announced.

But, as our readers know, many things have changed in the macroeconomic world during the last few years. First, a get tough with China trade policy was initiated by the Trump Administration. Then came China's trade response and its zero-Covid shutdown policy with the resulting global supply chain *kerfuffle*. In response, the U.S. pursued massive monetary and fiscal stimuli, but the rest of the world largely did not follow. Finally, Russia's invasion of Ukraine generated a U.S.-led embargo. Russia responded with new "friendships", altering the flow of energy, grains, and weapons to the consternation of the NATO allies.

Imagine, you are part of the leadership of a multinational corporation trying to decide how best to "live long and prosper"! By 2024, industry strategists learned and began putting into practice reshoring, nearshoring, and friendshoring.

§ 7.3 Early USMCA Macromarket Impacts

As the change in real GDP and unemployment data in the table below indicates, all three countries went through an initial downturn, followed by a recovery, during the 2020–2023 period.

% Change Real GDP / Unemployment Rate %

Year	Can.	U.S.	Mexico
2020	−5.2 / 9.6	−2.8 / 6.7	−14.4 / 4.5
2021	4.6 / 7.5	5.9 / 3.9	18.9 / 4.4
2022	3.8 / 5.1	2.1 / 3.5	3.0 / 2.8
2023	0.9 / 5.4	3.4 / 3.7	2.6 / 3.5

§ 7.4 Early USMCA Microeconomic Impacts

Agriculture. During NAFTA, the United States entered into few new trade agreements while Canada and Mexico continued to expand their trade relationships. Some farm organizations quickly applauded increased access to the Canadian dairy market, but analysts described the change as "symbolic." An ITC analysis concurred that the USMCA agricultural provisions were generally minor. There are no market access provisions in USMCA that address food and agricultural products trade between the United States and Mexico, so the predominant change in trade was between the United States and Canada.

Most trade in agricultural products among the United States, Canada, and Mexico was already duty free under NAFTA, However, some restrictions on agricultural trade remain. The United States maintains tariff-rate quotas (TRQs) on sugar and sugar-containing products (SCPs) and dairy products. Restrictions on trade in these products were slightly eased under USMCA. Canada maintains a supply management system including TRQs that protect its domestic producers of dairy products and poultry and egg-containing products from imports. By agreement the USMCA altered Canada's dairy management system, but the U.S. has twice challenged Canada's commitments in this area. See Chapter 6.

One small part of the Canada-European trade pact eliminated an eight percent European tariff on live lobster imports. U.S. lobster producers still faced the tariff, giving their Canadian counterparts a distinct competitive advantage. A mini-deal removing this tariff was negotiated by President Trump just in time for the 2020 elections. Another unique trade incident occurred in February 2021 at a Mexican factory. After a U.S. inspector was threatened, avocado shipments were temporarily banned by the USDA. The U.S. distributor assured U.S. consumers that there were sufficient supplies for upcoming Super Bowl parties! The dispute simmered until arising, again, in 2024.

Generally, during the NAFTA years, the U.S. ran small agricultural trade deficits with Canada and Mexico. Under the USMCA, North American total agricultural trade and partner trade deficits have risen. Since the USMCA made few changes in this sector, increased North American agricultural trade may have been influenced by U.S./China disputes.

Digital Trade and E-Commerce. USMCA is having a positive impact on U.S. industries that rely on cross-border data flows and digitally enabled trade, including e-commerce. In particular, the USMCA benefited North American computer services and digital platform services firms. While 75 percent of Mexican citizens use the Internet, security concerns (particularly fraud and fear of online banking), limit the potential impact of USMCA on Mexican e-commerce. A McKinsey & Co. study ranked Mexico 55th out of 151 countries in "digital maturity." The USITA continues to list digital solution opportunities in Mexican retail, financial services, logistical services, and lodging, food, and beverages.

Though the USMCA telecommunications chapter allowed greater access for competitors, analysts anticipated the USMCA would affect the business segment of the telecom services markets of Canada and Mexico more so than the consumer segment. In The consumer segments are either already facing competition (Mexico) or dominated by existing firms (Canada).

Changes in De-Minimis Thresholds (DMT), raising the value of cross-border purchases (usually business to consumer B2C) subject to duties were expected to have a modest, positive economic impact. The following de minimis values were specified in the USMCA:

- United States: U.S. $800 customs duty free de minimis value
- Canada: C$150 for duty-free shipments and C$40 for taxes
- Mexico: U.S. $117 for duty-free shipments and U.S. $50 for taxes

The Peterson Institute for International Economics analysis of *de minimis* policy suggested raising the Canadian minimum would increase consumer welfare through increased choice and lower prices. Critics, primarily Canadians, argued it would allow a backdoor entry into their country for competition from low-cost countries including China. No one anticipated the explosion of direct sale and delivery that has transpired.

U.S. Customs reported 1.1 billion BOLS (bill of ladings) valued at $54.5 billion in 2023. Increased *de minimis* allowances combined with COVID-induced isolation, led to a North American e-commerce boom, and a massive fulfillment industry expansion in border areas. Global firms quickly recognized the savings and ease of direct business to consumer shipping, primarily to U.S. customers. Tijuana, already the electronics assembly center of North America, benefited immensely from the de minimis provisions in USMCA. Amazon has a 400,000 square foot facility in Tijuana and a 1,000,000+ square foot distribution center just across the border. Retail e-commerce grew as follows:

NORTH AMERICAN RETAIL E-COMMERCE

(revenue $ billions, U.S.)

	2020	**2021**	**2022**
U.S.	**644**	**768**	**875**
CAN.	**43**	**54**	**61**
MEX.	**17**	**21**	**22**

Energy. Amidst the anti-USMCA rhetoric, little mention was made about energy trade. That may reflect the fact that, since NAFTA, the United States has dramatically reduced its energy dependence. Increased unconventional production of crude petroleum supported growth in U.S. and Canadian industries, while limited investment and declining output from mature fields constrained the Mexican industry.

The rise in crude petroleum production in Canada was largely due to growth in oil sands output. At the same time, Mexico's national petroleum company, Pemex, which had exclusive control over the country's industry, was prohibited, until 2013, from sharing ownership of crude production with foreign companies, limiting its ability to invest in exploration and production.

After 2013, within five years over 100 new oil and gas projects were initiated in Mexico. However, before even taking office President López Obrador announced a three-year moratorium on new bidding, and in the final 2019 USMCA negotiations, Mexico did not sign a side letter recognizing the importance of the integration of North American markets based on market principles.

The U.S. now has a surplus in energy trade with Mexico. U.S. firms send gasoline, diesel, and natural gas South while importing relatively small amounts of crude oil. In addition, Mexico imports almost all its energy production equipment from the U.S. and uses

U.S. electrical power as part of its burgeoning industrial production. In 2021, the Keystone pipeline addition to the U.S. oil imports was cancelled but, in 2024 the Trans Mountain pipeline across western Canada was completed.

North American energy industries are tightly integrated. In 2023, Canada and Mexico, respectively, accounted for 52 percent and 10 percent of all U.S. petroleum imports, while Canada accounted for 9 percent of U.S. petroleum exports and Mexico purchased 12 percent of U.S. petroleum exports. Canada's share of U.S. crude oil imports has risen significantly in the past five years replacing declining exports from Mexico and sometimes banned crude oil from Venezuela.

While the large increase in U.S. production of petroleum and natural gas, attributable to improved technology such as horizontal drilling and hydraulic fracturing, caught many trade administrators, oil industry and political leaders by surprise, under the USMCA, the prevailing sentiment seemed to have been "leave this sector alone." A *Forbes* magazine article declared "USMCA Solidifies Best Oil and Gas Alliance Ever."

Motor Vehicles and Parts. The most contentious part of USMCA negotiations involved motor vehicles and parts. The USTR described the automotive goals of the USMCA as to preserve current domestic vehicle and parts production, increase U.S. content, and decrease incentives to use low-cost labor. Industry representatives argued raising North American content rules above 65 percent (from the 62.5 percent NAFTA standard) would be difficult to achieve and undermine supply chain relationships and efficiency. Yet, when the 75 percent rule was announced, there was little vocal opposition.

The parties agreed to broaden the definition of what could be counted toward U.S. content, including items such as software, technological components, research and development, and some raw materials like steel. The goal was to discourage further erosion of U.S.-based auto manufacturing without a defined American-made content requirement.

Also looming over the failure of USMCA auto negotiations was the potential re-imposition of the so-called "chicken tax." In the 1960s, the U.S. imposed a 25 percent tax on all pickups and work vans imported into the country. The tax was a response to a dispute started when U.S. producers flooded European markets with farm products. European nations imposed a tax on U.S. poultry and President Lyndon Johnson responded by putting a tariff on foreign made pickups entering the country. NAFTA producers were exempt from the tariff but, during USMCA negotiations there were fears that things could change.

In addition, a USMCA 40–45 percent "labor value content" rule was established. Vehicles must be made using $16 (USD) per hour or more labor requirement. This seemed a difficult rule to document but, again, there was little comment from affected companies. Less frequently cited was the content clause requiring use of substantial steel and aluminum of North American origin.

In the end, USMCA's automotive provisions had seven major components (See Figure 3.1 below from the 2019 ITC Report). The first four components are regional value content (RVC) requirements for (1) vehicles, (2) core auto parts, (3) principal auto parts, and (4) complementary auto parts. The other three components are (5) labor value content (LVC) requirements for vehicles, (6) steel purchase requirements, and (7) aluminum purchase requirements.

For a Personal Vehicle (PV) or Light Truck (LT) to qualify for duty-free treatment, the vehicle must meet RVC, LVC, and steel and aluminum requirements. USMCA provisions were more complicated and required more regional content than those under NAFTA. They also required more parts manufacturer input into vehicle manufacturers' RVC and LVC calculations.

For the first five years under USMCA, a manufacturer can continue to meet a 62.5 percent RVC for up to 10 percent of its vehicles produced in North America. Unlike NAFTA, USMCA did not permit any parts to be "deemed originating," and it eliminated "tracing" as well. Automotive RVC requirements were slated to be staged over three years and vary for different categories. At least 70 percent of both the steel and the aluminum purchased by manufacturers for use in producing PVs and LTs must originate in North America.

A diagram of the USMCA automotive rules of origin is presented on the next page.

U.S.-Mexico-Canada Trade Agreement

Figure 3.1 Components of USMCA automotive rules of origin

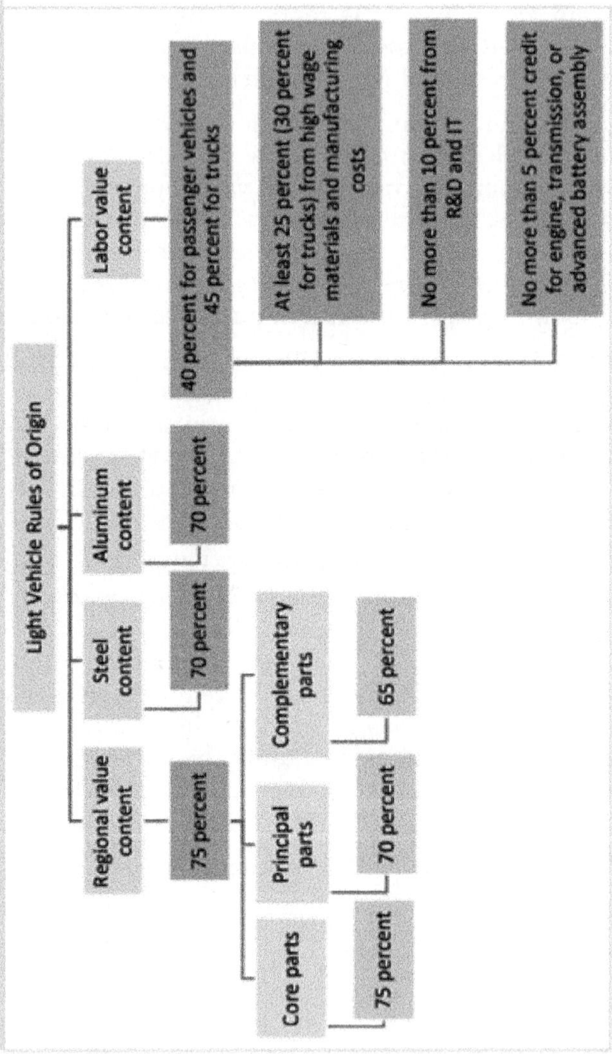

Source: Produced by USITC based on USMCA text.

Some reactions to the unbelievably complex micromanaged USMCA rules of origin for vehicles and parts were surprising. A Ford Motor spokesperson was quoted as saying:

> "Ford is very encouraged by today's announcement, and we applaud all three governments for working together to achieve free and fair trade in a strong regional agreement. We stand ready to be a collaborative partner to ensure this agreement is ratified in all three markets because it will support an integrated, globally competitive automotive business in North America. The benefits of scale and global reach will help to drive volume and support manufacturing jobs."

Similarly, an American Iron and Steel Institute representative stated:

> "We appreciate the administration's hard work to reach this trade agreement between the U.S., Canada and Mexico—especially regarding measures that ensure North American steel continues to be used in automobile production. We are pleased that the agreement is trilateral, as the relationship between our three countries has been extremely beneficial for the steel industry and resulted in robust trade and investment in the region over the past 25 years. This new agreement is significant as it will keep our manufacturing supply chains strong throughout North America."

The ITC 2019 report was not as optimistic. Their analysis found manufacturers fell into three groups: (1) Those that already comply with new rules of origin; (2) those who will likely adjust sourcing and assembly to comply; and (3) those for whom the costs would likely exceed the benefit of tariff preference. Their study predicted U.S. auto manufacturing employment would increase by 28,000 over five years and auto rules were likely to increase the costs of production and the price of cars available to consumers in the United States. One sceptic, the Cato Institute, predicted the increasingly restrictive rules of origin would cause more firms to pay the non-preferential tariff leading to reduced North American production and lower North American content. The result they suggested was one of USMCA's "biggest trumpeted gains, the new auto rules, are actually the worst part of the new agreement." Another commentator suggested USMCA is a "protectionist success, no matter the spin from the captains of industry."

By the time the final agreement was reached, automobile manufacturers seemed relieved, with comments including the agreement "makes the investment path for the auto industry more certain," "disaster avoided," "makes it more difficult to move jobs to Mexico," and "No Carmageddon."

NORTH AMERICAN VEHICLE PRODUCTION

(millions of vehicles)

	2020	2022	2023
U.S.	8.8	10.1	10.6
CAN	1.1	1.2	1.5
MEX	3.1	3.5	4.0

As the table above indicates, all three countries have expanded vehicle production since USMCA. On an absolute basis, the U.S. had the largest increase in production, but, on a relative basis Canada had the largest percentage increase. Since the agreement allows manufacturers to phase in compliance, it is probably early to assess the impact of USMCA requirements.

USMCA rules seemed to ignore huge changes emerging as the agreement was signed: The increasing demand for electric vehicles (EVs), COVID, and U.S.-China trade disputes. One analyst stated in 2022, that no one contemplated such a significant shift in such a short period of time. Thus, the USMCA rules were largely designed for internal combustion engines (ICE) vehicles. Then, in 2022, the Inflation Reduction Act (IRA) included EV tax credit incentives (up to $7,500 per vehicle) but with different regional content requirements from USMCA rules. See Chapter 6. While the USMCA vehicle rules are still being phased in, the impact of IRA's electric vehicle incentives combined with a "Push to counter China," changes are dramatic. This multi-million worker industry is shifting supply chains, expanding EV manufacturing capacity (following the Tesla model of vehicle and battery capacity coordination), and recognizing geopolitical risks.

At least eight international vehicle manufacturers are already assembling or planning to assemble EVs in Mexico, Tesla and BMW included. Mexico thus stands to benefit significantly from the EV wave of economic growth. In addition, General Motors, Stellantis and Honda have entered partnerships with Korean-based battery producer LG to create factories in North America.

Surprisingly, VW, Stellantis, and GM have announced plans to build EV operations in Canada, long considered the highest cost country for vehicle production among the USMCA countries. Analysts report natural resources for batteries, access to U.S. tax credits, green energy resources, plus government incentives as causes for new interest in Canadian automobile production. Experts also note EV production is less labor intensive than ICE vehicles offsetting one of the factors waying against Canadian operations.

On balance, numerous articles report auto manufacturers pursuing "nearshoring" and "friend-shoring" efforts as part of their goal to move away from China-based sole-sourcing. For fossil fuel and EV auto companies, Mexico is high on their radar screens. Likewise, Mexico is also attracting clothing, furniture and other production investments by Chinese parties seeking to take advantage of the USMCA, avoid shipping and U.S. tariff costs, and be closer to the North American market. Mexican wages are now significantly lower than those of the PRC!

Services. The services sector is a vital component of the United States' trade relationships with Canada and Mexico and the rest of the world. Over many years, the United States' major bilateral trade surplus has been in the services sector. Most notably, USMCA introduces binding obligations on market access that build on U.S., Canadian, and Mexican GATS commitments. In addition, USMCA makes some potentially important changes to provisions affecting certain industries including financial services and long-haul trucking. Though services trade in North America is expected to rise, USMCA provisions on services trade were not predicted to have a substantial impact on output in the U.S. services sector.

NORTH AMERICAN SERVICES TRADE 2022

($billions / rank among countries)

	Total U.S. Trade	Canada	Mexico
Exports	$924B	$56B / 2nd	$30B / 8th
Imports	$680B	$33B / 3rd	$28B / 7th

Labor. Not long after NAFTA was ratified, Harvard economist Daniel Rodrik warned that globalization was driving a wedge between workers who had the skills and mobility to prosper in a global economy and those who did not. At that time, the United States was still benefitting from the "brain drain" as eager, technology-focused young people flocked to the U.S. and never went home. They had the mobility, in part because educational visas provided relatively easy access to opportunities, "in the States."

Exactly when the brain drain reversed is hard to determine, but forces including post-9/11 education and security policy changes, increased opportunity, and incentives for talented students in their home countries, and growing global prosperity and communications encouraged "brains" to return home, shifting the global labor market for workers with skills.

In the United States leading economists, including Princeton's Alan Blinder, later confessed surprise regarding the importance of mobility or the lack thereof, in affecting towns and workers left behind in the race for globalization. Professor Rodrik observed the key challenge would be to make globalization "compatible with domestic social and political stability." He said it would not be easy as trade "unleashes forces that undermine the norms implicit in domestic practices."

In the U.S., increased trade, both a result of NAFTA and expansion of the WTO, weakened the explicit and implicit contract between workers and employers. Autobiographies including *Deer Hunting with Jesus* (2006) and *Hillbilly Elegy* (2017) described the pain, anger, and fear among workers who had "played by the rules," but were being left behind as technology and globalization changed their reality.

Most economists recognized there would be winners and losers but surmised that the benefits of trade would outweigh the personal and social costs. Belatedly, trade experts noted that business leaders and free trade advocates in Congress supported trade deals but opposed even modest trade adjustment assistance for displaced workers and abandoned communities.

Almost lost in the USMCA negotiations were early statements by the Trump team to try to enhance parts of the labor agreement. While seemingly incongruent with the Washington agenda in 2017, if Mexican collective bargaining increased workers' wages it would, in theory, reduce the cost differential and reduce corporate incentives to move work to Mexico. In fact, the Trump-Biden-Lopez-Obrador immigration policy blocking access to many refugees, has resulted in a huge increase in labor available in Northern Mexico.

Leaders of many multinational corporations supported USMCA based on supply chain synergies that have evolved over the last several decades. One analysis found that a 10 percent increase in employment at a U.S. multinational's Mexican affiliate led to a 1.3 percent increase in stateside employment, along with a 1.7 percent increase in exports and a 4.1 percent increase in R&D spending.

Robert Scott, author of the widely cited anti-NAFTA study said, during USMCA debates, that killing NAFTA would not bring the jobs back. With the higher costs, "multinationals like GM, Ford, and Toyota may just decide to shift production to Asia or Europe. The U.S.

benefits from having that production in North America, even if it is in Mexico."

The USMCA $16 per hour labor value requirement could induce a variety of responses. In theory, Mexican factories could increase workers' wages. Another response could be to shift production to U.S. and Canadian factories. A third option would be to shift production to lower cost countries and pay the import fee. Analysts predicted the clause would result in increased auto parts production in the U.S. and decreased domestic production of vehicles. With the three-year phase in requirement along with the many recent global and technological changes, it is too early to assess the business and economic impact of the $16 per hour requirement.

Unlike the NAALC, the USMCA included enforceable labor provisions that are subject to the same dispute settlement mechanism as other provisions in the agreement. While some observers contended these enforcement provisions could have a positive impact on labor conditions in Mexico, U.S. labor groups recognized that the impact of these provisions would largely depend on the parties' willingness to proactively enforce these obligations.

§ 7.5 USMCA Impact Summary

The near universal response to the USMCA agreement was a "sigh of relief." Many analysts described USMCA as NAFTA re-branded. The agreement updated most parts of NAFTA using revisions adapted from other trade agreements. See Chapter 6.

For economic and business leaders two critical unanswered questions remain:

(1) What will U.S. trade policy be in the future?

(2) Can we make long-term investment decisions in North America based on USMCA or should we look elsewhere?

Consider again, what transpired during the USMCA ratification years: Threats to terminate NAFTA, numerous meetings among heads of state, name-calling, face-saving gratuitous statements, imposition of protective tariffs, counter tariffs, triangulation of negotiations, and the threat of tariffs impacting immigration issues.

Next, consider the global impacts on the USMCA. With the combination of U.S./China trade disputes, Brexit, and COVID-induced supply chain disasters, many experts and business leaders say the era of globalization is over. On a macro level Bloomberg stated: "The U.S. and China are not engaged in wholesale decoupling of their economies, but both nations are hedging their bets by deepening trade flows with other nations." Add the invasion of Ukraine, the embargo of and withdrawal of multinational companies from Russia, Red Sea disruption of shipping, the Hamas/Israel war, and the fear of an uncertain future in Taiwan.

All these factors, and the U.S. 2024 Presidential election, make regional trade among geopolitical "friends" appealing. Despite its complexities and flaws, USMCA is emerging as one of the best deals available for business leaders.

Table of Cases

Index

References are to Sections and Chapters